INVITATION TO PHILOSOPHY

BY

DURANT DRAKE

BOSTON AND NEW YORK

HOUGHTON MIFFLIN COMPANY

The Riverside Press Cambridge

1933

The Riverside Press

CAMBRIDGE · MASSACHUSETTS

PRINTED IN THE U.S.A.

CONTENTS

iv CONTENTS

PART FOUR. LIFE AND MIND

PART FIVE. VALUES

INTRODUCTORY

WHAT PHILOSOPHY IS ABOUT

PROTAGORAS, if tradition can be trusted, coined the term 'philo-sopher,' lover, wooer, of wisdom. Certainly the word was used in this sense by Socrates and his disciples. Thus, by its earliest usage, *philosophy is the pursuit of wisdom*, and, we may add, its formulation in words.

What, then, is wisdom? Socrates was sure that it springs from knowledge — above all, from knowledge of oneself. And this knowledge is to be found, not by the easy acceptance of tradition, however venerable, not by any romantic flight of the imagination, or hopeful objectification of the heart's desire. Wisdom can be won only by wide acquaintance with brute fact. But wisdom itself is not a bare accumulation of facts, however encyclopedic and exact; it is not mere knowledge, it is its distillation. It is like honey, every drop of which is the result of many trips to many flowers. And, like honey, it finds its function in furnishing sustenance to life. True, philosophy, as Novalis said, bakes no bread. Rather, it has for its high concern the nature of man and of this mysterious world in which he finds himself; it tries to read the riddle of his existence, to weigh the claims of his multitudinous, often divergent interests, and, by so doing, to determine the direction of his highest good.

PHILOSOPHY AND THE SCIENCES

'Science' is the Latin name for 'knowledge.' We may say that knowledge, in any field, in so far as it is organized, is science. Scientific knowledge ripens, in its measure, into wisdom, and is applied in a thousand ways for the enhancement of life. How, then, does philosophy, the pursuit of wisdom, differ from science?

Some say that science deals necessarily with a world of mere appearance, whilst philosophy penetrates deeper and pictures to us the world of reality.

> Science investigates the world as it appears in our world-image and is not especially concerned with the relation of that world-image to some ultimate reality or the way it is produced in our consciousness. Thus science does not deal with the world of the Real so much as with the appearances or phenomena in our consciousness. It is satisfied to accept this world-image of ours as an independent reality and to forget or even deny its vital relation to our consciousness. The result is that science to a large extent is still subject to the limitations of our world-image and shares in its illusion. It does not deal with things as they are so much as with things as they appear; its laws are the shadows of living truth.[1]

A measure of truth there is in this, we must concede, and more than is realized by the unsophisticated. We must presently consider carefully the accusation that science is vitiated by irremediable illusion, and try to disentangle the exact truth in so sweeping an indictment. But for the moment we shall merely say this: science proves that it is dealing with reality by its practical success in shaping our fortunes, by fending off calamities and attaining for us what we seek. We need not be so humble as to think that only the few enlightened are in touch with the real world; every bit of science, yes, every bit of common, everyday knowledge, is, in its degree, actual knowledge of the world, though it may be symbolic rather than literal, and very far from complete. The in-

[1] J. J. Van Der Leeuw, *The Conquest of Illusion*, pp. 58–59.

sistence upon the untrustworthiness of science is usually, if not always, subtle propaganda in favor of some theology or metaphysics which would take us farther away from the world of obdurate reality rather than give us a clearer view. Amid the welter of such day-dreams, it is safe to cling to scientific fact. The conclusions of science are the surest knowledge we have; and *so far as science goes*, we can trust it more confidently than any other brand of truth.

Some eulogists of philosophy have it that while science gives us facts, philosophy concerns itself with values.

It is not the purpose of science to study meanings, values, and appreciations.... But since our primary interests relate to meanings and values, science must be supplemented by philosophy. My new motor car, for instance, is a thing of beauty, and it gives me joy just to contemplate its curves and its gloss and its correct proportions. It will have great *value* for me, as I imagine, enabling me to keep distant appointments, to economize time, to live more in the open air, to keep my family entertained, to maintain or increase my social prestige. It will have a *meaning* to my neighbors, revealing my unsuspected wealth and my taste and discrimination. The merely scientific aspects of the car, its physical causes and the laws of dynamics involved, are of less interest to most people; the values and meanings are the interesting things.... Hence it becomes necessary to go beyond science to philosophy. Life must be interpreted, not merely described.[1]

As a matter of fact, there are any number of sciences — or studies on their way to becoming science — which deal with values of various sorts: such studies as pedagogy, penology, political science, hygiene, jurisprudence, business administration; for that matter, history and psychology, so far as they deal with forms of happiness and pain. And, of course, there is the study of music and all the

[1] G. T. W. Patrick, *Introduction to Philosophy*, pp. 16–17.

arts. Philosophy is by no means unique in studying values. Nor are values its sole concern.

The point is, rather, that philosophy studies values, as it studies all things, *in their wider relationships*. By putting a given set of evaluations, as it puts a given set of facts, in a larger perspective, it may be said to 'interpret' them — for this is what interpretation is. Values are a kind of fact, and can be studied in detail by sciences developed *ad hoc*. Philosophy is the final umpire, the ultimate arbiter of evaluations and appreciations, as it is of all apparently conflicting conclusions of the understanding. Philosophy does not *extend* human knowledge, it clarifies, deepens, and integrates it.

The simple fact is, that human knowledge has become too vast to be grasped in detail by any one person; it has to be parceled out. The rule for savants, as for political tyrants, is *divide et impera*. All knowledge was originally one with philosophy; as it grew and grew it split apart, like protoplasm, until it has become in our day a whole family of sciences, each with its own sphere of interest. Each of these sciences deals either with some particular properties of things, as in the case of mechanics and chemistry, or with some particular field of events, as with descriptive astronomy and geology. *A science is any body of knowledge that is isolated and studied by itself.*

But in so far as we are occupied with the endless details of a science, we cannot see things in the large. Philosophy takes the results of all the sciences and seeks to harmonize them; it receives reports from every quarter of the field, and asks, What of it all? In the light of what these physicists, these biologists, psychologists, and the rest, say, What *is* man? What *is* this universe in which he lives? Whence came we, and it? Whither are we all going, and what is it all about? And — most urgently of all — What shall we *do* about it?

To vary the metaphor, philosophy tries to put this picture-puzzle of a hundred curiously shaped bodies of knowledge together, to see what sort of universe they make. This is the sense in which philosophy, as Bacon so audaciously said, "takes all knowledge for its province." It does not — it should not — presume to supersede, or to short-circuit, the laborious work of the scientists, the psychologists, the historians; it aims to synthesize their work and focus it upon man's ultimate needs. *Philosophy is the integration of knowledge, the synthesis of the sciences.*

There is no sharp line to be drawn here. Any scientist may philosophize, as well as investigate. "There is no teacher worthy the name, in whatever classroom he may be sitting, who does not at some point teach philosophy." But to reflect critically, to generalize, to see things in their widest bearings, requires a different temper and training from that which makes for successful detailed investigation. So it is that excellent scientists often make poor philosophers — though there is so much poor philosophy anyway that it is well not to throw the first stone! Anyone is free to lend a hand at any point; we need only say that the farther we get from particulars, the more we generalize, and the wider outlook we attain, the more philosophical we become.

In our day knowledge is becoming more and more fragmented, and almost inconceivably immense. We tend increasingly to become myopic, our eyes fixed upon the little plot of ground which we individually till. "The specialized functions of the community are performed better, but the general direction lacks vision." We lack co-ordination, we lack a general map and chart of action.

The need of philosophy grows ever greater, as an antidote to this specialization, to give us perspective and balance. Matthew Arnold wrote of the poet Sophocles that

He saw life steadily and saw it whole.

Philosophy seeks to see this world of innumerable miscellaneous things, this life-stream of so many diverse currents and cross-currents, as a whole, as a universe — to unfold before our eyes a synoptic panorama of life, to give us a general sense of the drift and import of existence, what the Germans call a *Weltanschauung*. No wonder philosophy has been called the Queen of the Sciences.

PHILOSOPHY, POETRY, AND RELIGION

The place of philosophy is not in the front-line trenches. The spade-work, the patient conquest of new terrain, is the job of the scientists, who are fighting ignorance simultaneously on a hundred fronts. The philosophers constitute a General Staff, whose business is to piece together their reports and tell us how the battle as a whole goes. This is the primary reason for so much less agreement in philosophy; we are here farther removed from the facts, and liable to generalize from misunderstood or inadequate data. But this work, too, must be done, if we are to weld disparate reports into unified insight. There are problems which transcend the bounds of any one field of science, or even of a group of allied sciences, problems which require a convergence of knowledge from the remotest quarters. There are discordances, which need to be critically weighed by a detached mind; the results of each science must be appraised in the light of all the others. And there is a No Man's Land beyond the trenches, where no science has as yet penetrated, which must be mapped, however uncertainly, and with whatever admixture of conjecture may be required.

Thus philosophy, in the nature of the case, is more speculative than science, and has more of the nature of poetry. It must reach out in imagination beyond the frontiers of discovered fact, into the vast unknown, toward the mysteries of life and death and destiny. It must give provisional answers to questions which science has not yet answered. It must be more than a summary of science to date, it must be a tentative completion of science, a shrewd anticipation of knowledge.

Thus, too, it must spend much time in defining and criticizing concepts, the tools of knowledge. It must scrutinize the terms found useful by this science and that, and question their underlying assumptions. It must deal largely with abstractions, and very much with mere words. For the sciences, happily, can go forward without clearly understanding what it is that they are investigating. If it is Space and Time, if it is matter, energy, atoms, electricity, life, or mind, it is not necessary to know what these entities actually *are*, to study them empirically and report very much *about* them. But to relate all these reports, to find out how these things go together and see them as constituting a universe, we must know, or guess, what they are. So philosophy has been, not inappropriately, defined as "thinking things through." As Tennyson said of the flower in the crannied wall, if we *keep on* asking questions, in any field of knowledge, we shall sooner or later get to ultimate problems, that is, to philosophy. We may be cursed as persistent pests and hair-splitting pedants. But it is only by such obstinate and searching inquiries that we can come finally to understand our world and ourselves.

Mr. C. D. Broad, one of the ablest of contemporary English philosophers, distinguishes 'critical' from 'speculative' philosophy.

> The analysis and definition of our fundamental concepts, and the clear statement and resolute criticism of our fundamental beliefs, I call *Critical Philosophy*.... The other sciences *use* the concepts and *assume* the beliefs; Critical Philosophy tries to analyze the former and to criticize the latter. Philosophy claims to analyze the general concepts of substance and cause; e.g., it does not claim to tell us about particular substances, like gold, or about particular laws of causation, as that *aqua regia* dissolves gold. Chemistry, on the other hand, tells us a great deal about the various kinds of substances in the world, and how changes in one cause changes in another. But it does not profess to analyze the general concepts of substance or causation, or to consider what right we have to assume that every event has a cause.
>
> Now there is another kind of Philosophy; and, as this is more exciting, it is what laymen generally understand by the name. This is what I call *Speculative Philosophy*.... Its object is to take over the results of the various sciences, to add to them the results of the religious and ethical experiences of mankind, and then to reflect upon the whole. The hope is, that by this means, we may be able to reach some general conclusions as to the nature of the Universe, and as to our position and prospects in it.... It must presuppose Critical Philosophy. It is useless to take our masses of uncriticized detail from the sciences and from the ethical and religious experiences of men. We do not know what they mean, or what degree of certainty they possess, till they have been clarified and appraised by Critical Philosophy.[1]

This distinction is useful, but seems to be merely a distinction between means and end. The same sort of critical work is constantly being done, within its limitations, in every field of science, as a necessary part of its procedure. Philosophic criticism is simply the final criticism, the criticism which takes *everything* into consideration.

[1] C. D. Broad, *Scientific Thought*, pp. 18–20. Harcourt, Brace and Company, Inc.

And this criticism does not, in philosophy any more than in science, exist *in vacuo,* as a separate study, for its own sweet sake; it exists in order to forward philosophy in its essential task of understanding the universe. Concern with concepts is concern with tools; they are sharpened in order to be used; they are used when they contribute to our vision of things as they are.

The philosopher is willing to do this tedious work of hair-splitting and defining, because he really wants to *know.* The poet, the literary man, as such, does not care so much about ultimate truth; he is content just to say how he feels, how things look to him. What he writes may thus be far more readable, and far closer to the popular taste. But *truth* is elusive, and is not to be won in any such simple way. The technique of distinguishing truth from error must first be learned; and that is an arduous task. Even when literature aims at a comprehensive view of things, as in the Bible, or the *Divina Commedia* of Dante, it lacks the rigorous method necessary to become truly objective; it remains this or that man's, or perhaps a people's, dream. It has not built itself up patiently upon the substructure of sound scientific and historical knowledge. It remains an impressive record of human aspiration and outlook, but it is a warped and specious wisdom in so far as it is divorced from the world of importunate fact.

But of course the poet and the litterateur rarely attempt the expression of a coherent world-view. They have other work to do. They are concerned with recording memorable aspects of experience. The power of the poets "is intensity rather than range; they do not give us the whole, but at a single point they do pierce through and touch the heart of life." They give us delightful and suggestive personal reactions to things, but leave to de-personalized science and philosophy the solving of problems, the formulation, in accurate terms, of objective truth. They commonly reach whatever philosophical views they hold through the absorption of current ideas, together with their own casual and one-sided experience; these views are almost certain to be heightened by their imagination and colored by their emotions. Moreover, their language is impressionistic rather than precise; they write to make their readers feel as they do, rather than to convince them by reasoned argument; and so they serve to stimulate and to delight rather than to instruct. But they stir and stretch a thousand minds for one that will listen to logic; they throw light upon the dark corners of life, they keep us aware of the inexhaustible wonder of the world; they bring into sharp relief all the kaleidoscopic turns of human experience which the philosopher must understand and explain.

We must hasten to add that many of the most reputed philosophers are really better poets than philosophers. Or at least, however good or mediocre their work may be as poetry, it is not very good as philosophy. For it is a product of the imagination rather than of the understanding, of the heart rather than of the head. And it would have been better put in verse, or in rhapsodic prose, than to masquerade in the form of what ought to be the wariest and most impersonal of disciplines.[1]

Occasionally there comes a man who is both philosopher and poet — a Plato, a Lucretius, a Santayana. But it is a

[1] Cf. Karl Pearson, *The Grammar of Science*, p. 17: "The poet is a valued member of the community, for he is known to be a poet.... The metaphysician is a poet, often a very great one, but unfortunately he is not known to be a poet, because he strives to clothe his poetry in the language of reason; and hence it follows that he is liable to be a dangerous member of the community."

rare combination of gifts. How can one seek a detached
and austerely factual view of things, expressed with
critical accuracy and restraint, and at the same time il-
luminate it with the glamour and glow of the imagination
and the magic of musical phrase? It is indeed possible,
it is urgently needful, to weave the web of poetry about
the dry bones of philosophy; and we shall hope not utterly
to fail in that precarious undertaking. But for the philosopher the philosophy should come first, formed by the
clear and unclouded mind, in stern resistance to the lure
of the appealing notion and the inspiriting dream. His
Kingdom of Heaven is the realm of substantiated, or at
least of objectively probable fact; he must seek that first,
with honest and unremitting endeavor, and only then
hope that these other things may be added to it — the
imaginative glow, the felicitous phrase.

This holds, likewise, of the opposing pulls of philosophy
and religion. The conflict between religion and science
has been, in the main, a conflict between particular entrenched bodies of doctrine, protected from criticism and
revision by various ecclesiastical organizations, and the
free spirit of critical inquiry, with the conclusions to
which, from time to time, that spirit has led. In this
conflict science has been essentially, and at almost every
point, in the right, as the gradual retreat of traditional
dogma concretely shows. Religious dogma represents
one form of the philosophy of its day, though it has
rarely, if ever, been based upon any rigorous technique of
truth-seeking. But dogmas in any case become rapidly
petrified by the veneration which they command; the or-
thodoxies of our day are vestigial remains of antique
ideas, in large part discredited and forgotten outside the
precincts of religion. Current religious belief consists,

for the most part, of philosophical and historical views which were uncritically accepted at the outset, without the painstaking work of examining the evidence impartially pro and con, and have been perpetuated by emotional propaganda accepted with a fine but misguided loyalty by the adherents of the several churches. With such partisan and propagandist doctrines a really critical and cautious philosophy must necessarily be at odds.

But this conflict has all been unnecessary and unspeakably tragic. For religion itself is as important as philosophy, and, indeed, of the two the more vital to man. And in the inevitable and necessary discrediting of antiquated theological dogmas, religion itself has been grievously hurt, so that it is like to die. The proper place of religion in life we shall consider toward the end of this volume. We may only say here that religion is in essence a spirit, an inner flame, a matter of the heart and the will, an integration of intent, a Way to live. As such it cannot be opposed to philosophy, which is a matter of the intellect or understanding. It is only the theorizing *about* religion, the doctrines which arise to explain and support this inner life, which oppose themselves to philosophy. And they are in opposition only if they are inadequate and erroneous explanations.

IS PHILOSOPHY WORTH WHILE?

That charming Englishman, Arthur Clutton-Brock, wrote, not long before his death, "Most people in England think of a philosopher as one who talks in a difficult language about matters which are of interest only to philosophers." To this we may add the familiar gibe to the effect that philosophy is "a search by a blind man for a black cat in a pitch-dark room — where there is no cat!"

By contrast, let us quote from another English writer, Gilbert Chesterton:

> It is foolish, generally speaking, for a philosopher to set fire to another philosopher in Smithfield Market because they do not agree in their theory of the universe.... But there is one thing that is infinitely more absurd and unpractical than burning a man for his philosophy. This is the habit of saying that his philosophy does not matter; and this is done universally in the twentieth century.... General theories are everywhere condemned.... A man's opinion on tram-cars matters; his opinion on Botticelli matters; his opinion on all things does not matter. He may turn over and explore a million objects, but he must not find that strange object, the universe; for if he does he will have a religion, and be lost. Everything matters — except everything.... But there are some people, nevertheless — and I am one of them — who think that the most practical and important thing about a man is still his view of the universe. We think that for a landlady considering a lodger, it is important to know his income, but still more important to know his philosophy. We think that for a general about to fight an enemy, it is important to know the enemy's numbers, but still more important to know the enemy's philosophy. We think the question is not whether the theory of the cosmos affects matters, but whether, in the long run, anything else affects them.[1]

Now which of these two so sharply antithetical ratings is correct? Is philosophy futile, and of merely esoteric interest, or is it of prime importance to us all?

We may admit at once that many philosophical problems are irrelevant to our daily concerns. Whether colors exist in the outer world, or in our minds, or whether they are non-existent essences, has no bearing upon industry or ethics or art. But this question is wrapped up with so many others, that the answer we give affects, and is affected by, our whole vision of the world in which

[1] Gilbert Chesterton, *Heretics*, pp. 12-16.

we live.   And to *have* a vision of that world, to understand, however dimly, our situation in it and the nature
of these surrounding forces that press upon us, is, for
many of us, a pure and abiding delight.   More and more,
as we grow older, and the passions of youth subside, this
theoretic interest, this yearning for insight, grows.   Aristotle, wisest of the ancients, had no doubt that its satisfaction is, for man, the Highest Good.

Much of our life, after all, goes beyond what is utilitarian in the narrower sense.   Many of our deeper interests are of little practical use.   They are for joy.   And,
for those whose minds have become accustomed to these
perilous seas of thought, there is a spaciousness, a sense
of far horizons, of the wind of the world blowing in our
faces, which we would not exchange for any of the snug
harbors of human knowledge and faith.   It has been perhaps of no use for men to seek, through years of effort
and failure, to discover the North Pole, or to conquer
Mount Everest, the highest point on this whirling planet.
But it is adventures such as these that kindle our imagination and make us something more than crawling and
industrious ants.   If minds were made for thinking, then
philosophy is its own excuse for being.   It shakes us out
of the mental ruts into which we so easily slip, and
makes us actually use our minds — provided, of course,
that we really have minds to use.   And whether or no
we ever settle these problems to our satisfaction, we have
at least been lifted for a while out of our little selves to a
region above that of our personal ambitions and worries
and conceit, the realm of sublime and eternal truth.

> Philosophy!   A game, no more; although
> World's keenest minds have toiled to pierce thereby
> The high-flung barrier of the boundless sky
> And find the cause of all.   It cannot show

A good more precious than the mystic glow
Of love; nor teach us how to prize more high
The living light that leaps from eye to eye,
The life we love, though vainly seek to know.

Philosophy! A game, no more; yet such
As dwarfs all other games to nothingness;
That plays with æons in its daring touch,
With stars for pawns, infinity to span.
Philosophy! A game for gods, no less,
That leaves man beaten, but a greater man.[1]

But surely many of the problems which we are to consider are of the greatest practical importance. What is
more needful for us than to learn which are the trustworthy roads to truth? or what is the proper criterion for
moral judgments? Far more than we realize, differences
in philosophical doctrine underlie our practical loyalties,
our divisions into parties and sects. Whether we are for
democracy or dictatorship or anarchy, whether we are
one hundred per cent Americans or members of the Third
International, Fundamentalists or Catholics or Modern-
ists, mystics or materialists, sinners or saints, depends in
large measure upon differences — however unconscious
— in our philosophy of life. Certainly, to understand
these warring groups, or to take sides intelligently ourselves, demands that profound study of first principles,
that detached and balanced reflective thinking about
ultimate matters, which we call philosophy.

Most people are content to have no explicit philosophy.
Nevertheless there is a philosophy implied in their practical attitudes, in what seems to them their common
sense. As Will Durant says, these are "questions which
few men ask, and which all men answer." They have
accepted answers to the world-riddles; or they simply act
in accordance with the answers which the people of their

[1] C. L. Goodrich, *Philosophy.*

set have accepted. And of course the chances are that these doctrines and attitudes into which they have so unconsciously grown are not the truest or best. It is not a question of having a philosophy or no philosophy. It is a question of having a vague, an inconsistent, a half-conscious, a blindly accepted and probably foolish philosophy, or a philosophy that is carefully thought out, consistent, and in line with the latest available information about ourselves and our world.

Today, as everyone knows, we are witnessing a rapid dissolution of dogma, a world-wide disintegration of established opinions and institutions. Complacent convictions are crumbling all about us. What an opportunity this offers for rebuilding something better! We have now a free field for the reconstruction of first principles and the development on their basis of a saner and happier life than any but a few fortunate human beings have ever known. If, then, here and there a philosopher avoids the press of practical affairs and spends his time in trying

> to see this sorry scheme of things *entire*,

it is that he may point the way

> to mold it nearer to the heart's desire.

It is true that philosophy often 'upsets' people. And if what you most want is to maintain your mental *status quo*, it is not wise to philosophize. You will sympathize with the Moslem who wrote the letter reproduced by William James in his *Psychology*: [1]

> Listen, O my son! There is no wisdom equal unto the belief in God! He created the world, and shall we liken ourselves unto Him in seeking to penetrate into the mysteries of His creation? Shall we say, Behold this star spinneth round that star, and this other star with a tail goeth and com-

[1] Vol. II, p. 640, footnote.

eth in so many years? Let it go! He from whose hand it came will guide and direct it.

But thou wilt say unto me, Stand aside, O man, for I am more learned than thou art, and have seen more things. If thou thinkest that thou art in this respect better than I am, thou art welcome. I praise God that I seek not that which I require not. Thou art learned in the things I care not for; and as for that which thou hast seen, I spit upon it. Will much knowledge create thee a double belly, or wilt thou see Paradise with thine eyes?

O my friend! if thou wilt be happy, say, There is no God but God! Do no evil, and thus wilt thou fear neither man nor death; for surely thine hour will come!

Imaum Ali Zadi.

Philosophy does upset such conservatism as this, whether Moslem or Christian. Of course. Wherever there are illusions, however prized, wherever there are prejudices — which are precious, too, to their owners, wherever people have made their judgment blind because of their loyalty to a belief which is sweeter to them than the truth, philosophy is ruthless. It upsets people, because they need to be upset. The breaking of idols is an ungracious task, but a necessary one. It is easy now to see that *past* dogmas needed clearing away; we are aghast at the blindness, the stupidities, the injustices, the complacent ignorance of past ages. Are we so sure that our ideas do not need revision too?

In short, if what you want is comfort, cling to your pet ideas, and *think* as little as possible. That is the program which most people follow; that is why they are what they are. If, on the other hand, what you want is to find ever more and more light, from whatever source, and to follow it whithersoever it may lead you, at whatever cost to your peace of mind; if what you want is to be a leader, to make your influence, such as it may be, count for progress and enlightenment, accept the invitation to philosophy, and join the ranks of those who make the pursuit of Truth supreme.

CAN WE HOPE TO SOLVE THESE PROBLEMS?

The history of philosophy is discouraging — as well as bewildering and hard to understand. There seems at first sight to be no progress, no forward movement, no knowledge securely won, no problem safely solved. Philosophical discussions seldom 'get anywhere'; there is in the end no more consensus of opinion than at the outset. A vogue for realism gives way to a wave of subjectivism, that passes over into absolutism, and presently realism is in vogue again. We might well paraphrase the French proverb about woman, and say, *Philosophie toujours varie; bien fou qui s'y fie.* Does this not show that these world-riddles are insoluble by man, at least by such means as he has yet at his disposal? How can we hope to succeed where so many greater than we have failed?

Well, these problems *are*, admittedly, the most difficult problems man has to face. Philosophy is, of necessity, so abstract, so far removed from the concrete facts with which its daughter sciences deal, that its results are not easily checked up; error can flourish long without being disproved. And, as that keen critic Ernest Renan once said, every one of the great philosophical doctrines "has so much to say for itself, and is so plausible from some point of view, that if a man could live long enough, and keep his mind fresh and virile, he would undoubtedly champion successively every doctrine and belong in turn to every sect."

But it is not true that there has been no progress. We have not yet agreed on the answers to the problems, but we have sharpened the issues, clarified our concepts, made many discriminations the lack of which blurred earlier discussions. We have collected relevant considerations and exploded many arguments formerly esteemed. We have explored the possibilities of thought in many directions, found some to be blind alleys and others of unexpected promise. In some cases, indeed,

> We seem merely to have got back to where we started from, and to have wasted our time. But this is not really so, for two reasons: (i) What we believe at the end of the process and what we believed at the beginning are by no means the same, although we express the beliefs by the same form of words. The original belief of common sense was vague, crude and unanalyzed... [it] consisted of a number of different beliefs, mixed up with each other.... [The] final belief... is much clearer and subtler than the *verbally* similar belief with which we began.... (ii) Our original belief was merely instinctive, and was at the mercy of any skeptical critic who chose to cast doubts upon it.... A belief that has stood the criticisms of an acute and subtle thinker... is more likely to be true than a merely instinctive belief which has never been criticized by ourselves or by anyone else.[1]

For such reasons as these, we are really far ahead of the philosophic thought even of the nineteenth century. Geniuses are rare; Plato, Spinoza, Hume, and the other immortals, will always be fascinating reading for the connoisseur. But the study of philosophy is far too generally the study of superseded systems. This interest in past ideas is a legitimate interest, but it is a historical interest rather than an interest in understanding our world. Within this century philosophical discussion has moved on to planes that leave these older thinkers hopelessly behind. Those amazing Greeks did indeed hit upon most of the key ideas of modern thought; but their ideas, though

[1] C. D. Broad, *Scientific Thought*, pp. 14–15. Harcourt, Brace and Company, Inc.

brilliant, were crude and ambiguous and mingled with much error, which has had to be patiently disentangled. They often lacked a precise understanding of their own terms, and they all lacked the vast accumulation of knowledge which makes the philosophic venture today so much more hopeful of success.

One reason why we do not realize our progress lies in the fact that ideas long since discredited still persist. The maintainers of doctrines do not know when they are beaten. It will be necessary to educate a far wider public in the art of reflective thinking before these exploded philosophies will disappear. As it is, many of those who pass for the best thinkers have really more interest in edification than in truth; their philosophy has been, as Bradley said, "the finding of bad reasons for what they believe on instinct" — or on tradition, or because they have hoped so hard that it may be true.

The public for the most part aids and abets this fault in philosophers. They applaud those who have an impressive and inspiring view to offer, some cosmic or ethical theory which intrigues their interest and satisfies their hearts. Meanwhile those who are doing the careful spade-work, resisting the glamour of alluring but unsubstantiated theories, and actually forwarding philosophy, usually write books which are hard to read, unedifying, unimpressive, of little interest to the general reader. People think they want the truth; but they want more effectively to be exhilarated and inspired, whether by fact or by plausible fiction. And so the search for truth is biased at the beginning; for we have no right to assume in advance that the truth is either edifying or consoling, or that the world is what we should like it to be.

At long last, the more scrupulous and clear-sighted

philosophers will no doubt receive their due recognition, while those who are more visionary and of looser logic will sink into oblivion. But many philosophers honestly believe that they are not philosophizing well unless their conclusions *are* edifying and inspiring; and therefore they reject *ipso facto* any doctrines which they find depressing. For the well-known British philosopher R. F. A. Hoernlé, for example, philosophy must be "a vision of reality which shall satisfy both heart and head." This demand meets with widespread acclaim.

By contrast with this let us listen to Bertrand Russell: "It is customary to demand of a philosopher that he should show that the world is good in certain respects. I cannot admit any duty of this sort. One might as well demand of an accountant that he should show a satisfactory balance sheet. It is just as bad to be fraudulently optimistic in philosophy as in money matters."

Whatever the ethics of this matter be, there is no doubt that the bias in favor of inspiriting and 'idealistic' conclusions has done, and is doing, a vast deal to retard the progress of philosophy. The history of modern thought in the West shows us one long struggle of the human mind to emancipate itself from the presuppositions of Christian theology, which had thrust its roots far deeper into men's very being than they ever knew.

But the emancipation is proceeding now with accelerated pace. A more scientific method is becoming current among philosophers. Traditions and dogmas which stand in the way of free thinking are rapidly losing their hold. A vast and rapidly growing body of knowledge offers the philosopher of today materials for his thought never available before. It looks as though the way were cleared for advance.

In any case, whatever our chances of success, we shall not be deterred by the failures of those who have gone before. What if Peary, or Lindbergh, had listened to counsels of despair? Suppose *all* past philosophy has failed — what then! We are only at the beginning of the quest. We may be very sure that men, while they are men, will never give up the intriguing and tantalizing task of trying really to understand themselves and this mysterious universe which is their home.

PART ONE
THE QUEST OF TRUTH

CHAPTER I

THE VOICE OF AUTHORITY

OUR first aim must be to discover the road to truth. We must learn to avoid the pitfalls and the *culs-de-sac*, and to find guide-posts for the trustworthy route. For strait and narrow is the way that leads to truth, and few there be that walk therein. In every matter of moment we are beset with floods of prejudice and propaganda; concerning every fundamental problem there are "fifty-seven varieties" of opinion. How are we to pick out the truth? How are we to know it, when we see it, from these manifold forms of error?

IS THERE ANY ABSOLUTE AUTHORITY?

The commonest way of attaining assurance of truth is to rely upon authority. Obviously all depends here upon the confidence which we may properly place in our Authority. And we shall ask first whether we may consider any Authority so absolute, so infallible, as to be beyond the range of doubt. The devout Catholic, or Fundamentalist, or Moslem, or indeed the devotee of almost every religion, holds the fundamental principles of his faith to be *guaranteed* by supernatural authority. There is, in these matters, no need of searching for the truth, it has been given us from Above. All we have to do is to accept it gratefully and believe.

If any one of these venerated Authorities *can* be absolutely relied upon, we have here a wonderful comfort and help. For though their pronouncements cover but a very limited range of questions, they usually deal with fundamentally important human concerns — the very matters upon which philosophy is laboriously seeking light.... But what a tremendous assertion it is, that for once in the ages a human voice was enabled to reveal the absolute truth about matters so difficult and obscure! It is a matter of such moment that any claim of this sort should obviously be submitted to the most searching scrutiny.

Yet, curiously enough, relatively few believers ever submit these amazing claims to the sort of scrutiny which they would apply in other realms — say, in a lawsuit or a business deal. The rest are content to accept, with little question, the Authority which they were taught as children to revere. In matters of everyday observation, their growing experience may presently counteract the momentum of their bringing-up — especially where their passions or pecuniary advantage are concerned. But in these high matters of the spirit they have little personal experience to add, and so the doctrines and beliefs early implanted in them remain, for the most part, unshaken. They see no practical need of rejecting the authoritative statements of priest or book, and it hardly occurs to them to inquire whether they are actually valid.

More than that, a believer comes to have a sort of vested interest in his beliefs. They are *his* beliefs, and he instinctively springs to their defense. To impugn them is as if you impugned his wife or his reputation. Even if his loyalty to the faith of his fathers, and of his youth, is subconscious, it is probably deep-rooted. To abandon it would be to become a spiritual vagrant and outcast, to exchange assurance for uncertainty and unrest.

If he belongs to a church, he hears these doctrines

categorically affirmed, and has them driven over and over again into his mind by a highly developed technique of 'suggestion.' For most churches use the prestige of the beautiful Christian tradition to indoctrinate their followers in their particular theological conceptions, and to prevent them from raising doubts of these doctrines. The following statements, for example, are typical of the Roman Catholic position:

> If the formulas of modern science contradict the science of Catholic dogma, it is the former that must be altered, not the latter... [That dogma] expresses real objective truth... Such truth is expressed in terms of sound philosophy, which will not be given up, *and which may be called the Christian philosophy.*[1]

> The fathers of the Church are unanimous in considering as outside the Catholic communion anyone who in the least degree deviates from even one point of the doctrine proposed by the authoritative magisterium of the Church.[2]

We cannot here discuss the ethics of such methods of securing allegiance and stifling free inquiry.[3] Unless the reader is himself a Catholic, he will probably resent the existence of such partisan indoctrination, such attempted immunization against contrary beliefs, on the part of the Catholic Church. But the fact is that a similar, though usually not so explicit or thoroughgoing, stand is taken by most Protestant churches, with reference, on the one hand, to Catholicism and alien faiths, and, on the other hand, to 'infidelity' and 'free thinking' — which sometimes seems to be deemed as dangerous as 'free love'!

But while resisting the pull of indoctrination and emo-

---

[1] From an address by the Bishop of Newport, reported in *The Tablet* for August 27, 1904. My italics.

[2] From an encyclical of Pope Leo XII.

[3] The present writer has discussed it in Chapter XVII, *Dogmatism and Indoctrination*, of his volume *The New Morality* (The Macmillan Co., 1928).

tional influences, we must attempt to analyze and appraise the most plausible of the arguments offered to support these various sacred Authorities. Of course we shall not presume, in so rapid a survey as ours must be, to *settle* any of these matters. As with all the further questions which we shall be raising, we shall merely suggest lines of thought which the reader must pursue for himself, and point to the sort of evidence which he should carefully weigh.

1. *The Argument from Intrinsic Worth*

This argument asserts that the teacher, or book, or institution in question is too wonderful to be merely human. He or it bears the stamp of divine origin, and can therefore be trusted at every point. For example, a contemporary writer says of the Christian Bible:

> The more we think upon it the more we must be convinced that men unaided by the spirit of God could neither have conceived nor put together, nor preserved in its integrity that precious deposit known as the Sacred Oracles.... The heavenliness of its matter, the efficacy of its doctrine, the unity of its various parts, the majesty of its style and the scope and completeness of its design all indicate the divinity of its origin.

Reduced to logical form, the major premise of this argument must be supposed to be, 'A book wonderful beyond a certain point can not be a merely human product'; while the minor premise would be, 'This book is wonderful beyond that point.' The burden of proof then rests upon the proponent of the argument to prove both premises.

Can any way be found to prove the major premise? Do we know the limitations of the human mind, so as to be sure that any work of a certain degree of worth must be superhuman?

As to the minor premise, it is clearly a subjective judgment. Not all readers find the Bible so transcendently
wonderful as this writer does. And the suspicion is
natural that this awe-struck attitude toward the Bible is
the *result* of a preconceived idea of its superhuman character, rather than a *reason* for formulating that conception. Would a reader who had never heard that the Bible
is the "Word of God" reach that conclusion by a dispassionate reading of its contents?... Similarly, the Koran,
Swedenborg's writings, Mrs. Eddy's *Science and Health*,
and the scriptures of various other religions, seem to
their devotees of supreme worth, and therefore of an authority not to be questioned. But readers outside of
the several folds are apt to find these books by no means
so supremely great.

Similar answers apply to the argument as used to authenticate a teacher or institution as divine. Who can
say how wonderful in genius or character a man may be,
and yet be human and fallible; how great and beneficent
an institution may be, and yet be entirely human, and
therefore liable to fundamental errors and mistaken zeal?
Who, moreover, has the right to say that a given man
(such as Jesus, or Gautama, the Buddha) *was*, actually,
as wonderful as the tradition of his followers has made him
out to be? or that a given institution (such as the Catholic
Church) *has* been so steadily in the right, so unerringly
beneficent, as its loyal followers assume?

The weakness of either premise would be enough to
make the argument highly dubious. With both premises
so far from proved, it is difficult to see how it can be
thought to have any weight at all.

2. *The Argument from Antecedent Probability*

This argument is succinctly expressed as follows:

> To those who believe in a living and personal God, the possibility of revelation is but the simple result of His existence. For how should He who is Love be silent?   Such a fact would be in contradiction with His nature.[1]

The argument frankly assumes the belief in a certain view of God, as its major premise, and presumes to say, in its minor premise, what such a God would do.... In view of the great variety of opinions as to the nature of God, and as to what His behavior may properly be conceived to be, it is evident that the argument will seem plausible only to a restricted group of believers.... The writer quoted, being a Christian, goes on to assume that the revelation which God, being what He is, would naturally give, is to be found in the Bible. A Moslem, if he accepted the argument would find it doubtless in the Koran. Clearly, it is not enough to prove the antecedent probability of a revelation; we must prove that this book, and not that, *is* the revelation.

It is also worth noticing that similar arguments can be used to reach all sorts of different conclusions. For example: "There exists a personal and loving God; such a God would not permit pain, and other forms of evil, to exist; therefore these evils do not exist." This is not brought up here for discussion, but merely to show the possibilities that lie in assuming such and such to be the nature and power and will of God.... All such assumptions, in the present state of human knowledge, must be said to be very precarious — *unless the fact of a supernatural revelation that this is the nature of God is assumed*. But it is precisely the assertion of such a revelation that

[1] C. E. Luthardt, *The Fundamental Truths of Christianity*, p. 193.

we are weighing; obviously the argument must not be circular, assuming, as a concealed premise, what it is setting out to prove.

3. The Ipse Dixit Argument

This argument, which is too common to call for quotation, runs, when rendered explicit, as follows: The teacher in question claimed to be divine, or divinely inspired. His character shows clearly that he was not a liar. Thus his teaching must be regarded as authoritative on his own say-so.... The argument may be applied to a book, such as our Bible, or to an institution, such as the Catholic or the Greek Orthodox Church.

The Bible, as a matter of fact, nowhere calls itself the Word of God; that is a later attribution. But the Old Testament prophets prefaced their utterances quite commonly with the phrase "Thus saith the Lord," or its equivalent. Jesus, according to the Gospels, called himself the Son of Man (a term taken generally as meaning a supernatural personage) and even the Son of God; various other sayings seem to make what amounts to an assertion of divine origin or nature.... Many other prophets, of many faiths, are reported to have made somewhat similar statements; most founders of religions are thought to have called themselves either divine or divinely inspired — and thus teachers of more than human authority.

The question of deliberate falsehood seldom enters in — though there is evidence enough that more than one founder of a religion was to some extent a faker. But it is always possible to hold that the prophet or saint was deluded in thinking himself supernaturally inspired, or of supernatural origin. The existence of such a delusion is a psychological phenomenon not at all uncommon. Thus the major premise of the argument, which asserts that a transcendently good man who claims divine origin or authority must be believed, is open to the serious objection that where religious experiences and emotions are intense, there is grave danger of delusion.

The question may also be raised whether the prophet or saint did actually claim to be divine, or divinely commissioned. Many modern historians doubt, for example, that Jesus thought of himself as in any sense a supernatural being. It is quite clear that it is an incurable propensity of believers to deify, or quasi-deify, the objects of their adoration. But there is, for our purposes, little use in studying the stories, in any case except where there is a pre-existing propensity to believe. For in all other cases the claim will simply seem absurd.

4. The Proof from Prophecy

This specifically Christian 'proof' has found artistic expression in such works as Händel's oratorio, *The Messiah*, and the paintings by Sargent on the walls of the Public Library in Boston. The idea is firmly embedded in the New Testament that the Jewish prophets foretold the coming of the Christ and some of the salient events of his life. The implied major premise of the argument is that such power to foretell proves supernatural inspiration, and thus indirectly authenticates the superhuman nature and authority of Jesus.

The implicit major premise may be questioned. There is a great deal of evidence for the occurrence in all sorts of quarters of strikingly prophetic visions and dreams, sometimes taken as supernatural manifestations, sometimes as occult but purely natural phenomena, occasionally as

a power normal to the human mind, though rarely exploited.[1] The skeptically minded reject all of these cases
as exaggeration or illusion or coincidence or fraud. In
the present stage of human knowledge no fixed conclusion
can safely be drawn. But it is evident that if the Jewish
prophets do actually seem to have foretold certain future
events, their case stands by no means alone. If a supernatural explanation is in order then, it may be difficult
to know how, in fairness, to reject it elsewhere.... Moreover, there is little logic in saying that a power to foretell
the future implies the truth of the ethical and religious
views of the successful predicter, or — in the case of the
Jewish prophets — of the Figure they foretold. The
early Christians were hypnotized by the idea of a prophetic adumbration of the events of Jesus' life. This
proved to their satisfaction that he was, indeed, the
long-awaited Messiah. But, granting that this was the
Figure of whose appearance the prophets had intimations,
we may well ask, Does that prove the authoritativeness
of that Messiah's teaching?

But here, as with the preceding argument, the minor
premise can be more fruitfully discussed. Is the supposed successful prediction by the Jewish prophets a
fact?... We must refer the reader again to the Biblical
scholars.[2] It is generally agreed by non-partisan historians that most of the so-called Messianic passages in the
Old Testament actually referred to contemporary or immediately impending events, and were unwarrantably

[1] See on this last point, J. W. Dunne, *An Experiment with Time.* The present
writer, while not subscribing to Mr. Dunne's theory, has had striking experiences
of the sort which he describes.

[2] See, e.g., J. Warschauer, *What is the Bible?* ch. V. C. H. Cornill, *The
Prophets of Israel,* ch. I. J. T. Sunderland, *Origin and Character of the Bible,*
ch. VII.

stretched by the early Christians to apply to supposed occurrences authenticating their faith. Vague similarities suggested intentional reference. Most of the 'fulfillments' of prophecy cited in the New Testament seem to the candid reader rather far-fetched, even supposing the events to have actually occurred as described. And when one studies the Old Testament prophets with no preconception of their rôle as precursors of Christ, one finds that they were not very much concerned about foretelling the future, except in the general way of threatening the punishment of Jehovah if the Jews failed to forsake their sins, and promising a Deliverer when they should do so. In so far as they did try to foretell the future, they were about as often wrong as right — or at least no more accurate in their predictions than any shrewd observer might be expected to be.

5. The Proof from Miracles

Perhaps the commonest argument for the authenticity of the Christian revelation has been the proof from miracles. The supreme miracle of Christian tradition, the Resurrection, has been, and still is, the glad tidings of the Church at Easter-tide, as the miraculous birth-stories still give a glamor to Christmas. If such marvelous events occurred, if Jesus had such prodigious powers, surely he was from Above, and his words must be taken as the absolute and unquestionable truth.

> We have the testimony of the Apostles. Their writings are pervaded by a spirit of sincerity.... Their sober-mindedness is also very evident.... The central point of their united testimony is the *resurrection of Jesus Christ*.... If any one event of history is certain, it is our Lord's resurrection. And it is this which is the seal and attestation of divine revelation.[1]

[1] C. E. Luthardt, *The Fundamental Truths of Christianity*, pp. 203–206.

A miracle served to authenticate as authoritative the teaching with which it is associated.... The divine power re- vealed in the acts of Jesus attested the divine authority of the words of Jesus.... The miracles of Jesus not only command attention but command belief.... To us, as to those disciples who heard him, the evidence of the authority of his teaching is found in the fact of his resurrection. It was not so much the beautiful farewell address to the disciples, as the empty sepulcher on Easter morning, that "brought life and immortality to light." [1]

Modern scholarship has long since ceased to regard the Gospels as written by the Apostles; they are anonymous compilations of stories and sayings which doubtless circulated long from mouth to mouth before they were committed to writing. Among these early Christian communities an almost negligible number had ever known Jesus himself. The atmosphere of the times reeked with marvels and portents. It is impossible now to trace these stories back to their sources. Quite apart from the a priori possibility, or probability, of miracles, the evidence of narratives written by believers a generation or two after the events, in so credulous an age, can hardly be accepted by any trained historian as convincing.... The Resurrection stories in the Gospels are among the later strata of the compilations. There are striking inconsistencies between one and another of them. They present a very different view of events from that which one would gather from the letters of Paul, which constitute our one early first-hand source. Paul gives no sign of believing in the emergence of Jesus' body from the tomb; the Resurrection for him means, clearly, the passage of Jesus' spirit from the underworld to Paradise. Paul mentions his own vision of the risen Jesus alongside the

[1] W. N. Rice, *Christian Faith in an Age of Science*, pp. 382–385.

others of which he had heard; one gets the impression of ecstatic experiences very different from the circumstantial physical events narrated in the later stories.... All this is, of course, a matter for the most meticulous Biblical scholarship, and is only alluded to here to suggest to the reader a line of research.[1]

But this matter of miracles is too long a story to start here; we shall devote to it a later discussion. The reader who is tempted to rely upon the record of miracles to attest the teaching of Jesus, or of the Church, is asked to turn at once to page 423 and read that section through, before proceeding with our argument.... We shall say here, in summary, merely this: miracles are related, in overwhelming numbers, to accredit every faith; it is extremely difficult to accept the Christian miracles without, in all fairness, accepting a thousand others, equally well — or ill — authenticated. And it is quite possible to hold that *none* of them happened — except in so far, of course, as they may have been merely natural events.... Usually, Christians who believe in miracles believe in them because the Bible, or the Church, *says* they happened. At another time, they find an added support for their belief in the Bible, or in the Church, in these miracles which prove them superhuman. Which is, obviously, to argue in a circle.

Jesus himself, according to the oldest strata of the Gospel record, seems to have rested the case for his teaching not upon any working of wonders, but upon its intrinsic appeal to the hearts of his hearers; he is even reported to have been impatient of those who were seeking a "sign,"

[1] Discussions of the alleged miracles wrought by Jesus will be found in J. Warschauer, *Jesus, Seven Questions*, ch. III, and in any good life of Jesus. The best scholarly study of the Resurrection stories is to be found in Clayton R. Bowen, *The Resurrection in the New Testament* (Putnams', 1911).

and to have called them an evil and adulterous generation.

We shall now briefly summarize the arguments *against*
accepting an Authority as absolute.

1. *The Multiplicity of Claimants*

Religious history is full of teachers and books and institutions for which absolute authority is, or has been,
claimed. In each case, the authentication fails to convince those outside the particular circle of believers.... It
is quite conceivable that one of these claims is valid and
the other false. It *may* be that while all other circles of
believers are merely gullible, *we* alone are so fortunate as
actually to have an inerrant source of truth. But the
study of comparative religion almost inevitably under-
mines that satisfying assumption. Objectively considered,
the evidence is so much of the same stripe! And our increasing knowledge of the psychology of belief reminds us
that gullibility may not be entirely restricted to people of
other faiths than our own.

2. *The History of the Development of the Idea of Revelation*

Wherever historical data are available, we can trace the
development of the idea that a certain person or book is,
in a peculiar sense, authoritative. In the case of the
Bible we have come to see pretty clearly the process by
which these books — and not other, more or less similar,
contemporary writings — came to be included in what
we call the Canon, and invested with a peculiar reverence
and awe. It took centuries for this process to be com-
pleted. Early canons included other books than those
we now accept, and rejected some which we include.

There were bitter debates as to the merits of this book and that, and at times the decision was by a bare majority. Yet the books which were, by this chance or that, accepted, are now regarded as the "Word of God," while their rivals for place, although in some cases of higher literary or religious value, now rest in relative obscurity. ... A knowledge of this more or less haphazard accretion of the writings that make up our Bible tends to lessen the likelihood that we shall look upon it as an oracle of supernatural truth.

Likewise, the conception of certain churches as authoritative had a gradual growth. The claims of the Roman Catholic Church, for example, were not widely accepted until the Roman hierarchy had actually won the supreme power. Rome was the capital of the dying empire. There was need of a united front to combat paganism. It was natural that the bishop of that city should assume the leadership. But the dogma of the infallibility of Catholic doctrine emerged only as the triumphant result of centuries of opposition and struggle. The idea that the Apostle Peter had been given divine authority by Jesus, had come to Rome, and handed on his authority to his successors, is evidently the rationalization of a *fait accompli*.

In such ways historical scholarship tends to discredit the claims of a book or institution to absolute authority.

3. *Inconsistencies in the Statements of an Authority*

In the case of the Bible:

Many inconsistencies exist between different traditions that have both been incorporated. When one verse flatly contradicts another, it is only by a difficult evasion that the believer can preserve his devout belief in the truth of both. For instance — to mention but a few — in Acts 9:7, speaking of Paul's vision, we read, "and the men who journeyed with him stood speechless, *hearing a voice*, but seeing no man," while in Acts 22:9, which narrates the same experience, we read, "And they that were with me saw indeed the light, and were not afraid; but they *heard not the voice* of him that spake to me." Again, the first three Gospels made Christ eat the Last Supper on the eve of the Passover, and die on that day, while the Fourth Gospel relates that he died on the day of preparation for the Passover. Of the same census we read in 2 Sam. 24:1, that the Lord commanded David to take it, and in I Chron. 21:1, that it was Satan who put it into his mind....[1]

Obviously, when two inconsistent statements are made, one of them at least must be untrue. And if a certain number of statements are thus proved untrue, what becomes of the infallible authority?

4. *Conflicts Between an Authority and Present-Day Knowledge*

The Bible declares that the world was made in six days, "morning and evening." It envisages a little world, centering about our earth. This earth is flat, and there are "waters under the earth"; the heavens are like an upturned bowl above it; above this "firmament" are other waters; through windows in it they come down as rain.... All of this, and much more that might be mentioned, was good astronomy in its day, but is now known to be mistaken. The coney is represented as chewing the cud. The zoölogist of today knows better than that.... Certain historical statements in both Old and New Testaments have been shown by historical research to be erroneous....

As for the authoritative churches, it is a matter of common knowledge that they denied for a long time, and in

[1] Durant Drake, *Problems of Religion*, pp. 269–270.

some cases still deny, various scientific discoveries and theories now generally accepted by intelligent people, such as the Copernican astronomy and the facts of organic evolution.

If Authorities make such mistakes, can they be accepted as absolute?

5. Low Moral Teachings of an Authority

Continuing to use the Bible as our example:

God's anger and desire for vengeance are repeatedly mentioned; and the picture the unprejudiced reader would form of this Jewish deity from many Old Testament passages is that of a cruel and bloodthirsty tyrant. He "hardens Pharaoh's heart" (Exod. 14:4–8) that he may punish the Egyptians in a spectacular manner; he throws stones down from heaven on Israel's foes (Joshua 10:11); he commands the sun to stand still that more of them may be slain before dark (Joshua 10:12–13); he bids his chosen people invade the land of a neighboring tribe, burn all their cities, slay all the males, adults and children, and all the married women, and keep the virgins for their own enjoyment (Numbers 31); he slays seventy thousand innocent Israelites for David's sin in taking a census of the people (2 Sam. 24:15)....

In the Book of Revelation, he that worships falsely "shall drink of the wine of the wrath of God, which is poured out without mixture into the cup of his indignation; and he shall be tormented with fire and brimstone in the presence of the holy angels, and in the presence of the Lamb. And the smoke of their torment ascendeth up forever and ever, and they have no rest day or night" (Rev. 14:10–11).... In one of the Epistles we read, "God shall send them strong delusion, that they should believe a lie; that they might all be damned who believed not the truth" (2 Thess. 2:11–12).

Surely such sentiments need no comment! In the light of them, to assert that the teachings of the Bible are throughout divine and authoritative is to barbarize our moral ideas; to claim that such words as these are inspired of God is to worship a God who is at times a very devil.[1]

[1] Durant Drake, *Problems of Religion*, pp. 271–272.

Some of the practices formerly sanctioned by the Roman Catholic Church, such as the Inquisition, are repugnant even to good Catholics today. And there are not a few attitudes taken by that church and other authoritative churches today which are sharply criticized by non-ecclesiastical moralists....

To save space, illustration of these arguments has been confined to the Bible and the Christian Church, since these are the Authorities best known to the great majority of readers of this book. But the arguments discussed, pro and con, apply, *mutatis mutandis*, to various other Authorities which have been offered for human guidance.

May we suggest, in concluding this discussion of absolute authority, that it is legitimate to hold to such an Authority *if* one has honestly decided that the arguments in favor of its claims are convincing, and the arguments against it weak. It is *not* legitimate to regard such an Authority as absolute simply because it is the easiest and most comfortable thing to do, or to save oneself the trouble of *thinking*.

TO WHAT EXTENT MAY WE LEAN ON AUTHORITY?

At this point we are probably in the mood to reject all authority whatsoever! But it is impracticable for us to question everything; we have neither the mental capacity, the necessary information, nor the time. What then! We know that we are beset by misinformation, by prejudice, by loose reasoning, by every sort of untruth. We know that the great progress of science in recent years was made possible only by the sweeping rejection of Authorities formerly accepted. The Middle Ages clung to tradition in every sphere — in medicine, in law, in science and philosophy, as well as in religion. It was the break with that reliance upon authority which ended the centuries of relative stagnation and gave birth to the modern world. We are now agreed that it is well that *somebody* should question *everything*. But we must individually take a good deal on trust.... *Whom*, then, can we trust? If we are to hold no Authorities sacred, what Authorities may we hold sound?

The present writer has two suggestions to offer:

1. *We should Consider Carefully the Qualifications of an Authority*

Is he a careful observer and reporter of facts? Has he full and expert knowledge of the subject in question? Is his thinking free from unwarranted assumptions? Does he seem to have considered contrary opinions without bias? Are his methods of reasoning logical, uninfluenced by his emotions, his interests, or his hopes?

We must beware of being too much impressed by genius or personality or even by mere intellectual power, in choosing the experts whom we are to trust. Men of powerful intellect have often gone far astray in their thinking. For the technique of sifting truth from error is not only difficult, it has been little *considered*. The genius is, of all men, most impatient of checks and cautions. The tide of his being runs too strong to be stemmed by any weighing and balancing of evidence, or any real sympathy for points of view alien to his own. The man of commanding personality has usually been a special pleader, too sure of his convictions, or too eager in his loyalties, to question his underlying assumptions. And so his thought, confined within their bounds, may have been vitiated by some initial error.

The great spiritual geniuses are, as a rule, particularly untrustworthy when it comes to impartial observation and logic; for great spirituality is almost incompatible with the development of the critical faculty. Such men are usually steeped in the moral and religious traditions of their people, expurgating or expanding them in the light of their own radiant intuitions, but never questioning their essential truth. Feeling, emotion, discipline of the will, are for them everything.... Such exponents of the spiritual life are of the greatest service to mankind; moral idealism, tenderness, courage, a quickened heart and a disciplined will, are of more immediate importance to individual men and women than the quest for wider and more accurate truth. Truth-seeking is perhaps, in the end, of even greater importance to mankind; and a rigorous devotion to the art by which it may be found is, in its way, also a great moral ideal. But this particular art is developed usually by a different type of person from the one who becomes a great artist, poet, or saint, the founder of a religion, or the leader of a cause. So, while we may well be heartened by the sight of such men, stirred by their vision, and helped by their counsel in our spiritual life, we should do well to be wary of their philosophical outlook.

We should also beware of being too much impressed by the antiquity of an Authority. There is a natural tendency in the human mind to pay respect to age, and to distrust innovation. But while age often mellows a tradition, and makes it more precious, as it does with wines and violins, it has nothing to do with its truth. The Constitution of the United States, the Apostles' Creed, the Ten Commandments, are simply the opinions of the men who formulated them; the reverence of generations adds nothing to their intrinsic value — whatever that may be — as expressions of truth.

When our ancestors uttered the opinions which are now hoary with age and which we are asked to revere, they were as young in years as ourselves, and the world in which they lived was much younger in the matter of racial experience. Their opinions, however old they may be, express the childhood of the race, not its maturity. And the age of an opinion or dogma actually affords a presumption against its truth rather than in favor of it.... In all that makes for wisdom we are not younger but older than our ancestors.[1]

Another point which must be noted is that a man may be an excellent Authority in one field and a very poor one in another.

Between statements of the same witness in different fields the correlation of reliability may be very small. It may in fact even be negative. I might, for example, give implicit faith to the utterances of a zealous socialist concerning the details of socialist doctrine, while at the same time I might be justified in regarding his evaluation of an opponent's objection to socialism as more likely to be wrong than right. This would be a case in which the correlation would be negative. Or again, I might accept on authority the statements as to his science of a great experimental physicist, rejecting at the same time as unimportant his opinions as to the accomplishments of a spiritualistic medium. The habits of trustfulness developed in him by work with his colleagues in the laboratory might easily make him a worse than ordinary judge of the trickery of charlatans. The same man can be very wise and good in our field, and very foolish and bad in others.... As the homogeneity of the fields decreases, there is a proportionate decrease in the probable degree of correlation. The authority of the great physicist would be quite trustworthy in chemistry, less so in biology, still less in psychology, and practically *nil* in literature or religion.[2]

[1] Wm. P. Montague, *Ways of Knowing* (By permission of The Macmillan Co., publishers, 1925), p. 44.

[2] *Ibid.*, pp. 41-42.

We must aim, then, to rely in every field of thought upon the authorities who are expert *in that field.*

2. *We should Consider how far there is Consensus of Opinion*

It is obviously not enough that the people in *our* church, *our* political party, *our* 'set,' believe thus and so. We should find most of these opinions to be minority opinions if we looked far enough afield. But on the other hand it is not mere numbers that count, it is *the number of those who are in a position to ascertain the facts.* How far, then, *is* there a consensus of opinion, among those who are in a position to ascertain the facts, as to the important matters upon which we need to know the truth?

The completest consensus of opinion is to be found in the realm of the physical sciences. If a scientific opinion reigns undisputed for years, we may be sure it is because it is based upon excellent evidence. The evidence is open to all; and if there is an error in observation or reasoning. it will soon be found.... There are, indeed, borderland re gions, on the frontiers of science, where there is frank disagreement, because the observed facts are as yet meager or uncertain. But if scientists agree in announcing some conclusion, we may be reasonably sure that it is so.

There is also a great deal of agreement as to the outstanding facts of history. But in details, especially as to causal influences and the relative importance of different factors, there is considerable difference of opinion; and one must learn to discount the nationalistic bias, the political, economic, religious leanings of historians.

There is a fair consensus of opinion among civilized peoples with respect to the simplest moral teachings. Thou shalt not (in general) kill, steal, tell a lie, etc. But the reasons here are so obvious that there is no need to accept such precepts upon authority. And when we get beyond this elementary agreement, we find the sharpest differences of judgment. There are many co-existing moral codes, each skillfully defended, and infused with fervent idealism by its proponents. If we accept any moral authority, we must realize that we are accepting a minority view. And while, for practical reasons, we cannot too cavalierly reject the conceptions of what is right and wrong which we find in our particular community, we should seek to form our own judgment as to the issues rather than repose too confidently upon any one teacher or any one code as authoritative.

In all other matters — political and social doctrines, religion, and philosophy — there is no consensus of opinion whatsoever. Millions of people in America believe in democratic capitalism, millions in Italy believe in the Fascist State, millions in Russia believe in Communism. Millions in the West believe in Christianity, millions farther East believe in Mohammedanism, Hinduism, Buddhism. There is no social philosophy, no metaphysical view, no religious doctrine, that is held by more than a minor portion of the human race.... Evidently, then, it is wise in these highly controversial matters to consider carefully the *arguments* advanced, rather than to rely upon some particular Authority. For no Authority has won, in these matters, anything approaching general acceptance; and so to choose an Authority *at the outset of our quest for truth* would be arbitrary. *After* we have investigated the qualifications of an Authority, as suggested above, we may legitimately accept one rather than another. But even then we can hardly feel as certain as if our chosen Authority commanded general assent.

SUGGESTED READINGS

G. L. Dickinson, *Religion, A Criticism and a Forecast*, I–II.
G. K. Chesterton, *Orthodoxy*, VIII–IX.
J. Warschauer, *What is the Bible?* I–II.
Durant Drake, *Problems of Religion*, XVI, XVII.
Columbia Associates, *Introduction to Reflective Thinking*, VIII.
W. R. Inge, *Faith and Its Psychology*, V–VIII.
W. P. Montague, *Ways of Knowing*, I.
H. Rashdall, *Conscience and Christ*, I.
G. S. Fullerton, *Introduction to Philosophy*, XXIV.
J. E. Haydon, *The Quest of the Ages*, VIII.
D. C. Macintosh, *The Pilgrimage of Faith*, II.
R. H. Thouless, *Straight and Crooked Thinking*, V, VI.
M. R. Cohen, *Reason and Nature*, pp. 23-33.

CHAPTER II

INTUITION AND FAITH

INTUITION

ONE of the common reasons offered for accepting a saint or seer as an authority is that he has had a special *intuition* of the truth. And many an obscure individual has believed himself to have direct intuitions, of genuine noetic value. A direct 'vision' of truth, it is sometimes called. But this is obviously a metaphor; intuition is not seeing, with the eyes, or perceiving with any sense organ. It is strongly imagining that something is thus and so, with an accompanying conviction that it really *is* as we imagine it. A distinguishing feature of intuition is that we do not know how we reach the insight. It is a leap in the dark, by contrast with the detailed observations and logical reasoning of an explicitly empirical method.

To be sure, the word 'intuition' has other meanings. It is sometimes used by philosophers (notably by Santayana) to mean our everyday awareness of the immediate data of consciousness, whatever they may be. In this sense we are all intuiting constantly, and without doing so we could know nothing.... But we shall use the term here in the specific sense above noted; for this is the sense in which the term connotes an alleged special avenue to truth, strongly contrasted with the more laborious and plodding empirical method. Women are often supposed to be better endowed with it than men, and geniuses than ordinary people. It often appears in the form of premonitions ('hunches') of impending events, or of immediate

convictions as to the character of people just met. For
the religious it may take the form of a sense that all is
well with the world, that God exists, or something of the
sort. For Bergson it is what the Germans are calling
Einfühlung and English-speaking estheticians are calling
empathy — a direct sense of the inner nature of an object
contemplated,

> A kind of intellectual sympathy, by which one places one-
> self within an object in order to coincide with what is unique
> in it, and consequently inexpressible... a means of possessing
> a reality absolutely instead of knowing it relatively, of plac-
> ing oneself within it instead of looking at it from outside
> points of view.[1]

In all these cases, the unique feature of intuition is
directness. It is, or purports to be, an immediate apprehension of something, and, moreover, an apprehension of
something *beyond* our immediate experience. Bergson,
and others, maintain that our most important knowledge
is to be reached by this route.

> No amount of thinking can lead to metaphysical realiza-
> tion. This can be attained only by the man who reaches a
> new level of consciousness. Metaphysical truth appears to
> this deeper state of consciousness as 'given' in the same direct
> way as outer nature is given to the eye, and the world of
> concepts to the intellect.[2]

> We must begin to realize that all man has ever thought
> of any worth in the history of philosophy, he has taught as
> the result of that inner and direct awareness of truth which
> we call intuition, and not as the prodigious result of weari-
> some reasoning.... As intuition becomes more widely recog-
> nized as a legitimate path to knowledge, the uncertainty
> which at present accompanies its occasional visitations will
> disappear; a new organ or function will ever be uncertain in
> its initial workings. It may reassure us, however, to realize
> that the greatest teachers of all times have ever presented

[1] Henri Bergson, *Introduction to Metaphysics.*
[2] H. Keyserling, *The Travel Diary of a Philosopher.*

their conclusions on their inner worth as intuitions; we do not find a Christ or Buddha proving conclusively that what he says is right, or reasoning out logically his doctrines. They can disdain to use such make-believe of proof and yet they spoke as no man ever spoke, and the hundreds of millions who have followed them have found sufficient conviction in their words through the very spirit of truth that spoke through them.[1]

Our question, then, is, *Have* we any such short-cut to knowledge? *Can* we "place ourselves within" an object, and thereby grasp its nature as it is not revealed to our sense organs or to our reason? *Is* there such a faculty as Intuition, and, if so, is it a trustworthy road to truth?

Experience does show that people, who, as we say, are intuitive, are often correct in their insights, their premonitions, their quick judgments of character. Bergson, who considers intuition an instinctive faculty, spends much space in showing the remarkable successes of instinct among animals; his conclusion is that his philosophy, based upon intuition, is more profoundly true than science, or than a philosophy based upon the scientific, empirical method.

To buttress his argument, Bergson attempts to show that observation and reasoning give us a world which is profoundly *un*real. The intellect falsifies whatever it touches; it is a purely practical faculty, useful for guiding us to appropriate reactions, but not of ultimate epistemological value. Logic schematizes, substitutes "a bony skeleton, a rigid framework," for the true nature of things, which is really too fluid, too infinitely various and changing to fit into this intellectual scheme, this "scientific construction."

[1] Reprinted from J. J. van der Leeuw, *The Conquest of Illusion*, pp. 56–58, by permission of and special arrangement with Alfred A. Knopf, Inc., authorized publishers.

The particular task which confronts the scientist in his dealing with the world of matter makes the intellect his instrument. But if the scientist in his philosophical moods were to go in search of reality, he would find himself in possession of another avenue of approach through direct intuition. The work of the philosopher here is somewhat like that of the artist, who *identifies* himself with the object, "putting himself back within the object by a kind of sympathy." It is as if, when we approach nature by means of the intellect, a certain "barrier" exists between nature and the mind, which intuition breaks down through sympathetic communication.[1]

Taking up this last point first, it is clear that observation and logic cannot give us *complete* knowledge of things. As we shall see in Chapters IV and XII, common sense and science can give us only a knowledge of the *structure* of things, not a knowledge of their inner nature (or substance, or quality, or *feel*). But this empirical knowledge of the structure of the world is not only extremely useful, as Bergson admits, it is the only kind of knowledge which would *be* useful. If it be possible, by intuition, to discover the inner nature of reality, that sort of knowledge may be interesting, and possibly inspiring, but it can be of no practical value. As a matter of fact, the more analytical and abstract science becomes, the more exact its grasp upon the nature of things seems to be — as is proved by its increasing ability to make successful predictions. The sort of inadequacy which science has is the sort of inadequacy which a map has; it is in some respects unlike the country mapped, but it gives us, so far as it goes, exact truth about that country. Why then should we refuse the name *truth* to that knowledge about things which is alone exact, and alone of actual use?

I am minded to ask: What difference would it make if his

[1] G. T. W. Patrick, *Introduction to Philosophy*, p. 45.

"scientific constructions" and "interpretations in the interest
of action" were renamed "knowledge" and the object of
them "reality"; if his "intuition" and "pure perception"
were labeled "esthetic experience" and their objects "subjective immediacy"?   Apart from some moral or religious
interest in setting intuition and its object higher than science
and the scientific (and social) object, what point [is there]
in this ascription of "knowledge" and "reality" to pure intuition and its object?   For Bergson, the scientific (the social
and the common-sense) interpretation is, theoretically considered, a misinterpretation made in the interests of practice.
But in what sense can it be misinterpretation if, follow it
however far, one never reaches any undesirable dénouement
which could be avoided by refraining?   Since conceptual interpretation serves the interests of action, why this invidious
denial to it of the term "knowledge"? [1]

Moreover, even if ordinary knowledge, and the whole
structure of science, should come to seem to us grossly
inadequate as knowledge of things-as-they-really-are, it
would remain to be proved that knowledge via intuition
is any more adequate, or truthful.... The plausibility of
Bergson's case lies in the fact that the world disclosed by
science — the world of atoms, electrons, and radiant
energy — is so different from the world of immediate experience.   But *is* this panorama of immediate experience
the real objective world, the world actually existing about
us?   Does it even *reveal* that world more truthfully than
science reveals it?   It certainly is very real in a sense,
namely, *as our conscious experience*.   And it is quite possible that it may carry within it clues, missed by science,
as to the inner nature of the things about us.   But to say
that this conscious experience of ours constitutes a direct
apprehension of this other-life, that this other-life about
us is like that, rather than as science describes it, is to

[1] C. I. Lewis, *Mind and the World Order*, p. 147.   Charles Scribner's Sons.

make a tremendous assertion.... This matter, however, we must leave to Part II of this volume.

When we look, now, at the positive arguments offered for the intuitional method, we note the concrete successes of what is called intuition. But these successful 'intuitions' reveal, in most cases, just the sort of world that ordinary knowledge and science reveal; they seem to be short-cuts to the same results, rather than a revelation of a different sort of world. And this is because what is called intuition is usually just the subconsciously reached or retained result of past experiences. Intuitions seem to well up out of some unknown deep; they are mysterious, inexplicable to the one who has them. But it is noteworthy that good intuitions come usually only to those who have considerable experience in the particular field where they appear. The man who is an 'intuitive' judge of character is one who has known and watched many people; he cannot say how he reaches his swift judgments, but they are clearly the result of a long accumulation of observations. Valuable intuitions as to the disposition of troops come to the experienced general more often than to the inexperienced, valuable scientific intuitions to the man of long scientific training rather than to the tyro.

> Poetic inspirations come, in anything like finished form, only to persons who have read poetry, studied it, and attempted to produce it; mathematical inspirations come to mathematicians only; musical inspirations come to musicians only.[1]

Prince Kropotkin, in his *Memoirs of a Revolutionist*, gives a good example of the birth of an intuition:

> To discover the true leading principles in the disposition of the mountains of Asia — the harmony of mountain formation

[1] G. A. Coe, *Psychology of Religion*, p. 273.

— now became a question which for years absorbed my attention....

Beginning, then, with the beginning, in a purely inductive way, I collected all the barometrical observations of previous travelers, and from them calculated hundreds of altitudes, etc.... This preparatory work took me more than two years; and then followed months of intense thought, in order to find out what all the bewildering chaos of scattered observations meant, until one day, all of a sudden, the whole became clear and comprehensible, as if it were illuminated with a flash of light....

There are not many joys in human life equal to the joy of the sudden birth of a generalization, illuminating the mind after a long period of patient research. What has seemed for years so chaotic, so contradictory, and so problematic takes at once its proper position within an harmonious whole.

But Kropotkin did not accept this new idea as true just because it came to him in a flash of intuition. No, any cautious scientist or philosopher will simply take his sudden intuitions as hypotheses to be tested empirically, not as self-guaranteed truths.

For nothing is plainer than that intuitions very often turn out to be *un*true. Evidently they need to be checked up by some more critical method. Indeed, different peoples' intuitions notoriously conflict. Bergson's intuition gives him one sort of world; other philosophers and seers have divined very different worlds. Usually we realize the untrustworthiness of other people's intuitions, but feel that our own are penetrating and reliable. For intuitions have a *feel* of convincingness, and at the moment when we have them it is difficult to distrust them.

There seems to be no reason for supposing that intuition has any special organ, that it is a separate 'faculty,' that it has any way of reaching truth save the ordinary ways. It is just swift, unconscious deduction from past experience. Or mere imagining, which may or may not hit the mark. Or it is a mere crystallizing of instinctive aversions and desires. In fact, the name 'intuition' is applied loosely to various types of swift conviction, the only point in common being that they are not the obvious fruit of remembered observations and explicit reasoning. So it would seem wise to accept them at most very tentatively, as hypotheses to be checked up by the more laborious but safer processes of empirical study.

MYSTICISM

Mysticism is the culmination, the glorification of intuition. The term may be used to denote the mystical experience itself, or to denote the theory that such experiences have noetic value, give us valid insight into the ultimate nature of things. This distinction is easily blurred, since one of the marks of the mystical experience is that it *feels* noetic, it has the appearance of a deeper insight, a revelation of truth. Under the spell of such an experience the subject feels himself "an initiate, one to whom has been granted a view of the Inside. To him the doors have been opened, from his eyes the veils have fallen." [1] The type of person who has such experiences rarely has also such an analytic and skeptical temper as to question the cognitive value of the experience. But it is *possible* to be a mystic, in the psychological sense, and yet to be entirely skeptical, after the glamour of the experience has faded, as to its value in revealing anything beyond the potentialities of vivid and ecstatic emotional experience.

By common usage the term 'mystical' is given to states of emotional ecstasy wherein the mind dwells, not on some particular object (as in the experience of being in love, or in the enjoyment of beauty), but on the glory of things

[1] C. A. Bennett, *A Philosophical Study of Mysticism*, p. 72.

in general.   In such states there is a sense of emancipation, of enlargement, of the merging of self with a larger whole. Reality seems, in the glamour of this emotional rapture, wonderfully different from the drab world of every day. All sorrow, frustration, limitation have vanished, everything is harmony and joy.   The mystic emerges from his rapture with a sense that he has penetrated the secret of things.   But what that secret is — save that it is ecstatically beautiful — remains usually ineffable.   If it is given definite form, it is in terms of the particular theology or philosophy of the particular mystic.   For the Hindu, the experience means oneness with Brahma, for the Christian it is union with Christ, or with one of the saints; for an agnostic like Richard Jefferies, it is a oneness with the ineffable beauty of Nature.

Prosaic folk, who have never had mystical experiences, find it hard to take them very seriously, just as those who have never been in love shrug their shoulders at the extravagant illusions of lovers.   It is, indeed, obvious that the mystic, like the lover, is not in a state of mind to criticize or discount his rapturous convictions.   How far, then, can we, as discriminating critics, accept their assurances that they have *seen*, they *know* — that all is well with the world, that Reality is One and Divine, that they have been merged with the World-Soul — or whatever traditional form their assurances may take?   Such assurances clearly contain *interpretation* as well as mere description of their experiences.   And interpretation of experience is always open to doubt, most of all when the subject is in an excited state of mind.   The completest psychological sense of certitude does not take us a step toward objective, logical certainty; the strongest convictions may be utterly mistaken.   It is easily conceivable that all these ecstatic experiences are hallucinatory, when considered as revelations of anything beyond themselves.

The *optimism* born of mystic experiences, the sense of the *glory* of reality, is of course the precipitate of the rapturousness of the experience. It can be matched by an equally violent pessimism born of experiences of a contrary sort. As William James concretely showed, there are what we might call *anti*-mystical experiences, emotional states as horrible as the mystical states are rapturous. Such dreadful experiences naturally crystallize into a sense of the unutterable horror of existence. Experiences of this sort have, naturally, not been cultivated and given a place of honor in religion and poetry. People who are so unfortunate as to have them usually wish to forget them as soon as possible. But have we, candidly, any reason for supposing that the rapturous experiences are any more *noetic* than the horrible experiences?

The mystic's sense of the *unity* of things is a natural result of the simplification of his field of consciousness. All other ideas drop out, all the multitudinous, harassing details of daily living; and nothing exists for him, for the time being, but God, Nature, the All — whatever he calls this sea of joy in which he feels himself bathed. His volition is suspended, his consciousness becomes 'automatic,' like that of a hypnotized person; he drifts on the great tide of being.... It is the supreme escape-mechanism from the perplexities and sorrows of life. Where such states are persistently cultivated, they tend to unfit the person for meeting his actual life-problems; mystics have been useful citizens only if they have tempered their mysticism with common sense.

Mystical experiences are so poignant, so memorable, and so glorious, that one hates to cast doubts upon their noetic value. But if we are honest, we must note the following points:

(1) The experiences of the mystic are, psychologically, very similar to experiences produced by opium, nitrous monoxide gas, and other drugs.[1] Can we seriously believe that these states of a drugged brain give a truer insight into the nature of things than a normally healthy, wide-awake brain? The mystical experiences are undoubtedly due, in some degree, to peculiar somatic conditions; indeed, the traditional techniques for cultivating them are largely concerned with producing the proper bodily condition. Whether the physical cause is a powerful drug or a combination of more subtle factors, it is difficult to believe, on reflection, that states of mind thus produced are more accurately cognitive than those of the normally poised organism. The drunkard *feels* closer to the heart of things, but the sober man discounts his assurances.

(2) The supposed truths reported by the mystics vary according to their antecedent beliefs. There is a certain degree of agreement among orthodox Christian mystics; their minds have been fertilized by their particular type of religious education, and their experiences come as a response to their expectations. But if we compare the mystical experiences of Hindoos, Mohammedans, Buddhists, Mormons, Christian Scientists, and so on, we find no agreement in their reports, save in their rapturousness. And as to that, we may say again, that these rapturous experiences are, themselves, merely a selection from a vastly greater number of experiences, many of which are repudiated as too depressing to pin our faith to, or even to record.... If, then, we are to accept the dicta of mystics,

[1] Cf. William James, *The Varieties of Religious Experience*, pp. 386 ff.

we must ask, Which mystics? And why mystics rather than other folk with vivid and convincing, but very different, insights?

(3) No coherent theory has ever been formulated as to *how* mystical experiences can yield knowledge of objective reality. We can understand, to some degree, how our sense-organs and our reasoning faculty can give us truth. But through what channels does the mystic's supposed knowledge come? It is generally said that the mystic's soul is in direct contact with God, or Reality, is One with it, during the experience. But how can this be? And what does it really *mean* to say that?... It all remains in the realm of vagueness and mere assertion. The mystic himself does not feel the need of answering such questions; he *knows* — and that is the end of it. But as reflective thinkers we can hardly be satisfied with so subjective and incommunicable an assurance.

(4) The essential conviction of the mystic is that Reality is gloriously *good*. But (as we shall see in Part V), goodness, beauty, gloriousness are not, except in a secondary and derivative sense, attributes of nature, they are attributes of conscious experience. When such qualities are attributed to nature, it is by an unconscious projection of our human emotions. Thus, all that the mystical experience *can* prove is that it is possible for the human spirit to live upon this emotional level, to respond to the Reality that encompasses it with this ecstatic acceptance, to maintain a state of rapture far above that of ordinary human experience. It is essentially an achievement in the *art of living*, rather than a help in the search for *truth*.

FAITH

From the Apostle Paul's famous trilogy, "faith, hope, and charity," down to the present day, Christian teaching has eulogized faith as a virtue and as a road to truth. *Credo ut intelligam*, said Saint Augustine — I believe in order that I may understand. 'Skeptic,' 'infidel' (that is, the man without faith), have been terms of reproach. Faith has seemed a positive, healthy, optimistic attitude, doubt the sign of a grudging, cynical spirit, or of a presumptuous, conceited temper, perhaps even a mere excuse for turning away from the religious life.... This follows the line of least resistance in average human nature. Faith is more natural to most men than doubt, and far more congenial. The human mind is instinctively credulous, while skepticism is an acquired characteristic. Faith is warm and soothing, doubt is cold, upsetting, a disturber of the peace. Faith stabilizes doctrine, justifies ecclesiastical authority and control; doubt threatens these interests and makes the doubter a homeless outcast, if not a dangerous rebel. It is no wonder that faith has been deemed a safer and nobler attitude of the spirit than doubt.

But we have been speaking of faith only in the sphere of religion. In other matters — in reading advertisements and editorials, in listening to political spellbinders, real-estate agents, or oil-promoters — faith is patently absurd and harmful. Faith in the upward course of the stock market has led to many a man's financial ruin. Why should credulity in matters of religion be any more sensible?... As a matter of fact, there has been a counter-current of opinion from early days which has labeled religious faith as folly, and even as sin. Faith, it has been said, is mere mental laziness, or cowardice, preferring the anodyne of some comforting belief to the arduous and perplexing task of sifting evidence and searching for tested truth. Faith leads to stagnation, skepticism to progress. As a modern Chinese writer, Hu Shih, puts it, "The most spiritual element in science is its skepticism, its courage to doubt everything and believe nothing without sufficient evidence.... The attitude of doubt is essentially constructive and creative."

Is faith, then, a virtue, or is it really a vice?... Before we can answer this question intelligently we must distinguish the various shades of meaning which may attach to this highly ambiguous word. It would be well if we had a different word for each meaning; for writers and preachers slip from one sense of the word to another without warning, and use arguments which have point with respect to one sense of the term to justify faith in a somewhat different sense.

(1) Perhaps the most primitive form of faith is *trust in a person or group of persons*, confidence that what they say is so because they say it. In this sense we *have* to exercise a great deal of faith — in our friends and business associates, in physicians, teachers, scientists, engineers, and all those upon whom we are dependent for safety, information, or help. The question at issue is whether it is reasonable to have faith in Jesus, or Buddha, or Mohammed, or the writers of the Bible, or the founders of our church and the formulators of its creed. The priest or preacher says, Trust the Church — its leaders have thought longer about these matters than you; trust Jesus — he *knew*.

Here, in particular, trust seems a more generous and loyal attitude than doubt. Yet doubt, in many a case, is wiser. It is sensible to trust people only in so far as experience suggests that our trust is warranted. We may, for example, trust a friend's willingness to help us in a crisis, yet distrust his financial advice. Similarly, we may trust Jesus' and Buddha's purity of motive, their insight into human nature, their judgment as to the best way of life in general, without trusting their cosmological views. They may have been profoundly convinced of the truth of their teaching on these matters, and yet have been completely mistaken — as, indeed, one of these two great spiritual teachers must have been, since their cosmic views are almost diametrically opposite.... The justification of faith in this sense, then, would take us back to our discussion of authority.... In general, we may say that trust, to be wise, must be discriminating, and *based upon reasonable evidence* that the object of our trust is really a competent and reliable guide in those matters with respect to which we are asked to trust him.

(2) But are we not begging the question in asking for "reasonable evidence"? If we have the evidence, do we need *faith?* Is not faith, precisely, *believing where we lack evidence adequate to convince the intellect?* Often, indeed, religious leaders have demanded faith in spite of apparently strong evidence to the contrary, so that there is actually some point in the little girl's definition of faith as "believing what you know ain't so" — or in Anselm's more dignified "Credo quia impossibile." The source of such a faith may be loyalty to a leader or church, it may be an emotional drive, the 'suggestion' derived from preaching or ritual or hallowed creed, or the unwillingness to surrender a precious belief. It may be an unconscious series of steps such as that which William James called the "faith-ladder":

Faith's form of argument is something like this: Considering a view of the world: "It is *fit* to be true," she feels; "it would be well if it *were* true; it *may* be true; it *ought* to be *true*," she says; "it *must* be true," she continues, "it *shall* be true," she concludes, "*for me;* that is, I will treat it as if it *were* true as far as my advocacy and actions are concerned."[1]

Faith of this sort was condoned, even espoused by James, in his famous essay, *The Will to Believe*, and has become the most popular aspect of the movement which he called *pragmatism*. Because of its connection with the other doctrines of that school, we will postpone discussion of 'faith' in this sense, to our chapter on Pragmatism, remarking here merely that, whether or not such a faith is morally justifiable, it will be a *reliable guide* only if it is an *intelligent* faith, a faith actually warranted by the *facts*. And whether or not it *is* so warranted cannot be decided by faith itself, but must be ascertained, if at all, by empirical study of those facts.

(3) But faith is not necessarily belief without evidence, or in spite of intellectual difficulties. In many cases it is hard to believe something for which we *have* good evidence, because some instinct or emotion shakes our confidence. Faith, then, may be *belief in despite of emotional obstacles*. The child learning to swim finds it difficult to have faith that the water will buoy him up, though he has ample evidence to justify that belief. A novice in an airplane, a savage taking his first railway ride, find it hard to have faith in their safety, though statistics show that the chances of harm are slight. A mountain-climber, forced into a position where he must leap a yawning chasm, may lose faith in his ability to make the leap, although past experience shows that

[1] William James, in the *Journal of Philosophy*, vol. 24, p. 198.

it is well within his powers. A parent witnessing his child perform some feat which is quite easy for him may find his faith faltering.... In these cases fear is the enemy of faith. But obviously such faith is only justifiable in so far as it is based upon solid evidence; otherwise it is mere recklessness and folly.

(4) Some of the cases cited above lead us to the final, and most important sense of 'faith,' the faith which is an expression of purpose, of idealism, of determination, as opposed to cynicism, pessimism, and despair. Faith in this sense is *the refusal to be discouraged*, the will to achieve, and *confidence in the possibility of achievement*. It is optimism, not in the sense of complacency, but in the sense of resolute hopefulness and courage. By contrast with the sort of faith which holds that something *was* thus and so in the past, or *is* thus and so now, it holds that something *can be made* thus and so in the future. It is a steady maintenance of interest and intent, in spite of temptation to slackening or diversion of zeal. Thus we may have faith in the League of Nations, or in Democracy, or in Communism, or Fascism, or in the Church, or in the Public School — in anything upon which we are willing to stake our efforts and our lives. Such a faith begs no question, and guarantees nothing; it is an expression of hopefulness and of intent. It believes in ideals because it is determined to realize them; it believes in the future, because the future is still, in part, pliable to our will.

Looking at these varying forms of faith, we may say, in summary, that faith is not a faculty that, in some mysterious way, sees deeper into reality than reason. It is not a method of discovering truth. Faith cannot tell us that Jesus rose from the tomb, that God exists, that water will buoy us up, that the League of Nations will work. It merely keeps alive and effective a conviction which we have reached by some other route. Whether or not it is warranted depends, therefore, upon the soundness of the reasons upon which the conviction in question is based. Clearly it should not be so obstinately held as to impede our sifting of truth from error. It should not be a premature faith; for premature faith is simply prejudice.

Moreover, faith of the right sort is not inconsistent with doubt. For doubting is simply using our intelligence; thinking fairly about things *involves* a goodly measure of doubt. What we call skepticism may, of course, be a mere expression of indifference, of lack of interest, of frivolity of mind, or of a despairing sense of the futility of the search for truth. But what is bad here is not the element of doubt, it is the moral slump — the inertia, indifference, mental paralysis, or slackness. The skepticism which is the expression of sincere devotion to truth, a sense of its importance, and an unwillingness to be duped, or to be content with specious comfort, is one of the noblest of human attitudes. Religious people have too often thought of all doubters as being of the former sort; they have failed to see the fineness of temper of the latter type — their scrupulous honesty, their disinterestedness, their courage. They should learn of the Apostle Paul — that ardent champion of faith — who said, "Prove [i.e., test] all things, hold fast to that which is good." Testing (the Latin *probare*) involves doubting; the faith (the "holding fast") is to be exercised with respect to that which meets the tests. *First* we must doubt all things, *then* we must hold faithfully to that which has commended itself to our best judgment as good and true.

Surely, then, faith has its place, and a very important place. We need, not less faith than our fathers, but a better-founded faith. One of the most pathetic things in life is the fact that people have pinned their faith to such illusions! We must not suppose that faith involves the abdication of common sense, or that it is the peculiar possession of fanatics and fundamentalists. We may have faith in the importance of doing right, in noble standards of life, even if they are dubbed quixotic and seem to demand more than they give. We may have faith in whatever ideals, in whatever causes have come, after serious thought, to seem sound and deserving of our allegiance. We may have faith in ourselves, in our latent potentialities, in our power to become what we want to be. We may have a similar faith in our fellows, in the goodness latent in them, and in the possibility of realizing a better life for man on earth. We may well have faith in our religion and faith in God — if our religion and our conception of God are such as intelligent and moral men may hold. Faith of such sorts as these is a great dynamic; by its power poor stumbling wayward man may some day realize his ideal, and society be made over into the likeness of our dreams.

SUGGESTED READINGS

H. Bergson, *Introduction to Metaphysics*.
Bertrand Russell, *Mysticism and Logic*, pp. 12–21.
George Santayana, *Poetry and Religion*, I.
J. B. Pratt, *The Religious Consciousness*, XX.
W. K. Wright, *Student's Philosophy of Religion*, XVII.
C. A. Bennett, *Philosophical Study of Mysticism*, Part II.
G. A. Coe, *Psychology of Religion*, XVI.
Margaret P. Montague, *Twenty Minutes of Reality*.

J. Middleton Murry, *God*, pp. 122–177.
H. E. Fosdick, *The Meaning of Faith*, pp. 38–50.
G. L. Dickinson, *Religion, A Criticism and a Forecast*, IV.
Leslie Stephen, *An Agnostic's Apology*, II.
H. Sedgwick, *Practical Ethics: The Ethics of Religion*.
W. R. Inge, in *Religion and Life*, I.
William James, *Some Problems of Philosophy*, Appendix.
J. H. Randall, *Religion and the Modern World*, last chapter.
M. R. Cohen, *Reason and Nature*, pp. 46–57.

CHAPTER III

A PRIORI TRUTH

WHEN people are pried loose from their comfortable reliance upon authority and intuition, they are apt to take refuge in the supposedly self-evident nature of certain basic truths. Certain propositions seem 'axiomatic' — compelling, by their intrinsic obviousness, the assent of all rational beings. Sometimes it is thought that we have an innate capacity to discern such truths, so that our knowledge of them is independent of the testimony of our concrete, but always fragmentary, experience, and is thus superior in certainty to all empirical knowledge.

This view seems the more plausible because of the general agreement as to the certainty and universality of logic and mathematics. Various thinkers, of whom the most noteworthy is Spinoza, have tried to import a mathematical certainty into their arguments upon matters of practical concern or of high theoretic interest, and to develop a theology or philosophy so rigorously logical, or even mathematical, as to command universal assent. Is such an undertaking feasible? If not, why not?

WHY ARE LOGIC AND MATHEMATICS SO CERTAIN AND SO UNIVERSAL?

We *know* that our logical syllogisms and our mathematical processes are universally and eternally valid. There is no possible doubt that $2 + 2 = 4$, that they always have equaled 4 and always will. And we feel equally certain of the conclusion of every operation in arithmetic, algebra, geometry, and all the other branches of mathematics — if it is correctly performed. If we add twenty-three units of *anything*, at *any time*, to thirty-one units, we do not have to count them to know that we have fifty-four units. If we have a plane triangle, we *know*, without measuring them, that the angles sum up to two right angles. In both cases, we can *see* that it *must* be so, *just by thinking about it*. If we were given the initial axioms and definitions of any mathematical system, such as those of the familiar Euclidean geometry, we could shut ourselves up in our closets and see for ourselves, in our mind's eye — if we were smart enough — the truth of every proposition in the system. And when we had seen the truth of these propositions, we could not possibly doubt them. No concrete experience could increase, or diminish, our assurance of these truths. This is what is called a priori truth, truth known prior to concrete sense-experience.

It is of the greatest importance to see clearly *why* the syllogisms of logic and the operations of mathematics give us such certain and universal truth.... In a word, it is because they give us simply knowledge of the *relations of implication* between different propositions; i.e., they tell us merely what statements imply what other statements. All that logic and mathematics tell us is that *if* something is so, and something else is so, *then* something else is thus and so. If y is z, and x is y, then x is z — where x, y, and z are *anything mentionable*. The conclusion *follows* from the premises. But logic cannot tell us that the premises are *true*; at best it can tell us only that they are valid implications of other premises, i.e., they are true *if* those other premises are true — and so on, *ad infinitum*.

The hackneyed example has it: "All men are mortal. Socrates is a man. Therefore Socrates is mortal." But, strictly, all that the syllogism tells us is that *if* the first two propositions are true, the third proposition is also true. All that is certain in the syllogism is the *linkage* between the propositions. This is commonly called 'formal truth.' It would be better to avoid the term 'truth' altogether in this connection, and speak only of logical 'validity.' For this *logical validity* is an utterly different thing from *factual truth*.

Reasoning is *valid*, even if all the statements are *false*. For example, the following is a sound syllogism: "All Americans are money-mad. John Masefield is an American. Therefore John Masefield is money-mad." But no one of the three assertions is *true*. On the other hand, a process of reasoning may be logically unsound, although all of the statements are true. For example, "All useful studies are hard. The study of mathematics is hard. Therefore the study of mathematics is useful." It is clear that although the conclusion of this argument is *true*, it does not *follow* from the premises. For, although all useful studies are hard, some non-useful studies are hard too; and for all our premises can tell us, mathematics may be one of these hard but useless studies.

Now, why can we be so certain of the validity of logical reasoning? Simply because to deny the conclusion and at the same time affirm the premises would be to make contradictory statements, which would cancel one another, and leave *nothing said*. The relation of 'implication,' which sounds so mysterious, is merely the relation which holds between propositions when the denial of one *means* a denial of the other or others. For example, a part of the meaning of the statement "All men are mortal" is embodied in the statement "Socrates is mortal" — since Socrates is (as we affirm in the minor premise) one of the units *meant* by the phrase "all men." Thus, if we deny the conclusion of the argument, that Socrates is mortal, we deny what we have already affirmed in our generalization about *all* men; we contradict ourselves.

The principle involved is commonly phrased as if it were a mysterious law of existence — "Nothing can be both x and not-x," "A thing cannot both be and not be."... But it is not necessary to assume any such a priori knowledge of the existing universe, to see the validity of the logical principle in question. For logic is merely a matter of consistency in our *meanings* and in our *assertions*. All that we need to say, so far as this principle goes, is, "You must not deny what you affirm" — because, if you do, you are contradicting yourself, and not really saying anything. Logic is a series of rules and checks to save us from inconsistency, to keep us from thinking (and so acting) at cross-purposes with ourselves.

Thus logic, *alone*, cannot give us any truth about nature. The laws of logic — i.e., of all valid reasoning — are a priori, prior to experience of the world, because they "impose no limitations upon it." [1] They would be what they are, *whatever* sort of world existed. Logic can only show us that certain *arguments* are valid, and others invalid. It cannot tell us what *exists*. Logical rules are not natural laws, they are rules of procedure, they are "addressed to ourselves."

And now, mathematics is simply a carrying-out of

[1] This phrase is from Professor C. I. Lewis, of Harvard University, whose book *Mind and the World Order* contains an excellent discussion of this matter.

logic in the fields of number and measure. The existing world does, as a matter of fact (i.e., of empirical observation), seem to be such that our logic and our ordinary mathematics apply very happily to it. But logic and mathematics themselves couldn't tell us that they would apply. And they would be just as valid, *as* logic and mathematics, whether or not they were of practical use in understanding nature. Arithmetic cannot tell us that there are four things in existence, or even that when you put two things with two things you will have four things. (You *won't,* if the things you put together are two drops of water and two grains of salt, or two tigers and two lambs.) It can only tell you that if you *have* two things plus two other things, and so long as you continue to have them, you have four things. For 'four' *means* 'two plus two'; and to say that you had two plus two, and that at the same time you *didn't* have four, would be to contradict yourself.

There are *numbers,* of course, far greater than the number of *things* we can ever find in the world, however we count them. And arithmetical propositions concerning them — their sum, difference, quotient, etc. — are just as valid and indisputable as propositions concerning numbers which we find illustrated in existence. In the nature of the case, empirical observation could never prove the truth of these propositions. But they are absolutely certain. Here is a priori knowledge of the clearest sort.... But *all* mathematical knowledge is of this sort. It is certain, because it is knowledge of our meanings, not of the existing world. We *need* no observation of the world to know that it is true, and no observation could increase the certainty of our knowledge.

In arithmetic we *define* 'two' as meaning 'one plus

one.' 'Three' is 'two plus one.' 'Four' is 'three plus one.' And so on. Taking these definitions *together*, we see that 'four' means 'one plus one plus one plus one.' And since 'one plus one' has another name, viz., 'two,' we can express the *same* meaning in other words by saying that 'four' means 'two plus two.' The term 'four' thus *means* 'two plus two.' There is no mystery about it. No knowledge of *things* is required. If, as John Stuart Mill suggested, there were a malicious demon who always added a fifth thing when we added two things to two things, that would not spoil our arithmetic in the least. We should have five things, but they would be *two plus two plus one* things. If, for example, we put two tigers with two lambs, the demon might add another tiger, or another lamb; but it would be obvious that our five animals were not two tigers plus two lambs, but were either three tigers plus two lambs or three lambs plus two tigers. If we turned our backs for a little while there might be, when we looked again, only two tigers, and no lambs. But it would still be just as true that if there *were* two tigers *and* two lambs, there would be four animals. For 'four' would be only a shorter way of *saying* 'two plus two.'

As for geometry, it is doubtful if there *are* any triangles, circles, or even straight lines in existence. But that does not affect the validity of the Euclidean geometry. For geometrical knowledge is of this form: "*If* there is a triangle (as defined), *then* its angles are equal to two right angles." All mathematics is an endless "if — then."

CAN LOGIC AND MATHEMATICS INFORM US
CONCERNING EXISTENTS?

If logic and mathematics are thus purely analytic, merely explicating our own meanings, how can they give us any information concerning the existing world? It is obvious that we do use them in furthering our knowledge of nature. But what right have *we* to legislate, in this a priori fashion, as to what can or cannot, does or does not, *exist?*

The answer is, that logic (including mathematics) can inform us of the nature of the existing world *only when it is used in conjunction with truths about the world got from other sources.* If your premises are true, then your conclusions are true too. But if your initial premises are not *true*, then your whole system of deductions is not *true*, although the logical *links* are impeccable. In recent decades a number of non-Euclidean geometries have been worked out in detail. They start from premises different from those adopted by Euclid, and are thus different throughout. Each of these logical systems is absolutely valid *as a logical system;* its 'truths' are just as certain and universal as the 'truths' of the familiar Euclidean logic. They just don't happen to apply so well to the existing world about us.... As a matter of fact, there is serious doubt as to whether the Euclidean geometry *does* apply to our world as exactly as we used to suppose it does. It may be that one of these other, non-Euclidean, geometries more faithfully portrays the actual nature of existents. The only way to find out is to study the world empirically, measure it, and judge which geometry is the best fit.

But whether or not Euclidean geometry applies *exactly* to figures in the existing world, it is at least so *approx-*

imately relevant that it may for all ordinary purposes be considered exactly true. It is empirically ascertainable that nature is either exactly Euclidean or so nearly Euclidean that we can use it in making measurements on earth without discoverable error; it is only when we consider astronomical distances that the discrepancy, if there be a discrepancy, between this geometry and the constitution of nature would be appreciable. If this familiar geometry *hadn't* proved to be so happily applicable to mundane measurements, it would long ago have been abandoned, except by lovers of mathematics for its own sake.

Systems of science and philosophy are much like systems of mathematics, except that when we go beyond the quantitative and measurable aspect of things our categories become much *more* doubtfully applicable to the existing world. For example, we may work out a philosophy of nature in terms of matter, energy, ether, atoms, or electrons. We formulate certain laws of the behavior of our supposed units. Then, *if* our categories really apply to the nature of things, *if* our laws are correctly formulated, and *if* our logic is sound, our whole conceptual system is *true*. All depends upon picking the right categories and formulating the right laws. But in any case, if our *logic* is sound, the whole system of thought hangs together, like a system of geometry; the conclusions do really follow from the premises.

Thus the history of science and philosophy consists in formulating and trying-out one conceptual system after another, to see which best fits the world in which we live. It is only by this trial-and-error procedure that we eventually hit upon the actual nature of things.

Of course the world might, conceivably, have been such that *no* logical or mathematical systems would be of any help in understanding it. If it were a world of queer and rapidly shifting shapes, one thing melting into another, like the colored shapes produced by Thomas Wilfred's color-organ, with no regularity, consistency, or dependability, our logics and geometries would be useless, except as mental exercise and diversion. But, fortunately for our practical life, our world, as William James put it, "plays right into logic's hand." Experience shows that it has an enduring structure, complex, baffling, perhaps beyond human powers to understand completely, but one which our logical-mathematical patterns can be made more and more accurately to fit.

Even so, it may not be clear why logic and mathematics are so valuable — and so difficult. Consistency in our own meanings sounds simple enough. Why are not these conceptual systems "an immense tautology"? Can we not trust ourselves not to contradict our own meanings, without all this fuss?

Well, in the first place, when you have a complicated pattern of meanings, it has to be unraveled step by step, by creatures with such minds as ours. For example, we define each integer, in arithmetic, as the preceding integer plus one. It is easy to show, then, that $7 \times 8 = 56$, just as we showed that $2 + 2 = 4$ (multiplication is just a short-cut to addition). But the number of logical syllogisms required to show that this is our meaning is very considerable; it is a great saving in time to learn the multiplication-table once and for all, and be done with it. To show that $34 \times 43 = 1462$ would require an *enormous* number of steps. Fortunately, human genius has discovered that set of short-cuts which we call arithmetic. And, of course, it can be shown, logically, that these short-cuts reach the same results as the long routes via the definitions of all the numbers from 'one' to the highest number involved.

Similarly, if certain laws of motion and of gravitation are assumed, and certain definite positions and motions and masses of the sun, earth, moon, and the other planets are likewise assumed, it is possible to prove logically what the relative positions of the sun and the planets will be at any future moment, if no disturbing factors enter in. The computations involved would fill many volumes and require years to make. And whether the heavenly bodies will actually *be* in those positions (so as, for example, to make an eclipse of the moon occur at a certain future moment) depends (supposing our logic-mathematics to be accurate) upon whether our initial assumptions accurately correspond to the actual physical facts. *If* we can know that they *do*, we can know a priori that the eclipse will occur as predicted. And, as a matter of fact, experience shows that these assumptions, as made by contemporary astronomers, *are* accurate within such a small margin of error that their predictions of eclipses do turn out to be accurate to the second. But even if the assumptions did not quite correspond to the physical facts, the system of astronomy thus worked out would be just as valid *as a logical system;* it would be a part of the *meaning* of the assumed laws and concrete motions that such and such positions would be attained at such and such moments.

Meanings may thus be so complicated, *must* be so complicated if they are to fit the extremely complicated nature of the existing world, that it requires the labor of a considerable number of people to trace their combined implications. It is possible to trace these consequences of certain combinations of premises once and for all, and to hold the results ready to use when occasions for their use arise. Thus we have the 'rules of the syllogism,' we have the multiplication-table, the tables of logarithms, and, in fact, all the formulas of mathematics, mechanics, and the other pure sciences. The bridge-builder can safely use these formulas in preparing his specifications. If he had to trace all the implications himself — not to speak of choosing the right premises — he would never get a bridge built. The practical work of a civilized community is thus necessarily co-operative, far more than we realize. The physicist formulates laws, and carries on elaborate experiments to see if these formulas actually fit the facts. The mathematician traces the consequences of these laws in detail. The steel-maker produces steel girders to certain specifications. The bridge-builder, by making further computations of his own, is able to see, without too great labor, that *if* the steel girders are really made as their description states, and *if* the physicist's laws actually hold of the physical world, and *if* the mathematician's operations are logically correct, *then* the girders ordered will support the stresses which traffic will bring.

In addition to the complexity of the job of tracing implications, it is often difficult to see what premises will yield us the knowledge we want. And if we can see what premises are relevant, we may not know whether they are true or not. An American may have discovered evidence that a certain supposition is true; a German, engaged in a totally different line of research, may have found reason for believing that a certain other supposition is true. An Englishman, having by chance read of both of these investigations, may, as we say, put two and two together, use these two suppositions as premises, deduce from them a logical conclusion, and publish his conclusion as a suggestion. A Frenchman may investigate and discover that this conclusion is a fact. The successful application of logic to life thus depends not merely upon logical skill itself, but upon finding the right premises and bringing them together.

The answer to the question which heads this section is, then, that logic (including mathematics) can give us knowledge of the existing world only when, and to the degree that, it has truths concerning this world to use as premises.

HAVE WE SELF-EVIDENT TRUTHS TO USE AS PREMISES?

If we are to have indubitable knowledge of our world, we must have indubitable premises upon which to build up such knowledge. Where can we get indubitable premises? Many people, including some philosophers of repute, have believed that some simple propositions are indubitable because self-evident; no one can possibly doubt them. They are apt to point to the 'axioms' of mathematics as instances of such self-evident truths. "A straight line is the shortest distance between two points." "Parallel lines can never meet." "Two straight lines cannot enclose a space." If we were blind and deaf, and cut off from all observation of the world, we could know these statements, and others of the sort, to be true, just by contemplating them.

A very considerable number of propositions have thus been offered by one person or another as 'self-evident' — e.g.: "Every event has a cause." "Nothing can act where it is not." "I am conscious." "Space (or Time) cannot be infinite." "Space (or Time) cannot be finite." "God is over all." The doctrine of evolution is declared untrue by Catholic logicians because it "contradicts the principles of metaphysics, which teach that things are *immutable in essence*, and that *the effect cannot be greater than the cause*." [1]

It is apparent, even from this brief list, that there is no consensus of opinion as to what propositions *are* 'self-evident.' Apparently 'self-evident' as thus used of a proposition means simply 'seems self-evident to me.' This would be an interesting psychological fact, an empirical truth about the working of a certain person's mind, or of the minds of a group of people dominated by a certain point of view. But is there reason to suppose that a proposition which seems self-evident to a person, or to a group, is necessarily *true?* Actually, many propositions which seemed at one time self-evident to practically everybody, have turned out quite clearly to be untrue. For example, it used to be considered a self-evident fact that if the earth were a sphere there could not be inhabitants at the antipodes, since they would be head-downwards and would fall off.

Those who believe that we have a priori knowledge of nature may argue that unless we do have such self-evident premises, we can never have *any* knowledge at all. Science could not *get going* without some such sure foothold at the outset. And they point out that we *do* feel more certain of these foundation-stones of our science than our very fragmentary experience could possibly warrant.... The answer to this is that we do not have to *assume* that these initial propositions are

[1] Quoted by William James, *Principles of Psychology*, vol. II, p. 670.

true; we may simply try them out, as working hypotheses. If all the deductions we make from them turn out to coincide with observed fact, so far as we can check them up, we have good empirical reason for thinking our hypotheses well chosen. If not, we will formulate other hypotheses. As a matter of fact, experience has given us overwhelming verification of many of the initial propositions of our sciences, and it is no wonder we feel sure of them. But our feeling of *certitude* is by no means the same thing as objective *certainty*, and is no warrant of it. We may have felt certain of these propositions *before* experience corroborated them. That is, we do often have a priori *beliefs*. But *beliefs* are not *knowledge*. There is no a priori *knowledge*, except knowledge of our own meanings.

As to the so-called 'axioms' of geometry, they are now more properly called 'primitive propositions.' That is, they are simply the set of propositions from which all the rest of the system of geometry *follows*. They are not necessarily *true*. Any number of sets of primitive propositions may be chosen, each giving rise to a whole elaborate system of geometry. Many of these primitive propositions, the 'axioms' of the system in question, will be anything but self-evidently true. Experience may show them to be grotesquely untrue. The geometry developed from them will be none the less a valid geometry, though it will not be of any practical use. In any case, our 'axioms' are merely arbitrary assumptions chosen for the sake of developing their implications.

Similarly, such propositions as "Every event has a cause," or "Nothing can act where it is not," may be excellent assumptions to try out. But we have no right to feel certain that they are true, in advance of our

study of the world.   As a matter of fact, the indeterminist (the believer in 'free will,' in the popular sense)
disbelieves the former proposition, as does the theologian
who believes that God's will to create the world was uncaused.   And many physical facts have seemed to belie
the other proposition.   It is true that no sane person
who says "I am conscious" can doubt the truth of that
proposition.   But *its* self-evidence is purely empirical;
you *feel* yourself conscious.... In short, there are *no*
propositions which we can *know* to be true, prior to the
experience which 'verifies' them.   (In what sense experience 'verifies' propositions we shall presently explain.)   We may *hope* that certain generalizations, such
as, "Every event has a cause," are true, because, if they
are true, our task of understanding the existing world
will be much simplified.   But if they turn out not to be
true, we must simply make the best of it.

The apriorist may fall back upon the contention
that certain propositions may be known to be true because their contradictories are *inconceivable*.   For example, a recent book on science by a reputable thinker
declares:

> The new discoveries have greatly extended our conception
> of the mutability of existence and modified our ideas of the
> fixity of matter, but they have not destroyed our faith in
> the constancy of existence as regards *amount*.   This convic-
> tion, known as the *law of constancy*, is not based primarily
> on experimental evidence.   Rather is it due to the inability
> of the human mind to conceive of the absolute beginning of
> substance or its absolute annihilation.[1]

Herbert Spencer's grandiose system of philosophy
rested upon a thoroughgoing use of this criterion.   One

[1] W. F. Cooley, *Principles of Science*, p. 114.

by one, scientific, religious, philosophical ideas were examined, declared to be inconceivable, and thereby dismissed. Contradictory suppositions, indeed, were *both* declared inconceivable:

> Of Space and Time we cannot assert either limitation or absence of limitation. We find ourselves totally unable to form any mental image of unbounded Space; and yet totally unable to imagine bounds beyond which there is no Space. Similarly at the other extreme: it is impossible to think of a limit to the divisibility of Space; yet equally impossible to think of its infinite divisibility. And, without stating them, it will be seen that we labour under like impotencies in respect to Time.... It results therefore that Space and Time are wholly incomprehensible.... [Moreover] Matter, in its ultimate nature, is as absolutely incomprehensible as Space and Time. Frame what suppositions we may, we find on tracing out their implications that they leave us nothing but a choice between opposite absurdities... All efforts to understand its essential nature do but bring us to alternative impossibilities of thought.... [Thus] in its ultimate essence nothing can be known.[1]

Spencer's argument is useful as a *reductio ad absurdum* of the argument for the truth of a proposition based upon the supposed inconceivability of its opposite. "We cannot conceive of space as infinite, therefore it must be finite." "We cannot conceive of it as finite, therefore it must be infinite." Take your choice!... If it is true that we cannot conceive either alternative, then it is obvious that our inability to conceive a supposition as true is no bar to its *being* true. For one or the other of two contradictory propositions *must* be true.... Why, indeed, should the psychological fact that we are unable to *conceive* of something as being so prevent it from *being* so? Why should we *expect* to be able to conceive everything that exists? If a given

[1] Herbert Spencer, *First Principles*, ch. III.

supposition seems inconceivable to someone, is that
not merely the result of the fact that his experience
hitherto has been of such a sort as to make it seem inconceivable? It seemed inconceivable to people in the
Middle Ages that anyone could live on the under side
of the earth without falling off.... In short, is the inability to 'conceive' something anything more than an
unfortunate psychological disability? And in view of
the great variety of beliefs which have been held by
some and branded as inconceivable by others, is it not
clear that the inability to 'conceive' something is a
mere individual idiosyncrasy?

But what do we *mean* by the inability to 'conceive'
something? Do we mean merely that we cannot *picture*
it in our mind's eye? There are certainly many aspects
of reality which are, in the nature of the case, unpic-
turable; so that would prove nothing.... Do we mean
simply that the supposition has no intelligible *meaning*?
There are such cases, of course, mere nonsensical combinations of words. But in such cases there is not a
supposition at all, of which it can properly be said that
it is conceivable or inconceivable. The succession of
words is simply meaningless.... Do we mean that the
supposition is *incredible*? That we find ourselves unable to believe it? But that, again, would be merely
a psychological fact. People vary indefinitely as to
what they find credible and incredible. All you can
fairly say is that a supposition is incredible to *you*. Or
you may say that it is incredible to all sane, or all intelligent, persons. But only if experience shows that
all sane, or all intelligent, people *do* find it incredible.
And that is not the case with any existential propositions
except those which are based upon familiar human ex-

perience — propositions which are empirical, not a priori.
Anti-logical propositions (such as, that $2 + 2 = 5$) are, indeed, incredible to all intelligent people. But such propositions, we repeat, do not constitute *existential* knowledge, concerning which we are here making inquiry.

In the proper sense of the term, we can 'conceive'
any entity that we can define or describe, and any supposition that we can frame. The very describing of the
entity, the very framing of the supposition *is* the process
of conceiving it. People *have* conceived Space to be
infinite. Other people have conceived it to be finite.
All that is necessary is to know what we *mean*. And
that is not difficult. We mean, in this case, that there
is some definite number of cubic miles, and no more, in
the space of our existent universe. Or, the number of
cubic miles is greater than any mentionable number.
Which supposition is true? That remains to be argued.
But the very fact that we can argue about it shows that
we know what we are talking about; i.e., we can *conceive* both possibilities.... Similarly, we can *conceive*
the 'amount of existence' as constant, or as diminishing,
or increasing. We can conceive of dragons and centaurs
and fairylands. We can conceive of a God-controlled
universe and of a Godless universe. We can *conceive*
of unlimited possibilities of existence. Whether we
can *believe* in them depends upon our particular mental
history; by study and thinking we can come to be able
to believe many things that were once incredible to us,
and to cease to be able to believe many things we once
believed.... All this is merely of biographical interest.
The important question is, What must we believe if we
are going to believe what is *true*? In what direction
must we *develop* our powers of conceiving and believing?

To sum up, we do have what we may call a priori truth. It is not 'innate,' it is not particularly 'self-evident,' or 'axiomatic,' it has no compulsive power over our minds, so that we find ourselves irresistibly believing it. It may be very difficult to grasp, and hard to believe. It tells us, in itself, nothing whatever about nature. It is merely an elaboration of our own meanings, as found within some conceptual system. Its truth (or, better, validity) is compatible with any sort of universe. It constitutes logic (including mathematics).

Our supposedly 'self-evident' truths are either merely propositions that hold *within such a conceptual system*, or they are generalizations from experience, or they are assumptions, working hypotheses, tentatively assumed for the purpose of tracing their implications. Or they are mere prejudices. In any case, they can tell us nothing about the existent world, except as they may be generalizations from our empirical study of that world, or logical deductions from such generalizations.

Our theology, our metaphysics, our ethics should, indeed, be as rigorously logical as we can make them — should be mathematically exact, if we can find significant numberable or measurable aspects of reality in these fields. But the 'primitive propositions' of such systems will remain doubtful. The system may hang together, logically, but be a mere coherent dream. Any number of such metaphysical or ethical systems can be constructed. To know which is *true*, or nearest to the truth, of the existent world, we must have some other criterion than the mere internal consistency of our structure. So we may admire the logical consistency of the medieval schoolmen, of Kant, or Spinoza, or Bradley, or Royce — or of Christian Science, or Mohammedan theology — and yet feel that all these beautiful systems of thought, so 'logical,' so persuasive to those who have adopted them, have little relevance to reality. Once get us firmly in contact with reality, and logic will help us stay there. But logic must be the servant of fact, and not set up as independent authority.

SUGGESTED READINGS

R. W. Sellars, *Essentials of Philosophy*, XII.
Columbia Associates, *Introduction to Reflective Thinking*, V.
Bertrand Russell, *The Problems of Philosophy*, VII–VIII; XI.
Betrand Russell, *Introduction to Mathematical Philosophy*, XIV–XVIII.
J. S. Mill, *System of Logic*, Book II, chs. V–VII.
Herbert Spencer, *Principles of Psychology*, Part VII, ch. XI.
A. K. Rogers, *What is Truth?* pp. 29–54.
M. R. Cohen, *Reason and Nature*, pp. 137–146, 171–198.
Cassius J. Keyser, *The Pastures of Wonder; Humanism and Science*, III; *The Human Worth of Rigorous Thinking*, XV.

Chapter IV
EMPIRICAL KNOWLEDGE

WE HAVE seen what logic can do for us. Now what can *observation* do for us?... If it is accurate, and accurately expressed, it can report what our concrete experiences are, one by one. We can amass such reports, collate them, compare them, and discover their general trends. This constitutes empirical knowledge. It is, at least, knowledge of the types and the history of human experience. But our experience is largely an experience of *things*. And if realism is true (we shall presently consider what grounds we have for believing it to be true), our empirical knowledge is also a knowledge of these things. The empiricist says that all knowledge of *fact* is of this sort; logic can be used to work over and clarify the knowledge thus got, can help us to see what must be true if what we have observed is so, but the only way to know what *is* so, is to look and see. However it may be with the Kingdom of Heaven, the attainment of truth cometh by observation.

WHAT IS THE EMPIRICAL METHOD?

Before making up our minds as to this, we had better see as clearly as possible what this empirical method of getting knowledge is. It is not always as easy as it sounds. For we must not only describe accurately such experience as we have — and that is a task beset by many difficulties — we must contrive to get the sort of experience that will tell us what we want to know.

Science is, of course, founded upon empirical observation. Many of these observations are what we call 'experiments.' Experimentation is the observation of isolated, partially controlled events. The stage is carefully set to get experience concerning what we want to learn about, and irrelevant factors are kept from intrusion. There is scope for great ingenuity in devising experiments. Our knowledge has not only been vastly increased thereby, but has been made far more accurate. For when observation is carried on under definitely known conditions, the *conditions* of various sorts of experience, the exact circumstances under which they can be had are discovered. And because of this definiteness, the experiments can be repeated, and the results checked up, by other observers, whose idiosyncrasies will counteract one another, and give us 'objective' fact.

Where such manipulation of experience is impossible, we must gather data in our chosen field of observation from as many angles as possible, using instruments of precision wherever we can. We must, of course, observe impartially, looking out particularly for discrepancies, for facts that are out of line with our expectations, watching sharply for new 'clues,' for facts hitherto overlooked, which may prove significant. We must state our observations as accurately and unambiguously as possible. We must classify the facts we have observed, analyzing out the various features of our complex experiences, seeing how these features fit together, *organizing* our miscellaneous data.

And then we must make tentative *generalizations*. For knowledge of particulars is not only endless, it is relatively useless. What we need to know, for most purposes, is not what happened in the past, but what may be expected to happen in the future. And it is only general knowledge, knowledge of the *kinds* of things there are, and the ways in which they behave, which can help us in this way.

But how is generalization *warranted*, on empirical principles? How can observation, which is always of particular occurrences, give us general truths? It might, of course, warrant us in saying that, for example, all the particles of matter we have studied so far tend to behave in the way which we formulate in the law of gravitation. But we have studied very few of the myriads upon myriads of existing particles. And our observations have extended over a very brief space of the world's history. What right have we to make a *general* statement, of the form, All particles of matter are subject to the law of gravitation (or, if you prefer, The law of gravitation holds for all particles of matter)?

The answer is, that all general statements of 'fact' (as contrasted with merely logical propositions, such as $2 + 2 = 4$) are, strictly, 'hypotheses'; they are suggested premises, from which observed facts could be deduced. If the facts which we can find do thus follow logically from our hypothesis, we call them the 'evidence' for the hypothesis, and we say that the hypothesis 'accounts for,' or 'explains,' the facts. For example, the law of gravitation 'accounts for,' 'explains,' the fall of an apple; that is to say, if the law is true, we can see that the apple *would* fall. Scientific hypotheses — and the ordinary assumptions of common sense — explain, in this sense, the observed trend of experience. They can, and must, be checked up, 'verified,' over and over again, by new observations. That is, we must keep on making logical deductions from them and then looking to see if the facts are as our logic tells us they must be if the hypotheses are true. The sciences consist of organized bodies of hypotheses which thus tally with observed facts.

It often happens that several contradictory hypotheses accord logically with all known facts. *Whichever* hypothesis is true, observed facts would be as they are. In that case, we must continue our observations until we find facts deducible from one but not from the other. For example, the Ptolemaic theory of the motions of the heavenly bodies fitted the facts known in its day quite admirably. It could, perhaps, by constant revision, be made to fit the facts since discovered concerning the visible motions of these bodies. But it could not have been deduced from that hypothesis, as it could be, and was, deduced from the Copernican hypothesis, that if there are stars not too distant, they will appear in slightly different positions at different times of the year. Such differences have been found; and the finding constitutes good verification of the hypothesis. Again, no one could have deduced from the Ptolemaic theory the existence of a hitherto unknown planet; whereas, working on the Copernican theory, the existence, mass, and position of such a planet (Neptune) *was* deduced, and discovered as predicted. Even if the Ptolemaic theory, by constant revision, could accept and describe these new facts, it could not *explain* them; i.e., they would remain brute facts, unrelated to anything else. Whereas the Copernican theory can link them all together, as inevitable consequences of its assumptions. That is, we can see that *if* it is true, and if certain other beliefs which are empirically based are true, these formerly unsuspected facts must, logically, be as they are.

Side by side with the elaboration of the Copernican

theory has gone a formulation of the laws of motion, and of gravitation. These too are, strictly, hypotheses. But the Copernican theory fits in with them admirably, while the Ptolemaic theory does not. The former also fits in with our growing body of hypotheses as to the size and complexity of the stellar universe and with the theory now carefully worked out by astronomers as to the *origin* of our earth and the other planets.... Thus scientific hypotheses win acceptance, not merely because they serve to explain a certain set of observed facts, but because they fit in coherently with *other* hypotheses which explain other sets of facts.

Can we say, then, that our empirical test of truth is, at bottom, one of *coherence*? In a sense, yes. Not the mere *internal* coherence, or logical consistency, of a set of beliefs, though that in itself is a valuable negative test. For if a set of beliefs *lacks* this internal consistency, we can be sure that something is wrong. People have a surprising ability to hold mutually contradictory beliefs; and it is a salutary work, to do as Socrates used to do, go about pointing out these contradictions, and awakening in men the realization that they do not know *what* they believe.... But this is not a sufficient test of truth. For a creed may contain no contradictions, may be internally consistent, and yet be a mere dream, not a picture of the actual world. It may be perfectly coherent, yet false.

But if we extend the application of the term 'coherence' to mean that our test of truth is consistency with all our other hypotheses which are empirically founded, and with all known facts, we could not have a better. Our religious beliefs, for example, must be compatible with the most securely founded hypotheses of geology, anthropology, psychology, and history, our moral convictions with the findings of economics, sociology, and political science.... If each of our beliefs accords logically, so far as we can see, with all observed facts in its field, and is not logically incompatible with our beliefs, similarly tested, in other fields, then they *may* all be true. But we must not rest content with mere absence of discovered contradiction; we must try to fit our hypotheses together in such a way that one of them can be seen to follow logically from another. For logical implications are the surest things we have. So the more extensive a structure of observed fact and hypothesis we have *hanging together* logically, the more unlikely it becomes that this whole structure of supposed knowledge is false.

Even so, our empirical knowledge, as soon as it goes beyond a statement of what has actually, already, been observed, cannot be said to be *certain*. We can never know that some ugly fact, discovered tomorrow, will not upset our confident generalizations. Or — to be more subtly skeptical — we can never know that things which hitherto *have* always acted in such and such ways may not tomorrow turn round and act in somewhat different ways. Thus, no amount of evidence can ever prove a factual generalization to be universally true. It remains possible that further observation would have discovered a discordant fact. Or that *future* facts may be discordant.... In short, all generalizations concerning matters of fact remain, strictly speaking, hypotheses.

Even our knowledge of *particulars* is not certain, save, perhaps, for a knowledge of the sort of experience we are having right now, at the present moment. And that is, quantitatively, negligible. With respect to all past experience it is always possible that there are errors of memory, or errors of record, in detail, or that the whole supposed experience is a memory-illusion. And so far as our knowledge of particulars purports to be a knowledge of objective *things*, it remains conceivable, as we shall presently see in discussing idealism, that our supposed contact with objective things is always illusion.... Thus there is no possible way of attaining certainty, either by logic or by observation, or by a combination of the two, with respect to *fact*. In other words, *proof*, in the strict sense, is merely the internal aspect of a logical system. All knowledge of fact is, and must remain, hypothesis. If my memory is trustworthy, and my descriptions of my experiences accurate, such and such occurrences really happened. If I have accurately analyzed the situation, overlooking no relevant factor, and if things do always happen in exactly similar ways under exactly similar conditions, and continue to do so into the indefinite future, and if there is no alternative hypothesis conceivable which would equally well explain these facts, then my hypothesis is true.... It sounds like the familiar "If we had some eggs we could have ham and eggs, if we had some ham."

It seems as though all our hard-won knowledge were very dubious. And, indeed, one can see why there has been a recurrent drift, among philosophers, toward skepticism, the denial that we can have any knowledge at all.... But, after all, our empirical knowledge does function admirably as knowledge. It enables us to build skyscrapers and to predict eclipses many years ahead. It works. In fact, though we do make many mistakes, the great bulk of our empirical knowledge is *overwhelmingly probable*. When we consider what vast numbers of observations have been made in every field, and are being added to from day to day, what vast numbers of logical deductions are being made, and what continual applications are being made of these deductions, when we realize that a single fact inconsistent with an hypothesis would upset it, or a single practical application that turned out to be mistaken (if no error could be found in the process of deduction or in some other hypothesis used as premise), and that, in spite of all this accumulating experience, our scientific hypotheses, and our common-sense knowledge, stand unshaken year by year, century by century, we shall realize that our confidence in them is well placed.

Another way to put this is to say that all human knowledge, except knowledge of logical implications and of what is immediately present in one's momentary field of consciousness, is knowledge of probability. We *know* that it is probable, considering the available evidence, that the sun will rise tomorrow, that we were alive yesterday, that the law of gravitation is true, etc. Probability, like logical implication, is a relation between a conclusion and the grounds upon which it rests. Knowledge of *probability* is thus actual *knowledge*, not mere belief, or hypothesis. Such knowledge is not contradicted if the facts turn out not to sustain the hypothesis. The hypothesis *was* probable, just the same, if it was properly based upon observation. It *is* safer to bet upon accumulated experience, though any one bet may conceivably turn out to be wrong, and though, conceivably, *all* our betting upon past experience might turn out some day to be upset by some sweeping alteration in the course of nature. We have no positive reason for supposing that the great bulk of our empirical knowledge is *not* knowledge of *fact* (as well as knowledge of probability).   And we have an enormous amount of evidence, constantly increasing, that it *is* knowledge of fact.

WHY IS THE EMPIRICAL METHOD NOT UNIVERSALLY ACCEPTED?

It is by the empirical method that we have amassed all of our generally accepted knowledge.   All common-sense knowledge and all scientific knowledge is empirical.   Why, then, should some people try to undermine confidence in it?   And what have they to say? As to the why, there are a few philosophers, and would-be philosophers, who take a sort of malicious pleasure in destroying people's confidence in science or in common sense.   But most of the attack comes from those who hope, by discrediting science, to rally people again to some religion, or some metaphysical view, which the advance of empirical knowledge has imperiled.... However, the important thing is not the motives of these writers but their arguments.

1. *Are there fields to which the empirical method does not apply?*

Some religious people, not hostile to the empirical method in general, wish to keep it out of religion, some philosophers wish to keep it out of philosophy — or, rather, to relegate it to a subordinate position.   They offer another method as more useful within their particular field.   The question is, then, chiefly as to the adequacy of this other method — authoritarian, a priori, or intuitional.   These methods of seeking truth we have discussed in earlier chapters.   If the reader goes with the writer of these pages in discarding these methods as highly uncertain tests of truth, the problem resolves itself into the question whether or not there are any facts in the field open to empirical observation. If there are, they can be studied empirically. If there are not, we must be content to forego knowledge in that field. We may have conjecture, fancy, hope; but we cannot have knowledge. There are many fields as to which we are in that situation — the history of peoples who have left no records, the craters on the other side of the moon, the possible satellites of distant stars, etc. To the writer, however, it does not seem that religion or morals or philosophy constitutes such a field. There are in these realms many facts which can be studied empirically, and already much empirical knowledge has been amassed.

The protest against empirical conclusions concerning religion is based partly upon the fact that there seems to be no satisfactory empirical evidence for certain widespread beliefs, the result of the historical development of ideas, which are very precious to their believers. With this dread of the invasion of sober reflective thinking into these realms of precious belief we may sympathize. But for those who wish to know what the situation really *is* — whether their beliefs are mere speculative possibilities, mere fancies, mere hopes, or well-grounded probabilities — there is no recourse but to study observed facts in the sober scientific way.... The protest is based in part upon the one-sided array of facts sometimes presented by empirical investigators. It is true, in a sense, that "spiritual truths are spiritually discerned"; that is, they are discerned by people who have had first-hand experience of the spiritual life. Such facts may be overlooked or minimized by people incapable, by nature or experience, of properly understanding or evaluating them. In the older days it was only the radical, the rebel, who ventured to study religion empirically; and such men tend naturally to underline the iconoclasm of their results. But nowadays all the fields of human values and ideals and hopes are being studied by competent scholars, and against their carefully weighed conclusions the assertions of Authority, of Intuition, of Faith cannot stand.

No competent investigator will deny the possibility of the existence of facts for which he has as yet found no convincing evidence. And the briefest survey shows an enormous amount of miscellaneous evidence for the existence of all sorts of things which do not seem to fit into the accepted body of our knowledge. It is well to be very humble, as yet, in our attitude toward the universe. Any simple believer *may* have hold of some truth which is not yet empirically verifiable. Clairvoyance, clairaudience, telepathy, spirit-communication, prophetic dreams... by all means let us welcome, and scrutinize, the evidence for every as yet inexplicable occurrence. But nothing is to be gained by swallowing the glib conclusions of the credulous, or making a cult of the occult. There is no short-cut to knowledge. We must learn to labor and to wait — to labor at the job of collecting and collating observations, to wait until we have verified facts before we presume to say we *know*.

Philosophy, to save its face, has invented a theory that scientific knowledge is not real knowledge, but that there is an extra-superfine brand of knowledge to be obtained in philosophy.... This is to my mind a complete delusion. I do not believe that there is any way of obtaining knowledge except the scientific way. Some of the problems with which philosophy has concerned itself can be solved by scientific methods; others cannot. Those which cannot are insoluble.[1]

[1] Bertrand Russell, *Journal of Philosophy*, vol. 19, p. 646.

*2. Does not the natural origin of our sense-organs and
reason discredit them as means of attaining truth?*

After all, we are animals. Our senses and our reasoning powers have been developed, in the struggle for
existence, not because of their value in yielding us theoretic knowledge, but because of their practical usefulness in helping us to cope with our environment. Is it
not over-optimistic to suppose that they give us insight
into the ultimately real? [1]

To this argument the simple answer is that the evolutionary process *has*, obviously, developed in us all sorts
of organs which are useful and reasonably trustworthy —
eyes that see, throats that swallow, stomachs that digest,
and so on. And these organs would not be useful and
trustworthy if they were not adjusted to the actual
nature of surrounding objects. If eyes are to serve
their practical purposes, they must reveal things to us, in
sufficient detail, as they really are. Otherwise they
would mislead us. Stomachs must be adapted to digest
or reject the particular chemical substances which are
swallowed. There is no line between practical and
theoretic knowledge; beliefs (including the beliefs which
are implicit in action) are not, generally speaking, *useful*
unless they are *true*. This is only a rough generalization;
there is room for considerable illusion which, not being
harmful, or even, on occasion, being salutary, might
persist in spite of the pruning effects of natural selection.
But plainly, unless objects which look round really are
round, and those which we take to be square really are
square, unless bread is really good-to-eat, and water
really will float ships — and so on in infinite detail —

[1] For an elaboration of this argument, see A. J. Balfour, *The Foundations of
Belief*, p. 304 ff.

unless our supposed knowledge really *is* knowledge, and not mere illusion, we could never get along with our world as comfortably as we do.

To put it another way, the trustworthiness of our senses and our reason is *verified* daily. However loath to trust them we might be, antecedently, we find, as a matter of fact, that they are reliable — to a degree — and increasingly reliable as we sharpen our scientific method and correct the errors of one observer by the co-operation of many observers. When, for example, by using modern telescopes, amassing a considerable number of observations, and reasoning from these observations, we can predict an eclipse of the moon years ahead to a fraction of a second, who can possibly doubt that our senses and reason are, in this field, trustworthy? And if in this field, and the many other fields where we have similar verification, why not also in the fields where verification is more difficult or impossible?

3. *Are not the data of our senses hopelessly subjective?*

We shall presently call attention to the 'subjectivity' of our sense-data (see pp. 110 ff. and 200 ff.). A study of the physiology of perception, and a comparison of our sense-data, show that these data reflect the nature of the perceiver as well as the nature of the object perceived. There is reason for believing, for example, that the objects about us do not have, themselves, the colors which we seem to see in them. Considerations of this sort have led some critics of science to discredit it, from a purely empirical point of view — to show, that is, that the empirical method discredits *itself*.

> We need only to consider carefully our perceptions regarded as psychological results, in order to see that, regarded as sources of information, they are not merely occasionally inaccurate,

but habitually mendacious. We are dealing, recollect, with a theory of science according to which the ultimate stress of scientific proof is thrown wholly upon our immediate experience of objects. But nine-tenths of our immediate experiences of objects are visual; and all visual experiences, without exception, are, according to science, erroneous. As everybody knows, colour is not a property of the thing seen: it is a sensation produced in us by that thing. The thing itself consists of uncoloured particles, which become visible solely in consequence of their power of either producing or reflecting ethereal undulations.... From the side of science, these are truisms. From the side of a theory or philosophy of science, however, they are paradoxes.... What sort of a system is that which makes haste to discredit its premises? In what entanglements of contradiction do we not find ourselves involved by the attempt to rest science upon observations which science itself asserts to be erroneous? [1]

Anticipating our future conclusions, we may say here that our human knowledge *is*, to a considerable extent, infected with a subjective coloration. But scientists have realized this, and discount it. We correct sight by touch, ordinary vision by microscopic and telescopic vision, and by all sorts of other instruments. Thus we have slowly learned to sift the subjective from the objective elements in our experience, and to construct a picture of an objective world which can be believed to be independent of perceivers and by its detailed construction to account for the variations in the sense-data of various observers. There is no need, then, to be disturbed by the discovery of the subjective elements in knowledge. They make the work of science more difficult, but do not make it impossible.

It remains theoretically possible that there is no external world at all. We all irresistibly believe in such a world (unless in some moment of ultra-sophisticated

[1] A. J. Balfour, *Foundations of Belief*, pp. 111–113.

reflection), and inevitably act on that belief. As we shall see, there is strong theoretic justification for that universal belief. But even supposing the belief to be false, science would not thereby be discredited, or any other method shown to be superior. Science would then simply be the study of possible human experiences under varying circumstances, and would still be as practically useful, and as *true*, in this revised sense, as we commonly take it to be.

4. *Does not science rest upon unproved assumptions?*

All the fundamental conceptions of science — self, sub-stance, cause, force, life, order, law... are assumed at the very outset.... The authority of science is not in itself. All its laws and generalizations derive their validity from the ulterior truths which they assume and upon which they rest.[1]

This argument reveals a misconception of the scientific method. Science *rests* upon concrete *observations*; its building-stones are empirical facts. True, hypotheses are devised, categories are applied, but tentatively, to see whether the observed facts fit them. Categories and laws are not *assumed*, arbitrarily; they are suggested, as convenient labels, as means of apprehending great masses of fact, and are freely discarded when they fail to apply to these discovered facts. Experience quickly reveals that there is *something* to which the terms 'self,' 'substance,' 'cause,' etc., apply. Such terms are, at first, vague or of varying interpretation. Attempts at precision are repeatedly made, until some definite mean-ing is found which fits in with our concrete observations and already accepted hypotheses. Such great general-izations as the doctrine of evolution, the atomic theory,

[1] F. S. Hoffman, *The Sphere of Science*, p. 39. See also A. J. Balfour, *The Foundations of Belief*, pp. 126–132.

or the principle of the conservation of energy, are not foundation-stones upon which science is built, and whose falsity would therefore imperil the whole edifice; they are the domes that cap the structure. If they should be shown to be untenable, some other formulations would be found; and meanwhile the vast mass of scientific data would rest undisturbed.

5. Is it true that science can describe but not explain?

There is a rather widespread feeling, especially among those who accept some supernatural religion, that science, with its empirical method, can *describe* accurately what it finds to exist, but cannot *explain* its existence — as a religion can.

> Science will never wholly satisfy the heart of man, nor will it ever thoroughly exhaust reality. This fact it will acknowledge more readily, the safer it feels itself against encroachments upon its own domain. At the same time, science will confess its inability to supply the place of religion; it will admit that in addition to its own problem there is room for another which it cannot solve. Besides the question concerning the What and the How, man inevitably raises the question as to the Wherefore... This undertaking cannot be accomplished with the means of scientific knowledge... The physical explanation is necessary, but it does not settle everything; the question concerning the meaning remains.[1]

In considering this point, we must note that there are several senses of the term 'explain.'

In the first place, to explain may be to show what intent, purpose, plan is fulfilled in an event. We explain the Great War by unraveling the motives of the rulers and diplomats, showing what they were after, and why they chose to commit their peoples to war.... Can we explain natural events, in this sense? *Is* there pur-

[1] F. Paulsen, *Introduction to Philosophy*, Eng. tr., p. 10, 162.

pose or plan behind the course of nature? Unless we
are sure there is, we must not blame science for not
disclosing the plan. And if there is, how can it be detected, or guessed, except by empirical study of the
course of events? It is by such empirical study, performed by historians, that we arrive at our judgments
as to the purposes behind the War. Unless we have
an authentic supernatural revelation of God's will, there
seems to be no way of reaching any conclusion as to a
possible intent fulfilled in nature, save in the form of
an hypothesis such that from it the course of events can
actually be deduced. In other words, if there *is* a purpose running through things, the only hopeful way of
finding it would seem to be the scientific way.

A second sense in which we may be said to explain
events is by pointing out the results they achieve. Thus
I explain why hens sit on eggs by showing that thereby
chickens are hatched. I explain why we have eyes by
pointing out that they enable us to secure food, escape
our enemies, etc. This does not imply that the hen has
any *intent* to hatch out chickens; probably such an idea
never occurs to the setting hen. Nor are the causes
that gradually produce eyes in living organisms conscious
of the end they are serving. Nevertheless, the ends
are achieved, and the value of the ends may be considered,
in a sense, a justification for the events that led to them.
... The discovery of the results achieved by various
series of events is, of course, purely a matter for empirical study.... If, however, we raise the question
whether the ends-to-be-achieved somehow affect the
process, so as to steer it toward achieving them, the
answer seems to be that no such method of affecting
events has been discovered, or even clearly conceived,

in any detail. But if there *is* any such effect of ends upon means, there would seem to be no way of discovering it save by ordinary empirical research.

The commonest sense of 'explaining,' however, is to show how a law that has been discovered is the inevitable result of laws already formulated; or how a particular event is an instance of such a law. To explain a phenomenon is to show that, the pre-existing configuration of events being what it was, and the laws of nature being what we take them to be, this particular phenomenon would inevitably (i.e., logically) be what we find it to be.... To explain why a hen sits on eggs *may* mean to point out that eggs are hatched thereby. But the most fruitful sense in which we are said to explain the act is in terms of animal psychology and physiology. The hen has a certain internal mechanism which can be studied in detail. This mechanism drives it to certain types of behavior under certain recurrent conditions — quite without reference to what the result of that behavior may be.... So to explain why a watch goes may be to say that a watchmaker made it with the intent that it shall go; or it may be to point out that by going it keeps step with the sun and enables its owner to keep his appointments. But in the most useful sense, to explain why a watch goes is to describe its mechanism and show that, its structure being what it is, and the laws of physics being what they are, it *will* keep time.

In this sense, to explain an event is simply to assimilate it to the rest of our experience. It is the exceptional event that needs explanation, the event that has not yet been fitted in to the rest of our knowledge.

Mystery is the isolation of a fact from all others. Explanation is the discovery of agreement among facts remotely placed: it is essentially the generalizing process, whereby many widely scattered appearances are shown to come under one commanding principle or law.[1]

'Explanation' in this sense is, of course, the very life of science.

SUGGESTED READINGS

Columbia Associates, *Introduction to Reflective Thinking*, III.
Durant Drake, *Problems of Religion*, pp. 254–258.
G. W. Cunningham, *Problems of Philosophy*, III.
F. S. Hoffman, *The Sphere of Science*, III.
J. A. Thomson, *Introduction to Science*, III.
B. W. Bode, *Outline of Logic*, XII–XIII.
H. A. Aikins, *Principles of Logic*, XXXV.
Hugo Münsterberg, *On The Witness Stand*.
J. S. Mill, *System of Logic*, Book IV, ch. I.
G. A. Coe, *Psychology of Religion*, III.
H. B. George, *Historical Evidence*, I, IV, VIII.
Karl Pearson, *The Grammar of Science*, I.
A. J. Balfour, *Foundations of Belief*, Part I, ch. III; Part II, ch. I.
H. N. Wieman, *Religious Experience and Scientific Method*, VI.
H. N. Wieman, *The Issues of Life*, VII.
R. H. Dotterer, *Philosophy by Way of the Sciences*, X.

[1] Alexander Bain, *Mind and Body*, p. 121.

CHAPTER V

PRAGMATISM

PRAGMATISM is, as William James said, "a new name for an old way of thinking." But because of the new name, and the prestige of its proponents, it has come much more explicitly into favor in this twentieth century than ever before. We must ask, therefore, What is this pragmatic method of attaining truth — or of justifying belief? And is it deserving of our espousal?

In some people's mouths 'pragmatism' seems to mean little more than empiricism. The pragmatists have been the most uncompromising enemies of the authoritarians and the apriorists; they have insisted upon a relentless analysis of every theory and principle, to discover its "cash value" in experience. They have turned their backs upon problems which promise to make no practical difference, and put their energies, in truly American fashion, into clarifying and forwarding our concrete purposes. This is the very apotheosis of empiricism.

But three developments, or twists, of empiricism give the particular flavor of pragmatism. First, it is asserted that a belief is accredited as true if it 'works,' not merely in the ordinary empirical sense of fitting observed facts, but in the sense of meeting our needs, or satisfying our desires. Secondly, it is even asserted that if a belief works, in either of these senses, it *is*, *ipso facto*, true; the fact that a belief works is what *constitutes* its truth, what we mean by calling it 'true.' Or, thirdly, it is asserted, less radically, but more persuasively, that if a belief satisfies us, inspires, comforts, helps us, we have a moral right to hold it.... These three positions shade into one another, and are commonly confused. But they need to be considered separately, for they by no means amount to the same thing.

It is not difficult to understand the enthusiasm with which the gospel of pragmatism — which blends these three doctrines in varying proportion — has been hailed. It confers a right to hold many comforting beliefs which people conversant with modern knowledge had supposed they could not honestly hold. It gives a sense of assurance, of having truth, to people who had been bewildered and were drifting toward skepticism.... But is this assurance warranted? Is pragmatic truth really *truth*? We must examine with some care the three views above defined.

IS THE FACT THAT A BELIEF SATISFIES OUR NEEDS EVIDENCE THAT IT IS TRUE?

Religious postulates need confirmation as much as those of science. The true claim of religious experience is that they receive it, after their kind; that, e.g., prayer works, that it really uplifts and consoles.... The truest religion is that which issues in and stimulates the best life.[1]

In the degree that religious doctrine... ministers to the practical and inner life of man, is its validity assured.[2]

Of course the kind of life that religious belief creates must be the ultimate judgment pronounced upon the truth of the religious philosophy involved.[3]

From such conclusions [that the universe is Godless] the mind instinctively shrinks. It prefers to think that there is something beyond.... Only the infinite satisfies; in that

[1] F. C. S. Schiller, *Riddles of the Sphinx*, p. 468. *Studies in Humanism*, p. 369.

[2] G. Galloway, *Philosophy of Religion*, p. 367.

[3] H. A. Youtz, *The Enlarging Conception of God*, p. 15.

alone the mind finds rest.... We are driven, then, to believe....[1]

On pragmatic principles we cannot reject any hypothesis
if consequences useful to life flow from it.[2]

The above excerpts are typical of a very widespread
habit of argument. Another way of presenting the
argument is to say that our 'hearts' are to be listened
to as well as our heads. That is, if the affective, emotional side of our nature cries out for a certain belief, it
has its rights in court as well as the intellectual side of
our nature; *its* testimony must not be ignored.[3]

In plain English, all this seems to boil down to the
following proposition: A belief is to be deemed true (*a*) if
it cheers or consoles us, if it makes us happier or healthier
to believe it; (*b*) if it inspires us to live a good life; (*c*) if
it is in line with our ideals, i.e., with what we should
like to have true; or, generalizing, if it is in any way
practically useful to believe it to be true.

Of course, in practice it is only just this particular
belief or that which is accredited because of its desir-
ability. But it is clearly inconsistent to use this criterion
for validating one belief without being willing to use
it to validate any belief which consoles or inspires anyone. Are we really ready, then, to say that all beliefs
which satisfy their believers are thereby proved to be
true? On what possible grounds could we defend that
delightful proposition? Is there not, in fact, overwhelming evidence to the contrary? Do we not see on
every hand beliefs which console and inspire people and
yet are plainly untrue? Have not almost all of the

[1] G. P. Serviss, *Curiosities of the Sky*, p. 13.
[2] William James, *Pragmatism*, p. 273.
[3] William James elaborated this argument effectively in his essay *Reflex Action and Theism* in the *Will to Believe* volume.

infinite variety of religious beliefs held by different races of men been in some degree comforting and inspiring to them?   And does not everyday experience constantly show us people blindly, pathetically believing what it comforts and fortifies them to believe, though their beliefs, as we can see, are not true?   It hardly seems necessary to labor the point.

Nevertheless, the pragmatists insist that our beliefs must satisfy our whole natures, our hearts as well as our heads.   Beliefs are 'verified' by the practical effects they produce as well as by logical deduction and successful prediction.... But *is* the 'heart' an organ for the discovery of truth?   *Has* our emotional nature any means by which it can discover the nature of things?   We can see how truth can be reached via empirical observation, coupled with logical reasoning.   This is branded as a one-sided, 'intellectual' road to truth.   But is there any other road?   If so, it is not enough to assert that there is such a road; it must be pointed out.   It must be shown *how* our emotion, our needs, our desires, ascertain what is true.... What is 'verified' by the beneficent effects of believing something to be true is merely the proposition that *believing* it to be true has such effects, not the proposition that it *is* true.   Since, whether or not the belief is true, *believing* it to be true consoles or inspires the believer, it is evident that that beneficent effect is no evidence that the belief is *true*.

In fact, to hold that a satisfying belief must be true (or even that it is more likely to be true) is a practically dangerous doctrine — and so *untrue* on pragmatic principles!   Such easy-going belief, prior to a scrupulous investigation of the evidence, inevitably warps our mental processes so that we cannot estimate the evidence impartially. As Alice in the Delighted States says, "Sometimes you believe something because you see it, sometimes you see something because you believe it. It's a poor rule that doesn't work both ways!"... Pragmatism doesn't hurt us in our everyday life, because we don't *use* it in our everyday life. We don't believe that stocks are going up because it consoles us to think they are; we don't believe that a business venture is going to succeed because that is an inspiring belief. Or, if we do, we come quickly to grief and learn to be more solidly empirical. But in regions where it does no obvious harm to accept error, where we can pretty safely live in happy illusion, many people feel it to be rational to use precisely this same criterion of truth that is so obviously misleading where it can be checked up by an empirical test.

For clearness of thinking it is too bad that the pragmatists have chosen this word 'works,' which has a precise scientific meaning, and used it in this sense, which is so different that it seems hardly more than a pun or a play on words. To say that the Copernican theory 'works' is one thing. The theory that prayers are heard and answered by God might be said to 'work' in the same sense of the term, if experiment showed that the number of cases where what was asked for came true so decidedly outweighed the number of contrary cases as to rule out chance, and no alternative hypothesis fitted the facts as well. To say that the theory 'works,' in the sense that believing it to be true inspires and consoles people is to make such an utterly different sort of statement about the theory that some other term than 'works' ought to be used.

There is no need of proceeding further along this line.

The contention that a belief is true because believing it to be true has beneficent results is obviously silly *if we mean by 'truth' what we usually mean.* Pragmatism deserves a hearing only in its more radical form, where it says, It is precisely the fact that a belief has beneficent results that *constitutes* its truth. That is what we *mean* by *calling* it 'true.'... We proceed to consider this pragmatic conception of Truth.

DOES THE FACT THAT A BELIEF WORKS CONSTITUTE ITS TRUTH?

True ideas are those that we can assimilate, validate, corroborate and verify. False ideas are those we cannot. That is the practical difference it makes to us to have true ideas; that, therefore, is the meaning of truth, for it is all that truth is known as.[1]

To look upon a belief as true, is, in other words, to look upon it as a belief that 'works'; this defines the meaning of the word 'true,' as used in such a context; this describes what we have in mind when we use the word 'true.'[2]

According to this conception, the fact that a belief 'works' is not a (more or less fallible) *test*, by which we ascertain whether or not a belief is true, it constitutes the very meaning of the term 'truth.' The two senses of 'works' — the scientific sense, and the sense we have just been discussing — are very different; but most pragmatists declare that for a belief to 'work' in *either* sense is for it to be true. When they use the term in the scientific sense, the doctrine is more plausible; when they use it in the beneficent-result sense, it is more eagerly welcomed by people generally. But is 'working' in either sense a proper definition of 'truth'?

[1] William James, *Pragmatism*, p. 201.
[2] H. Berkeley, in *Mind*, vol. 21, p. 85.

In the first place, we must note that to define 'truth' in this way is to assert by implication that contradictory propositions may both be simultaneously true, one 'for me' and another 'for you'; and that a proposition may be true today, and untrue tomorrow, although the facts to which it refers have not changed.   The belief that the earth is flat and stationary 'worked' well for Ptolemy and the medieval world; for them, therefore, it *was* true, in the pragmatic sense of 'truth.'   Even today, there are those, in Zion City for example, for whom this geo-centric theory works; for them it still *is* true.   For educated people today this Ptolemaic theory is *untrue*; for us it is true that the earth is spherical and rotates on its orbit once in twenty-four hours.... Take *any* plausibly supported belief, concerning past events, concerning people's motives, the nature of the world we live in, or of God.   *Innumerable* theories in all these fields have 'worked.'   On pragmatic principles all are, or have been, true.

> If all religions work, all are true; and what is wrong is the rigidity of an idea of truth which cannot tolerate such *plural truth*.[1]

This pragmatic usage involves us in saying (for instance) that the *belief* that centaurs existed was *true* (since it 'worked,' for the Greeks) even though centaurs *didn't exist*.   The belief that Sacco and Vanzetti were murderers was true (for the judge and jury who tried them, and for most Massachusetts people) even if, in fact, they had murdered no one.   The belief that the Germans were primarily responsible for the World War was true for the Allies, while a contrary belief was true for the Germans.   The belief that you have died will be

[1] F. S. C. Schiller, *Riddles of the Sphinx*, p. 469.

true for me, if I am ever presented with what seems to me sufficient evidence of your decease, even though you are actually still very much alive.

On the other hand, where no evidence is available to support a proposition, and no beneficent consequences can be found, that proposition, according to pragmatism, is not true — since there is no reason for saying that it 'works.' So it is not true that there are a hundred craters on the other side of the moon, and it is not true that there are *not* a hundred craters on the other side of the moon. Ordinary logic tells us that there either are or are not a hundred craters there. Ordinary people believe that one or the other of the propositions is true, although they do not know which. Pragmatism says that *neither* is true, though one or the other would *become* true, if we ever got a look at the other side of the moon. Thus any liar can make his lies true, by simply making them so consistent that they 'work' perfectly for those who accept them. And anyone, by destroying the evidence that a certain event occurred, can make a ''ef in that event henceforth false.

This is obviously a radically different use of the term 'truth' from that which customarily obtains in good society. In fact, 'true,' to the pragmatist, means merely 'seems to be evidenced' — seems so to this person or that, at this time or that. Substitute 'seems to be evidenced' for 'true,' in the preceding paragraphs, and the paradox disappears.... But then, why not stick to ordinary usage? Why not say, The belief in centaurs accorded with the facts known to the Greeks, was a tenable working hypothesis, which they thought they had reason to suppose true? Why say it *was* true? Why not say, The belief in Heaven and Hell, in Reincarnation, or whatever you please, inspires, stimulates people, is a salutary working hypothesis? Why say that all these beliefs are *true?*... Simply because, if they said merely what we suggest, they would be saying nothing new, nothing of particular interest. By calling these working hypotheses *true*, they quiet people's doubts, and give them the comforting satisfaction of feeling that they possess truth.... But is this not a specious, and dangerous, satisfaction?

The pragmatists, however, have their case. They say, There is no possible way in which we can find out anything about the truth of our beliefs *except* the fact that some work and some do not. As a matter of fact, it *is* the beiiefs-that-work which we call 'true,' and the beliefs-that-do-not-work which we call 'false.' There is no higher sort of truth discoverable. If you examine instances of what you call 'true' and of what you call 'false,' you will find that the fact of working or not working is the sole differentia. And since we can never discover whether a belief accords with all the facts there are, we *have* to call it true if it fits the facts we *find*.

> Does a definition of valid knowledge have any meaning — to say nothing of validity — save as based upon the specific detectable traits of those instances of knowledge-enterprises that have turned out valid, in contrast with those which have turned out invalid.[1]

This contention becomes more plausible for most people when they are confronted with the question, What else do *you* mean by 'truth'? Is a true belief one that correctly copies, or corresponds to Reality? But how *can* a belief copy, or even correspond to, an outer Reality? It is not so simple as it sounds! What *is* a belief, any-

[1] John Dewey, *Journal of Philosophy*, vol. 7, p. 173.

way? It is a very protean sort of thing, never at any two moments clothed in the same psychological or physiological stuff. Is it anything more than a certain 'set' of the organism, a tendency to act in this way rather than that, to say "Yes, this," "not that," and so on? A visual picture may arise in the mind, or it may not; certain words may frame themselves — and, of course, in any language; all that seems necessary is a certain specific sort of motor adjustment. A person believes correctly if he adjusts himself correctly. The correct belief may be, psychologically, anything that serves as a cue to this correct adjustment. The truth of propositions is merely the fact that they guide us aright, they enable us to make appropriate adjustments to things as they are.

All this the anti-pragmatist may well accept. But the pragmatist continues: We can never get out of ourselves, to discover some 'outer reality' to whose nature we are making appropriate or inappropriate adjustments. All we can possibly discover is that certain adjustments practically help us, enable us to get forward with our purposes. If they 'work' in this way, we call them true; and the only reason we ever have for calling them false is the discovery that they do not work so well as we thought, that some other belief-adjustment works better. In so far as this happens, we change our labels; what we formerly labeled 'true' we now label 'false.' Tomorrow we may have to change some more labels. But this uncertain, possibly-to-be-discarded-tomorrow truth is the only kind of truth mortals can ever have. The apparent paradox of truths that are changing and contradictory is the inevitable result of our human limitations. An Absolute Being might be supposed to have an eternal fixed truth; but we must be content without it.

All this presupposes, however, that truth must be defined as a certain *kind of experience* — lest, otherwise, we should be untrue to empiricism. The only difference *that falls within experience,* between true and untrue beliefs, is the difference between their working and not working.... But the trouble with this is, that many beliefs which, in ordinary usage, we call false, also have worked, and some beliefs which work well today will doubtless turn out false, while some beliefs which do not seem to work now are probably, all the time, true. In this everyday sense, truth is a goal to be reached; it is what it is, whether we know it or not. What changes, what presents contradictions, is not the truth, but our *beliefs.* In short, truth is not a specific, describable kind of experience — for error is often just the same kind of experience; truth is a *relation* between a belief (or supposition, or proposition) *and the object to which it refers.* A belief is true if it adjusts us properly to *things as they really are.*

Whether a belief works or not, in our experience, is an empirically discoverable fact. Whether it will continue to work, in the face of further experience, remains an open question, to be decided by that further experience. But the pragmatist does not consider the question *why* some beliefs work, or why they cease to work. Common sense says it is *because* true beliefs are adjustments to things *as they are.* Beliefs work *because* they are true; the fact of working does not *constitute* their truth. For a complete experience, rubbing up against every side of the object in question, only an accurately true belief would work perfectly. Since, however, our experience of things is very fragmentary, untrue beliefs may often work well enough; the maladjustments which a more rounded experience would disclose have not had occasion to appear. In other words, truth is the sort of thing that would work perfectly, under all conceivable circumstances — instead of being merely what happens to work well enough in our meager experience. A proposition may *be* true even if it isn't *believed* to be true, even if it hasn't even been *thought of*. And a belief may be false even if it has, so far in human experience, worked perfectly.

If this is so, it means, as the pragmatists point out, that we can never be absolutely sure that we have truth. All that we can ever *know* is, that our beliefs work well so far as our experience has yet gone.... True. But how much better off is the pragmatist? He has his 'truth,' to be sure, i.e., his beliefs made 'truth' by definition. But your 'truth' may be contradictory to my 'truth'; and both 'truths' may be errors tomorrow. Indeed, for this 'radical empiricism' there *is* no fixed and stable truth for our beliefs to reach toward and approximate, there *is* nothing but a world of fluctuating experience and fluctuating belief. Whereas the ordinary realist holds that truth itself is stable, and we may have great confidence (though never absolute certainty) that we have attained it. What we call our knowledge is *probably* true, often to a high degree of probability; and if it *is* true, it is eternally and unchangeably true.

Empiricism is properly a method of testing suppositions to see which are probably true. Suppositions concerning objects outside of our experience may thus be tested, by considering what consequences may be expected, within our experience, if they are true, and what if they are false. The evidence by which we test suppositions must fall within experience, but the objects or events in which we believe need not, and in many cases could not, fall within our experience. When we say the earth is a sphere, we do not *mean* by that statement anything discoverable within experience, we do not mean that it 'works,' in the scientific or in the popular sense, to believe the earth round; we mean that there *is* an earth, prior to and independent of our experience, and that this earth *has*, itself, the character of being a sphere. If there is an earth, and it does have this character, the belief is true, and was true long before anybody thought of it.... If I believe you love me, and my cynical friend believes you only pretend to love me, both of us may find our beliefs 'working,' in both senses of the term. For pragmatism both beliefs, then, are true. But common sense says that only one of the two beliefs is true — and *you* know which one.

Our conclusion is, then, that it is a mistake for pragmatism to define truth as a discoverable characteristic of our experience. Truth is a relation between a supposition, or proposition, and the object or event to which it refers. That relation must, no doubt, be defined, ultimately, in terms of adjustment. But the true supposition is not just any one that chances to serve our purposes so far; it is the one suppositio⸗ (whether as yet held by anyone or not) which *would* serve to adjust us to the object in question without any misleading, under all possible circumstances.

IS THE WILL TO BELIEVE LEGITIMATE?

As popularly espoused, and indeed as expounded by some thinkers of note, pragmatism is a moral rather than a factual doctrine. Instead of saying, Whatever works is, *ipso facto*, true, it says, Whatever works for you, you have a moral right to believe. In other words, instead of being a method of defining truth, it is, in this version, merely a method of justifying belief. It declares that wherever the evidence is inconclusive, wherever you find yourself presented with alternative beliefs either of which may, so far as you can see, be true, you may — and indeed should — choose the belief which is more helpful or inspiring to *you*, the belief which works best in your practical life.

William James is the classic exponent of this doctrine. His famous essay, *The Will to Believe*, is, as he says,

> a defence of our right to adopt a believing attitude in religious matters, in spite of the fact that our merely logical intellect may not have been coerced... Can we (as men who may be interested at least as much in positively gaining truth as in merely escaping dupery) always wait with impunity till the coercive evidence shall have arrived?... *Moral* questions immediately present themselves as questions whose solution cannot wait for sensible proof... Religion offers itself as a momentous option. We are supposed to gain, even now, by our belief, and to lose by our non-belief, a certain vital good. Secondly, religion is a forced option, so far as that good goes. We cannot escape the issue of remaining sceptical and waiting for more light, because, although we do avoid error in that way *if religion be untrue*, we lose the good, *if it be true*, just as certainly as if we positively chose to disbelieve.... If religion be true and the evidence for it be still insufficient, I do not wish, by putting your extinguisher upon my nature (which feels to me as if it had after all some business in this matter), to forfeit my sole chance in life of getting upon the winning side, — that chance depending, of course, on my willingness to run the risk of acting as if my passional need of taking the world religiously might be prophetic and right.[1]

In appraising this alluring doctrine, let us consider first the cases in which we are urged to believe on the ground that to refuse belief is to paralyze *action*. We

[1] William James, *The Will to Believe*, p. 1 ff.

cannot stand still forever, at every fork of the road, waiting for evidence to turn up as to which is the right road. We must choose a road, even at the risk of error. And, in lack of objective evidence, why not let our hopes, or our emotional needs, determine our decision?

The first thing to say to this is that we do not need to *believe*, in order to *act*. Why not admit, frankly, "I do not know which is the right road to take, but I will *try* this one. I will adopt the supposition that this is the best course, as a working hypothesis. But I will keep my mind open and alert for evidence *on both sides*." In short, what we need for action is not the will to believe, but merely the will to experiment, the will to try out an hypothesis. We need courage and self-confidence, instead of an indecision-complex and too great a fear of making mistakes.

But even this self-confidence may easily go too far. For after all, it is not action at any price that we want, but *right* action. The man who is cautious in adopting a belief may act as energetically as the believer; he is far more apt to act intelligently. The pathos of human life consists, to no inconsiderable degree, in its conscientious blundering. About us on all sides are people too readily believing what is not so, and, in consequence, *pushing the wrong way*. In some cases action based upon a will to believe is obviously dangerous, as in the instance given by Clifford of the shipowner who believed his ship to be seaworthy; without substantial evidence he had no right to his comfortable belief, whereby human lives were endangered. And though in most cases the peril is not so plain, there are always dangers lurking in mistaken belief. In the long run, men will clearly be better off if they learn to see things as they are. But what is needed for this is, in Bertrand Russell's words, "not the will to believe, but the wish to find out, which is the exact opposite."

Moreover, belief, once given, is hard to revoke. The man who has willed to *believe* has committed himself; his loyalty, his pride, become engaged. If the belief comforts him, or justifies his course of action, he comes to *lean* upon it. Thereafter he is not in a state of mind to entertain contrary hypotheses fairly or to reverse his course if new evidence turns up. He is greedy for evidence that will sustain his course and has a blind spot for contrary evidence. The man who, in a doubtful matter, has merely *entertained a supposition* and tentatively acted upon it is likelier to entertain contrary suppositions fairly and to reverse his course if new evidence turns up. By contrast with his mental flexibility and alertness, the will to believe seems mere snap judgment or pig-headedness.

So far we have been cautioning against over-hasty and over-confident belief. An even graver danger, however, lurks in the factors by which pragmatism persuades us to fashion our beliefs. It is the more comforting or more inspiring supposition that we are urged to will to believe. But we have failed to find reason for supposing that a belief which comforts or inspires us is, in general, any more likely to be true than one which does not. So, to allow our hopes or our emotional cravings to bias our belief is to blind our judgment and make us less able to estimate impartially such evidence as there is. If any practical issue is at stake, we had better be *particularly* on our guard against the distorting effects of our passions and our hopes.

It may be said, however, that in most cases no important difference in outward behavior is at issue. It is a question merely of adding the inspiration or comfort of the belief, with (it is felt) no harm done if the belief is mistaken. As the small boy in Mark Twain's story said, in defending himself for telling a whopper, "But maybe it *was* so; we didn't know anything about it, but we judged it would please him, and it did; and it didn't cost us anything." Or, as an evangelist is reported to have said, "There may be no such place as Hell, but, anyway, we're all better off for believing in it."

We may at once agree that the attainment of truth is not the only human good. Personal consolation has its rights. And especially may we condone the clinging to unevidenced beliefs on the part of elderly people, to whom they have become, by long association, too precious to lose. But should we not frankly admit that this is a form of self-indulgence? The attitude of the man who refuses to bias his judgment by his hopes is a braver attitude, and more useful for human progress. For there is nothing which so stands in the way of our finding out the real truth about things as this habit of believing what it is pleasant and inspiriting to believe.

There is only one force that makes a bad mind out of a good one or a tolerable one, a force that has been able to accomplish this result in the majority of civilized minds. That force is "the will to believe"; more fully expressed, the willingness to believe on insufficient evidence, because the belief is attractive, or the opposite unattractive, or the labor of further thinking unattractive. To believe by attraction instead of believing on test, that is the temptation.... The prevailing errors in reasoning, responsible for most of the harm of false conclusions, are obvious errors. We should all see and avoid them, except that we are looking the other way.[1]

[1] Dickinson S. Miller, in *The New Republic*.

The critical spirit, the habit of looking sharply for the evidence on both sides of a debatable question, discarding loose arguments, and proportioning belief to discovered facts, is one of the most difficult of habits to develop. We all admire it in a Newton, a Darwin, a Pasteur. Their patient years of hunting for evidence, their refusal to commit themselves to theories not yet fully substantiated, shame our easy credulity. Still, most of us rather frankly prefer for ourselves the comfort of believing heartily in our pet doctrines to the uncertainty — and perhaps the social stigma — of doubt. We are perhaps subconsciously afraid that if we were perfectly candid we should have to admit that some of our dearest beliefs are *not* well substantiated. We want to believe them nevertheless. We are afraid we could not stand their loss very well; our spirits, and perhaps our morals, would collapse. And so we label hearty belief a virtue. We stop thinking those troublesome facts that do not quite fit our belief, we dwell thankfully upon any argument we can find which fortifies it, we associate with those who proclaim it. And soon we find that we do not have to will to believe it; it has come to seem obviously true, and we join in impatient rebuke for those who do not share it.

Is not this clinging to a pleasant belief essentially dishonest? Is it not importing partisanship, prejudice, personal desires, into what should be a matter of strictly objective tests? Does that not undermine one's intellectual integrity?... And again, is it not essentially absurd? As if we could alter the inexorable facts by choosing to believe them to be thus and so?... The main point, however, is not that it is dishonest, or that it is absurd, but that it is practically harmful and ob-

structive. For there are no beliefs that do not, somehow, affect our action. Why do we not get ahead with
religion, consolidate our fantastically numerous sects,
patch up the ancient quarrel with science, and make
religion the vital force for redeeming civilization which
it might be? Precisely because the members of each
separate religious body are obstinately, selfishly clinging
to their particular beliefs, which, largely because of long
use and association, are comforting and inspiriting *to
them*. Why do we not get ahead with morals, with
political and economic improvements, curing the many
curable stupidities of our present social order and living
like rational beings together? Largely because we cling
so *willfully* to our pet beliefs — in individualism or in
communism, in sex-restraint or in sex-freedom, in pro-
hibition or in freedom-to-drink, with very little serious
effort to discover whether our beliefs are really warranted by the facts.

True, the line between illegitimate willfulness in belief and a reasonable willingness to adopt an hypothesis,
or the legitimate faith of which we spoke in an earlier
chapter, is not always easy to draw. Certainly we want
courage, optimism, hopefulness, rather than cynicism
or indifference; and certainly these virtues, being attitudes of the spirit, are compatible with the most
scrupulous restraint in belief. But in practice it is
difficult to prevent faith, or tentative espousal, from
passing over into belief, and belief from passing over into
dogmatism. One has spent one's life as an adherent of
this church or that; one cannot bear the thought that
one has, perhaps, been following a false light. One has
lived a chaste life, forswearing many beckoning delights;
one cannot endure the thought that one has, possibly,

been making a needless sacrifice. Or one has lived a gaily sensual life, and feels the need of justifying oneself in one's own eyes. One has made a fortune in business, or is still hoping to; to question the essential morality of this system of private profiteering would be to question one's own status as a good citizen. Or (in Russia) one has sacrificed one's opportunity to make money, and devoted oneself without reservation to a communal enterprise; to doubt that communism is the proper ideal for society is to question the value of all one's effort and sacrifice.... How *can* human beings renounce their will to believe what they have to believe to be at peace with themselves?

Probably the majority never will renounce it. But at least the philosopher should point out the selfishness and cowardice of such self-indulgence. A generous and sympathetic lover of mankind, like William James, may crystallize into a phrase this common failing, and condone it. The present writer wrote sympathetically of it in an earlier volume,[1] which the curious reader may compare with this discussion. But his mature view is that those who care deeply for the future of mankind should combat to the best of their ability this tendency to willfulness in belief and urge the contrary habit of submitting all suppositions ruthlessly to the most rigorous objective tests, and proportioning belief to the evidence thus obtained.

SUGGESTED READINGS

W. James, *Pragmatism*, especially ch. VI.
E. S. Brightman, *Religious Values*, III.
Bertrand Russell, *Philosophical Essays*, IV–V.
G. E. Moore, *Philosophical Studies*, III.

---

[1] Durant Drake, *Problems of Religion*, ch. XXV.

Durant Drake, *Problems of Religion*, XXI.

W. H. Mallock, *Religion as a Credible Doctrine*, XII–XIII.

J. B. Pratt, *What is Pragmatism?*

D. L. Murray, *Pragmatism*.

W. E. Hocking, *Types of Philosophy*, IX–X.

W. James, *The Will to Believe*, title essay, and *Reflex Action and Theism*.

E. H. Rowland, *The Right to Believe*, I.

W. K. Clifford, *Lectures and Essays*, vol. II: *Ethics of Belief*.

G. S. Fullerton, *The World We Live In*, XVIII.

W. R. Inge, *Faith and Its Psychology*, IX.

Bertrand Russell, *What I Believe*, I.   *Sceptical Essays*, I–II.

PART TWO
KNOWLEDGE AND ITS OBJECTS

CHAPTER VI

THE INADEQUACY OF NAÏVE REALISM

RELIABLE truth, we have decided, is to be reached by the empirical method, i.e., via perception, conception, and memory. But before we can formulate what we know about the universe, we must examine these processes, and determine *what sort and degree of knowledge* they can give us. Is it knowledge of a world of *things*, existing independently of our perceiving or conceiving them, an immense world about us, existing in its own right? Everyone except a few philosophers and mystics takes it for granted that this is the case; i.e., we are all instinctively *realists*. But there are some philosophers who hold that *things* have no existence except *for experiencers*, that experience itself (or consciousness) is the only reality. This is subjectivism, or phenomenalism.... Before considering this possibility, we must inquire why anyone should abandon realism of the simplest, most naïve sort. We shall soon see that the world is much more complicated than the unreflective man supposes. All the epistemological theories which seem so strained and far-fetched to the plain man have their origin in the fact that any simple, naïve realism can be quickly shown to be inadequate, because of incontestable facts.

The most natural supposition, at first sight, is that things — chairs, tables, trees, stars, and all the rest — exist in their own right, prior to and independently of anyone's perceiving (or conceiving) them (this is *realism*); and that, when we do perceive them, we are directly aware

of them, we perceive them as they are, as they would be
if we were not perceiving them (this is *naïve* realism).
For example, this table is really, physically, here, in a
certain definite position in my room, whether anyone is
looking at it or not; it is really oblong, of a certain definite
size; it is really (when light falls upon it) brown and
shining; it is really hard and smooth-surfaced, *in itself*.
When I look at it, the sense-data (or sensa) which I
thereupon have (the details which constitute an oblong,
brown patch in my field of vision) are actually *there*, in
the physical world so many feet from my body, real
qualities or characteristics of the physical table itself....
Consciousness may thus be likened to a searchlight,
lighting up (in perception) various physical things in
turn, around (and including) the perceiver's organism,
and *revealing* their nature. "Things sail into it and out
again without any break in the continuity of their being." [1]   And as two searchlight spots may move toward
each other and partly overlap, so may two fields of
consciousness include identical sensa; in such cases we
actually have elements of our experience in common,
our fields of consciousness overlap, or interpenetrate
each other, in physical space.

The argument for a naïve realism of this sort is that
perception shows that it is *so*.   All other theories seem
forced, by comparison, seem to do violence to the
empirical facts.   Only this theory "takes the universe
at its face-value, and gives credit to whatever it *finds*."

However, everyone must admit that perception is
often illusory.   The sun and stars *seem* to rise in the east,
circle the heavens, and set in the west, behind a stationary earth.   When we put on yellow spectacles, the

[1] F. J. E. Woodbridge, *Journal of Philosophy*, vol. 7, p. 416.

landscape about us *seems* to become yellow-bright; if we change to blue spectacles, everything seems sober-blue. Surely these familiar experiences suggest — what is, in any case, an obvious logical possibility — that, though things do exist about us, affecting us in various ways, they may be in some degree different from what they seem. In other words, the data of our perceptual consciousness (*sensa*) may *not* be the actual qualities of the physical things about us, but merely qualities produced *in our conscious experience* when we look at (or touch, etc.) these physical things. A theory that should adopt that supposition, and explain how that can happen, would be, by comparison with the naïve view, a sophisticated or critical realism.

As a matter of fact, the arguments against naïve realism are overwhelming. We shall summarize five such arguments.

1. *The causal dependence of sensa upon organisms*

(*a*) Look at what you call a red apple. Your sensum (what you see) is red; you assume, naïvely, that the apple itself is red. But to your neighbor, who is 'red-blind,' the apple looks gray. You think *you* see the apple as it *is*; for *your* eyes are normal. But what is a 'normal' eye? The physiological fact seems to be that if your eyes were constructed in the appropriate way, you would see the apple as yellow, or blue, or black. Perhaps some of the lower animals see quite different colors from those which we see; certainly some of them see objects by ultra-violet light, which gives us no color-sensations at all.... It is clear that the color we see depends upon the nature of our *eyes*. How then can it be an inherent character of the physical thing we are looking at?

(*b*) If you put on blue glasses, the apple looks bluish — just as truly, objectively, bluish as it looks bright red when you take the glasses off. But nothing has happened to the *apple*. Evidently, the fact that an object *looks* a certain color does not prove that it *is* that color.

(*c*) If you shake your eyeball with your finger, you have a *shaking-sensum*. But you have not shaken the physical apple.... If you push your eyeballs in the right way, you can see *two* apples. But you have not created a second physical apple by pushing your eyeballs.... Do not such facts show that our sensa are *different* entities from the physical things of which they seem, at first sight, to be merely features, or qualities?

(*d*) When a whistling locomotive rushes by you on a station platform, the pitch of the whistle seems to change abruptly. What you *hear*, your sensum, does, obviously, change. But the objective, physical pitch has not changed, as the engineer can testify; you have an altered sensum because the sound-waves have come to your ears spread out by the receding motion of the train, instead of compressed by its approaching motion. It would seem that *one*, at least, of your two differing sensa must be different from the whistling-event-as-it-is-in-itself. Probably *both* are different from that physical event.

(*e*) If you heat one hand over a fire, and simultaneously chill the other hand on a cake of ice, then plunge both hands into a pail of what would ordinarily be called lukewarm water, the water, in every part of the pail, will feel cold to one hand and warm to the other. Obviously *one* of these thermal sensa must misrepresent the physical fact. Is it not obvious that *both* sensa are subjective — i.e., conditioned by the nature of the observer, instead of being objective, i.e., truly characterizing the outer object as it is when unobserved?

All the above cases show the part played by our sense-organs (together with events taking place between the outer object and the organism) in determining the nature of our sensa.   But what *directly* determines their nature is apparently certain events in our brains (together with reactions of the organism thereby initiated). Unless a nerve-current of the appropriate sort reaches the proper part of the brain, we have *no* sensum of the sort which we have when we are thus stimulated.   And many observations indicate that we should have a sensum of that sort if such a nerve-current were sent to the brain, even though there existed no physical object of the sort which the sensum seems to reveal.

(*f*) Thus a man who has lost a limb sometimes *feels* it there, as before the amputation; in such a case his sensum is clearly subjective (nerve- and brain-engendered), and not an actual event in his (non-existent) limb. Similarly, many patients have seen an apparently objective bright patch of light, though they were in a pitch-dark room, when their brains have been stimulated by an electric current applied to the optic nerve.

(*g*) It has been suggested that if we could successfully cut the nerves going from the eyes to the brain, and those going from the ears to the brain, and splice them up so that the currents coming from the eyes reached the auditory area of the brain, and the currents from the ears reached the visual area, we should hear what we now see and see what we now hear!

It seems an overwhelming and inevitable conclusion from all the experiments above mentioned, that our sensa, being what they are because of the particular nature of our sense-organs and brains, are, in some sense, *organism-produced*, and therefore are not an actual part of the antecedently existing physical things themselves, which, as realists, we believe to surround us in space.

2. *The nature of the process of perception*

Another set of considerations re-enforces and extends the above conclusion. A study of the physical processes causing perception shows that it is not a *revelatory* but a *productive* process. In the case of vision, certain jumps made by electrons near the surface of the physical object in front of the eyes send out pulses of energy, of certain definite sorts. These energy-pulses hit the eyes, set up processes there, which cause nerve-currents to go to the brain along certain specific nerves. The events in the brain thus initiated set off various minute organic reactions. And the brain-events (together with further cerebral events caused by the organic reactions) determine the nature of the visual sensa which thereupon appear.... There are several things to note about this complicated causal process.

(*a*) *Identical events* in the outer object affect various observers. The energy-pulses traveling to all are exactly similar. The *differences* between the sensa of the various observers are caused at, or approaching, the *terminus ad quem* of the process, they do not exist at the *terminus a quo*, the outer object. There are not several qualities in that object, one affecting you, and another affecting me. There is *one* event out there, affecting us

both, but in different ways. The two different sensa
are therefore not *revealed* as out there, they are *produced* in, or upon, or somehow in connection with, you
and me, respectively.

(*b*) This causal process is a *one-way process,* proceeding from outer object to organism. There is no evidence of any reverse process, by which sensa produced
at the organism-end of the causal chain get thrown back
into the outer object (or into any outer space). So, although our sensa do *seem* to be out there, where the
outer physical things are, we know of no way in which
they could *get* there.

Moreover, it is noteworthy that no one but the perceiver of a particular sensum even *seems* to see it out
there; it is his private appearance. Whereas, if perception is really a boomerang, throwing the organism-
engendered sensum out into the object, it would be
natural to ask why others do not perceive it to be there.
... And if these sensa really do clothe the outer objects,
they are perfectly inefficacious there; they have no
part in the physical life of those outer objects, as physicists describe it.

Finally, if our sensa are really, in some mysterious
way, projected *out there*, upon the physical things which
are affecting our eyes, they are still the effects of events
going on in the particular perceiving organisms, and so
exist in, or upon, the outer objects only while perception
lasts, and only for the particular observer. They are
not qualities of the independent object itself, as it is
when unperceived. Nothing is gained for knowledge,
therefore, by supposing this mysterious (and instantaneous) projection to take place.

It is far simpler, then, to suppose that our naïve attribution to the objects about us of the qualities with which they seem to be clothed is an illusion. When we look through blue glasses, the bluish color which the landscape seems to have does not really exist out there in the landscape. Similarly, when we look through our eyes, the colors which the landscape seems to have do not really exist out there.

But where, then, *do* these colors, and other sensa, exist?... Well, that is one of the most puzzling of philosophical questions. We will consider the matter awhile yet before presenting the various possible answers.

(*c*) It takes *time* for outer objects to affect perceivers in such a way that sensa appear to them. Hence, sensa appear at a time appreciably later than that of the events in outer objects which started the process resulting in their appearance. In the case of very distant objects, stars and nebulæ, the time amounts to years, even thousands of years. The star which you now see may, therefore, have exploded and ceased to exist years ago. Yet this sensum — the twinkling point of light — appears to you *now*. Obviously, if a sensum exists *now*, it cannot be any part or quality of a physical object which no longer exists. But apart from this dramatic instance, it should be clear that the time of the appearance of a sensum to a perceiver is not the time of the event in the outer object which, in one sense, we may be said to be seeing; it is the time (or else a time slightly later than the time) of the brain-events produced by the causal process emanating from that outer event. Therefore, *every* sensum must be distinguished from the physical fact which, in some sense, it reports.

Another striking illustration of this fact may be found in an experience like the following. A bugle-call sounds, causing a regiment of cavalry to charge. If you stand some distance away, you see the regiment charge *before* you hear the sound of the bugle. That is, your visual sensa (the moving patches of color) appear before your auditory sensa (the bugle-call) appear. Not only are *both* sets of sensa *later* than the events they picture for you, the *order* of their appearance reverses the order of the outer, physical events.

And now, just as sensa never appear at the *time* of the events which we seem to be perceiving, so they often appear to be at a *place* which cannot be the place of the outer, physical events. The star, if it has not exploded, has probably *moved* so far, during the centuries which the light-waves have taken to reach our eyes, that it no longer exists in the direction from us in which we see it.... When we look down a railway track, we see *converging* rails; that is the sort of sensum we have. But the physical rails are parallel, not convergent.... Looking through a magnifying-glass, we see objects much nearer to us than they are; i.e., our sensa appear to be at a place where the object looked at does not, itself, exist.... Such instances show that many, at least, of our sensa cannot be parts or qualities of the physical objects to which they seem, at first sight, to belong, since they do not even appear to be *in the place* where those physical objects are. Does it not seem likely that sensa are *never* parts or qualities of those objects, but another set of existents entirely?

3. *The difficulty of superposing contradictory characters*

If we were to waive the preceding arguments, and insist that our sensa exist out there in the objects which we believe to surround our bodies, we should run up against still another difficulty. We should find that our various sensa constitute contradictory reports as to the nature of those objects. I see an apple as red; my neighbor, who is red-blind, sees it as gray; another, having taken santonin, sees it as yellowish; if we had a wide enough pharmacopeia, we could doubtless, by internal dosage, make ourselves see it as any color we pleased. If naïve realism were true, the apple would be *all* these colors at once; for every shade of color that any man or animal sees in it would be *there*.... Such a view makes sharply against common sense, which views objects as having just one definite color, size, shape, etc. It blurs the world into a welter of superposed qualities.

The difficulty lies not so much in supposing that physical objects are so extraordinarily manifold, as in believing that they have innumerable qualities so nearly alike and yet different. It does not strain our imagination to suppose the apple to be at the same time red (of a certain definite shade) and also hard, round, and shiny. But to suppose that it is at the same time a hundred different shades of color (in the same place) is not easy. It seems, indeed, logically possible, when one is discussing epistemology. But can anyone who has studied biology, or anyone who has watched an apple growing in his orchard, and thought of it as a living thing, with a definite nature of its own, a thing formed out of earth and air and water, really believe that it possesses such a mist of qualities? At any rate, it is well to realize that this is a necessary corollary of naïve realism. Montague is doubtless right in asserting that the multifold-quality view (which has been seriously advanced by certain epistemologists) "will ruin the realistic movement if it is not repudiated. Any one place at any one time must contain but one non-contradictory set of qualities. Such a set of qualities is what we mean by an object; and its occupancy of one space at one time is what we mean by its existence." [1]

Some writers seem to think they have solved the difficulty by saying that our sensa are out there on the object (or somewhere out there in space) only "*from* certain directions," or "*for* a given observer," or "in relation to" him.... Such phrases need clearing up. If they mean merely that only an observer in a certain position, with a certain sort of eyes, will have the sensum in question, and that it will seem to be out there where the physical object is, they add nothing to what everyone admits. The difference of opinion is as to whether the sensum really exists out there where it seems to him to exist. The answer must be yes or no; it is either out there on (or in) the object, or it is not. In either case, the qualifying phrases "for" some one, or "from" a certain direction, are meaningless.

4. *The difficulty of locating non-perceptual sensa*

So far we have been speaking of the ordinary data of perception, and chiefly of visual data. This is the natural stronghold of naïve realism. For it is difficult to rid ourselves of the illusion that our visual sensa are really out there, clothing the objects about our bodies. In the case of sound, it is somewhat easier to believe that the sound we hear is not the external event itself. And in the case of touch, taste, and smell, it is still easier to think of our sensa as subjective, our own sensations, rather than qualities of the external objects.

[1] W. P. Montague, in *The Philosophical Review*, vol. 23, p. 55.

But now consider hallucination. We commonly agree that, though the hallucinated person may see what he sees just as clearly *out there* as we ever see anything, yet what he sees is not *really* out there.... Well, if his sensum is not really out there, in the space in front of him, *where* is it? And wherever it is, may not ordinary sensa be in the same place, or have the same sort of existence, as these hallucinatory sensa? (The *difference* would be, that in the one case there are real physical objects in front of the body, affecting the sense-organs, while in the other case there are not.)

When we consider, further, what we may call the sensa of dreams, a similar question may be raised. Where are these visual objects which we see (sometimes so vividly) in dreams? Nowhere, most people would say; they are simply *imagined* to exist, they do not really exist. And so in day-dreaming, in imagining.... But if we can *imagine* objects to exist in front of us, so vividly that we really seem to *see* them, when there are no such objects there, may it not be that in the case of ordinary perception we are similarly *imagining* our sensa — on the occasion of being stimulated by real outer objects? (The impact, and the precise nature, of the incoming nerve-current may be supposed to account for the vividness and the precision of these perceptual sensa.)

Notice this: it is impossible to draw a sharp line, psychologically, between perceptual sensa and the sensa of dreams, imagination, and hallucination. That is, there are borderline cases, where we are in doubt whether what we have just seen or heard is objectively real or subjective. And there are cases where the subject himself is convinced that he has seen or heard something objectively real, while bystanders are convinced that he has *not*.... This suggests that all sensa are in the same boat, have a similar existential status — whatever that may be — and that the difference between perceptual and non-perceptual sensa lies in the fact, extrinsic to their nature, that they are generated by outer stimulation, on the one hand, or by organic events alone, on the other hand.... At any rate, epistemological theories must keep these non-perceptual sensa in mind, and not concern themselves merely with admittedly perceptual sensa.

5. *Cases where knowledge is obviously mediate*

Further, epistemology must consider not merely the perceptual, and the quasi-perceptual, data of consciousness, it must consider our knowledge of the past, of the future, and of other people's minds. In the case of perception, it is natural to suppose that what appears in our field of consciousness is the very physical thing itself, to suppose that consciousness is like a searchlight, somehow reaching that physical thing in front of our bodies, and *revealing* it. But when we *remember* a past event, can we suppose that what appears in our field of consciousness *is* the past event itself? How *can* it be, since the past event is past and gone, is no longer in existence? Must it not be that there is a duality here between the past event, with its date, and the present memory-image, with *its* date? And *where*, then, is the present memory-image, what sort of status has *it*? May it not be that sensa and memory-images have a similar status (whatever that may be), sensa giving us knowledge of objects now existing in the neighborhood of the body, and memory-images giving us knowledge of objects, or events, that existed in the past, but both being distinguishable from the objects themselves of which they give us knowledge?

Similarly, in anticipation must we not admit a temporal duality between the anticipatory image of a future event, and that event itself, which has not yet happened?... Moreover, in anticipation, as in memory (and as, indeed, in perception), there is usually some *error*; the present images in the mind are more or less different *in character*, as well as in temporal status, from the events themselves which they imagine, and so, obviously, cannot be identified with them.

So with *your* knowledge of *my* conscious experience. I can tell you, in detail, of my experience. But your experiences, thus engendered, are different from my experiences, forming as it were, a separate realm.... May it not be that our knowledge of trees, desks, etc., is really as *mediate* as our knowledge of other minds? We often have good reason to believe our echoes of other people's conscious experiences to be *veridical*, reporting those experiences truthfully, just as we have good reason to believe that our sensa often report correctly the nature of physical objects. But they are not those experiences themselves.

Must we not, then, distinguish, in all cases, the colors and shapes and sounds which confront us, as conscious beings, from those independent existents, or events, of which, in some sense, and in some degree, they give us knowledge? We mean nothing more than this, at present, when we use such terms as 'subjective,' 'in the mind.' What sort of status our sensa, and other data of consciousness, have, whether they are 'physical' or 'mental' (whatever those terms may mean), and where, if anywhere, they exist, remains to be discussed.

SUGGESTED READINGS

R. W. Sellars, *Essentials of Philosophy*, II–III.
Durant Drake, in *Essays in Critical Realism*, pp. 3–32.
G. T. W. Patrick, *Introduction to Philosophy*, pp. 366–372.
C. D. Broad, *Perception, Physics and Reality*, I, IV.
Durant Drake, *Mind and Its Place in Nature*, I–II.
D. S. Miller, in *Essays in Honor of William James*, VIII.
R. W. Sellars, *Evolutionary Naturalism*, II.
Bertrand Russell, *The Problems of Philosophy*, I–III.
W. P. Montague, *Ways of Knowing*, VIII.

CHAPTER VII

SUBJECTIVISM

THE upshot of the preceding chapter was that our sense-data — the items that make up our perceptual experience — cannot, upon reflection, be taken to be actual parts of the physical things which, as realists, we believe to be existing about us and affecting our bodies. They are *our sense-data*; their status seems to be similar to the status of our memory-images, the content of our dreams, and the pictures woven by our imagination — except that they, presumably, in some sense and in some degree, reveal to us the nature of those physical things surrounding our bodies.

But now we must question this presumption. How do we know, after all, that those extra-mental things really exist? Perhaps these data of our experience, these sensa, memory-images, and the rest, are the only sort of existents there are. Perhaps all real knowledge, after all, is merely knowledge of the sort of experiences that actually occur, or of the sort of experiences that *would* occur under various circumstances — i.e., given certain combinations of antecedent experiences. Perhaps *nothing* actually *exists* outside of experience itself.

This view is commonly called 'subjectivism,' or 'phenomenalism.' It is never the view of the active man, who always feels himself to be dealing with *things*, that have their own independent, continuous existence, apart from anyone's experience of them. But though subjectivism may seem a highly artificial and preposterous doctrine to one who is unused to philosophical reflection, it grows in plausibility as we brood upon it; and it has been advocated, under varying names, by some very able thinkers. Certainly no one is competent to maintain any metaphysical theory who has not felt its spell. It requires a certain wrench of our natural mental habits to take this point of view. But our natural mental habits may be only serviceable, not metaphysically trustworthy. And once the subjectivistic way of looking at things is acquired it may become a new habit of mind, almost as difficult to shake off as the old.

THE SUBJECTIVISTIC POINT OF VIEW

Let us, then, lay aside our common-sense belief in a world of physical things, and take a fresh start. What do we actually *know* to exist? Why, our conscious experience, as we *feel* it. Or rather, *I* know *my* conscious experience. For example, yesterday I was (realistically speaking) in a railway car. What did I then know of existence? For a few moments, something like this: A rumbling noise, a faintly jarring sensation, color- and form-sensations, a rim of dark red, and between the red bands a mass of blue above, various shades of green below, with a quality of 'out-there-ness'; simultaneously some half-formed thoughts, a wish, a pain perhaps, a memory or anticipation. All these elements of experience in continual change, except the red bands (the window frame), which were continuously present. This is all that existed *for me* at that time. Other existents there undoubtedly were, simultaneous with this stream of my conscious experience; but they were not present with or in it. In contrast with the whole universe, if it exists, or in contrast merely with the conscious experience of all human beings contemporaneous with me, that stream of my experience was a very narrow one, a tiny microcosm of a reality. But everything beyond it *was* beyond it and could only have had, for me, a hypothetical existence.

Suppose I call this flux of immediately present items my 'stream of consciousness.' May it not be that reality consists merely of a number of such streams of consciousness — mine, yours, other people's, the consciousness of animals, and of superhuman beings, if such there be? To be sure, some of my items of experience are sensa, and these seem to be 'external' to me. But does that mean anything more than that these sensa are external to my *body*-sensa? And on the view we are considering, my *body* is simply one group of sensa, particularly persistent. *None* of my sensa are external to my conscious *experience*. In short, *all* that I have is a succession of ever-fluctuating visual, tactile, auditory, motor, kinesthetic sensations, woven together, by a certain ease of transition, into whatever degree of unity and continuity my conscious experience has. And *my* stream of consciousness is sundered sharply from the similar jumble of contents which make up *your* stream of conscious experience.

If this is all, if nothing exists but these streams of consciousness, of ever-changing, kaleidoscopic mental life, how comes it that we so generally believe ourselves to be living in a world of relatively stable extra-mental *things?...* Well, we do find *recurrences* in our flux, particularly among those items which we call sensa. Variable as our sensa are, they fluctuate about fixed points. And they *go together* in groups, so that one sensum is a sign of the potentiality of the appearance of other sensa of that group. May it not be that these *groups* of actual and potential sensa constitute all there really is to *things*? For instance, I have a brown-shiny-oblong sensum. I say I see a table. For I know that if I make certain movements (i.e., have certain motor and kinesthetic sensations), I shall have a certain sort of smooth-hard tactile sensum present in my experience, and so on. So, while on the one hand we form the conception of a stream of consciousness by grouping our experiences *as they occur*, in their context with our other experiences, on the other hand, by grouping these data according to their *kind*, and according to the *pattern* to which they seem somehow to belong, we form the conception of physical *things*.

Thus *things* are merely "permanent possibilities of perception" (*relatively* permanent, by contrast with our changing sensations). The whole physical universe is just a concept in our minds, the order, or pattern, of possible experiences. The laws of physics, after all, are verifiable simply as formulas which serve to point out the regularities in past experiences and to predict future experiences. When the chemist asserts that all acids turn litmus-paper blue, all he means (or should mean) is that, if we go through the particular series of experiences which result in the visual experience of litmus-paper-and-acid-together, we shall have the visual sensation of litmus-paper-now-blue. This is just a possible or actual *experience*.

Any group of actual and possible sensa that hang together, as it were, come to seem a stable and independent *thing*, by contrast not only with the *evanescent* character of each actual sensation, but also with the *incompleteness* of each individual sensum. It is the group-of-potential-sensa that demands our attention, rather than any particular sensum. So we seldom have a sensum without, subconsciously or consciously, referring it to its group; if we name it, we give it the name which applies to the *group* of sensa.... And we discover that other people's sensa fall into similar groups; and thus larger, inter-personal, groups of sensa can be demarcated, which form, as it were, common, public, objects. The actual sensa present in your experience are, slightly or radically, different from those present in mine; but the two groups of sensa occupy the same position in that vast pattern of sensa which we call the physical world. This name, this concept, of a world that is (relatively) stable and public and infinitely vaster than anybody's actual sensa, has ingrained in us the belief that another *kind of reality* exists, a physical world somehow different from our little mental worlds, a macrocosm of insentient things surrounding our microcosmic mental worlds. But perhaps this is a mistake. Perhaps, when pruned of illegitimate connotations, the physical world turns out to be merely a name for the totality of the possibilities (or perhaps we should say, the conditional certainties) of experience.

A group of nineteenth-century British philosophers, notably Bishop Berkeley and John Stuart Mill, were the first to give clear utterance to this conception. Somewhat later, Karl Pearson, in his widely read *Grammar of Science*, spoke of our discourse concerning the physical world as "mental shorthand" — the actual *reality* being concrete *experiences*. Similarly, Hans Vaihinger calls our concepts of matter, energy, atoms, etc., "indispensable fictions," useful but not literally true. D. L. Murray writes, "The 'real' thing is a coincidence of various people's perceptions, similar enough to enable them in practical life to speak of perceiving the same. Such a serviceable coincidence of perceptions may well (and for practical purposes must) be called a single real object." [1] And M. P. Mason declares, "'Possible experience' is the only adequate conception of reality. It gives us a sufficient ideal basis for science, and at the same time keeps within the bounds of experience." [2]

George Stuart Fullerton, an American philosopher of the generation just past, repeatedly declared that the only intelligible *meaning* of the concept "the physical world" is "the objective *Order* of experiences," the Order which we gradually construct in our minds by fitting together our multitudinous sensa — the latter alone being the stuff of reality.

> It is not a question of denying 'things' and their positions and operations. It is simply a question of what can intelligibly be meant by such, and of the grounds upon which they are to be accepted.... No plain man, no man of science, hesitates to talk of things as existing and as having qualities as yet undiscovered. [But] in looking for such, no one expects to come upon anything save appearances [sensa]. The thing, as apart from all appearances, seems to be a mere nothing. All that we have a right to say about it, all that we seem able to think about it, seems to be drawn from the objective order of phenomena, where we abstract from the fact of a phenomenon's actually appearing at a given time, considering only its belonging to the order. Why regard the thing as a something 'in itself' at all? Why not find the thing *in* phenomena...? [3]

A certain objectivity there is, indeed, in any case, about this Order which has been conceived, vaguely by the plain man and in elaborate detail by the scientists, whether

[1] *Mind*, vol. 18, p. 382.
[2] *Journal of Philosophy*, vol. 3, p. 457.
[3] George Stuart Fullerton, *Journal of Philosophy*, vol. 22, pp. 33, 31.

it is *merely*, as Fullerton believed, a man-conceived Order
which enables us to predict, and, to some extent, control
our sense-experience, or whether it is *also*, as realists
believe, a picture (more or less adequate) of a world of
entities which exist in their own right, independently
of our experience.   But the subjectivistic interpretation
of physical concepts is certainly not that of the plain
man, or of the actual working scientists.   And whichever
interpretation is correct, we must at least keep the two
views sharply distinct in our minds.   If subjectivism
is true, to put an end to all conscious experience would
be to put an end to *everything*; the term 'physical things'
has *meaning* only with reference to forms of actual or
possible *experience*.   Whereas all realists believe that
the existence of physical things would be none the less
a real existence if there were no such thing as conscious
experience at all.

CAN WE KNOW OF ANYTHING BEYOND EXPERIENCE?

Subjectivism is conceivably true.   Our question now is,
Have we any reason to believe that it *is* true?... Perhaps
the chief reason why thinkers have taken refuge in subjectivism has been their realization of the difficulties
inherent in common-sense realism.   For, as we have
seen, our conscious experiences cannot be made to fit
together to form a coherent realistic world.

Moreover, it is *simpler*, it requires less assumption, to
accept merely 'states of consciousness,' mental realities,
and let it go at that.   Why bother to assume anything
else?   Are not our little realms of conscious experience
(with all their possibilities of extension) *enough*?   There
may, conceivably, be things-in-themselves, outside conscious experience; but, if so, why should they interest

us? The subjectivist "applies the law of parsimony to ontology," as Lovejoy says, refusing to multiply entities beyond necessity.... But the philosopher *should* be interested to know whether or not extra-experiential entities exist, i.e., whether subjectivism or realism is true. And we must not rule out the realistic hypothesis even if we cannot find proof that it is true, unless we can find proof that subjectivism, or some *other* view, is true. Bertrand Russell calls realism an "audacious metaphysical theory." But then, so is subjectivism. To say that independently real physical things do *not* exist is as dogmatic as to say that they *do* exist, unless we can show good reasons pro or con.

But now, the subjectivist insists that, in the nature of the case, it is impossible to *know* anything about extra-experiential entities, if such there be; hence we should ignore the possibility of their existence.

It is hard to see how observation can ever lead us to the unobservable, or how experience can ever prove the unexperienced and inexperiencable.[1]

In philosophy, if we mean to get on, we must adhere to the methodological postulate that what can't be known shan't count.[2]

The plain man, however, *supposes* himself to know a good deal about things that exist outside his experience. He believes that his house exists, with all its furniture, when no one is looking at it or thinking of it. And by that statement he certainly *means* more than the fact that he, and other observers, *could have had* perceptual experiences of the house and its contents, if they *had* been there. If he starts a fire on the hearth, goes out,

[1] J. B. Pratt, *Journal of Philosophy*, vol. 9, p. 579. (Pratt, however, is not a subjectivist.)

[2] D. L. Murray, *Mind*, vol. 18, p. 380.

and comes back after an hour, he believes that certain events actually took place during his absence, in the realistic sense.... The scientist believes that he knows a great deal *about* myriads of events which never fall directly within anyone's experience.... Which is right — the subjectivist or the plain man and the scientist?

The following is offered as an exact statement of the situation: *If* realism is true, our physical knowledge *is* knowledge, in some sense and degree, of extra-experiential existents. If it is not true, our physical knowledge is merely knowledge of our potential experiences. In Chapter IX we shall give strong reasons for believing realism to be true. But it will be confessed that we cannot *know* that realism is true. Hence all we can say is that it is *highly probable* that our physical knowledge is actual knowledge of a realistic world. We may confidently believe that we know a great deal about that world; but we cannot *know* that we know it! However, to know something about the physical world, it is not necessary to *know* that we know it. For if so, it would be necessary to know that we know that we know it; and so on *ad infinitum*. No, *verification* of our knowledge is often, as in this case, impossible; but knowledge is already knowledge, prior to verification.

If we are honest, the subjectivist says, we shall limit ourselves to saying that experiences occur *as if* the physical world were real.

[Atoms, etc.] should not be held for literally real. It is *as if* they existed; but in reality they are like co-ordinates or logarithms, only artificial short-cuts for taking us from one part to another of experience's flux. We can cipher fruitfully with them; they serve us wonderfully; but we must not be their dupes.... They are all but ways of talking on our part, to be compared solely from the point of view of their use.

The only literally true thing is *reality*; and the only reality we know is sensible reality, the flux of our sensations and emotions as they pass.[1]

But since experiences constantly occur *as if* the world of nature were real, why is it not simplest to believe that it *is* real? The subjectivist never seems to ask how these scientific formulas *can* help us to predict experience so exactly, unless they are descriptions of the way things are really acting, in a real world.... Strictly speaking, all our *historical* and *autobiographical* knowledge is as truly an 'as if' knowledge; we can never get back into the past to verify our ideas about it, we can only pile up evidence in the present; and the belief that such and such past events happened remains merely a highly probable hypothesis. That is the sort of thing most knowledge *is*.

This, however, does not quite dispose of the subjectivist's argument. He asks us how it can be conceived to be *possible* to have knowledge of extra-experiential existents? Whenever we know anything whatsoever, does not our *knowledge* of it bring it *within* our experience?... No, whatever is directly present within our experience we may be said to be *aware* of; but that awareness does not constitute *knowledge*. Knowledge always has to do with the absent. We know, a moment after having an experience, that we have had it; we know what experiences we had yesterday and last year; we know, to some extent, what other experiencers there are, and what experiences they are having; we know, if realism is true, what physical things exist, what physical events have taken place at various past moments, and what may be expected to take place in the future. If

[1] William James, *Pragmatism*, pp. 189–190.

realism is not true, our supposed knowledge of physical things is illusory. But whether veridical or illusory, it is the same general sort of thing as those other types of knowledge which *everybody* believes in; it is a relation of the knower to objects or events not at the moment present to his awareness. And there is no more difficulty, a priori, in knowledge of physical objects external to the present field of consciousness than in knowledge of past events in one's own life.

The arguments which support our natural animal faith that we are living in the midst of a realistic world will be presented in Chapter IX. In the meantime, we agree with the subjectivist that in the nature of the case we can never absolutely *know* that our physical knowledge is knowledge of such a real, independently existing world. But neither can we know that it is *not*. And the moral to be drawn from this is not that we should sternly refuse to believe in that world, but that we should let our beliefs be guided by *probability*, so far as we can estimate it. And if we cannot make up our minds which hypothesis, the realistic or the subjectivistic, is the more probable, we had better follow our animal faith in our actual living (as we surely shall, anyway!) and leave the philosophical corner of our brains open and unbiased, one way or the other.

CAN WE CONCEIVE OF ANYTHING BEYOND EXPERIENCE?

The subjectivist, however, may go on to say, It is impossible even to *conceive* any other sort of existence than experience. Trans-empirical reality of any sort may be ruled out a priori.

I am driven to the conclusion that for me experience is the

same as reality. The fact that falls elsewhere seems, in my mind, to be a mere word and a failure, or else an attempt at self-contradiction.[1]

[To conceive] an existence which is prior to thought [is] self-contradictory, inasmuch as that very thing-in-itself is only conceivable by, exists only for, thought.[2]

It is only within the experienced world that the terms 'existence' and 'reality' have any applicability. Carried beyond that world they are empty sound.[3]

A predication of reality to what transcends experience completely and in every sense, is not problematic, it is nonsense.... A hypothesis which in the nature of the case is incapable of any conceivable test is the hypothesis of nothing.[4]

Non-empirical realities are nonentities.[5]

It was pointed out in Chapter II that an inability to conceive something would imply nothing but the weakness of our powers of conception; and, moreover, that, as a matter of fact, we do conceive anything that we talk about. Realists, certainly, do *conceive* extra-mental realities; they even suppose themselves to know a great deal about them.... The fact that these things are only "conceivable by thought" (a tautology!) does not imply that they "*exist* only for thought."... Why, then, should it be said that we cannot conceive extra-experiential objects? Why are they "nonsense"?

The assertion seems to rest on the supposed empirical fact that everything we conceive turns out, upon inspection, to consist of experience-stuff. If we are aware of it, it is, *ipso facto*, an item of experience, a datum of consciousness, a mental state.

Objects as known have been found — not assumed — to

---

[1] F. H. Bradley, *Appearance and Reality*, 2d ed., p. 145.
[2] John Caird, *Introduction to the Philosophy of Religion*, p. 149.
[3] R. F. A. Hoernlé, *Idealism as a Philosophy*, p. 113.
[4] C. I. Lewis, *Mind and the World-Order*, pp. 32, 64.
[5] John Dewey, *The Influence of Darwin on Philosophy*, pp. 230, n., 238 n.

be forms of experience. [To speak of any such objects in abstraction from the relation of knowledge is] as inherently incredible as if one should speak of ether vibrations abstracting from motion.... No description of matter [or ether] can be made except in terms of sensible quality and relation.[1]

To such assertions the simple answer is that although, whenever we think of anything, that something is, necessarily, at the moment, an object-of-thought, that fact, the being-an-object-of-thought (or, for that matter, an object of sense-experience), may be a mere *adventitious* fact, a new relation into which the object has been brought, and not a *constitutive* fact. One cannot, indeed, speak of vibrations without implying motion; for, by definition, vibrations are a form of motion. Similarly, the subjectivists *define* all our objects of sense and thought *as* objects of sense or thought, and thereby, by very definition, exclude the possibility that these same objects exist when unsensed or unthought of. If they were consistent, they would define their percepts and concepts of you and me as objects-of-their-sense or thought, and thereby exclude the possibility that we exist when they do not perceive or think of us! But is this not a *reductio ad absurdum* of subjectivism? You and I are not dependent for our existence upon being perceived or conceived by anyone else; we have our *own* existence. Then why may not physical things have *their* own existence?

So when we think of a number, the number we think of is, at the moment, an object-of-awareness. But, whatever the number of living subjectivists may be, it is clear that there *is* such a number; and that that number actually finds illustration in existence, whether or not

[1] M. W. Calkins, *Journal of Philosophy*, vol. 8, pp. 454–455.

anyone ever counts the subjectivists or so much as thinks of that particular number. A number, clearly, is not intrinsically and in the nature of the case an object-of-awareness. So may it be with the whole world of physical things in which the realist believes.

It is, indeed, obvious that there are many numbers (very high numbers, numbers with very complicated fractions, etc.) which no one ever thinks of, which no one ever *has* thought of, or in any way experienced. It seems obvious, too, that spatial and temporal relations are independent of anyone's awareness of them. London is just so many miles from New York, the earth is just so many miles from the sun, whether anyone knows how many miles, or so much as raises the question. It is just so many years and days since a certain meteorite fell on earth, though no one knows how many, and even though no one has ever seen or heard of the meteorite. When these numbers and these spatial and temporal relations are thought of, they are, *for the time being*, objects of consciousness. But they are none the less real if they are never thought of.

When it comes to colors, sounds, smells, etc., it is, again, logically possible that just these qualities exist unperceived and unconceived, and that the realistic world contains innumerable qualities of the sort. It may be a mere adventitious fact that anyone is *aware* of these qualities. But we shall see presently that physicists find no reason for supposing that such qualities exist outside of conscious experience. So it may well be that all this warmth and color of our conscious experience *is* the contribution of consciousness itself. In so far, the subjectivists would be right as to the fact. But they would be wrong in their assertion that it *must* be so.   The fact that whatever we find in experience is, necessarily, an object-found-in-experience does not in the least prove that those very objects cannot exist prior to, and external to, experience.

Or, there may be more or less *similar* objects existing outside of experience.   There are all sorts of possibilities. The only point we need make here is that the subjectivistic attack has not disproved the possibility of the existence of a real physical world, independent of experience. Positive reasons for believing in such a world we shall adduce in Chapter IX.

SUGGESTED READINGS

R. W. Sellars, *Essentials of Philosophy*, V.
J. S. Mill, *Examination of Sir William Hamilton's Philosophy*, XI.
G. S. Fullerton, *Introduction to Philosophy*, III–V.
G. S. Fullerton, *The World We Live In*, III.
R. F. A. Hoernlé, *Idealism*, II.
W. P. Montague, *Ways of Knowing*, X.
C. D. Broad, *Physics, Perception, and Reality*, III.
G. E. Moore, *Philosophical Studies*, I.
W. E. Hocking, *Types of Philosophy*, XX–XXII.
R. B. Perry, *Approach to Philosophy*, IX.

CHAPTER VIII

IDEALISM

SUBJECTIVISM itself hardly constitutes a philosophy; it is a 'methodological postulate.' But upon it as a base have been built the various systems of philosophical idealism, which have played so prominent a part in the thought of the past century or so. Subjectivism rules out everything beyond experience. But the question arises, Whose experience? To this question there are two types of answer, the pluralistic and the monistic, personal idealism and absolute idealism. The former gives us a world consisting of a number of separate *minds*, each with its private experience. The latter gives us a single all-inclusive *Mind*, of which our individual minds are fragments, and calls the apparent isolation of our minds from one another an illusion.

FROM PLURALISTIC TO MONISTIC IDEALISM

For pluralistic idealism, reality is a society of persons (or selves, or minds) — and nothing else. It goes beyond subjectivism, since it believes not only in the data of consciousness which are empirically *present*, and therefore indubitable, and in other, more or less similar data of other people's consciousness, which are assumed, or inferred, but also in entities called selves, or minds, which *have* these data. These minds do not exist in Space; on the contrary, Space is merely an idea of ours (arrived at by fitting together our various sensa, with their *felt* spatial relations) and so has its only existence *within* minds. Similarly, Time is merely our *sense* of duration; it exists within minds, rather than minds within Time. God may exist, a perfect mind. But there is no *universe*, there are just a great number of separate minds, superhuman perhaps, certainly human and sub-human. They are not in a common Space and Time, for there *is* no Space and Time, except as experiences in the several minds. And, similarly, there are no *other* relations between them, since there is no reality to relations but the experience-of-relatedness within each separate mind. Each mind is a little universe in itself, while in between and beyond them is *nothing*.

The first question one wishes to ask is, If there is no physical universe, how does it happen that each individual's experience unrolls *just as if there were* such a universe? If each person's stream of experience is just a sort of private 'movie,' why should these hints and clues of extra-mental reality be so continuously present? And how does it happen that separate minds have such closely similar, yet significantly different, experiences, so that they *seem* to be living in the midst of a *common* non-mental world?

The personalist may point out that in dreams we seem to be confronted with such a real world, and yet we all agree that our minds are creating these phantasms. So it is conceivable that our own minds create all our waking sense-experience. But this would not explain the regularity of the pattern of this experience, its obvious independence of our will or mood, or the fact that this pattern is, apparently, common to all minds. The further explanation is, therefore, natural that we have the sort of experience we have because God wills us to have it, in just this detail. God tunes our minds to a common melody, so to speak, and practices upon us this

magnificent deception of an apparent universe which
does not really exist, in order that by wrestling with the
obduracy of this non-existent world, we may develop
our mental life in ways that have moral worth.

One may wonder, in passing, why, if God can do all
that, he did not create a real physical world and be
done with it, instead of having to create in us perpetually
the illusion of such a world!

But most idealists have been no more content than
realists would be with these isolated monads, this collection of minds with no *medium* between them, no cosmic setting. They, too, have felt the irresistible urge
to believe in a *universe*. But since they have accepted
the subjectivistic postulate, that experience and reality
are synonymous terms, that things exist only for minds,
they can get a universe only by assuming the existence
of a universal Mind which experiences everything.
The universe exists as the experience of this Absolute
Mind, this all-inclusive Experiencer.... Such a conception gives contemplative satisfaction, appeals to the
imagination and the religious feelings. But since these
satisfactions constitute no evidence of its truth, we will
say no more about them, but consider what evidence is
offered.

Josiah Royce, one of America's most famous philosophical idealists, used as illustration the case where
two oarsmen find themselves in the same boat. The
data present in the two streams of experience are different. Can we then truthfully speak of their both
seeing, or being in, the *same* boat? Only, Royce asserted,
if there is an all-inclusive Experience of which these
two finite sets of experiences are partial aspects, their
two minds being conjoined, so to speak, in the Absolute

Mind.   For to affirm the existence of the same boat is to assert that this *common* boat has some sort of real existence.   But if only experience, consciousness, can be conceived to be ultimately real, the only sort of continuous, common existence it *can* have is as a continuous percept in an all-embracing Experience.

> We are driven to assume an ultimate consciousness to sustain the universe in the absence of any other, to hold time and space together and resolve their contradictions; to unite the personal perspectives of the finite selves.[1]

Otherwise our lives would be, as William James put it,

> a congeries of solipsisms, out of which in strict logic only a God could compose a universe even of discourse.... The incredibility of such a philosophy is flagrant.[2]

In so far, the common-sense universe of physical things would seem to serve the purpose more simply than an assumed Absolute Mind.   But the idealist argues that a collection of separate physical things would no more constitute a *universe* than a collection of separate minds.   Why, for example, should the particles making up the supposed physical earth cohere, obey common laws, revolve together about the sun?   Why should they all work together so marvelously to form a system, a cosmos?   Why should the earth obey the pull of the sun, ninety million miles away?   Why, and how, could any *cause* produce an *effect*, somewhere else, in another physical thing?... In short, the supposed realistic world would be merely a great number of utterly separate worlds; only in consciousness is there wholeness, continuity, unity.

What other medium do we know of but a thinking con-

---

[1] May Sinclair, *The New Idealism*, p. 314.   By permission of The Macmillan Company, publishers.

[2] William James, *Essays in Radical Empiricism*, p. 77.

sciousness in and through which the separate can be united in that way which constitutes a relation? [1]

In unminded Space-Time, powerless to retain its own past and future, there is incurable disintegration. Introduce consciousness that joins instant to instant and holds past, present and future together in one duration; that joins point to point and holds length, breadth, and thickness together in one extension; that links point with instant and point-instant with point-instant in one Space-Time; see Space-Time once for all as existing, not in and by and for itself, but as the simplest and most universal form of consciousness, so that all events happening in Space-Time are *ipso facto* happening in consciousness, and contradiction disappears.... In consciousness and consciousness alone is there continuity; and only so far as Space-Time *is* consciousness has it duration. [2]

The belief in matter is no intelligible explanation of the facts. Matter may be said to be solid, extended in space. What is there about this concept to make the motion of matter intelligible? Why should mere solidity move? Why should the impact of one solid electron on another result in the motion of another electron? In short, what is there about matter as defined to explain its properties as observed? There is no doubt about the laws of 'matter'; there is no doubt about the fact that in dealing with physical things we are dealing with something real; but there is a great deal of doubt about whether the concept of matter is an intelligible explanation of the order of the universe. 'Matter' as defined fails to satisfy reason.... Without this hypothesis [that what we call matter is really just God's experience], the order and interaction of nature becomes a mystic miracle, an inexplicable fact. [3]

In short, the thoroughgoing idealist feels that only *within a mind* is unity-in-plurality intelligible. He cannot conceive how separate physical things, or how separate minds, could communicate with, or influence, one another, could constitute a *universe*; whereas we can

[1] T. H. Green, *Prolegomena to Ethics*, § 70.

[2] May Sinclair, *The New Idealism*, p. 227. By permission of The Macmillan Company, publishers.

[3] E. S. Brightman, *Introduction to Philosophy*, pp. 233, 246.

see that a stream of consciousness has precisely this unity-in-plurality. Therefore the universe, if there *is* a universe, is probably a single stream of consciousness.

However, the fact that the idealist deems it easier to understand such a universe does not prove that that is the sort of universe that exists. Perhaps the universe is very *difficult* to understand.... But, as a matter of fact, it is not clear to most of us that the unity-in-plurality exhibited by a stream of conscious experience is any easier to *understand* than the unity-in-plurality of a physical universe. We *find* a sort of unity in our field of experience, but do we understand how it is possible? ... Many contemporary psychologists would say that this unity-in-plurality of consciousness can best be explained as the result of the manifold stimulation of an organism, and its unitary *reactions*. In so far as we react to a set of impressions as to a single object, or scene, we *give* our conscious life a sort of unity. In so far as we do not, we have discontinuity. And there is far more *dis*continuity in our conscious life than we commonly realize. In short, it seems to many of us easier to understand the unity of consciousness in terms of the physical organism than to understand the unity of the physical universe as a unity of consciousness.... And it is very difficult to see, in detail, how a *cosmic* consciousness *could* have the unity-in-plurality that a small private field of consciousness has. To this point we shall return in a moment.

A somewhat subtler form of the idealist's argument runs as follows: We agree that there is such a thing as objective *truth*, independent of our subjective apprehension of it. We agree that the entities which make up the universe exist in some sort of *relations* to one another.

We agree that certain logical, mathematical, physical *laws* hold throughout nature. But if the universe is composed of separate individual entities (whether mental or physical), none of them knowing, at best, more than a fragment of this eternal Truth, or knowing that for more than a brief span, *what sort of reality* does this eternal Truth have? How could it be eternally true, except as the content of a universal, all-knowing Mind? And what sort of reality do the relations between things, or between persons, have, when these relations are unknown to *them*? Must we not postulate a universal Mind for which these relations have reality, a Mind for which the whole system of "natural law" holds? We do not *devise*, we *discover* logical truths, mathematical laws, of which perhaps no man has ever before been aware; yet these laws, we admit, have been always *there* to discover. But *where*? What sort of being have they had when no finite mind was aware of them? How can they be eternal and universal laws, except as the expression of an eternal and universal Mind?

To such questions as these realists give somewhat varying answers, which we shall briefly consider in Chapter X. But they agree that truth is, *in some sense*, eternally valid, relations and laws are in some sense objectively real, whether or not they are known by any consciousness, finite or infinite. In fact, they assert that an *awareness* of this truth, or of these laws, even by an all-embracing Mind, would be a secondary fact, an *additional* fact to their *reality*. An omniscient Mind would, by definition, *know* all truth; but the truth would have to be *there* to be known. It would be aware of the existence of spatial, temporal, causal relations, but its awareness of them would be veridical only if they were really *there*.... In short, the realist asserts that to conceive the existence of an all-knowing Mind does not in the least help to solve any of the problems which the idealist raises.

SOME DIFFICULTIES OF IDEALISM

It may be granted that *if* the subjectivistic postulate is sound, if we have no reason to believe in, and cannot even conceive, any sort of extra-mental existence, some variety of philosophical idealism must be accepted; that is, *if* we are to believe not merely in our fragmentary and evanescent experiences, but in some sort of a continuously existing, larger universe. The realist, however, not accepting the subjectivistic postulate, believes in a physical universe surrounding our finite selves and acting as a medium of communication between us. Moreover, for reasons which we shall summarize in the following chapter, he finds this familiar concept easier to accept than the more artificial concept of a universe which has existence only in God's mind. But before considering those arguments for realism, we may pause to point out some difficulties which idealism must meet.

(1) All idealists, in addition to accepting the manifold objects-of-consciousness, which alone are empirically given, postulate the existence of minds, or selves, which *have* these data, are aware of these objects. For the personalist, these are strictly separate, non-overlapping minds; for the monistic idealist they are fragments, or aspects, of the One absolutely real Mind.... But what *is* a mind? How does the One Mind, or how do the many minds, *have* experience? What is this relation of *being aware of* objects-of-consciousness?... If personalism is true, where do new-born minds come from?... *How* do

minds affect one another?... If monistic idealism is true, what is this relation of being-an-aspect-of the Universal Mind?... Perhaps these questions are answerable. But they are seldom, if ever, answered by the idealist. He balks at believing in the existence of independently real physical things, but he seems aware of no difficulty in understanding the existence of minds, with their mutual influence, or of One Mind with many subsidiary foci.... But actually, this picture of a mental universe is as truly an *hypothesis* as the familiar conception of a physical universe, as much in need of evidence to support it, and as bristling with questions which, the realist feels, have not been satisfactorily answered.

(2) If the subjectivistic analysis is correct, the logical result would seem to be solipsism — the view that only one's own experience exists. For that is all that anyone *finds*, all that is 'given,' that is a datum, for *him*. It is just as truly accepting an *hypothesis*, for me to believe in other people's experience as it is for me to believe in physical things outside of anyone's experience. True, I see other people walking around. I hear them speak or cry out in pain. But from the subjectivistic standpoint (upon which all idealisms rest) these are just objects-of-my-experience, which may conceivably be as insubstantial as the people in my dreams. If I am going to let myself believe that this stream of my experience reveals to me *other* experience, outside of mine, why not just as well assume that it reveals to me other non-experiential existence, i.e., physical things? Both sorts of reality are equally transcendent to my experience, both equally involve assumption, faith, or hypothesis, as well as mere acceptance of what is actually experienced. Indeed, the belief in a vast Universal Mind

seems to the realist far less forced upon us than the belief in chairs and tables, earth and sun and stars. And idealism of every stripe seems to him an arbitrary half-way skepticism, since it accepts our natural belief in other minds and rejects our equally natural belief in physical things.

Indeed, if we were to reject, consistently, belief in everything not empirically *given*, we should have to reject belief in our own *past* experience. For all we ever *have*, actually given, is just what is now present in our conscious field. True, we have what we call memories. But these are present experiences, and may conceivably be illusory, not revealing any real past. I may have but just begun to live, a moment ago. My experience is of a sort that suggests irresistibly that it has been going on for years. But it also suggests, with almost equal irresistibility, that I am in the presence, and at the mercy, of independently real physical things. If we may trust one appearance, why not trust the other?

In short, the idealist believes in the *literal* truth of human biography and history (as the record of past *experience*); he takes psychological records at their face value. But he refuses to take physical science at its face value; he interprets it in a forced and Pickwickian sense.... Obviously, we *must* believe in our own past, to live at all. And we should die of loneliness if we did not believe in the reality of other sentient beings. Whereas we can get along without believing in the independent reality of physical things, if we accept an idealistic substitute for that belief. But all three beliefs are *logically* in the same boat, equally hypothetical, equally in need of substantiation.

(3) We have seen that most idealists feel driven to

postulate an all-conclusive Consciousness, to weld our various finite minds into a *universe*. If there is such an all-inclusive Mind, your mind and mine are parts, or aspects of it. How then does it come about that we seem to be so separate? By no possibility can I become aware of your mind, or explore it, as I can my own. The chasms between minds are among the surest of empirical facts. Even if we call this separateness an illusion, the illusion would be none the less a fact, to be accounted for.... In short, can we have our cake and eat it? Can we have separate minds, as we seem to, and yet be parts of one all-embracing Mind? If there is such an all-embracing Mind, must it not be *another* mind than ours, knowing perhaps all that we know, but still being distinct from us? And if so, how does the existence of such a Mind serve, after all, to weld us into a single universe?

(4) If the Universal Mind really embraces all experience, yours and mine and everyone else's, it must include my prejudices and mistaken ideas, my experiences of ignorance and suffering and sin — and those of all the billions of sentient beings. What a welter of follies and errors and cross-purposes it must be! One aspect of this Divine Mind is ignorant of what another fragment of the Mind knows, one bit of the Mind is striving to thwart another bit of the One and Only Mind!... The idealist insists that this is not so, that in the Divine Mind these clashes and prejudices and errors are reconciled and constitute a wondrous harmony.... But if so, again the Absolute Mind is *different* from the finite minds, and cannot serve as an explanation of their existence, or weld them into a universe. Or so it seems to the realist.

If we say [reality] is a single, all-inclusive, rational consciousness, how shall we reconcile this with the fact that ignorance and error are real in our experience?   As real they must be included in the experience of an all-inclusive Mind, and yet there can be no ignorance and error in an all-knowing Mind.   Ignorance supplemented and error corrected would not be ignorance and error.   Manifestly a single mind cannot be both absolutely rational and absolutely all-inclusive.... If my experience must be transmuted to be included in the Absolute, it cannot be my experience which is included there; it must be something else.[1]

(5) This is apparent even in the matter of sense-experience: As we saw in Chapter VI, your sensa and mind do not fit together to form a coherent object.   If the Divine Mind includes the sense-experience of all the men and animals that are simultaneously perceiving (as we realistically say) the same object, *its* experience of that object would be a hodge-podge of the differing-but-more-or-less-similar sensa of all the observers.... The idealist contends that this is not so, that the One Mind is the standard, so to speak, which our minds feebly and distortedly reflect.   But if so, this Divine Mind is, once more, something different from our minds, and not a container and unifier of them.

To conceive the world as being one vast consciousness, having one coherent meaning, telling one story, so to speak, is esthetically and religiously alluring.   And at a stroke we should solve the puzzling problem of the relation of mind to matter — by denying the existence of matter.

The problem of the realist is how to account for mind as a part of a system in which mind was not present from the be-

[1] D. C. Macintosh, *Journal of Philosophy*, vol. 26, p. 226.

ginning.... This attempt to get mind out of the mindless lands us in endless difficulties and contradictions.[1]

If mind cannot be a product of nature, nature must be a function of mind.[2]

But the realist finds it impossible to reconcile this simplified and glorified picture of a universe with the concrete details of the realities that confront him. The *real* world, he insists, is this world of separate minds, with their feeble intelligence and their conflicts of purpose; their environment and medium of communication is the world of atoms and electrons and chemical processes, the world of stars and nebulae, the world of measurable spatial relations. It is in such terms that we are gradually coming to understand and deal with our world. *Concretely studied*, this world seems very different from the idealist's dream, as the following chapter will attempt to show.

SUGGESTED READINGS

R. F. A. Hoernlé, *Idealism*, V.
May Sinclair, *A Defense of Idealism*.
May Sinclair, *The New Idealism*.
E. S. Brightman, *Introduction to Philosophy*, IV.
Clifford Barrett, ed. *Contemporary Idealism in America*, esp. II, III.
H. A. Larrabee, *What Philosophy Is*, VIII.
W. E. Hocking, *Types of Philosophy*, XX–XXIII.
R. B. Perry, *The Approach to Philosophy*, XI.
Frederic Harrison, *The Philosophy of Common Sense*, VIII.
William James, *A Pluralistic Universe*, II.
C. E. M. Joad, *Mind and Matter*, III.

---

[1] May Sinclair, *The New Idealism*, ch. VIII. By permission of The Macmillan Company, publishers.

[2] W. E. Hocking, *Types of Philosophy*, p. 287.

CHAPTER IX

THE GROUNDS OF REALISM

EVERYONE, except a few philosophers and their disciples, believes in the realistic world; the belief is implied in all our science and all our ordinary discourse. There is considerable variation of opinion among reflective thinkers as to the fundamental stuff of which things consist, but there is an almost complete agreement that the physical world is made up of electrons and protons (whatever they may be) combining in complicated structures to form atoms, chemical compounds, biological organisms, and astronomical bodies. Causal interactions are going on in this intricately patterned world, quite independently of our experience; indeed, to a great extent, these processes are not yet known by any human observer, or even imagined. External as these physical things are to our bodies, and to our minds, we can, somehow, know a good deal *about* them. And other people can know about them; they are objects of common, public knowledge. We can also know a good deal about one another's *minds*. And we can see that these things which physics studies are *different* from minds, that minds (i.e., such minds as we quite definitely discover about us) are immersed, so to speak, in a great sea of what is quite different from mind.... Such is the world of common sense, the familiar world of mind *and* matter.

The subjectivist is right, however, in protesting that we have no *guaranty* of the existence of this world. It is conceivable that our supposed knowledge of it is illusion and our experience but a coherent dream. As cautious thinkers we must beware of trusting common sense; we must see whether we can *justify* our instinctive realism — just as we have insisted that the idealist justify his idealism. Belief in *any* sort of universe, belief, for that matter, in anything whatever beyond the passing data of experience, is, in the nature of the case, *hypothesis*, and not unquestionable *datum*.

Well, how do we set out to justify any hypothesis? If we use the empirical method, we accept an hypothesis when it seems to cover the facts of experience more adequately than any other hypothesis that we can frame. And our belief in realism rests, in the end, upon our discovery that it fits, it explains, the peculiarities of experience better than any form of idealism. In fact, there is no scientific hypothesis which serves to tie together and explain so many otherwise inexplicable facts as this hypothesis of realism. The following paragraphs will summarize the most notable peculiarities of our experience which serve in this way as the *evidence* for realism — in the same sense as that in which the sense-data accumulated by the astronomer are evidence for the truth of the Copernican hypothesis, which covers and explains them.

1. *The Difference between Perceptual and Non-Perceptual Experience*

Within our experience itself there is an observable difference between our sensa and the images which appear to us in our dreaming, thinking, imagining. There is, indeed, a borderland where it is difficult to distinguish the two types of data, but in general they are clearly distinguishable. Sensa are relatively vivid, clear, steady, coherent, whereas these other images are, by contrast, faint, blurred, flickering.... If realism is true, this difference is easily intelligible.   Sensa are produced in our experience by causal processes coming from the outer world, they are sharply defined by the definite nature of the messages that reach us from without, and are as stable as those processes — which, in turn, reflect the stability of the outer objects which initiate them. Our non-perceptual experience is engendered from within the organism, lacks the shock-effect of the experience provoked from without, and lacks its steadiness, since it is not subject to this outer control.... This suggests, with force, that physical things are not mere "potentialities of perception," but are *realities*, of a very definite nature, capable of affecting our experience in definite ways, pretty clearly distinguishable from the ways in which our non-perceptual experience develops.

2. *The Mechanism of Perception*

Sensa are obtained in a different way from that in which non-perceptual experience is obtained.   The latter can be had with eyes shut and all the other sense-organs slumbering.   To get sensa we have to have sense-organs functioning, and a whole series of events proceeding from the outer object to the brain.   If any link in this chain of events is broken, the perceptual experience will not be had.   Now it is conceivable that our experience of this complicated series of events is merely one kind of *experience*, not actually revealing a series of real events *preceding* the appearance of our sensa.   But if so, the question insistently arises, Why do we find, so regularly, this particular series of experiences obtainable, whenever we have sensa of each particular sort?

The whole business *looks* as if these experiences (our knowledge of light-waves, eye-events, and optical-nerve-events, for example) reveal to us a real series of events going on outside our minds and necessarily preceding the appearance in our field of consciousness of each definite sort of sensum. If there *are* no physical things, if there are only minds, why this constant illusion of a complicated inter-mental medium? If there is, in reality, only One Mind, why should one part of it affect another part in this roundabout way, instead of in the way one part of my mind affects another part, without the complicated mechanism of sense-perception? Is not realism the most sensible hypothesis to cover these facts?

3. *The Continuity of the Physical Order*

Our sense-experience is very fragmentary. But the pieces strongly suggest a continuous, coherent set of processes back of them, giving them their precise nature. For example, I start a fire on the hearth and then leave the room. Ten minutes later I return and find the wood partly consumed. An hour later I return and find nothing but hot ashes. It *looks* as if a continuous process was going on during that hour of which my sensa reveal definite phases, whenever I put myself in a position to receive effects from it. I can construct in my imagination such a series of physical events, external to me, the events making up the fire itself. My sensa invariably report the stage due at each moment of that series of events. When I enter the room they jump into my conscious field, unrelated to anything antecedently there; they apparently obey, not laws of my mind, primarily, but the laws of that external series of events which I have imagined. That external order is a changing order. Relatively few of its changes are reflected in my direct experience, but they serve nevertheless as controls of the experience which I actually have. After dreamless sleep, my experience picks up the pattern, so to speak — the pattern of processes which apparently have been going on while I slept.... Are not these facts *explicanda*? And what explanation of them can we give half as plausible as the explanation that the processes we have imagined really *are* going on in the world about us, even when we are not aware of them?

4. *The Converging Testimony of Differing Senses*

Physical objects are usually perceived by several senses. I can see my table, I can feel of it, push against it, lift it, hear the sound I make when I hit it. In subjectivistic language, I have groups of very different sorts of sensa, which, in spite of their differences, fit together to form my concept of this table.... Why should our experience be thus analyzable into groups of sensa which combine to form the picture of a physical *thing*?... Various other people have somewhat similar groups of sensa, which seem, as we describe and utilize them, to reveal this same table.... What meaning can these facts have, if not that there *is* a single physical table, which affects several of my senses, thus producing several differing groups of sensa, and similarly affects other people's senses, producing in their experience more or less similar groups of sensa?

5. *The Time-gap when Mind Affects Mind*

When I speak to you, *my* experience-of-speaking occurs at a certain time. Then an interval of time elapses.

Then you hear my voice. The time-gap varies exactly with our distance apart.... Now, if only minds exist, why should there be this interval between the event-in-me, the cause, and the event-in-you, the effect? What happens during that interval? And what is the real meaning of what we call distance? If Space is only a form of experience, something *within* minds, not something existing *between* minds, and separating them, why should it take longer for my mind to influence yours when we are, as we commonly say, farther apart than when we are nearer?... If the reality is One Mind, and nothing else, the matter becomes, if possible, still stranger. Why should one part of the Divine Mind require half a second to influence another part, and two seconds to influence another part? And what happens during the interval, when neither part is conscious of speaking or hearing, when apparently *no* (relevant) conscious experience is taking place?... Surely it *looks* as if distance were real, and a real series of events were taking place *between* the two minds, requiring time to occur, in proportion to the distance.

6. *The Dependence of Minds upon Matter*

Our ideational-volitional life — our thinking, dreaming, planning, willing — is, to some degree, self-contained. Our ideas follow one another along the lines of traceable associations; they are, in part, modifiable at will, and depend upon the state of our mind at a given time. But with sensa it is quite different. We are *confronted* by them. They appear suddenly in our field of experience, often quite unrelated to anything antecedently there. We cannot banish them by effort of will. They evidently obey other laws than those of our minds.... And we are at their mercy. A cold wind blows on me (i.e., I have sensa thus described in realistic language), and I suffer, perhaps become ill. The sensa implied by saying that a bullet has hit me are followed, perhaps, by the complete and permanent cessation of my consciousness.... Is it not clear that we are in the grip of a world of realities vastly greater than ourselves? To see a man freezing to death, or dying of a bullet wound, is, inevitably, to be a realist, at least *pro tem*.

These extreme experiences — which come to us all, in some form sooner or later — make us realize that even our ideational and volitional experience is at the mercy of this environing world. A bottle of whiskey alters the whole tone of my mental life, a whiff of chloroform brings it to an abrupt end for the time being, a clotting of blood may drive me insane.... Specifically, as we shall see in Chapter XVIII, our whole mental life is dependent, point by point, upon the functioning of our *brains*.... But if our brains are but a name for a certain group of potentialities of experience, or even if they are a certain specific group of images in a Universal Mind, it seems curious that our whole mental life should be dependent upon them.

7. *The Facts of Cosmic History*

It is generally agreed that the universe existed for long ages before any minds appeared on this earth, or, so far as we know, anywhere. The events of this cosmic history are known by astronomers and geologists, in considerable detail.... But what *meaning* is there in this long story, on idealistic premises, if there were no experiencers present to experience these events? It will be said that we have here the story of the unfolding

of the Divine Experience.   And this is conceivable.
But when one reads the story in detail — the evolution
of stars from nebulæ (a monotonous process consuming
trillions of years), the (apparently accidental) formation of our solar system, the laborious laying-down of
rocks, the slow development of chemical compounds,
the seething of currents of wind and water, the breeding
of endless varieties of microbes, worms, reptiles, and all
the strange profusion of vegetable and animal life, one
creature warring upon and devouring another creature,
with volcanic eruptions, floods, droughts wiping out
countless millions at a sweep — the story surely sounds
far more like a realistic story of separate *things* and organisms, than like the unfolding of the story of a Divine
consciousness.

It is quite evident that our fragmentary and evanescent
data of experience can never be *understood* except as an
enclave within a far greater, independent reality, which
we call Nature; and that this Nature is, in detail, just
what the sciences report it to be.   Our experience is not
only fragmentary, it is, by itself, a jumble, a chaos.
Only by constructing, with infinite patience, this picture of a vast environing Nature, can we replace this
chaos with order, predict future experiences, and learn,
in increasing measure, to control them.   The belief in
a Universal Mind inspires and consoles some people;
but it does not help us to predict and control experience.
Thus realism is, at least, pragmatically justified.

And what more *could* we have in the way of proof?
As we saw in studying the empirical method, there is
no such thing as guaranteed proof, of the Q.E.D. sort,
except in the purely hypothetical realms of logic and

mathematics. An independently existing physical world
is proved to exist in the same sense, and with as great
certainty, as *anything* can be proved to exist. The
idealist accepts as proved the facts of human history.
But these facts, and indeed the facts of the idealist's
own earlier life, can be proved to be actual facts by no
other method, and with no greater certainty, than the
facts of the life of the physical world.

RADICAL EMPIRICISM

It is, to be sure, an impregnable position, to refuse to
believe in anything beyond immediate experience itself.
There is today a group of philosophers who content
themselves with *describing* experience, and refrain from
postulating any environment, or substructure, for experience. They call themselves variously radical empiricists, experimentalists, or instrumentalists, instead
of subjectivists or phenomenalists. For 'subjectivism,'
of the traditional type, they tell us, *falsifies* experience.
We do not experience ourselves as little isolated streams
of consciousness; we experience objects *as* outside us,
we experience other people *as* having minds of their
own, we experience the past, in memory, *as* past. And
so a philosophy which would limit itself to experience,
but would describe experience accurately, needs a better
name than 'subjectivism.'

William James spoke of the "autonomy of experience."

[Experience] leans upon nothing. [It is] self-sustaining...
to be radical, an empiricism must not admit into its constructions any element that is not directly experienced....
We should be wise not to consider any thing or action [beyond
experience], and to restrict our universe of philosophic discourse to what is experienced, or, at least, experiencable....
[This view] gets rid of the whole agnostic controversy, by

refusing to entertain the hypothesis of trans-empirical reality at all.[1]

The experience-philosopher today admits permanent objects, believes in the past history of the world, and in other personalities than his own, quite as earnestly as the realist. He simply defines them in terms of actual or possible experience, as felt or suggested goals or sources of thought, emotion, or conduct, whose value and meaning consist wholly in their actual or possible effects on our own experience.[2]

Things — anything, everything, in the ordinary or nontechnical use of the term 'thing' — are what they are experienced *as*. Hence, if one wishes to describe anything truly, his task is to tell what it is experienced as being.... [This is not to deny] the existence of things temporally prior to human experiencing of them. Indeed, I should think it fairly obvious that we experience most things *as* temporally prior to our experiencing of them.... Books, chairs, geological ages, etc., are experienced *as* existent at other times than the moments *when* they are experienced.... We experience them *as* that sort of thing, *to be* that sort of thing... when we think of the event as just past-event, we neglect the factor in it, that it is a part of *present* experience, of immersion of a knowledge-object in an inclusive experience.[3]

But now let us consider this doctrine that things are what they are experienced as being. I experience you, perhaps, as a bluish-looking person — but that is because I am wearing blue spectacles. I experience you as speaking faintly — but that is because I am hard of hearing. I experience you as admiring me — but that is because I am egotistical. The lover experiences his beloved as all that is lovely — but that is because he is in love. In short, things are plainly *not* always what they are experienced as being; our experience of people and things quite commonly distorts and falsifies them.

[1] William James, *Journal of Philosophy*, vol. 3, p. 648. *Essays in Radical Empiricism*, pp. 243, 195.

[2] W. S. Sheldon, *Journal of Philosophy*, vol. 3, p. 183.

[3] John Dewey, *The Influence of Darwin on Philosophy*, pp. 227, 240. *The Journal of Philosophy*, vol. 16, p. 419; vol. 3, p. 256.

The fact is, the radical empiricist, confining himself rigidly to describing experience, never gets beyond psychology. For to say that he experiences an event *as* a past event is not to say that there *was* a past event; it is merely to say that he is having a certain sort of present experience. To say that he experiences an object *as* an independent object is merely to say that he is having that sort of experience, and is by no means to say that there *is* an independent object. An hallucinated person experiences an object *as* an independent object, a person suffering from a memory-illusion experiences an event that never happened *as* a past event in his life.... So long as we talk only in terms of the data present within our experience, we do not raise the epistemological question at all, i.e., the question at issue between the realist and the non-realist. But we must not suppose that we have solved a problem by refusing to raise it.

If consistently carried out, this cognitive timorousness, this will-not-to-believe in anything beyond the immediate data of experience, leads to curious conclusions. Remember that for the radical empiricist, afflicted as he is with a sort of reiphobia, all truth about absent objects is really a truth about our present experience of such objects *as* absent. If you take this whole-heartedly, you must assert that all the truths which you formulate about me, and about all other persons, are merely truths about certain experiences of your own. You experience me, to be sure, *as* an independent person; but to say that is merely to describe certain data of *your* experience. Even if you say that you experience me *as* having experiences of my own, you are still only describing the sort of experience *you* have.... But *I* know there is a great deal to *me* that never falls within the purview of *your* experience.

There are myriads of facts about me which, being hopelessly transcendent to any experience that you have, must simply be ruled out as unreal by your philosophy.

Likewise, the reality of past events is, for the consistently radical empiricist, merely the reality of certain present memory-data, which are experienced *as* past.... But how about all those myriad events which have vanished and left no memory in anyone's experience? They are hopelessly trans-empirical; and the fact that any such events ever existed cannot be acknowledged.... So, if today's vivid experiences, not being recorded, are known to no one after our death, they will be hopelessly trans-empirical to our descendants; and it will not be admitted by them, if they are consistent radical empiricists, that there ever could have been any such events.

In short, the world of the radical empiricist is merely the world that he can experience. The vast unexplored realms of time and space which common sense, and the realist, believe to extend far, far beyond the feeble perspectives of our human experience, shrink, in this philosophy, into the background, the stage-setting, of that sole reality, that all-important drama, *our* experience. Or, strictly, it all dissolves, for you, into the dream of your *own* experience; since *my* experience, so far as it escapes your knowledge, is as transcendent to your experience as are the events transpiring on the remotest stars.

What is radical empiricism, then, but subjectivism over again, dressed in a new terminology? What was 'subjectivism' but the refusal to believe in anything beyond experience? The radical empiricist talks, indeed, of chairs and tables and stars, of past events and material things. But *his* stars are not those vast complexes of a myriad events, mostly unknown to us, which the realist

believes to be happening beyond our ken, and to have
been happening long before any man ever saw even their
far-off glimmer; *his* stars are these faint twinkling points
of light, plus the knowledge gleaned by astronomy; i.e.,
they are the relatively slight and distant *effects* produced
by those stars in the flickering and very limited field of
our human experience.

> The world which instrumentalism allows us to know is
> man-made, like the scenery on the Underground: there are
> bricks and platforms and trains and lights and advertise-
> ments; but the sun and stars, the rain and the dew and the
> sea, are no longer there — sometimes we seem to catch a
> glimpse of them, but that is a mistake, we only see a picture
> made by some human being as an advertisement.[1]

The radical empiricist is apt to claim for his theory the
prestige of science, since science is empirical in its method.
But science does not restrict itself to describing the data
of experience, it dares to believe (humbly, of course, and
always seeking further evidence) in hypotheses which
far transcend experience. Experience, for science, is
evidence of the existence of these trans-empirical realities.
Science pores over our jumbled, chaotic experience, sorts
it out, accepts this as veridical, rejects that as subjective,
and gropes its way to the conception of *Nature*, a vast
existing realm, through the understanding of which,
alone, can our little islands of experience be understood,
and, in some measure, brought under our control. The
great work of *intelligence* is to discover this framework
of reality behind the passing show of experience. The
'discovery' remains, indeed, an hypothesis. The vast
world of Nature cannot be dragged down within the spot-
light of our consciousness, so that we can be actually

[1] Bertrand Russell, *Journal of Philosophy*, vol. 16, p. 20.

aware of it, as we are of the data present within our experience; it must be, to the end, merely *believed* in.   But the belief in *Nature*, in a vast environing reality of which *experience* gives us only hints and clues, is what differentiates the *understanding*, and *mastery*, of life from a mere esthetic appreciation of it.   Understanding and mastery require not merely an acquaintance with experience itself, but a reasonably correct theory as to the larger realities upon which experience depends.

As a *reductio ad absurdum* of radical empiricism, let us suppose that a cloud of cosmic poison gas has suddenly wiped out all life on earth.   Experience — that is, all the experience we know anything about — has ceased. The earth keeps on revolving, the oceans still beat on their shores, the sun still shines — But no!   For outside of *experience* — which, by hypothesis, is ended — there *is* no reality, and so nothing *can* happen.   Indeed, the fact of our death would not *be* a fact; for there would be no one left to experience it *as* a fact.   Our conscious experience *could* not be ended, for it could not be *experienced* as ended.   And what is not experienced is not so.

Does not this bring home to us a truth which everyone but the radical empiricist knows, that conscious experience is only an episode, a flower that grows out of the soil of Nature, an incidental feature of reality, and not the whole of it?   It is, to be sure, the seat of our values, and the *starting-point* for all reflection.   But to shut ourselves in its home-vistas forever would be as if the Lady of Shalott had taken the reflections in her mirrors to be the only realities, or as if a man locked up within a *camera obscura* were to suppose that these little figures moving about on the ground-glass were all there is to the universe.

SUGGESTED READINGS

Durant Drake, *Mind and Its Place in Nature*, III.
George Santayana, in *Essays in Critical Realism*, pp. 163–184.
Bertrand Russell, *The Problems of Philosophy*, II–IV.
R. B. Perry, *The Approach to Philosophy*, IX.
R. H. Dotterer, *Philosophy by Way of the Sciences*, pp. 243–259.
Bertrand Russell, *Philosophy*, XII–XIII.
G. E. Moore, *Philosophical Studies*, II.

CHAPTER X

POSSIBLE FORMS OF REALISM

WE MUST now try to synthesize the results of Chapter VI with the results of Chapters VII–IX. In Chapter VI we found ourselves driven to give up the naïve idea that our sense-data are simply parts, or aspects, of that physical world which we believe to surround us and to be reported, in detail, by the various natural sciences. Those sciences construct a coherent picture of that world, but they find no place in it for our sensa. And numerous considerations suggest that our sensa are rather *effects produced in our experience*, through our sense-organs, by certain events occurring in that physical world.... In Chapters VII–IX we considered whether we are warranted in retaining our instinctive belief in the existence of that physical world. And, after weighing subjectivism, idealism, and radical empiricism, we have found that *realism*, the belief in the existence, independently of experience, of the physical world, explains the peculiarities of our experience far better than any alternative theory, and is therefore to be accepted as probably true.... We remain realists, then, but we cannot be naïve realists. So we must now consider what *sort* of realistic theory we can hold, in view of the considerations adduced in Chapter VI.

The difficulty lies in conceiving *where* our sensa (and our other data of consciousness) exist, if they are not parts, or aspects, of the physical things about us. We have said that sensa are effects produced in our experience. But *where* are these items-of-our-experience, in relation to our organisms or to outer objects, i.e., to those complexes of electrons and protons which make up the physical world? We have first-hand acquaintance with the former, we cannot ignore them; and we have excellent reasons for believing in the latter. But the two sets of entities do not seem to fit together to make a single universe!... This is perhaps the most puzzling problem of philosophy. We can do no more than to indicate briefly the principal solutions which are given by contemporary philosophers. Of course it is not easy to classify these theories, presented as they are in very varying terminology. But it may be hoped that the following six types of theory pretty well cover the ground. Somewhere among these six answers the truth probably lies.

1. *Sensa exist in the outer physical world, independently of being sensed*

There are a few realists who cling obstinately to the naïve belief that sense-qualities exist, independently of perception, in or upon the physical objects about us, where they *seem* to be. They are, indeed, often dislocated in space from the complexes of electrons and protons of which they are, in some sense, aspects; and they may persist as after-echoes, long after those objects-of-physical-science have ceased to exist. In either case, they occupy points of space simultaneously occupied by other physical existents. Thus physical things interpenetrate, or overlie, one another, so far as their sense-qualities go.... And there are an infinite number of these sense-qualities at every point. For there is no other place for sensa than out there in the physical world where they seem to be; and so every sensum that any sort of sentient creature, with any sort of sense-organs, *might*

have, when sensing a given physical thing, must be supposed to be already existing out there where it would
seem to that creature to be.

In consistency, this pan-physical theory must hold,
also, that images-seen-in-mirrors, hallucinatory objects,
objects-seen-in-dreams, as well as colors-seen-in-objects
when looking through colored glasses, and all mirages
and illusory sensa, exist out there also, all the time, waiting
to be sensed. For if it be granted that *any* of these sensa
— all of which *seem* to the perceiver to be out there in
the physical world — have some *other* locus, and are not
really out there, the camel's nose has been admitted to
the tent, and reflection will conclude that all these other
sensa likewise may have that other locus.

This theory evidently owes whatever plausibility it
possesses to the fact that it is in line with the initial *look*
of things. Sensa do *seem* to be 'out there.' So do the
objects of hallucinations and dreams. But the considerations adduced in Chapter VI show with overwhelming
force that all sensa are, in reality, organism-engendered,
and not antecedently existing qualities of outer objects.
And in any case, it is a preposterous doctrine that the
physical world, which seems to the physicist so clean-cut
and fixed in its nature, should really be cluttered up with
an infinite number of contradictory qualities at every
point.

2. *Sensa are created in the outer physical world by the perceiver*

There are a few realists who, admitting that sensa are
"produced in and through the processes occurring in a
particular psycho-physical organism," hold that the
perceiver, by an unconscious and instantaneous "psychic

process," creates these sense-qualities in the outer physical object, so that they really exist there *while they are
being sensed.*

> The sense-qualities are not first 'in the mind,' or intra-
> organic, and then 'projected'; they are created, in each case
> of sensing, in the particular location in which they are found.
> Sometimes the qualities produced are not placed accurately
> upon the object from which the stimulation first proceeded.[1]

The chief objection to this theory is that it assumes the
existence of a mysterious 'psychic' creativity at every
moment of perception, a process of which we are not
aware, and of whose existence we have not the slightest
evidence.   Indeed, it would be completely out of line
with every *discovered* aspect of the process of perception.

Moreover, if these sense-qualities, thus mysteriously
created, really exist out there for the time being, it may
be asked why no one can sense them there except the one
perceiver who has put them there.   And it may be asked
why they are utterly inefficacious there, having no part
in the life of the object as portrayed by physics.   And
it must be realized that when many observers are perceiving the same object, the object must, on this theory,
possess simultaneously, in the same place, as many different sense-qualities as there are observers.

This theory does not give us such a preposterously
cluttered universe as the preceding theory.   But, on the
other hand, it does require the assumption of an unintelligible out-reaching 'psychic' process which seems a
mere *deus ex machina* invented to fill a gap in explanation.

3. *Sensa exist in private spaces*

Some contemporary realists, impressed by the incon-

[1] D. C. Macintosh, *The Problem of Knowledge*, p. 313.

gruity of sensa with the objects-of-physical-science, and yet convinced that sensa are real objects of a sort, existing out there where they seem to be, have concluded that sensa exist, not in the physical world, but in a realm of their own. Or rather, each perceiver's sensa exist in a private realm, really *out there*, but not in the *same* outerness that physical things inhabit, or that other people's sensa inhabit.

There are two varieties of this theory, paralleling the two views we have just discussed. One holds that all the sensa which could possibly be sensed by any sort of organism exist, antecedently to perception, in one of these infinitely numerous realms (or 'perspectives'). The other view holds that there is "a peculiar kind of transphysical causation, according to which the occurrence of certain events in a certain brain and nervous system determines the occurrence of a sensum with such and such a shape, etc., in a certain sense-field of a certain sense-history." [1]

Both of these views save the 'uniplicity,' the clear-cut nature, of the *physical* world. But the former view makes the *universe* extraordinarily complicated, with an infinite number of non-dovetailing realms, each inhabited by myriads of similar-but-different sensa. The latter view, like the one discussed on pp. 169–170, involves the assumption of a mysterious and instantaneous process of creation and projection, by which each perceiver creates an evanescent group of really existent objects, some of them at great distances from himself, in a private, but real, and 'objective,' realm, whose objects, though really existent out there, he alone can sense.

In either case, we have the apparently insoluble prob-

[1] C. D. Broad, *The Mind and its Place in Nature*, p. 219.

lem of the relation between physical space and the spaces
of these groups of sensa. We have two sorts of space-
filling existents, which are saved from jostling one another by occupying totally different spaces. But all
these spaces *seem* to be in the *same place!* Is there room
in the universe for so many spaces?... Surely this theory
seems rather a desperate expedient!

4. *Sensa exist in the brain of the perceiver*

Some realists, impressed by the fact that sensa are
organism-engendered, and, indeed, engendered only when
nerve-currents from the sense-organs reach the brain,
consider that all sensa exist really in the brains of their
several perceivers. By recurring to Chapter VI, it will
be seen that this theory avoids all the objections there
raised to naïve realism. It saves the simplicity of the
physical world, it assumes no mysterious projective
creation, and no collection of non-dovetailing spaces.

Perhaps it will be said that your sensa cannot be
thought to exist in your brain, because no observer
would ever find them there. All he could find would be
cells, fibers, gray matter, etc.... But we must remember
that, according to this theory, the sensa that an observer
would sense when he looked at your brain (the 'gray
matter,' etc.) would not *be* in your brain, but would
exist in *his* brain, as *his sensa*. The observer could never
sense the qualities of your brain, all he could ever sense
would be *effects* produced on *his* brain by the events
going on in yours. So there is nothing in perception to
conflict with the hypothesis that what exists in your brain
is (among other things) *your* sensa.

A more serious objection appears, however, when we
realize that physical science tells us that our brains are

composed, like the rest of the world, of varying structures of very rapidly moving electrons and protons. If we are realists, we take this knowledge literally. Is, then, this knowledge of our brains as composed of whirls of myriads of tiny units, all alike (or so nearly alike that physics can detect no differences, save that between protons and electrons), *compatible* with the theory that our brains are, in part, composed of the sensa which we find in our experience? Carrying out the theory, we should undoubtedly have to say that *all our experience* is in our brains, *is* the very series of events which physics describes, from the outside, as an enormously complex dance of electrons and protons. The difficulty lies in the apparent incongruity of the two sorts of knowledge of one and the same events. As described by science, those events are merely changes in *place*, changes of *pattern*; whereas changes in our experience are *qualitative* changes. Electrons are in unceasing rapid and complex *motion*; the items of our experience are relatively stable. The electron-patterns are inconceivably complex; the items of our experience are relatively simple.... How can these two sorts of reality go together?

Moreover, even if these two sorts of knowledge of our brain-life can be shown to be compatible, the question remains, Can we really ever squash up into our brains, so to speak, these landscapes, these objects so evidently *outside* of us, and often far distant? What *may* exist in our brains we may hesitate to deny. But surely not *these* entities! When I see an automobile-like sensum, apparently a hundred feet away, and moving away from me, how can I say that *that* entity is in my brain?... In short, do we not *mean* by a sense-datum (a sensum) something external to us? Perhaps this complex of qualities that we sense is not really a *physical thing*, or any aspect of a physical thing. But it is a *supposed* physical thing at least, it is what we *take to be* a physical thing, or an aspect of a physical thing, out there in the world.

At least it seems so to most realists. A recent volume by one of the acutest American realists contains the following comment:

> One of the most curious developments in the entire history of thought is the invention in our day of what may best be named the Hypodermic Philosophy.[1]

5. *Sensa exist in the mind of the perceiver*

Confronted with these difficulties, many realists find it simplest to take refuge in a dualism of mind and matter. Our sensa (and the other items-of-our-experience) exist neither 'out there' in the physical world about us, nor in our brains, nor in quasi-physical sensa-realms, but *in our minds....* To grasp this theory, one must go back to the subjectivistic point of view, and think not in terms of sensing-qualities-out-there-in-the-world, but in terms of having-such-and-such-sense-experiences. The whole panorama of my experience is a private 'movie,' unfolding itself on the screen of my mind. But beyond this private panorama lies the physical world, really existing there (as the subjectivist will not admit), and causing, through my sense-organs and my brain, this mental reflection, distorted but useful, of its nature.

This theory does away, at a stroke, with all the difficulties we have considered. But it presents us with a new set of difficulties. What sort of existence do these mental events have? How do they interact with bodies?

[1] A. O. Lovejoy, *The Revolt Against Dualism*, p. 13.

How, specifically, does my mind receive impressions from my brain, and, in turn, give orders to it? If minds are not in space, how does it happen that my mind travels round, in some sense, with my brain?

We shall discuss this supposed dualism of mind and matter at length in the chapters following this. At this point we shall merely say that to many realists such a dualism in existence seems unintelligible, and the belief in it a mere verbal solution for a difficult problem.

6. *Sensa are merely supposititious existents*

The newest realistic theory, and probably the most difficult to grasp, holds that sensa do not exist at all, anywhere. What happens is that certain brain-events are caused by the nerve-currents from the sense-organs, and these brain-events incite the organism to react *as to* certain supposititious external entities. All the warm *sentient* character that sensa have is the character of the brain-events. But the *specific* characters that our sensa have depend upon the specific nature of our organic *reactions*. We react as to an object so big, so far away, of such and such a shape, because our brain-events, excited by just such characteristics in the physical object in front of the body, act as signals to produce such specific reactions. And because we are reacting as to external objects, we quite fail to realize that the *feel* of our sensa is the feel of our own brain-life. In short, we project our brain-states into the world about us. Not literally. Nothing is actually *put* out there in the physical world. We simply *take* our brain-states to be out there, *imagine* this substance of our own life to be outside our bodies. And in that process of imaginative projection we have to falsify the nature of our brain-life. For what is really within us is now taken to be spread out before us, just as we take the color of blue spectacles to be spread out on the landscape.

A simple illustration of the process which, upon this theory, takes place in all perception, may be found in the familiar experience of after-images. After looking at the sun, for example, I turn my eyes upon some other part of my environment, and see a bright disk there. If I look at a near-by wall I see the disk upon its surface, relatively small. If I look at a far-off mountain I see the disk on its side, far away and as large as the mountain.... The after-effects of the intense stimulation of my eyes really exist only in my eyes and in my brain. There is no mechanism by which a bright disk can be created out there upon the wall, or upon the distant mountain. But the brain-state produced by the lingering agitation in my eyes causes me to react *as if* a bright disk were in front of my eyes, whichever way I happen to turn them, and at whatever distance my eyes chance to focus. The *brightness* of my sensum is due to the intrinsic nature of my brain-events. The direction and distance from me, and apparent size, of my sensum are due my reactive mechanism. The *bright disk out there on the wall* (my sensum) is a fictitious product of the imaginative projection of my brain-state.[1]

So when we dream, or have an hallucination, the ob-

---

[1] Note that the after-image is merely a continuation, somewhat dimmed, of the perceptual sensum, the sun-that-I-see. It is altogether to be supposed that the existential status of the sensum in its earlier stage and in its later stage is the same. But the *later* sensum (the 'after-image') cannot plausibly be supposed to exist out there on whatever object I focus my eyes upon, whereas the *earlier* sensum (what I see when I look at the sun) *is*, naïvely and naturally, supposed to exist out there.

This illustration, as well as many other points in the analysis of the epistemological situation, I owe to Mr. C. A. Strong, one of the keenest of contemporary students of the problem.

jects that we seem to see in front of us do not exist there, or *anywhere*. They are merely *imagined* objects, with no locus in any existential world. What exists is certain brain-states, caused by preceding brain-states together with nerve-currents from other parts of the body. These brain-states initiate highly complex organic adjustments; we act, in some degree (though there may be no gross, visible movement of the body) *as if* certain objects were in front of the body.

Now in veridical perception the situation is exactly the same, except that in this case there are existing things stimulating the sense-organs. The result is that we imagine objects which are (more or less) of the same nature as the objects which are really existing out there. But our *sensa*, in this case, have exactly the same status as those other sensa which are present to us in dreams, or in hallucinations, or as 'after-images.' That is, they have, *as described*, no existence whatever. For our description, in each case, is a description of something-out-there-in-the-outer-world. But if we were to describe what *exists*, in each case, we should have to describe our brain-states and our bodily reactions. Sensa are, thus, purely supposititious existents. They are, as described, concrete, particular things, which *might* very well exist. But they are, actually, purely fictitious things, taken as existing simply because our bodily reactions (including our tendencies to describe) are directed *outward* instead of inward.

A sad mistake this, from the point of view of the philosopher who wishes to understand the exact situation in perception. But for practical purposes it is the happiest possible mistake. For what concerns us, as animals living precariously in the midst of an environing world, is not the nature of our own brain-life, but the nature of these other existents about us — so that we may distinguish those which threaten us and those which, in various ways, may be of use. And the slow process of evolution has developed in us a mechanism of extraordinary value for this purpose. There is no way in which our own conscious life could actually get out and *include* events or existents outside of us. What happens is that a 'message' comes to me from, say, a table ten feet away, in the form of a definite pattern of light-waves. These produce in me a pattern of brain-events which have a one-one correspondence with the events from which the message has come to me. These brain-events, in turn, incite delicate and complicated organic reactions which, taken together, constitute a reaction as to a-table-ten-feet-away. And since, in the case supposed, there really *is* a table ten feet away from my body, my reaction is the *correct* reaction. My *sensum* is an imaginative projection of my brain-states. But in this case my imagination hits the mark; I imagine out there what really *is* out there.

Conscious perception is, then, *initially*, a perpetual self-deception, a perpetual romancing. What we suppose ourselves to be confronted with, and take to be so real, is a mere distorted projection of our own inner life. It has its *roots* in this organic life; but the organic life, itself, is not *external* to our bodies, as these fictitious entities, our sensa, describably are. On the other hand, these initially fictitious sensa *may* coincide in character with the real existents about us. But that happy coincidence does not alter their status *as sensa*, which is obviously the same whether the physical things about us happen to have or not to have just such a character.

Sensa, *as such*, are fictitious entities. So we can say, with Santayana:

> The immediate... is always specious; it is peopled by spec-
> ters which, if taken for existing and working things, are illu-
> sions; and although they are real enough, in that they have
> definite character and actual presence, as a dream of a pain
> has, their reality ends there; they are unsubstantial, volatile,
> leaving no ashes... Thus immediate experience of things, far
> from being fundamental in nature, is only the dream which
> accompanies our action, as the other dreams accompany our
> sleep; and every naturalist knows that this waking dream
> is dependent for its existence, quality, intensity and duration
> on obscure processes in the living body, in its interplay with
> its environment.

Even with the disproportionate amount of space given to describing this theory, it is likely that most readers will not clearly grasp it; to make it intelligible, not to say plausible, a volume would be required, instead of a few paragraphs. But it is the conviction of the writer that the truth lies here. If the truth were simple, and easy to grasp, philosophers would have agreed upon it long ago, as scientists have agreed upon vast reaches of accepted truth. Each of the other five realistic theories is easier to grasp. But each of them is open to grave objection.... However, if this last theory is true, each of the other theories has some truth in it, has laid hold of some aspect of the situation.

The first theory holds obstinately to the conviction that we directly perceive the very objects about us, as they are antecedently to the act of perception. And that is true, *in so far as perception is veridical.* I perceive a penny as round; the existing penny really *is* round; *in so far* I perceive what really exists, and existed before I perceived it.... In another sense, too, I am

directly perceiving the really existing penny, viz., my eyes are focused upon it, my body is reacting to it, I am talking about *it*, meaning *it*, and not some additional existent, an 'idea,' or a 'sensum' existing in some other realm.

The second theory has an inkling of an important aspect of the truth in its conception of 'projection.' But this projection is not an existent process; nothing is really *put out there* upon the antecedently existing physical things. The projection which takes place in perception is a merely imaginative projection; all that really happens is that we imagine certain qualities to be out there, and act as if they were there. In other words, we *see* them there (in the case of visual perception). For this is what seeing *is*; it is vividly imagining certain visual characters to exist in front of our eyes, in the direction and at the distance upon which our eyes are focused. The imagining is involuntary; and the nature of what we imagine is determined by the nature of the physical thing which exists at the place upon which our eyes are focused — as well as upon the nature of our eyes and brains and reactive mechanism. But it is none the less imagining, in the sense that *what we imagine* does not thereby leap into existence. All that *exists* is — whatever *does* exist in the physical thing at which we are looking, the light-waves radiating from it, and the organic events caused by the light-waves which strike the eyes, culminating in the events which we may lump together and call imagining-such-and-such-an-object-out-there.

The third theory results from an attempt to reconcile two insights; first, that sensa are, describably, *out there*, and not in our brains or in a non-spatial mental realm;

and secondly, that they cannot be put into the same world in which physical things exist; each person's sensa are private to him and constitute, in some sense, a separate, private world.... The error lies in assuming that because sensa are, describably, this and that object, or quality, out there, they really *exist* out there. *Of course* each person's sensa form a private world, for they are the fictitious entities imagined by that particular person.

The fourth theory is right in holding that it is our *brain-life* which reflects the nature of the world about us, and has that *feel* to it that we call 'sentience.' All the feel of our conscious life resides there, and all the characteristics which make us imagine, specifically, just this and that sensum. But the process of imagining takes place, in part, by means of a reactive mechanism which involves a considerable part of the body, and the *sensa* (the *whats* that we imagine, what we seem-to-see, etc.) do not exist in the brain, or anywhere.

The fifth theory may be taken as *true*, if we understand by the "mental realm" in which sensa, etc., are located, the purely imaginary realm in which these non-existing entities have their being. Such language is misleading, however, since 'mental' items are usually supposed to *exist* as truly as physical things; and a purely gratuitous problem arises as to the relation between these mental existents and physical existents.... In the best usage, the *mind* is the really existing mechanism possessed by each organism for coping with the world in which it lives, by initiating useful bodily reactions, and, incidentally, giving rise to these misdescriptions, the objects of which are our sensa.

This whole matter will be clearer when we have discussed, from another angle, in chapters XVIII to XXI, the relation of mind to matter.

SUGGESTED READINGS

Durant Drake, etc., *Essays in Critical Realism.*
R. W. Sellars, *Essentials of Philosophy*, IV.
R. W. Sellars, *Evolutionary Naturalism*, III.
Bertrand Russell, *The Problems of Philosophy*, II–IV.
Bertrand Russell, *The Analysis of Matter*, XX–XXI.
W. P. Montague, *Ways of Knowing*, IX.
Durant Drake, *Mind and Its Place in Nature*, I–IV.
C. D. Broad, *The Mind and Its Place in Nature*, IV.
G. E. Moore, *Philosophical Studies*, V.
C. A. Strong, *Essays on the Natural Origin of the Mind*, I–III.

PART THREE

THE COSMOS

CHAPTER XI

TIME, SPACE, AND STARS

WHATEVER conclusions we may reach when we discuss epistemology, we are pretty sure to be realists in everyday life and when we study the concrete data of science. It is impossible not to believe that the world exists in its own right and that it is, in detail, what physics and geography and astronomy report it to be. So we turn now to these sciences to learn what they have to tell us, in the most general terms, about the universe.

ARE TIME AND SPACE OBJECTIVELY REAL?

The first thing to note is that they tell us of a world existing in Space and Time. And in this they are keeping close to everyday experience — with a difference.

In our conscious experience objects appear as above or below other objects, larger or smaller than other objects, nearer or farther, of this shape or that. Events happen before or after other events, and are of longer or shorter duration. These spatial and temporal experiences fuse into a general awareness of Space and Time.

But a little reflection shows that these sense-data of ours do not really fit together into a coherent spatio-temporal order. An object that seems above another object from one point of view may seem below it from another. The larger object will seem smaller as we walk away from it toward what had seemed smaller before. All will seem nearer or farther according to the clearness of the atmosphere. And their shapes will vary in our conscious field with our changes of position. Similarly, a period of time that we call an hour or a day may go like a flash or may drag out to an interminable length. A dream that has seemed to cover hours, or years, may occupy but a few minutes, or seconds, by the clock.

Further, when two or more people compare their spatial and temporal experiences, they will be found to differ in detail. A period of time that seems long to you may seem short to me. An angle that looks obtuse to you is a right angle to me.... And, of course, *all* our spatio-temporal experiences depend upon the scale of our bodies. A fly must have a very different sense of the size of objects from ours. Doubtless if we were small enough to live on a molecule in the air about us, a single second (in which it has many millions of near-collisions and changes of path) would seem like an eternity.

In one sense, then, our spatio-temporal experiences are subjective; that is, they are what they are because of the nature and position of our sense-organs and reactive mechanisms. They are mere *pictures* of the world about us. But in spite of that, they may have objective validity, revealing to us, however distortedly, a real order of relations between the objects and events that exist about us. Have we good reason to believe this to be so? Do the physical things of which science tells us have, themselves, spatio-temporal relations? Are Space and Time in some sense objectively real?

Actually we all (except a few ingenious philosophers) believe in the objective reality of spatio-temporal relations. More than that, we believe that physical things and events fit together into a single, coherent spatiotemporal order. We learn to correct the idiosyncrasies of personal perspective and the incommensurabilities of our capricious sense of time. Men long ago invented measuring-rods and clocks; we all believe that they, rather than our ordinary sensations, tell us the truth about Space and Time. One mile is as long as another, however long or short the distance may seem to our fresh or tired bodies. One hour is as long as another, whether we are at play or at the dentist's. Science builds upon this belief in the evenness of objective Time and Space, and gives us universally accepted measurements of both.

There is good reason for holding that this objective spatio-temporal order is not a mere 'construct,' an invention of our minds, but is actual fact. For all experience shows that it makes a great difference *where* and *when* anything exists, i.e., in what spatio-temporal relations to other things. Our universe is one of mutual influence, not a mere collection of entirely separate reals; and everything that happens, happens in strict conformity with its locus in Space and Time. Think of the importance of *proximity* in the case of a spark and tinder, or of the movement of a hammer and dynamite. Remember that gravitation, and electrical forces, vary, according to ascertained laws, with *distance*. It requires a predictable *time* for far-off things to affect one another. In general, causal influences are a function of Space and Time. Even you and I are made what we are by our spatio-temporal environment, and could not possibly have been quite the same in any other locus of Time or Space. A change of place, and a duration in time, are changes in this order of affectability, and are therefore real events. Spatio-temporal relations are important factors in determining what shall happen, and what experience we shall have. They are thus important facts in the constitution of the universe.

But we must explicitly discriminate between our spatial and temporal *experiences* and the objective set of relations which these experiences reveal. Our *sense* of space has been developed; its psychogenesis can be more or less clearly traced. Our sense of the passing of time is likewise a psychological fact. Objective Time and Space existed long before there were animals to sense them, and would continue to exist if all animal-minds were snuffed out. Our space-perceptions and our sense of duration *represent* the order in which events exist, they *are* not that order; they are qualities of experience, representative of relations which cannot themselves enter our experience.

The relations between existents have a different status from that of the things which they relate. The *order* of existents is a fact *about* existents, not an inherent quality of them. Space and Time must remain among our ultimate indefinables. But the point to note is that a full description of existing things at every point and at every moment would not be a complete description of the universe; there would still remain to be described their relations of coexistence and succession. These too are objective facts.

These two sets of relations seem to be equally objective. But there is obviously an important difference between Time and Space, in that the temporal order is irreversible. Objects may change their relations back and forth in Space; but Time is a one-way street. Temporal relations, when put into equations, look like spatial relations. But these equations leave out the essential aspect of Time, the fact that it keeps sliding forward, on and on, so that only the present moment ever exists.

There are, indeed, some philosophers who hold that

Time is not in itself essentially different, in this respect, from Space; and that it is merely owing to our nature that we have to traverse it point by point in one direction, just as a bug crawling along a tight rope would experience it point by point in the direction in which he happened to be traveling.   So Eddington says, "Events do not 'happen,' they are just there, and we come across them successively in our exploration." [1]   Conceivably, other Beings might traverse Time backwards, or might experience temporally separated events as together.   On this view the past is, in some sense, still existent, and the future already exists, though not yet traversed by us.

But, in spite of the allure of this paradoxical conception, it seems clear that the one-way direction of Time is not merely a matter of our experience, but is an objective fact.   For it is obvious that history *would not make sense* if read backward.   The evolution of organic life, the biography of a man, or of a nation, or of the earth, if reversed, would be the sheerest nonsense.   Causation works always forward.   Imagine the story of a battle told backwards, with the dead and mangled soldiers rising to their feet, receiving their wounds, shooting vigorously, and walking off, in good order, backward! Run any 'movie' (especially a 'talkie'!) backwards. Effects would always precede causes, the cart be always before the horse.   The end of every spoken sentence would precede its beginning.   There would be no reason for anything that happened; all the sense would be taken out of it.   No, Space can be looking-glassed without absurdity, Time cannot be.   Nor can it reasonably be considered as a fourth 'dimension' of co-existent fact.   For

[1] *Report on the Relativity Theory of Gravitation*, p. xi.   Also, *Space, Time, and Gravitation*, p. 51.

Time is not merely a pattern of events; its irrevocable going-on-ness is of its very essence.

THE STELLAR UNIVERSE

What, now, is it that exists in Space and Time? What are the existents that, enmeshed in their spatio-temporal relations, make up the physical universe? The word 'matter' we may use as a colorless term for the stuff that exists, the content of the Space-Time universe, without implying any antecedent idea of what that stuff *is*. In the following chapter we shall ask what the physicists, with their microscopes, can tell us about sample bits of it. In this chapter we shall ask what the astronomers, with their telescopes, can tell us about its large-scale pattern and its total amount.

To the astronomer the universe lies revealed as a vast abyss of Space sown very sparsely with stars, and with what Shapley calls the cosmoplasma — meteors, dust-clouds, gases, single molecules, atoms, and electrons. Disregarding these minute and miscellaneous bits of stray matter, as well as such few satellite planets and moons as may exist here and there, we may think of the universe as consisting of globular masses of gas, enormous in size as compared with our earth, but the merest pin-points, floating like so many dust-specks, in the black ocean of Space. They are, to be sure, hundreds of thousands of miles in diameter; but their distances from one another are a matter of trillions (i.e., millions of millions) of miles. Light, which travels 186,000 miles in a *second*, takes anywhere from a few years to millions of years to go from one star to another. It is convenient, therefore, to speak of interstellar distances in terms of light-years — a light-year being about six trillion (6,000,000,000,000)

Our own sun is a moderate-sized star belonging to a star-group which, in turn, belongs to a vast system of stars, usually called the Galaxy, because the Milky Way (Greek, *galaxias*) is its apparent boundary.   There is still considerable disagreement among astronomers as to the dimensions of our galaxy; but work now in progress should settle the undecided questions before very long. At present (1932) our galaxy is rather generally thought to be, in shape, something like a bulgy lens or round sofa-cushion, about two hundred thousand or three hundred thousand light-years in its long diameter, and perhaps forty thousand light-years thick, if outlying clusters of stars are included in both measurements.   Within this system is the local star-group to which we belong, a group seven thousand to ten thousand light-years in length, some distance from the center of the galaxy along the long diameter.   *We*, then, are close to the long diameter of the galaxy (which gives us the effect of the Milky Way as we look out toward its rim), some fifty thousand light-years out from the center of gravity of the system.

Our Galaxy contains many billions (thousands of millions), perhaps hundreds of billions of stars.   And beyond it lie other galaxies of stars, on and on to the farthest reach of our largest telescopes.   The Andromeda 'nebula,' which is one of the very nearest of these 'island-universes,' about eight hundred thousand light-years away according to recent estimates, is the most remote object visible to the naked eye.   But beyond and beyond, our telescopes have photographed millions of these star-systems, perhaps thirty million of them to date; and there seems to be no sign of thinning out.   It is expected that the two-hundred-inch telescope now in process of construction will penetrate three times as far into space

as the hundred-inch telescope (which is as yet the largest)
and so open up to our view many times as large a volume
of Space, and, very likely, many hundreds of millions of
galaxies.   And what might not a four-hundred-inch
telescope reveal!

All these measurements are, of course, subject to correction.   But it may be mentioned that the long diam-
eters of these galaxies, as now measured, run from eight
to forty thousand light-years, whereas our own Galaxy
seems much larger.   A theory gaining in favor, therefore,
is that what we have called our Galaxy is really a collection of several galaxies, a super-galaxy; perhaps what
we have called our local star-cluster is properly to be
called a galaxy, belonging to this group of galaxies.   A
number of groups of galaxies have been discovered far
out in Space, so our situation would be by no means
unique.   But this is merely mentioned in passing, because of its intrinsic interest; it is of no philosophical
importance.

The galaxies seem to be separated pretty evenly, being
in the neighborhood of a million or a million-and-a-half
light-years apart, on an average.   The farthest ones as
yet detected are (if contemporary estimates are at all
reliable) about one hundred and fifty million (some say
two hundred and fifty million) light-years away.   The
two-hundred-inch telescope should enable us to detect
galaxies at least five hundred million light-years away
(i.e., about three sextillion miles = 3×10^{21} miles [1]).

If we may reckon at least a billion stars to a galaxy

---

[1] It will be noted that I am following the American usage, which calls a
thousand million a billion, a thousand billion a trillion, and so on.   The most
convenient method of symbolizing large numbers is in terms of the powers of
ten: 10^{21} means ten-to-the-twenty-first-power; 3×10^{21} is the same as 3 followed
by 21 zeros.

(which is doubtless an underestimate), a hundred million galaxies would contain a hundred quadrillion stars ($= 10^{17}$). There are probably *at least* as many as that. According to Sir James Jeans, there are at least as many stars as grains of sand upon all the seashores of the earth. *And yet*, Space is so vast that they are very, very thinly strewn. As to this, Jeans says that if there were three wasps in Europe, the air of Europe would be more crowded with wasps than Space with stars; and, again, that if the stars were ships at sea, the average ship would be well over a million miles from its nearest neighbor. Eddington says that the average distance between stars can be represented by thirty cricket balls roaming through the space occupied by our earth.

If our sun were a globe two feet in diameter, our earth would be a small pea two hundred and fifteen feet away, Jupiter an orange a quarter of a mile away, Uranus a cherry a mile and a quarter away; the *nearest* star would be seventy-five hundred miles away. And this is rather close, as interstellar distances go.

The force of gravitation apparently holds throughout these unimaginable spaces; and it is only the motions of the stars that keep them apart. Our own sun is moving at a speed of about thirteen miles a second with respect to the average positions of the stars in our cluster. The motion of the cluster as a whole with respect to the center of gravity of our Galaxy (or super-galaxy) seems to be in the neighborhood of two hundred miles a second. This is doubtless to be conceived as a rotation of the Galaxy; the period of rotation would be, at the speed mentioned, about three hundred million years. Also the galaxies are moving relatively to one another at high speeds. So the phrase 'the fixed stars' expresses only a convenient neglect of stellar motions; the stars are so remote that, except to delicate measuring-instruments, they do not seem to change their position in an observer's lifetime. But they are all whirling through Space. Hence, to state the approximate position of our sun in the Galaxy is of no importance; it was in quite a different place when primitive man roamed the earth. And the constellations will look totally different to our remote descendants. *Everything* we know of is in swift and ceaseless motion.

IS THE UNIVERSE INFINITE IN EXTENT?

If present-day astronomers are to be trusted, there are some quadrillions of stars already revealed by photographic plates. (They assume that certain faint blurs are to be interpreted as galaxies roughly similar to those nearest to us, which can be studied in considerable detail.) And there is no astronomical reason to suppose that there are not quintillions, or sextillions of stars.... May we believe, then, that their number is *infinite?*

It is argued that if there were an infinite number of (bright) stars, however far away, we should receive an infinite amount of light from them. For if every star sent to us even the most infinitesimal amount of light, an infinite number of such infinitesimal amounts would be greater than any finite amount of light. We should not see them as separate stars; for our eyes, and even our camera-plates, are not sensitive enough. But we should see a diffused light all over the sky — as we now see certain patches of the Milky Way where we cannot discriminate the multitudinous but remote separate stars.

But we do not know enough yet about the interstellar spaces, or about light, to find this argument convincing. There is undoubtedly a great deal of more or less opaque dust and gas strewn irregularly through Space; and there are known to be a considerable number of dark stars. There is not enough of this opaque matter to hide extremely remote stars and galaxies from us, except in certain spots in the sky. But there may be enough, quite widely dispersed, to veil the light from still remoter stars. And, of course, there may be *more* opaque matter in distant regions than near by.... Then, we do not yet know enough about light to be sure that it does not peter out eventually in Space, or that it does not travel in more or less discrete and eventually diverging rays, like the spokes of a wheel, so that at very great distances it could not affect all points on the surface of its continually expanding sphere.

More arresting is the argument that an infinite number of stars would radiate an infinite amount of heat. The absorption of this heat by our earth would heat it rapidly to incandescence. On the contrary, there seems to be only a very limited amount of radiant energy of all sorts loose in the universe.... But we still know too little of what happens to radiation to stress this argument too confidently. And both these arguments apply only to the existence of hot, bright stars; there might be, for all they can say, an infinite number of dark, cold stars.

A further question remains. Can we suppose Space to be infinite in extent? If so, a star or meteor that got up enough speed to escape from the gravitational pull of its galaxy might go flying outwards, away from the stellar universe, forever. And if so, light and heat are radiating out, away from the stars, and being hopelessly lost, at every moment. This process would mean the loss of all the heat (and, incidentally, of much of the mass) of the universe within a finite time.

Apart from this unpleasant consideration, it is impossible to *imagine* Space as infinite; many people have said they could not *conceive* it to be infinite, and therefore it could not be infinite. However, it is perhaps even more obviously impossible to imagine Space as bounded — as coming to an end, with no Space beyond. So we can set one 'inconceivability' against another, remembering that the criterion of inconceivability proves nothing at all. For centuries the discussion of Space resulted in this *impasse*.

Quite recently certain mathematicians, of whom Einstein is the best known, have offered us a conception of Space as 'curved,' and so finite but unbounded. Such a Space, too, cannot be visualized; but it can be conceived by analogy. The surface of a sphere is finite in area but unbounded; if you go on and on, you come back to the neighborhood of your starting-point. Space may be conceived to have its *three* dimensions curved, as the surface of a sphere has its two dimensions curved, and a circle has its one dimension curved. If you went on and on in Space, in the closest approximation to a straight line that you could possibly find, you would eventually get back, from the other side, to somewhere near your starting-point.

If such *is* the nature of Space, it is clear that there can not exist, in reality, any absolutely straight lines — just as there cannot be a straight line on the surface of a perfect sphere. Every 'straight' line really shares, however infinitesimally, the curvature of Space. And all of Euclid's geometry is only approximately, not absolutely, true of our Space — as it would be only approximately true on the surface of a perfect sphere. Thus we hear many physicists saying nowadays that

Space is non-Euclidean; and that this deviation from Euclidean geometry enables it to be finite in extent, though unbounded.

The Einsteinian theory is that Space is curved because, and in so far as, it contains *matter*. The presence of matter curves, or warps, Space; or, as some say, matter *is*, precisely, a collection of warps in Space. Thus, near large masses of matter Space is more sharply curved. The presence of matter is everywhere felt (we call it 'gravitational force'), and Space has a total curvature which is a function of the total amount of matter in the universe. But it is not evenly curved; its geometry varies from point to point.

If Space is finite in extent, we ask at once, How big is it? What is the longest line that could be drawn in it? Such a line (called a 'geodesic'), if prolonged, would return to its starting-point, if Space were evenly curved, and would, in any case, return to the general neighborhood of its starting-point and then go on round again. It has been suggested that we may actually be able to see round the universe — that an extremely remote galaxy seen in one direction may be the same galaxy that we see from the back side in the opposite direction. If this were so, a geodesic could be not much more than three hundred million light-years. And, in fact, Einstein, De Sitter, Eddington, and others have estimated that the 'diameter' of the universe is of this order, 10^{21} miles. Eddington estimates that a ray of light would make the round-trip in a thousand million light-years, which gives us 6×10^{21} miles.

With such a diameter, the total volume of Space would be of the order 10^{63} cubic miles. Steinmetz, in one of his lectures, accepting this estimate, told his audience to imagine a check made out for the total money-value of everything on earth, and such checks paid out, over and over again, as fast as a man could handle them — two to a second — for a person's whole lifetime, from birth till death. If every human being who has ever lived, since the time of the ape-man, had never done anything but pay out such checks at that rate, paying for Space at the rate of one cent a cubic mile, the amount of Space yet paid for, compared with its total amount, would be as large as an acorn compared with the earth.

However, there are many who feel that this whole account of 'curved' Space is merely metaphorical. We shall return to the matter in the following chapter. We may note here, however, that what the actual *shape* of Space is cannot be ascertained from any geometry, however successful it may prove in furthering calculations. Euclidean geometry holds for a cylinder, or cone, or a crumpled sheet, as well as for a plane surface. And these complicated non-Euclidean geometries are compatible with all sorts of possible 'curvatures' for Space. It is doubtful if the word 'curvature' is warranted at all, to express the application to Space of these mathematical formulæ.

If it *is* appropriate to call Space 'curved,' we cannot help asking, Is it curved *in* a fourth dimension? If you curve a plane surface, it must be curved in a third dimension; and apparently, if a three-dimensional Space is curved, it can only be in a fourth dimension. It seems impossible to get an even 'curve,' not to say uneven 'warps' or 'puckers,' without calling in at least one extra dimension. And, actually, Einstein seems, at times, to be asking us to believe in *ten* dimensions! We may well ask if it is any easier to imagine such a world than to imagine Space as infinite, or as bounded!

The whole matter is terribly confused, in current discussion, by the introduction of the principle of relativity, which we shall presently discuss, and by the relativists' fusing of Time and Space into Space-Time. We are told that Time is the fourth dimension, and that it is Space-Time which is curved, not Space alone.... But if we are right as to the one-way direction of Time, it is difficult to conceive Time as 'curved,' and, therefore, returning on itself, like the supposed geodesic of curved Space. For if Time were thus to return upon itself, it would keep on going. There would be a finite *pattern of events* in Time, but Time itself would be (at least potentially) infinite. The pattern of events would be *repeated* over and over again. Time keeps moving on; and each time round would be *another* series of events, even if exactly similar to earlier series.

We have not yet studied the universe in its Time-order, so we must postpone further discussion of the question whether Time is finite or infinite to a future chapter.

SUGGESTED READINGS

G. T. W. Patrick, *Introduction to Philosophy*, VI.
Carl Snyder, *The World Machine*, XXV–XXX.
H. S. Jones, *General Astronomy*, pp. 351–371.
J. C. Duncan, *Astronomy*, XIV.
F. R. Moulton, in *The Nature of the World and of Man*, I.
J. A. Thomson, *The Outline of Science*, I.
A. S. Eddington, *Stellar Movements, etc.*, I, XI, XII.
J. H. Jeans, *The Universe Around Us*.
R. H. Baker, *The Universe Unfolding*, VI–VII.
J. H. Jeans, *The Stars in Their Courses*, VI–VIII.
Harlow Shapley, *Flights from Chaos*, XII–XIII.
Albert Einstein, *Relativity*, Part III.
R. W. Sellars, *Essentials of Philosophy*, XVII–XVIII.

CHAPTER XII

MATTER AND ENERGY

WE TURN now from the telescope to the microscope. We ask, What is the stuff of which the stars consist? What *is* this matter of which the universe is made?

FOUR ILLUSIONS CONCERNING MATTER

1. *The Diversity of Matter is an Illusion*

The spectroscope has revealed the fact that the matter which constitutes the stars — and all the interstellar 'cosmoplasma' — is the same sort of stuff that we find on earth.... At first sight, there seem to be innumerable *kinds* of matter — air, water, soil, solid rock, and all the rest. But a little observation shows that many, at least, of these substances change into one another — wood into smoke, gas, and ashes, soil and water into leaves and flowers, wheat of the field and juice of the grape into our own heart's blood and vigor of life. The Ionian sages, twenty-five centuries ago, had the intuition that everything is made of one underlying substance which merely changes form. Democritus put it most clearly when he conceived that all things are made of extremely tiny atoms which, by combining in different ways, produce the differences in things. The whole history of modern physics has been a vindication of this theory, reducing the diversities of objects to a matter of differing *structures* of a few elemental units.

Chemistry has shown that all known substances are composed of ninety-two 'elements.' Some of these elements, and certain of their compounds, are very stable under terrestrial conditions; we cannot yet break them up into their component parts. But the spontaneous natural process called 'radioactivity' changes certain elements into others; and it is probably only a matter of time before man will be able to break up and manufacture most or all of these 'elements.' For it is now definitely known that each element is composed of a vast number of similar 'atoms,' and that these atoms are complex structures of two underlying units, electrons and protons. Their differing 'properties' are due to the differing number and arrangement of these electrons and protons. The hydrogen atom is the simplest, with one proton and one electron. The uranium atom is the heaviest, with two hundred and thirty-eight protons and as many electrons. A great deal is already known about the structure of these atoms, and their arrangement in bits of visible matter.

It is difficult to realize that mere differences in spatial arrangement and motion of similar units can produce such different *qualities* (i.e., effects in our conscious experience when we look at them or touch them), and such different *properties* (i.e., causal effects upon and from other things). But a great deal has already been learned about the mechanisms of causation involved. And it becomes increasingly clear that there is no *other* way to produce changed causal effects *except* through changes in structure. A diamond, for example, is pure carbon, made of exactly similar units to those which make up a bit of lamp-black; its very different qualities and properties are due simply to the crystalline *arrangement* of its atoms. So, the difference between one element and another is, apparently, due merely to the differing number, spatial arrangement and motions of their constituent

electrons and protons.   Perhaps these, in turn, are but
different arrangements, or motions, of still more elemental units.   So far, we seem to have reduced the diversity of matter to a difference in arrangement of two
underlying units.   It is irresistible to imagine a further
reduction to one sort of unit.   We shall return to this
speculation later.

2. *The Simplicity of Matter is an Illusion*

The analysis of matter into electrons and protons reveals the fact that the simplest, most apparently homogeneous bit of matter is really an extraordinarily complex little world in itself.   A single atom has, as we have
noted, anywhere from two to nearly five hundred electrons
and protons, in a complex and changing configuration.
And the combinations of atoms which we call 'molecules' have anywhere up to ten thousand atoms, arranged in intricate patterns which chemists are beginning to understand.

These atoms and molecules are, in spite of their complexity, far too small to be seen in any microscope.   A
cubic inch of copper, we are told, has some septillions of
atoms (i.e., some trillions of trillions, some multiple of
10^{24}), each atom being a system of sixty-three protons
and sixty-three electrons.   Some of the atoms are likely
to be minus and plus the normal number of electrons;
and free electrons are probably swinging about from
atom to atom.... An ordinary bit of mixed matter,
such as wood or cloth or paper, or ordinary dirt, is far
more heterogeneous in its complexity.   A single cell of
our bodies has an architecture so intricate that we are
only just beginning to learn a little of its detail.

The atom, evidently, must be very small! and the

electron quite a bit smaller! The protons, curiously, seem to be much smaller still, yet much heavier than the electrons, so that by far the greater part of the *mass* of an atom is the mass of its protons. A human body contains in the neighborhood of 10^{29} electrons and protons. The biggest stars contain about 10^{58}. So a man's body is about halfway between the mass of a proton and the mass of a star.

So numerous are the atoms in any small piece of matter that if a single glass of water (where, however, the atoms are not so crowded as in solid matter!) were emptied into the sea, and so stirred around that its contents became equally dispersed among all the oceans, lakes, and rivers of the earth, any random glassful of water, salt or fresh, anywhere on earth, would contain about two thousand of the atoms from the original glass.

For all we know, every electron and proton may be extremely complex, may be a world in itself. But at least, every smallest bit of matter that we can see, every drop of water, every breath of air, is comparable in its detail to a whole universe of stars.

3. *The Solidity of Matter is an Illusion*

Matter in its fine texture is like the stellar universe not merely in its complexity but in being, likewise, extremely porous. We saw in the preceding chapter that the stars are separated by distances which are enormous in comparison with their size. If the known universe could be squashed together, so that the stars formed one solid mass, it would occupy only the minutest fraction of Space. And if the squashing were continued until all the electrons and protons touched each other, the whole mass would occupy only a few cubic miles. You and I would squash down into invisibility — yet we should *weigh* as much as ever! So much of the universe, both without and within what is called solid matter, is empty of matter that its average density has been computed as one hundred septillionth (10^{-26}) the density of water.

The diameter of an electron is estimated to be about a tenth of a trillionth (10^{-13}) of a centimeter. The atom has no definite diameter, since it is something like our solar system, with most of its mass near the center, and outlying electrons in distant orbits. But we can compute the distance between the centers of adjacent atoms. In a diamond, where (as in all crystals) the atoms are systematically arranged, the distance between the centers of atoms is something over a hundred millionth of a centimeter (10^{-8}). In a gas there is perhaps ten times as much distance between adjacent atoms.

The best way to realize the meaning of these figures is to imagine matter tremendously magnified. C. G. Darwin states that if a drop of water were magnified ten billion times (10^{10}), it would be two or three times the size of the earth. The centers of its atoms would then be about six feet apart, all the way through. The constituent electrons would be about a hundredth of a millimeter in diameter, the protons still smaller; so *nothing* would yet be large enough to be visible to the naked eye. A microscope could find individual electrons and protons — if they would only stand still to be seen, and if there were any way of seeing them! All the rest of this great volume would be empty space (whether really *empty* we shall presently inquire).

Our sense of the solidity of matter is thus another illusion. Matter seems solid to our senses because in the smallest bit that we can distinguish there are millions of millions of atoms to reflect light and oppose the touch of our hands. But actually, the solidest bit of matter is, like the open sky, a vast void with inconceivably tiny specks flying about, very, very far apart in proportion to their size.

4. *The Stillness of Matter is an Illusion*

On a windless day in the country, or on a still night even in the city, a man without scientific knowledge would never suspect that we live in a whirl of omnipresent and incessant motion. Rest seems as fundamental as motion. But it is not so. Apparent quiescence is a mere matter of our blindness; ours is not a static but a dynamic world. Of a few of these changes we become indirectly aware through sensations of heat, light, and sound; other motions our instruments reveal. The rest escape us entirely, save by inference. But the inference is hardly less certain than the assurance of perception.

That the molecules of matter in a gas are in motion is obvious enough, from the rapid diffusion with which an odorous gas, released in one corner of a room, will permeate the whole room. In fact, the molecules of a gas are incessantly flying about, in a zigzag course, deflected from a straight line by their near approach to other molecules, and making some thousands of millions of turns a second.... In liquids, the molecules may be better described as sliding about among one another. They are near enough to be never free from their mutual influence, and so their paths are never straight.... In a solid, the molecules, being more closely packed, retain their relative positions as a rule, and only oscillate to and fro. But there are usually a good many free-lance electrons roaming at large from atom to atom; upon them depends the electrical conductivity of a body — an electric current consisting of the passage in one general direction of great numbers of free electrons.

Within the atoms planetary electrons are revolving about the atomic centers at rates well over a thousand miles a second. So tiny are the orbits that a single revolution takes what seems like almost no time at all! It is said that the electron in a hydrogen atom, when in its shortest orbit, circles about the proton about seven million times in every millionth of a second. This is about a one-hundred-and-fortieth of the velocity of light. Free electrons, under certain conditions, fly much faster, approaching, on occasion (for a very short distance), pretty close to the velocity of light.

When we remember that the earth is rotating about its axis once a day, revolving round the sun once a year, traveling with the sun in the direction of the star Vega, rotating with the sun about the center of our galaxy, and journeying with the galaxy through Space, we realize that there is no rest in the universe, for the tiniest particles or the largest mass. The motions which we *see* are insignificant upon a cosmic scale; they are sporadic and slow. Stellar motions run to hundreds of miles a second, electronic motions to many thousands of miles a second. ... A concrete description of the world about us would have to record the ever-varying motion of every particle in this sea of incessant change. But such a description is not only hopelessly beyond our formulation, it would be of no practical use. To understand and master our environment, we need to analyze these motions into their simple components. But we must remember that what actually occur are not these component motions, as separately described, but a resultant motion at every

point and moment of the universe, of such a nature that
it could be deduced if we could weave together the sub-
atomic, atomic, molecular, mass- and cosmic motions
which our analysis seeks to describe.

RADIATION AND THE ETHER

What we commonly call 'matter' occupies, we have
said, a very small portion of Space.   But all the intervening 'empty' space seems to be full of *something*.
Matter is continually sending out pulses, which radiate
like ripples on the surface of a pond.   There are the long
radio-rays, the shorter heat-rays, the still shorter light-
rays, ultra-violet rays, and, shortest (and therefore most
penetrating) of all, the 'cosmic rays' which are believed
to come from the interstellar spaces.[1]   The only difference between the 'rays' is in their wave-length (and,
therefore, their 'frequency'—the number of 'crests'
that appear at a given point in a given time).   They all,
the longest and the shortest, travel through Space at the
same rate, about 186,000 miles a second.   We may call
them all 'electro-magnetic rays,' or 'ether-rays,' or
'radiant energy.'

Radiant energy is still a great puzzle.   Certain facts
indicate unmistakably that radiation is like a ripple,
spreading out in a circular wave-front.   Other facts indicate that it flies in individual darts or particles.   Eddington has recently coined the word 'wavicles' to express this dual nature.   And now, to add to the confusion,
electrons have also been found to have wave-properties.
Further, it has been discovered that radiation decreases
the mass of the radiating body.   So it seems probable that

[1] There is doubt, however, as to the existence of these 'cosmic rays'; they
may be merely electrons bombarding the earth from outer space.

'radiant energy' consists of tiny bits of the one universal substance, much smaller than electrons, which are shattered off from the atoms in radiation. The term 'photon' is being used in some quarters for the units of radiation. Photons exert pressure when they impinge upon a body; they are subject to gravitation. They carry energy in fixed amounts, always an exact multiple of 'Planck's Constant' (6.56×10^{-27} ergs). So it looks today as if 'matter,' the stuff that exists in Space, should be classified under *three* heads — electrons, protons, and photons. All have wave-properties, all have definite mass, and carry definite amounts of energy.

The *causes* of radiation are only slightly understood. It seems to be generated by, or associated with abrupt changes in speed or direction of motion of electrons. The sharper the jerk, the shorter is the wave-length of the resulting 'ray.' Heat consists of a continual succession of such rays, originating in the quick changes of motion of the atoms and molecules in a 'hot' body. The faster the atoms fly, the jerkier the pulses they emit, and the 'hotter' we call the object. Certain nerve-organs in the skin of our bodies are affected by these rays so as to send specific nerve-currents to our brains, whereupon we have the sensation of heat. But, indeed, all bodies have their molecules set into faster motion by the impact of these rays, and thus become 'hotter.' Temperature is thus a measure of the rapidity of motion of the molecules of any given bit of matter.

The mechanism of our eyes is so arranged that radiations measuring from about thirty-four thousand to sixty-four thousand to the inch affect them, in a way somewhat similar to that in which longer pulses affect the heat-organs in our skin. But the nerve-messages from our eyes to our brains engender in us a very different sensation, that of light. The color of the light seen depends upon the wave-length of the ray; white light is a mixture of many wave-lengths. Some of these rays result, according to one theory, from the jerk made when a revolving electron drops to a shorter orbit. When light is 'absorbed' by the body it hits, the photon disappears, and an electron is lifted to a wider orbit.

But now a further question plagues us. All radiation has a wave-character. *Something* seems to be *oscillating*. This something, in the vast spaces between bits of matter, has usually been called the 'ether.' Its existence has been assumed as the medium through which the pulses of radiant energy radiate. As Sir Oliver Lodge puts it, "If ripples are travelling from distant objects, there must be something which is rippling." On this view, Space is full of *substance* everywhere; so that, as Descartes suggested, there is as much substance in an empty jar as in a jar full of gold. Some theorists have surmised that the ether is the one and only substance, and that electrons and protons are opposite forms of condensation and rarefaction, or oppositely moving whirlpools, or 'warps,' in its mass, while photons are traveling quivers. As W. C. D. Whetham put it, "Matter is a persistent strain-form flitting through the universal sea of ether."

The ether, to be sure, has fallen on evil days. It seems impossible to conceive a substance with the necessary properties! Yet, as Eddington says:

We need an æther. The physical world is not to be analysed into isolated particles of matter or electricity with featureless interspace. We have to attribute as much character to the interspace as to the particles; and in present-day physics quite an army of symbols is required to describe what is going on in the interspace. [1]

Einstein corroborates this by saying that the view

that space is physically empty is finally disposed of. [2]

It is clear that something is *happening* constantly in the interatomic and interstellar spaces. What, for lack of a clearer comprehension, we call 'waves' of light, heat, and the rest, are everywhere crisscrossing through Space, in inconceivable confusion.

In addition to this omnipresent radiation, 'attractions' and 'repulsions' somehow carry across Space. All electrons repel one another and are attracted by protons, according to the inverse square of their distance. Magnetism, too, affects objects which are not contiguous. And gravitation affects the most distant objects. Must we not assume some medium through which these 'forces' exert themselves? Physicists offer us diagrams showing the 'lines of force' surrounding bits of matter, in great detail, and with great assurance. Surely, we may think, there must be something *there*, corresponding to these diagrams. But before trying to decide what it is, we must decide what we mean by 'force.'

WHAT DO WE MEAN BY 'ENERGY' AND 'FORCE'?

The terms 'energy' and 'force' have two distinct fields of application. In their *psychological* sense, they denote certain familiar kinds of sensation, the sensation of energetic action or strain; or the potentiality of such sensations. But we must beware of reading these sensations into the physical world, just as we must beware of

[1] *The Nature of the Physical World* (1928), p. 31.
[2] *Sidelights on Relativity*, p. 18.

reading our sensations of hotness and brightness into
the physical things and vibrations that engender them.
For physics, energy is simply 'motion or the potentiality
of motion'; force is 'the capacity to produce motion.'

The convenience of the term 'energy' arises from the
fact that motions of the various types that are found in
the physical world occur in fixed quantities under given
conditions, and are interchangeable with one another
in fixed proportions. A definite quantity of one sort of
motion will produce a definite quantity of another sort.
So exact is this quantitative equivalence, that if we could
take a definite quantity of 'energy' in any form, and keep
it from leaking away, we could change it into another
kind of energy, and then another, and finally back into
its original form, and find precisely the amount we started
with — i.e., an exactly similar set of motions. This
fact is called the 'conservation of energy.'

The 'quantity of energy' is thus simply a convenient
scale by which to measure and predict motions. It is
proportionately greater when there are more particles
in motion, when the particles are of greater mass, or when
their motion is swifter. The heat-motion of burning
coal, for example, an extremely swift movement of the
molecules, is transformed in the locomotive into a very
much slower motion of the mass of the railway train.

But there is a complication to the story! Motion of
certain sorts may pass over into what, so far as we can
see, is a mere *potentiality* of motion. For example, when
a pendulum reaches the top of its swing, the swinging
motion disappears, and leaves no visible trace, except
in the changed *position* of the pendulum. The total
amount of motion in the world is, apparently, less than
it was a moment before. But the new position is fraught

with the potentiality of motion — which, in the case of
the pendulum, immediately proceeds to become actual
again. This latency of motion we call 'potential energy.'
And we have to amend our understanding of the 'conservation of energy' by saying that, in any closed material
system (i.e., where there are no leaks) the amount of
kinetic energy (actual motion) plus potential energy
(latent motion) remains constant.

In addition, however, to the 'kinetic' and 'potential'
energy of masses of 'matter' (in the usual sense), there
is the vast amount of 'radiant' energy, of which we have
been speaking. If the law of the conservation of energy
holds of the universe as a whole, it must be the sum of
these *three* kinds of energy that is constant. Some
physicists think that more energy exists now in the form
of radiation than as the kinetic or potential energy of
what we commonly call 'matter.'

Why should there *be* definite potentialities of motion
when matter is in certain positions, or states? What is
the meaning of this exact equivalence of motions, some
actual, some, so far as we can see, merely potential?
Why should one body 'exert force,' i.e., produce motion,
of a quantitatively predictable amount, in another body?
What is really happening in situations which we describe
by the words 'attraction,' 'repulsion,' 'strain'? All that
physics can *discover*, in all these cases, is motion, and the
potentiality of motion. But that is doubtless a mere
limitation of our means of discovery. Most of us believe
that there is something behind the scenes, a *push*, a *go*,
to the world-life, which the words 'energy,' 'force,' etc.,
may properly connote.

There are two sharply contrasted viewpoints here.
One group of theorists are looking for dynamic explana-

tions, seeking to find, in every case, a mechanism by which one body affects another, and one motion passes into another. Gravitation, for example, is explained as a result of differential radiation-pressure — so that bodies are *pushed*, by direct contact, instead of being mysteriously 'attracted' at a distance. 'Potential' energy is really a form of etherial motion, interchangeable with the motions of material particles. And so on.[1]

The other group declare, as Bertrand Russell puts it, that "the whole conception of 'force' is a mistake." The cause of the varied motions of bodies is simply the curved nature of Space. 'Gravitation,' for example, is the result of the warping of Space in the neighborhood of matter. Bodies take the easiest paths at every moment, and only *seem* to be attracted by other bodies. A 'field of force' is simply a portion of Space intricately curved. This view Eddington speaks of as a geometrical instead of a mechanical theory of fields of force. Einstein, more than anyone else, has elaborated it; his ultimate aim is to describe all motions, and all 'forces,' in terms of what he calls the metrical properties of Space.

The members of this group point triumphantly to Einstein's success in making more accurate calculations than had yet been made of the deflection of starlight in the gravitational field of the sun, and of the movement of the perihelion of Mercury. But the greater accuracy of Einstein's calculations seems to have resulted from his taking into account certain factors in the situation of which the classical theorists were unaware — in particular, the fact that gravitation is propagated at a finite rate instead of instantaneously, and the fact that

[1] See, for vigorous defense of this view, James MacKaye, *The Dynamic Universe*, New York, 1931.

mass increases and length decreases with velocity.[1] These were triumphs of Einstein's mathematical genius, although the 'verifications' are sharply disputed by some astronomers.[2] But they cannot support one view of 'force' rather than another, since the two theories are simply two interpretations of the same facts; whether we speak of 'forces' or of 'curves' in Space, our equations have to be equivalent, to express the observed facts. The issue is metaphysical rather than observational.

WHAT, THEN, DO WE KNOW ABOUT MATTER?

Various as are the theories concerning matter and Space, one conclusion emerges clearly from our survey. All our physical knowledge reduces to a knowledge of 'structure,' 'configuration.' All physical changes of which we know are redistributions of units; all differences are differences of pattern of distribution. As Eddington puts it:

> Although we seem to have very definite conceptions of objects in the external world, those conceptions do not enter into exact science, and are not in any way confirmed by it....
> Whenever we state the properties of a body in terms of physical quantities, we are imparting knowledge as to the response of various metrical indicators to its presence, and nothing more.[3]

There is, to be sure, in addition to physical knowledge, psychological knowledge, knowledge of the 'qualities' produced *in our experience* when we look at or touch matter. But it is important to note that physics does not find any of these qualities in the things them-

---

[1] The Lorenz-Fitzgerald contraction, of which we shall speak in Chapter XIV.
[2] Cf. C. L. Poor, *Gravitation vs. Relativity*.   The whole matter is still open.
[3] *The Nature of the Physical World*, pp. 253, 257.

selves, or anywhere in outer Space. Our 'sensations' are merely symbolic of the structure of physical things, not (so far as we have any reason to know) replicas of qualities which exist also in them. We have already noted, in chapter VI, that our sensations, and our perceptual experiences, are produced at our end of a long and complicated causal process, and are effects of outer events, rather than aspects of those events themselves. We have now to note that the events in physical things which cause our sensations are always motions, or potentialities of motion (forces).

'Color' ('visibility,' 'brightness,' 'light') in the outer object, is simply the fact that certain electrons within it are swerving from one path to another, causing radiation-pulses which happen to be of the frequency to affect our eyes. In no other sense is there any light or color, outside of our conscious experience.

'Heat,' in the physical sense, is simply the rapidity of motion of molecules in a body, and the radiation-pulses thereby caused, pulses of lesser frequency than light-waves, and so incapable of affecting our eyes, but capable of affecting certain sense-organs in our skin. In no other sense are bodies hot.

'Hardness' is simply the fact that one group of units of matter will not readily interpenetrate another group, or dent its contour very much. The 'hardest' objects are, as we have seen, mostly mere Space; there is plenty of *room* for them to interpenetrate. The 'hardness' consists merely in the cohesive forces between their molecules, which keep them rigidly in position, and the forces of repulsion which keep other groups of molecules away.

All 'chemical properties' are names for the ways in which atoms hang together with other atoms — chiefly because of the number and arrangement of electrons in their outer rings of electrons.

'Electricity' and 'magnetism' are simply names for certain types of attraction and repulsion between electrons and protons, i.e., tendencies to motion. An electric current is a flow of electrons through a conductor.

We must, therefore, resist the tendency to think of the units of matter, the electrons, protons, photons, as little hard visible grains. A single electron could not have visibility or color, or hardness. These are all, in the physical sense of the terms, mass-phenomena, requiring the presence of a great number of material units. In the psychological sense, they refer to *kinds of experience*, and do not apply to matter at all.

Physics, then, merely discovers the size and shape of bits of matter, i.e., the *volume of space* they occupy; their relative *positions* and *distances* from one another; the direction, velocity, and acceleration of their *motions*; their *potentialities* of future motions, as expressed by the concepts of potential energy, force, stress, etc. And it seeks to formulate laws which express the ways in which bits of matter move under varying conditions. Its goal would be reached if it gave us a complete map of the units of matter in Space and Time, and a set of equations which would enable us to infer all later distributions from earlier distributions.

The units of matter seem at present to be electrons, protons, and photons, with outlying 'fields of force' — which may possibly be only a name for the complicated 'curvatures' of Space. At any rate, whether we speak of fields of force, or the ether, or Space, it is clear that the *medium* which separates the units of matter is itself a reality with definite properties. If we should succeed some day in reducing these apparently different types of existence to differing structures or motions of one underlying substance, we should have pushed the frontiers of our knowledge farther, but we should have got no different *kind* of knowledge.

What is the *substance*, the stuff, of which electrons, protons, photons, and the spatial medium are made? To that physics can give no answer. For these entities are known only by the *effects* they produce upon our senses and our instruments. And those effects are always produced simply by their position and motion. 'Matter' is — simply the x's, y's, and z's that are in such and such positions and move in such and such ways. 'Energy' and 'force' are, for physics, merely the quantitative aspects of those motions. 'Mass' is, for physics, only one factor of energy (the other factor being velocity). But it is natural to suppose that 'mass' stands really for 'quantity of matter,' the 'amount of substance' in a given place.

There are those who decry the category of substance as meaningless, since physics cannot tell us what it is. But most of us will continue to feel that if certain parts of Space are occupied, there must be *something* that occupies it; if there is motion, there must be *something* that moves. In a later chapter we shall discuss a speculative theory as to what the substance of things *is*. But we can only speculate; its inner nature remains private. We can only say, definitely, that matter is — whatever *exists*, in the atoms, and throughout Space; whatever occupies space, moves, acts, exerts force (if there is such a thing as force) and causal effects (if there is such a thing as causation). This seems to be very meager knowledge! But, after all, the configurations of the units of matter are so enormously complex that scientists will have their hands full for the indefinite future in unraveling them. And it must be remembered that a knowledge of the inner nature of matter would be of only sentimental interest. What matters is, how matter may affect us, and how we can affect it. Such knowledge is always knowledge of the *structure* of matter in Space and Time.

SUGGESTED READINGS

Bertrand Russell, *Philosophy*, IX, XV.
Bertrand Russell, *The A B C of Atoms*.
R. A. Millikan, *The Electron*, IX.
G. W. Cunningham, *Problems of Philosophy*, Part III.
Comstock and Troland, *Nature of Matter and Electricity*, Part I.
H. S. Lemon, in *The Nature of the Universe and of Man*, IV.
J. A. Thomson, *The Outline of Science*, VIII.
Wm. Bragg, *Concerning the Nature of Things*, I.
Harlow Shapley, *Flights from Chaos*, IV–V.
R. W. Sellars, *Essentials of Philosophy*, XIX.
W. S. Gamertsfelder and D. L. Evans, *Fundamentals of Philosophy*, pp. 299–316.
R. H. Dotterer, *Philosophy by Way of the Sciences*, IV, V.
C. G. Darwin, *The New Conceptions of Matter*.

CHAPTER XIII

FIRST DEGREE RELATIVITY

IN ORDER to understand current doctrines of relativity, we must grasp clearly the distinction between absolute and relative characters of things.

An absolute character is a character that something has in itself, without reference to anything else. A relative character is a character that it has only with respect to something else. The possession of an absolute (or inherent) character of a certain order is logically inconsistent with the possession by the same thing of any other character of the same order; whereas it may have any number of relative characters of the same order. For example, the fact of my being a man (having the character 'manhood') is an absolute fact, and is incompatible with my being any other sort of animal; but the fact of my being a brother is a relative fact. I could be a man if I were the only living creature, but I can be a brother only *to* someone. And my being a brother to someone is not incompatible with my being a son to someone else, an uncle to another person, and so on. Again, the fact that I am feeling a pain is an absolute fact; the pain is an absolute character of my conscious experience. But the fact that the date of my feeling it is August 10, 1932 is obviously relative to the particular calendar now in use.

Now, what are relative facts concerning the constituents of an aggregate are absolute facts concerning the aggregate. My *family* has the absolute character of containing one, and only one, brother-sister relation.

So, although all spatial and temporal facts are relative facts about the units which are related, the fact that a given unit has a given spatial or temporal relation to a certain other unit is (generally considered to be) an absolute fact; this particular manner of relatedness, and no other, is an absolute character of the aggregate which they constitute.   If I live in America, that is an absolute fact, incompatible with my living, at the same time, anywhere else.   If you live nine miles due west of me, that is an absolute fact, incompatible with your living, at the same time, at any other distance or in any other direction from me.   Hence, the conclusion reached in the last chapter, that our knowledge of nature is almost wholly, when analyzed into its elements, a knowledge of the *structure* of things — i.e., a knowledge of *relations* — does not mean that it is not knowledge of absolute facts. Every visible body is a complex structure of myriads of units in intricate spatio-temporal relations; but that does not prevent that particular pattern of relations from being an absolute character of the body as a whole.

So far, then, we have taken it for granted that the facts which we have presented concerning the spatial structure of the universe are absolute facts.   We have assumed, with common sense, that everybody has, at any one time, a definite size, shape, and mass.   We have not supposed that it can have a certain mass 'with respect to' one observer or point of view, and another mass at the same time with respect to another observer or point of view.   We have not supposed that it has one size, occupies a certain volume of space, 'relatively to' some particular point of view, and that, at the same time, it occupies a different volume of space 'relatively to' another point of view.   We know that the size and shape of an object may *look* different from different stand-points; but we hold that it has just one size and shape intrinsically, in itself. Otherwise, what do we mean by saying that science gives us definite, objective knowledge of the structure of the universe?

Similarly, we have supposed that every motion of a body is really in a certain definite *direction*, and at a certain definite *speed*, even though, because we live on a moving earth, and can set out no stake in Space, we cannot determine with assurance what its actual speed and direction is. We have supposed that every event has its definite *duration*, takes up just so much time and no more, and that any other estimate of its duration would be mistaken. We have supposed that one event must happen unequivocally either before or after or simul-taneously with another event. To say that an event was an hour long as correctly judged from one standpoint, and an hour and a half long as correctly judged from another standpoint, seems to us a logical contradiction. And to say that one event preceded another with respect to this 'frame of reference' and followed it with respect to that, seems, if possible, even worse.

But this common-sense belief in the absolute nature of things and events, and therefore in their *singleness* of nature, has been rejected, in varying degree, by many physicists and philosophers, in favor of a belief in the *relativity*, and therefore the infinite *multiplicity*, of their characters.

We have already discussed, in Chapter VI, the episte-mological theory called 'objective relativism.' That doctrine asserts that the qualities and forms which objects have *in our conscious experience* are relative char-acters of the physical things themselves. The grass itself is really green, the water in a basin is really cold; but only 'for' a given observer, 'relatively to' a certain type of organism.   A penny is really elliptical, as well as round; it is elliptical 'with respect to' an observer (or, for that matter, a camera) at a certain standpoint. Railway tracks really do converge in the distance, 'with respect to' an observer, or camera, properly placed. An oar dipped into water really is bent, 'in relation to' our eyes, and visual experience, though it is not bent 'in relation to' hands that feel of it, and tactile experience... In short, the qualities and forms of physical things are relative, not absolute, characters.   And therefore every physical thing has, simultaneously, an infinite number of sets of characters, one set 'for' each possible point of view from which it may be perceived.

However, we saw that these are not true cases of relativity.   The greenness of the grass, the coldness of the water (i.e., the *qualities* which we label by these terms), are *not* relative characters of the grass, the water.   They are *effects* produced in our conscious experience via a complicated series of events proceeding from those outer objects.   A single, definite, clean-cut event in the external existent produces diverse effects upon different organisms, and, through the organisms, upon the diverse streams of conscious experience associated with them. The sense-qualities thus produced are absolute, intrinsic characters of these several streams of conscious experience.

Similarly, the convergence of the railway tracks is not a character of the *tracks*, it is an *effect* produced upon our eyes, or upon a camera-plate.   The bentness is not a character of the *oar*, it is a character present in our experience when we look at the oar, or a character of a *picture* of the oar... Thus, so far as epistemology can

tell us, things have their own absolute, inherent characters.   There is *concomitant variation* between certain
events in the physical world around us and the effects
they produce in our experience and in other physical
things.   But there is no relativity of characters, in the
sense in which theories of relativity use that term.

THE ALLEGED RELATIVITY OF MAGNITUDES

But we come now to a more plausible case of relativity.
It is obvious that our *measurements* of length, size, mass,
duration, etc., are relative to our standard *measures*.
If our yardsticks all shrank a little, every length would
be a greater number of yards (or a larger fraction of a
yard); every distance would be longer, in yards (or miles),
everything would be larger in size, and velocities of moving objects would be greater, *as measured in our units*...
We can, of course, correct our yard-measures by other
lengths, say the diameter of the earth.   But now, suppose our earth and everything on it shrank uniformly.
How could we know that anything had happened?   By
contrasting unchanged cosmic distances with shrunken
earth-distances?   But how could we know whether the
earth and everything on it had shrunk or whether everything outside the earth had expanded?   We could not
know.   The relativist goes further and says, There is
no meaning in the alternative.   For 'size' analyzes
down to the relations 'larger than,' 'smaller than'; it is
always a purely relative fact.   Earth-sizes would have
become smaller than cosmic sizes, and cosmic sizes larger
than earth-sizes, in either case.   So there is no difference
between the cases.

Suppose, again, that the whole universe shrank to half
its present size, with all our measuring instruments and

velocities sharing the change.   Would anything have happened?   The relativist says, No; there is no meaning, whatever, in the supposition.   For size, length, distance, are merely relative characters; and no change in them has any meaning except *in relation to* some other size, length, and distance... And, of course, the same view is held concerning mass.

We measure time by clocks.   We check up our clocks by the earth's daily rotation and its annual revolution round the sun.   But suppose we found presently that there were 367 days in a year; should we know whether the day had become shorter, or the year longer?   Certainly, by measuring the duration of other events, we might discover that the earth's revolution was keeping its former temporal relations to them, while its rotation was taking a shorter time relatively to them.   What then?   We should simply have learned that the day was now shorter than formerly, relatively to other durations, and other durations were now longer relatively to it. And that, according to the relativist, is all there is to it... And if you suppose *all* events in the universe (including, of course, the movement of the hands of clocks) to be speeded up, so that, as we should be tempted to say, time was going faster, the relativist will say there is no meaning in the supposition.   For time-lapses, like distances and sizes, are merely relative.   Time is just a name for the duration of events relatively to one another.

THE ALLEGED RELATIVITY OF MOTION

We naturally suppose that every moving object is really moving in a certain definite direction with a certain definite velocity, no matter how it may seem to us to be moving.   But consider:

A man sitting on the top of a fast moving autobus throws a ball up into the air; it falls back into his hand. To the thrower the ball seems to go straight up and down. An observer standing on the sidewalk sees the ball start upward just opposite him and fall into the thrower's hand some feet beyond where he is standing; he sees its course as a curve like that of water in a fountain. This path is longer than the path observed by the thrower; so the velocity of the ball is greater, as judged by the man on the sidewalk... But the observer on the sidewalk is moving too; he is moving eastwards with the earth's rotary motion, speeding through Space as it follows its orbit round the sun, and flying, at a still faster rate, with the solar system toward Vega. A spectator in Space, who did not share these motions, would see the ball make a much flatter and longer curve, at a much higher speed.

Now we know much about the earth's motion relative to the sun, the stars, and the galaxies. But we do not know what further motions it may have. So, even if there is such a fact as absolute motion, we do not know what the earth's absolute motion through Space is. Thus we do not know what the 'real' path of the ball is. We cannot compute it with respect to the 'fixed stars,' for all the stars are moving far faster relatively to the ball and one another than the ball is moving relatively to the earth. We can find no fixed reference-frame in Space. All we can ever *discover*, it would seem, is the motion of a body relative to some other moving body.

We naturally believe that every body has a certain definite *position* in Space. And if it has, it would be true to say that a body moved from position *x* in Space to position *y*, at such and such a speed. This would be its *real* motion, from which its changes of position with respect to other bodies would *result*. But how can we define position in Space? In a universe where everything is in motion, must we not agree that the only meaning we can give to the statement that a star is at a certain place is that it has such and such a position with respect to other stars?

The relativist draws this conclusion. He says there is no reality corresponding to such phrases as 'the real velocity and direction of a motion,' or 'the real shape of the path' of a moving object. The path and velocity as seen by one observer is just as real as that which would be seen by any observer who might be moving in any direction at any speed. Every moving object has an infinite set of paths and velocities, each as 'real' as any other, although we are usually interested only in one or two of them, such as, in our illustration, the path and velocity of the ball relative to the autobus, or relative to the street.

Bertrand Russell declares, speaking of a trip from London to Edinburgh:[1] "You therefore say and think that you have traveled to Edinburgh, not that Edinburgh has traveled to you, though *the latter statement would be just as accurate.*" If motion is nothing but the reciprocal change of position of bodies, Russell is right. And so is Eddington, when he declares that there is no meaning at all in saying that a star might slow down and come to rest; because a decrease of velocity relative to one frame is an increase relative to another frame, and coming to rest in one frame would be getting increased motion in some other frame.

If a meteor comes rushing toward the earth, it is exactly as true to say that the earth rushes to hit the meteor;

[1] *The A.B.C. of Relativity*, p. 5.

and that, in succeeding moments, or at the *same* moment, it rushes in a hundred other directions toward a hundred other meteors.   If an electron in a tube flies at a speed of 100,000 miles a second, it is just as true to say that, for that brief moment, the walls of the tube, and the earth, and all of us, rush the other way at that terrific speed — and then abruptly stop.   If I shoot a bullet into the air and it falls back to the earth, it is equally true to say that the earth falls away from it abruptly and rushes back to meet it.

So with rotary motion.   Russell, as a consistent relativist, declares:[1] "There is no difference between the two statements: 'The earth rotates over a day,' and 'the heavens revolve about the earth once a day.'   The two mean exactly the same thing."   Copernicus was mistaken in thinking that his doctrine was true and the geocentric theory false; all that we are warranted in saying is that the earth and the stellar universe have a relative rotation.

Suppose all the bodies that comprise the universe of matter were eventually drawn together into one huge lump.   Could this one body rotate, or move in any direction?   Is there any *meaning* in the supposition that it could?   The relativist says, No.   Such a universal motion could not possibly be detected, and would make no difference of any sort; therefore there would *be* no difference.   If there were no other body relatively to which the unique lump could move, it should not be called moving, as a whole, though, of course, parts of it could move relatively to other parts.

In short, all that motion *is*, on this view, is a reciprocal change of position of two or more bodies.   Bits of matter change their position with respect to one another, they

[1] *Op. cit.*, p. 10.

have no 'real' motion of their own, no absolute motion
in Space.

THE ARGUMENTS FOR RELATIVITY

Some relativists insist that the concepts of absolute
Space, Time, motion, mass, etc., are *meaningless*, so that
it is foolish even to raise the question whether there are
realities corresponding to them. One of these, P. W.
Bridgman, in a recent widely discussed volume, *The Logic
of Modern Physics*, declares, "If a specific question has
a meaning, it must be possible to find operations by
which an answer may be given to it" (p. 28). For
example, "We do not understand the meaning of absolute time unless we can tell how to determine the absolute
time of any concrete event, i.e., unless we can measure
absolute time. Now we merely have to examine any of
the possible operations by which we measure time to see
that all such operations are relative operations. Therefore the previous statement that absolute time does not
exist is replaced by the statement that absolute time is
meaningless" (p. 6).

It is, indeed, a fairly simple matter to define relative
facts, and very hard to define what we mean by absolute
facts. But at least we are sure what we mean *negatively*.
By 'absolute mass' we mean mass considered not in its
relations to other masses, but in itself. By 'absolute
Time' we mean Time not merely as the relative durations
of different events but as it passes during any one event,
considered alone. By 'absolute motion' we mean something that could occur if there were only one body left
in the universe — rotating, let us say, alone. We may
believe, also, that a body's absolute motion is motion
relative to Space itself, or to something immaterial in

Space (which we may call the 'ether,' or, with Einstein, the 'intermediary medium') which serves as a set of landmarks by which absolute motion could, theoretically if not practically, be gauged. If there is nothing fixed in Space, absolute motion could still be gauged by its relation to light-rays, or other immaterial events, if these events have, themselves, a fixed, absolute *rate* of motion through Space. But even if there is nothing fixed in Space, we may still believe that bodies have 'real' motion (as distinguished from the merely apparent motion of bodies 'moving relatively to' them), and that this real motion is a dynamic fact, with its causes and its effects. If there is such 'real' motion, there must be an absolute Time and Space in which it occurs.

Surely, then, whether or not we have any reason to *believe* in absolute Time, Space etc., the concepts are not *meaningless*. And, in fact, even Bridgman, when pressed, admits as much, but asserts that "the meaning has no connection with reality." This, then, is an assertion about reality, instead of about the meaninglessness of certain concepts. And the ground for the assertion is that there is no way of discovering whether or not reality has characters corresponding to the concepts. As C. G. Darwin puts it, "If a thing is essentially unobservable, then it is not a real thing, and our theories must not include it."

But *is* the fact that we cannot observe something which, in the nature of the case, we could not observe even if it existed, a sufficient reason for asserting that it does not exist? Atoms and electrons are never *observed*; we believe in their existence because the hypothesis that they exist, with such and such properties, helps us to

[1] *Op. cit.*, p. 29.

explain many facts which we do observe. For that matter, our realistic belief that physical things in general exist, outside of our conscious experience, is a mere hypothesis. And so with our belief in the past. None of us has ever observed the facts of past cosmic history; yet we all believe they happened. Again, none of us has ever observed any one else's conscious experience, or can possibly prove that there *is* any conscious being but himself. Your belief that I am conscious, and not an unconscious automaton, is, logically, a hypothesis, justified because the peculiarities of your own experience are better explained by it than by the contrary hypothesis. Similarly, the hypothesis of absolute Time, Space, and motion is a hypothesis which we shall be warranted in holding, in spite of the fact that all our measurements must obviously be relative, if that hypothesis serves to explain certain facts better than the relativistic hypothesis.

Many physicists will prefer to shelve the question as to absolute motion, etc., because it does not matter for their experiments. And if they theorize on the subject, they may prefer a relativistic theory because, as C. D. Broad puts it, "it keeps closer to the observable facts."[1] But as philosophers, we wish to know what sort of a world we are living in. And that quest is bound to take us very far from observable facts — though our theories will be accepted only because they *explain* observed facts. Incidentally, a carefully elaborated relativistic theory, such as Einstein's, with its hummocky non-Euclidean Space-Time and its many startling implications, takes us at least as far from observable facts as the view that Time and Space are absolute. But in any case, we should

[1] *Scientific Thought*, p. 91.

beware of assuming that a limitation of our knowledge is a limitation of reality. That is a very anthropocentric delusion. To paraphrase Xenophanes, horses or oxen — or fishes or earthworms — might as rightfully assume that whatever is "essentially unobservable" by *them* cannot exist.

THE ARGUMENTS AGAINST RELATIVITY

So, then, we ask the believer in absolute Space and Time, What is it that can be better explained by the theory that motion, mass, distance, and duration are absolute facts than by the relativistic theory? His answer is, all the facts concerning the *causes* and *effects* of motions. The causes producing motion act on this or that particular body, initiating or changing *its* motion; motion with respect to other bodies is a by-product, so to speak. And a body's own changes of motion produce effects upon *it* which are not produced upon other bodies moving relatively to it.

All our experience points to the generalization that motions occur only when *caused*. A great many causes have been, and are, at work, of which the actual motion of a body is the resultant. But causes operate upon individual bodies, or upon a number of bodies in varying degree. So, although there is, inevitably, a reciprocally equal shift of position with respect to one another, it is one body more than another which is responsible for it.

One billiard-ball rolls toward another. Their approach is mutual. But only *one* of them has been *pushed*. Because of that, the relative shift of position is due to *it*, and not to the other ball.

A bullet is shot into the air. To content ourselves with saying that there occurs a relative motion between the bullet and the earth is to ignore the *cause* of this relative motion. The cause changes the bullet's path, not (to any appreciable degree) the earth's. It is quite true that the earth may, possibly, be moving in a direction away from that in which the bullet is fired, at such a rate that the bullet (which shares the motion of the sun and earth) at the end of a few seconds is actually farther along in that direction than when it started. Like the Red Queen in *Alice in Wonderland*, it has to run hard to stand still. In that case, what the gunpowder-explosion did to the bullet was to violently retard the motion it had had as an earth-object. But that does not alter the situation. It is the bullet, not the earth, that has had its path so radically altered; the rapid separation of earth and bullet is due to a new absolute motion of the *bullet*, whereas the earth's path is scarcely changed.[1]

If a hundred people toss up balls in varying directions, at varying speeds, the earth moves relatively to them at a hundred different speeds and in a hundred different directions, at the same time. There is no contradiction in this. But it is evident that all these new relative motions of the earth with respect to the balls are not due to any changed motion of the *earth*. They occur because forces of varying degree have been applied to the *balls*.

It takes *force* to produce and change absolute motion. If I go to visit you, *I* have to expend the energy, not you. If an electron is shot out in a cathode tube at a speed approaching that of light, it is because a force is available to make so infinitesimal an object move at that speed. We may say that the earth moves, for an instant, at that

[1] To be strictly accurate, the earth has had an infinitesimal motion imparted to it also. But that is negligible, for the question at issue. That question is whether the half-mile-high jump of the bullet can equally well be called a half-mile-long drop of the earth.

same speed, relatively to the electron. But this is only relative motion. No available force could make the huge bulk of the earth *really* move at that tremendous speed. The event which the experimenter produces is essentially one-sided, though the resulting shift of position is, in the nature of the case, reciprocal.

If, with Einstein and the relativists generally, we abandon the conception of force and substitute metric properties of Space as the cause of accelerations, we have not got rid of the one-sidedness. We have to recognize that different parts of Space are differently 'curved.' And so, of two bodies that experience a relative acceleration, one has had its motion altered directly, by coming into a region of Space that is 'warped,' whereas the other body has its motion relative to the first body altered only because the first body's motion is altered.

It is particularly clear that rotation is an absolute fact. We may say, if we choose, that the heavens are 'rotating with respect to' the earth. But the earth is *really* rotating, the heavens are not. For there were causes, a few thousands of millions of years ago, which produced this rotary motion of the earth; no causes could possibly make the stars and galaxies rotate (at speeds far greater than that of light) about the earth, every twenty-four hours... Similarly, if I spin a top, I spin the *top*, and not the whole universe in the contrary direction.

In short, whenever we can see the causes that have *produced* motion, we can see *which* body has been *given* the motion. It is only where we cannot unravel the complex causal factors that we have to content ourselves with describing relative motions. The measurement of relative motions is not the goal of science, it is just a first step toward finding what has actually happened.

Can any one really suppose that if all the stars were drawn together into one lump, that lump could not move? Obviously it would have whatever translatory and rotary motion resulted from the motions of its component parts before they coalesced. Suppose one atom remained outside the one great lump. Even the relativists must admit that it could move relatively to that atom. But then suppose the atom was dissolved into radiation. It is preposterous to say that the one big lump could not *keep on* moving! It could not *stop* moving.

Again, when the relative duration of events changes, the affair is really one-sided. If earth-time slowed up, relatively to extra-terrestrial events, we should look for some cause affecting the *earth*. And whether we found it or not, we should be confident that there was some definite cause which had lengthened the time of the earth's motions, and that it was not equally true that all other cosmic events were taking a shorter time. If my watch loses time, I do not say, Time is merely relative, and history is now proceeding more rapidly with respect to the time which my watch measures. No. I look for the cause that has affected my watch and not the rest of the universe.

And now we must note also that we can get on the track of absolute motion by finding its *effects*, as well as by finding its causes.

You and I are approaching each other rapidly in motor-cars. I put on my brakes suddenly. Our relative motion decreases abruptly. The decrease is as great, and as sudden, for you as for me. But I alone feel a jerk; I may even be thrown out. Nothing whatever happens to you. Similarly, if I swerve to one side violently, or pick up speed too suddenly. Our *relative* change of motion is symmetrical. But *I* feel all the effects. The *causes* of the change of motion are one-sided, and so are the *effects*. May we not conclude that it is *my* motion, and not yours, that is *really* changing? These effects are not due to the fact that I change my velocity relatively to the earth, while you do not. If we were flying past each other in rockets, far out in Space, exactly similar one-sided effects would be produced, supposing I had a way of suddenly accelerating my rocket, or swerving its course.[1]

All sorts of other effects might be mentioned. If I walk ten miles to see you, I get tired, not you. If I go in my car, it uses up fuel, and gets wear and tear. It is not equally true that you have come to me; you are not tired, and have no bills to pay.

In the case of rotation, the one-sided effects are noticeable too. The earth is flattened a little at the poles by its rotation, certain prevailing winds and ocean-currents are produced. Some relativists have suggested that these effects are produced by rotation "relative to the fixed stars." But what have the fixed stars to do with it? They are far too distant to have any share in these effects. If there *were* no "fixed stars," would not the rotation of the earth itself produce these effects? They are effects of the rotation itself, needing no reference to any other body.

It is well known that if a free-swinging (Foucault)

[1] Since writing the above, I note that Professor W. P. Montague, in the paper referred to in the following chapter, called attention to these one-sided effects of the *intrinsic* acceleration of a body. In his illustration one of two bodies approaching each other in Space undergoes a spurt of acceleration; loose objects on its surface, such as marbles, roll *backward*; no such effect occurs upon the other body. In my illustration one of the two bodies is suddenly *retarded*, and loose objects upon it (but *not* objects upon the other body) tend to move *forward* (relatively to it). The principle is, of course, exactly the same in both illustrations.

pendulum is set swinging toward, say, the star Vega, it will continue swinging in that direction while the earth rotates under it. If it were swung at the North Pole, it would point to slightly more western points at each swing, till, after twenty-four hours, it pointed to the meridians toward which it was started swinging... Now what we actually *observe* is merely that pendulums rotate their planes of swing with respect to the earth, but keep to the same plane of swing with respect to the stars. The relativist is content with that observed fact. But this fact needs to be *explained*. The stars, again, have no causal connection with the case; they have a faint gravitational attraction in all directions, but that has nothing to do with these effects. Nor is there any force causing the pendulum to keep changing its plane of swing. As a matter of fact, the pendulum does *not* change its plane of swing. The *cause* of the relative motion of earth and pendulum is obviously the rotation of the *earth*, which does have causes... If the *heavens* were revolving about a stationary *earth*, the pendulum would rotate its plane of swing *not* with respect to the earth, but with respect to the revolving heavens. This little pendulum is a pretty good detector of absolute motion!... A gyroscope would do, too.

A reply sometimes made by relativists, with respect to such cases as have been adduced, is that they are all cases of *acceleration*, i.e., *changes* of motion. Uniform motion in a straight line is merely relative and reciprocal; but accelerations are absolute. A body may rotate, or swerve, or go faster or slower, on its own hook; but uniform rectilinear motion is meaningless, except as motion relative to some other body... What makes this reply plausible is, of course, that in the case of unaccelerated relative motions there is no way of telling which body is really doing the moving; whereas, relative accelerations always have causes, and often have discoverable effects, which serve to locate the real seat of the acceleration. Accelerations are every bit as reciprocal as uniform motions; we simply have evidence in their case of a one-sidedness which we lack in the cases of uniform, undisturbed motion.

Moreover, if it is permissible to believe in absolute rotation (or an absolute push-forward or retardation of a body) it cannot be said that the conception of absolute motion is *meaningless*. For it is as easy to see what we mean by absolute motion of translation as what we mean by absolute motion of rotation. If we can properly say that the earth is 'really' rotating, and the stars are *not* revolving round the earth once a day, we can equally well say that the electron in the cathode tube is 'really' moving at a tremendous rate, and the earth is *not* moving at such a rate in the opposite direction... In such cases it is easy to see which body is doing the moving, or most of the moving. In other cases, as with stellar motions, the determination of real motion may forever be impossible. But the fact that it is not *determinable* by us does not prove that it is not *determinate*. We must not erect the limitations of our knowledge into limitations of the universe.

And there are two important points to be noted: First, *every* real motion, even if uniform, is the *result* of acceleration, and is a measure of the force (or of the shape of the 'field') that produced it. If we could trace back the motions of two stars, we should find their causes; and then (if we could discover *all* the causes that had accelerated both stars), we should know how much of their relative motion was due to one star's actual motion and how much

to the other's... The second point is, that uniform motion
in a straight line probably does not exist.   If it does, it is
certainly very rare in the universe.   The notion of it is
a mere limiting case.   So if the relativistic doctrine applies only to it, it has little relevance to the existing world.

SUGGESTED READINGS
See list at end of the following chapter.

CHAPTER XIV

SECOND DEGREE RELATIVITY

A RELATIVISM of the sort that we have been discussing is an old and familiar view. But Einstein has shown us that the implications of relativism, when fully unfolded, are far more startling than had been supposed. The old doctrine asserted that size is merely relative to other sizes, mass to other masses, duration to other durations. But it left the relations of the magnitudes of each sort to one another a set of absolute facts. If one body was twice as long as another, it *was* twice as long, for any one's accurate measurement. If its mass was twice as great, it was unequivocally twice as great, and any statement to the contrary was false. If one event lasted twice as long as another, no change of viewpoint could alter that fact. But now we see that relativism, when consistently carried out, implies that *these relations are themselves relative*: there is no meaning to a statement even of the relative sizes and masses of bodies, or of the relative length of time-lapses, except as the standpoint is given with respect to which the statement is true. This we may call Second Degree Relativity.

THE MICHELSON-MORLEY EXPERIMENT

To see why, if we accept the ordinary sort of relativism, we are driven to make these startling deductions, we must first understand the famous Michelson-Morley experiment. This experiment was an attempt to discover the earth's absolute motion, by finding its motion relative to the motion of rays of light. Light-rays may naturally be supposed to travel in all directions through Space at an invariant rate, whatever the direction in which our little earth happens to be headed on any given day. If so, they should *seem* (to exact measurement) to go more slowly when the earth is traveling in the same general direction, and more rapidly when the earth is traveling against this direction. We know that the earth is moving at about 18 miles a second in its annual orbit round the sun. If, then, we could measure the time taken by a light-signal sent parallel to the earth's surface in the general direction of the earth's motion, and the time taken by a signal sent in the reverse direction, we should be able, by subtracting one time-lapse from the other, to discover quite exactly at what speed the earth is traveling, from month to month, relatively to light-rays flying freely through Space.

Unfortunately, our clocks and recording-instruments are not delicate enough for this direct experiment. The velocity of light has to be measured on earth by a round-trip; and this defeats the end we have here in mind. But Michelson and Morley, about fifty years ago, devised a method which, it was thought, would detect the difference in the velocity of light in different directions relative to the earth's motion. The following simplified account gives the principle of the experiment.

In the figure, a lamp is at A. A beam of light is sent from it to B, and at the same time to C, the same distance from A, but at right angles to the line AB. At B and C are mirrors, reflecting the beams back to A. According to a well-known optical law, if the two beams traverse exactly the same distance, they will be in identical "phase" upon their return to A. If one path is even infinitesimally longer than the other, an "interference-effect" will be produced, which will shift if the relative distance of the two paths shifts.   Now, if the earth were *stationary*, the distance through Space which the ray traverses from *A* to *B* and back, would be the same as that from *A* to *C* and back. But if the earth (carrying the machine with it) is *moving*

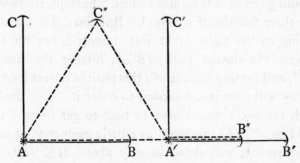

FIG. I. SIMPLIFIED DIAGRAM OF MICHELSON-MORLEY
EXPERIMENT

If   (*a*) *AB* = *AC* = 9 ft.
  (*b*) The machine moves to the right @ 12 ft. per sec.
  (*c*) Light travels @ 24 ft. per sec.
Then (*a*) The round trip *ABA* = *ACA*, 18 ft., takes ¾ sec.
  (*b*) The round trip *AB"A'* is 24 ft., takes 1 sec.
  (*c*) The round trip *AC"A'* is about 21½ ft., takes about ⅞ sec.

in the general direction of *B*, the distance from *A* to *B* and back is really *longer* than the distance from *A* to *C* and back; and there should be a marked "interference-effect." As a matter of fact, it is impossible to make the two distances *AB* and *AC* exactly the same. But that is not necessary. The point is, that if the earth were stationary, the *relative* length of the two paths would remain exactly the same, when the machine is slowly rotated. But if the earth is moving, in *any* direction, the relative length of the two paths will be altered as the machine rotates, and a *shift* in the interference-bands will occur.

For the sake of making the matter clear in a diagram, we shall suppose that light travels 24 feet a second, and that the machine is moving to the right (in the direction AB) at 12 feet a second. The two mirrors, B and C, are both 9 feet from A. Then, if the machine were stationary, ray no. 1 would go from A to B and back, 18 feet; ray no. 2 would go from A to C, also 18 feet. Both journeys would take three fourths of a second. But since the machine is moving to the right at 12 feet a second, ray no. 1 will traverse the dotted path $AB''A'$, hitting the B-mirror at B'', and getting back to A'; this path is 24 feet long, and the ray will take just a second to cover it. But the path which ray no. 2 would have to take to get from A to A' would be $AC''A'$; this path, as a little geometry, or actual measurement, will show, is only about $21\frac{1}{2}$ feet. So, actually, the ray that reached A' via C'' at the *same* instant that ray no. 1 reached A' had to leave the lamp A a little *later* than ray no. 1 left it. Its path is even shorter than $21\frac{1}{2}$ feet. The two rays, on meeting at A', will be in markedly different phase. As we rotate the machine slowly, the difference in length between the two paths should increase, then decrease, then increase again, with shifting and reshifting of the interference-bands.

Of course the speed of light is really so much greater than any speed we can attribute to the earth that the two paths will be only very slightly different in length. Still, the earth is *known* to have an orbital velocity in excess of 18 miles a second, and this is more than enough to produce the effect expected.

The disconcerting result of the experiment was that *no* shift in the bands took place as the machine rotated.[1] This can only mean that light travels to both mirrors

---

[1] As a matter of fact, slight varying shifts were observed. But they were taken to be observational errors. Some observers think they have evidence of a genuine objective shift. But the overwhelming majority of physicists accept Michelson's and Morley's conclusion that there is no real objective shift.

and back in the *same* time, just as it would if the earth were standing still. It does *not* prove (as relativists universally assume) that light travels, relatively to the earth, in all directions at the same speed. The velocity of the machine relative to that of light may be as different as you please in the opposite direction *AB* and *BA*; in any case the *round-trip AB″A′* will be of the same length when the machine is turned round into the reverse direction. The experiment simply proves that the back-and-forth round-trip takes (to a very close approximation) the same time as the transverse round-trip. And this is certainly in need of explanation.

NON-RELATIVISTIC INTERPRETATIONS

A. The most natural interpretation of this unexpected result is to hold that *light-rays share the motion of their source*. If this is the case, the velocity of the ray taking the path *AB″A′* is slightly greater than that of the ray taking the path *AC″A′*; and there *would be* no difference in the time of the two round-trips. There are three varieties of this hypothesis, as follows:

1. *The Corpuscular Hypothesis*

All material particles on earth share the earth's motion. Their paths and velocities are exactly the same in all directions, with respect to the earth, as if the earth were at rest. Similarly, if light-rays are corpuscular, consisting of vast numbers of photons, like tiny bullets, this is just what we should expect. But if light-rays are *waves*, we should *not* expect it. Sound-waves do not share the velocity of their source. It has been assumed in physics for some generations that radiation consists of waves, and so a positive result was expected from the experiment. But now that light seems to be in some respects corpuscular and in some respects wave-like, no antecedent expectation seems justified.   Ritz, a brilliant young Swiss physicist, whose death in 1908 was a great loss to physics, believed that light-rays are essentially corpuscular, and that they share the motion of their source.

We must await a more exact knowledge of the nature of radiation before forming a judgment as to the plausibility of this theory.

2. *The Ether-Drag Hypothesis*

A second hypothesis is that the ether close to a material body is dragged along by that body, and that all ether-waves (including light-waves) share this motion.   This, too, would explain the negative result of the Michelson-Morley experiment.   The term 'ether' is unpopular to-day.   But there does seem to be some *medium* between bits of matter, to carry the 'stresses' and 'strains,' which are very real facts, whatever their intrinsic nature may be.   Even Einstein agrees that there is some sort of "intermediary medium."   The question is, whether radiation consists of waves in this medium, and whether, if so, the medium is dragged about by material particles and imparts to its waves this additional component of velocity.

The phenomena of aberration are generally taken to disprove this hypothesis.   At two seasons of the year six months apart, when the earth is, in turn, nearest to a certain star and farthest from it, it is necessary to point a telescope at a slightly different angle to see it, though its actual direction from the earth is the same.   For the earth at the two seasons is moving (in so far as its orbital motion goes) in opposite directions, at right angles to the star's rays; and while the light-rays are traveling down the telescope-tube, the tube has been moving sidewise. The angle through which it is necessary to turn the telescope, first to the right, and then to the left, is a rough measure of the relative speed of light-rays and of the earth in its orbit.   But if the star's rays were dragged sidewise as they got near the earth, as the ether-drag hypothesis implies, this aberration-effect would not occur... There is at least one experiment (the Airy experiment) which points in the other direction.   But the consensus of opinion of physicists is strong, at present, against any sort of 'ether-drag' hypothesis.

3. *The Field-of-Force Hypothesis*

Professor W. P. Montague, in a brilliant Presidential Address to the American Philosophical Association in 1923,[1] suggested a third variation of the general theory that the velocity of light varies with the velocity of its source.   According to his view, each particle of matter carries with it its own field of force, which extends indefinitely in all directions, interpenetrating, but not fusing, with the fields of force of all other particles. Light-rays are periodic oscillations in the particular field of force connected with the particle from which they have their origin.   No matter how far they travel from their source they share the motion of that particular field of force.

This theory does away with the necessity of assuming the existence of a mysterious puzzling 'ether,' and the necessity of assuming light-rays to consist of *particles*. In some sense, 'fields of force' do exist.   But whether each of the innumerable fields of force preserves its own identity,

[1] This address was published in *The Philosophical Review* for March, 1924.

as the theory requires, is highly dubious. It is more natural to suppose that the field of force between material particles is a single resultant field, made what it is by the various component forces acting upon it. But in that case there would be no foundation for Montague's theory.

The assumption, common to the three theories just discussed, that light-rays share the velocity of their source, could be tested if we could measure accurately enough the velocity of the light-rays which come to us from variously moving stars. Some astronomers have thought they had decisive evidence against the assumption, from observations made upon eclipsing double-stars. But the matter is very delicate and the evidence uncertain. Montague suggested, in the address referred to, an experiment by which it might be possible to decide the matter; the experiment would discover whether rays proceeding in parallel lines from incandescent wires moving rapidly in opposite directions on a revolving globe reached a point some distance away at the same instant. The experiment would be difficult, however, and costly, and has not yet been attempted. In the meantime, most physicists are convinced that light does *not* share the motion of its source.

B. Quite different is the *Lorenz-Fitzgerald hypothesis*. This hypothesis supposes that all light-rays, whatever their source, move at one and the same absolute velocity in all directions. Since the earth has *its* velocity (different at different times of the year), light-rays have a different velocity relative to the earth in opposite directions. But there is a *compensating factor* which makes the two round-trips in the Michelson-Morley experiment take the same time, viz.: the motion of matter shrinks all lengths in the direction of motion, in increasing degree as the velocity increases, and to the degree necessary to make the path $AB''A'$ in our diagram the same (or very closely the same) length as $AC''A'$. Such a shrinkage would be infinitesimal at ordinary speeds; and even if it were appreciable, could not be detected on the moving body, since all measuring-rods would shrink exactly as much as the objects measured.... As a matter of fact, just such a shrinkage might have been predicted from already accepted electro-magnetic principles.... There seems to be no way to get positive verification of the shrinkage. But a concomitant increase in inertial mass, which was deduced from the same principles, was actually found to occur in the case of very fast moving electrons, causing their deflection in a magnetic field to be less than would otherwise occur, quite in line with the prediction of the Lorenz-Fitzgerald formula.

Very recently a theory has been worked out by Professor MacKaye of Dartmouth College (published in *The Dynamic Universe*, New York, 1931), offering a brilliant explanation of the underlying causes of these phenomena. In a word, he takes electrons to be wave-like (in line with much recent theory), and the compression caused in them by motion to be analogous to the compression supposed to be caused in light-waves by the motion of their source (the Doppler Effect). It is too early to judge of the probability of this particular theory. But if it proves vulnerable, other causal theories will doubtless be proposed. Meanwhile, the Lorenz-Fitzgerald contraction is in harmony with the accepted facts of electro-magnetic theory, and would, no doubt, be generally accepted as an absolute physical fact, were it not for the popularity of the relativity-theory.

It is a pity we cannot discover by experiment whether light does or does not travel at the same velocity in opposite directions relatively to the earth's motion. The Michelson-Morley experiment does not decide that question, since there are a number of hypotheses offered to explain its negative result. The best hope for deciding the matter would seem to lie in taking radio-waves, which are universally admitted to travel at the same velocity as light-rays, but, unlike light-rays, follow the curvature of the earth, so that very much longer paths are available for experiment. If radio-signals were sent, say, from New York to Seattle,[1] some three thousand miles, and the exact time of sending and of receiving the signal were recorded, and if the exact time of east-bound signals between the same points were recorded, the signal traveling in the general direction of the earth's orbital motion should take slightly less time than the signal traveling in the opposite direction, if the earth's motion does make a difference in their relative speeds (and if the opposite signals follow an identical route, which is highly doubtful, since radio-paths are known to be zigzag). If we were to take the motion of the earth *with* the sun (which is thought to be some two hundred miles a second), and chose our two points on the earth's surface to lie in that general direction, we should, apparently, have a still better chance of succeeding. But even so, our clocks would have to keep step to a one hundred thousandth of a second, and our

[1] Montague suggested, in his Presidential Address, a triangular experiment, with a trained Eskimo at the North Pole to synchronize the east- and west-clocks by a radio-signal. Synchronization of the clocks would not be necessary, however, if they were going at the same *rate*.

recording apparatus to be equally efficient, to detect the very slight difference in time of the two radio-signals, if such there is. So we shall have to give up this hope for the present, simply noting that if a difference in the time taken by two opposite signals is ever *found*, it will definitely disprove the relativity-theory. It will also disprove the various hypotheses which make the velocity of light vary with the velocity of its source, and leave us, apparently, with the Lorenz-Fitzgerald contraction as an *absolute* physical fact, not a relativity-effect.

EINSTEINIAN RELATIVITY

Einstein's theory is strikingly different from those we have considered. Yet it is merely a logical deduction from the relativistic view of motion, when that is combined with the Lorenz-Fitzgerald contraction-formula (and the parallel formula for the increase in mass of a rapidly moving electron, which has been experimentally verified). If the doctrine of the relativity of motion is true, when body *A* moves, it is only relatively to body *B*, body *C*, body *D*, etc., that it moves; and it has a *different* velocity with respect to each of these variously moving bodies. Just what degree of contraction shall its lengths have, then, and what degree of increase its mass? The degree that would be calculated for its amount of motion relative to body *B*, its amount of motion relative to body *C* — or what? What can a relativist say but that its shrinkage in length and increase in mass are merely relative facts: it has one length and mass with respect to one body, other lengths and masses, with respect to other bodies. And, since relative motion is always reciprocal, these other bodies must have these same manifold contractions of length and increases of mass relative to body *A* and the other moving bodies. This might seem to some people a *reductio ad absurdum* of relativism. But Einstein boldly accepted the implication.

Now, if the Lorenz-Fitzgerald contraction is only a *relative* fact, there is *no* contraction relative to observers who have no *motion* relative to the Michelson-Morley machine. With respect to such observers, the light-rays in our illustration do *not* follow the paths $AB''A'$ and $AC''A'$; they simply follow the paths ABA and ACA; there is no shrinkage in length (and no increase in mass). But if we were observing the machine from a moving railway train, or from a distant star, we should see that with respect to *that* reference-frame the rays were taking paths of the $AB''A'$ and $AC''A'$ type; and so with respect to *that* reference-frame there has to be a Lorenz-Fitzgerald contraction, to make the light cover both paths in the same time. With respect to a faster-moving train or star, the machine (and the earth, and everything else on it) must have a *greater* contraction in length (and increase of mass). But the (relative) contraction is always proportionate to the (relative) motion, so that from *any* point of view the rays naturally would, and do, take both paths in an equal length of time.

The acute reader will have noticed that there is an implicit assumption here, the assumption that the velocity of light is the same in all directions for all the observers.... Well, if there is no absolute motion, but only the motion of bodies relative to one another, there is no reason for holding that light would travel faster with respect to one body than with respect to another, or faster in one direction than in the opposite direction. For we can just as truly consider any body as at rest, or as moving this way, or that, according to the reference-frame we choose. So

Einstein makes the assumption which we see is required by the theory, viz., that *the velocity of light is always the same, in all directions, with respect to every body.* No matter how a body changes its motion, the velocity of light relative to it remains invariant. This would be a preposterous assumption for a believer in absolute motion; but it is difficult to see what other assumption a thoroughgoing relativist could make. For in a relativistic world, there is no 'privileged' motion...The result is, that one and the same set of light-rays is traveling at its one, fixed rate *relatively to each one* of the variously moving bodies that make up the universe.

Note, now, that to keep our two paths equal to each other, we must refrain from making lengths in the *transverse* direction relative. The result is that *sizes* and *shapes* of objects are relative to the motion of the observer. A figure that is a square relatively to the body on which it lies will be an oblong relatively to a body moving with respect to it — a differently shaped and sized oblong relatively to every differently moving body. A man lying down will be shorter for people walking past him than he is for himself; standing up, he will be narrower, or thinner, for them, according to their direction of motion. The faster another person is moving past him, the shorter, or narrower, or thinner he will be for that person... Thus there is no 'real' shape or size to anything, any more than there is a real length or mass; there are simply the innumerable different shapes, sizes, and masses which it has with respect to the innumerable moving bodies in the universe. This is not a paradox, according to the relativist. For length, size, and shape "are not things inherent in the external world, they are relations of things in the external world to some specified observer." [1] In

[1] A. S. Eddington, *Space, Time, and Gravitation,* p. 34.

other words, they are relative, not absolute, characters of things; relative not merely to standard *measures*, and to other magnitudes of the same order, but *also* relative to the speed and direction of motion of the body from which they are observed.

A further implication of the theory is even more startling. Take our illustration once more. Seen from a body with respect to which our machine is moving at the rate of twelve feet a second, the transverse ray takes the path $AC''A'$, which is about 21½ feet long. Because of the contraction in the direction of motion (relative to the space-frame of our observation-post), the ray that goes forward and back, $AB''A'$, covers that same distance, 21½ feet. Since the velocity of light has been assumed to be the same for all observers, in all space-frames, light must take over seven eighths of a second to take each of these paths, *relatively to the observation-body*, although, its path being 18 feet, it takes just three fourths of a second, *relatively to the space-frame of the machine itself*. Thus, although the motion of a body does not affect time on that body, as it passes on that body itself, it does affect the time-rate on that body *relative to the time-rate on all bodies moving with respect to it*. When a hundred years have passed on earth, by our clocks, only seventy years, or twenty, or two, relatively to our time-scale, have elapsed on bodies (if such there be) moving relatively to the earth at certain calculable (but of course extremely high) velocities. Durations, like spatial magnitudes and mass, are not absolute facts, but are merely what they are relatively to the particular space-frame from which they happen to be measured.

We must never forget that all relative motion is reciprocal, and that, therefore, all changes in magnitude which are relative to motion are reciprocal. All lengths-in-the-direction-of-motion are contracted on that other body relatively to *our* lengths, at the same time that *our* lengths are contracted relatively to *their* lengths. Our clocks are going more slowly than theirs, as truly judged from *their* observation-post (since our clocks count three fourths of a second for the same event that their clocks say took over seven eighths of a second). But it is equally true that their clocks are going more slowly than ours, as truly judged from *our* observation-post.

Relative motions of visible bodies on earth are so slow that these relativity-effects cannot be detected. But the *principle* must hold in every case, if the theory is sound. Every time we walk or drive past one another, you and I must be thinner for everyone else than we are for ourselves, at the same time that they are all thinner for us than they are for themselves. Each man's watch must be going slower, from these other people's point of view, than he sees it to go, although their watches are all going lower than his, from his point of view. The hands of his watch are making a smaller number of revolutions for them than for him, and theirs a smaller number of revolutions for him than for them. Moreover, since not merely clocks and watches, but all physical processes, go at these different relative rates, each man realizes, if he is a good relativist, that all these other men are growing old more slowly than he is. Of course it is only if we could travel at tremendous speeds relatively to one another that our relative rate of senescence would be *appreciably* different. And even then, since their slower rate of senescence would be merely from our point of view, and we should be, all the time, growing old more slowly from *their* point of view, there would be no occasion for envy.

It follows from all this that there is no one universal Time or Space. There is the spatial order which is relative to the earth's tangential motion at any moment. In this frame the stars have certain shapes, sizes, and masses, and the whole stellar universe has a certain definite (though unknown) mass, occupying, altogether, a certain total volume of space. But the measurements made from any other planet, or star, would be different, and would give a different total for the mass and volume of the universe of stars. And each of these myriad sets of measurements would be equally valid, since there would be no reason for calling one list of volumes and shapes and masses any truer than another. In short, dwellers on different planets or stars dwell in measurably different spatial worlds... They dwell, likewise, in different time-orders. For observers on any planet or star would find, if they could observe events on the other planets and stars, that time is going at a different rate upon each of them, relatively to the time-rate upon the observation-body. And these time-rates which *we* establish as true for each body are different from the rates which each of *them* would establish as true... Neither in the case of Space or of Time are these mere perspective *distortions*, or subjective *appearances*. For no vantage-post in the universe has a right to call *its* measurements truer than those of any other post. If all motion is merely relative, all these sets of measurements are equally (but, of course, only relatively) true.

However, it is apparent that there is a systematic correlation between the *lengths* which are true for one frame of reference and the *durations* which are true for it. Clocks go slower as lengths grow shorter, *pari passu*. So it is possible, by lumping spatial and temporal measurements together, to find a mathematical quantity which remains constant for all frames — a constant obtained, by a similar process, whatever frame of reference is chosen. Thus, by fusing spatial and temporal measurements, Einstein has been able to find a mathematical statement for them, *in combination*, which holds true for all possible space-frames in uniform rectilinear relative motion. These are the equations which form the subject-matter of his *Special Theory of Relativity*. With their aid, if any one true set of measurements of a group of things moving together is made, the measurements which will hold for them with respect to a differently moving body can be calculated — so long as the two bodies are moving, relatively to each other, with uniform velocity in a straight line. Of course, they seldom or never are; they move in complicated curves. But even so, if all the factors that enter into their motion can be found, it should be possible to devise mathematical constants such that from true measurements for one space-frame, true measurements can be calculated which will hold for *any other* space-frame, moving in any exactly describable way with respect to it. To find such (vastly complicated) equations, is the task that Einstein has set himself in the *General Theory of Relativity*.

The mathematical constant which is obtained when spatial and temporal measurements are fused is called the "interval." If the theory is true, this is an *absolute* fact, whereas all spatial and all temporal measurements are relative. The one common Space and the one universal Time having disappeared into the jaws of relativity, we are offered Space-Time in their place... But we need not bother trying to make out what this new sort of universe is. For it is evident that no new physical reality is offered us, but merely a set of mathematical transformation-equations, which enable us to calculate one set of measurements of distances and durations from another set. The mathematical statement has become so generalized, even in the "special" theory, that it has ceased to symbolize any concrete reality; it symbolizes only a constant *relation* between reals.

SOME IMPLICATIONS OF THE THEORY

In order to make vivid the meaning of Einsteinian relativity, we will consider a few concrete implications.

A. The Multiple Centering of Light-rays

Suppose that a number of automobiles (or airplanes, or bullets, or electrons), moving in different directions, at different speeds, converge toward a point, *A*, so that they are all close to it at an instant when a light is flashed from it; they pass one another without collision, change of course, or retardation, diverging in various directions at their various speeds. Ten seconds after the flash, every point on the hollow sphere constituted by the out-traveling light-rays from the flash will be 1,860,000 miles from *each* of the moving bodies, as judged (correctly) from that body, no matter how far from one another they are by that time. One and the same set of light-rays is thus centered in many places at the same time — except, of course, that there is no "same place" or "same time" for relativity.

This is merely a concrete illustration of Einstein's fundamental postulate, the invariance of the velocity of light for all observers. But it means that being-at-the-center-of something has become a merely relative fact. And this certainly upsets our ideas of the determinateness of location in Space.

B. The Agelessness of a Beam of Light

The Lorenz-Fitzgerald contraction-formula gives the result that a body moving with the speed of light would lose all its length-in-the-direction-of-motion, and become a thing with breadth but no length. At the same time it would become infinite in mass. Relativity-theory adds to this the assertion that its journey would take *no time at all*. For all its clocks would be slowed down to the point of stopping. Nothing would *happen*; a man would never grow an hour older. For no time would elapse… But these would, of course, be only relative facts — relative to reference-frames with respect to which the body in question had this velocity.

We do not need to worry about this, however, since physical bodies, we are told, never move with that relative velocity. But light-rays do move with that velocity, relatively to *all* physical bodies. Hence time on a light-ray (relatively to *all* observers) has come to a standstill. A light-ray is a series of periodic changes. But all these changes happen at the same point-instant in Space-Time! "When two events are parts of one light-flash… the interval between the two events is zero." [1] "We must not allow ourselves to talk about the age of a beam of light." [2]

To a believer in absolute Time this is the sheerest nonsense. It helps to show that "time" has, for the two theories, two quite different meanings.

C. The Impossibility of Adding Velocities

Another implication of the theory is that we must not add velocities in a straightforward way. The speed of

[1] Bertrand Russell, *The A.B.C. of Relativity*, p. 55.
[2] P. W. Bridgman, *The Logic of Modern Physics*, p. 76.

light seems to be a limiting speed for matter. But on relativist principles, all velocity is merely relative, and no *relative* velocity can be greater than 186,000 miles a second. So when an electron in a cathode tube is shot at a speed of 150,000 miles a second, if another electron near by is shot at a similar speed in the opposite direction, their speed *relative to each other* is *not* 300,000 miles a second, but something less than 186,000 miles a second. In ordinary radioactive matter electrons (β rays) may be shot out in opposite directions simultaneously at a speed nine tenths that of light. Yet their speed relative to each other must, the theory insists, be less than that of light; their speed relative to their starting-points is already so nearly that of light that their speed relative to each other *can* be only a very little greater! And their distance apart, while moving away from each other, is scarcely greater than the distance of each from its starting-point! It would have to be so. For the theory has it that time, as well as size, vanishes at the (relative) speed of light; there is nothing worse left to happen! Indeed, nothing more can *happen*, because time has already reached a standstill.

If, however, we believe the Lorenz-Fitzgerald contraction to be an *absolute* fact, there is nothing to prevent *both* electrons from having the contraction, and their relative speed from being what ordinary mathematics would make it.

D. *The Multiple Ages of People*

To illustrate the theory of the relativity of time, let us take an imaginary case; the *principle* involved is no different from that in everyday life. Let us suppose two extremely long express trains speeding past each other at enormous velocities in opposite directions on parallel tracks extending far out into Space. As car no. 1 on train *A* passes car no. 1 on train *B*, babies are born in each of the two cars. On that same day, in train *A*, a number of babies are born, say in every millionth car. And so in train *B*. The babies grow up; the trains are still passing each other, at unaltered speed. When on train *A* sixty years have passed, by their clocks, these babies, now become gray-bearded men of sixty, think about the people on train *B* as they whizz past. Supposing the relative speed of the trains to be fast enough, it is true for them that only two years have elapsed on train *B*, and that the babies born on train *B* are now two years old.

But *on* train *B* — i.e., with respect to their *own* space-frame — those same babies are sixty years old. And as *they* look across to train *A*, they calculate that the men on train *A* are two-year old babies... According to relativity-theory, all four of these judgments are equally true. For there is no "privileged" reference-frame. It is just as true to say that these men are two years old as to say that they are sixty.

Let us venture to ask just this: Suppose cameras are pointed through the windows, as they fly past one another, at the men (babies) in the opposite trains; and suppose snapshots are possible, on super-sensitive films, at that relative speed of passing. Would the *pictures* reveal the people in the other train as they are for themselves, sixty-year-old men, or as they are for the people who are *taking* the pictures, two-year-old babies? Suppose the day on each train when all the babies on that train were born was called January 1, 1900. Then, on the day when the pictures are taken, it is 1960 on each train, for the people on that train. But it is 1902 on train *A* relatively to the time-scale of train B, and *vice versa.* Suppose calendars hanging in each train opposite the windows. Would snapshots taken from train A reveal the calendars in train B as marked 1960, or would they show the date as 1902, which it *is* there *for* the photographer? And *vice versa?* It is contrary to all sense to say that a camera could make the figures 1960 look like 1902, or make a man who is, and looks, sixty years old, for himself and his fellow-travelers, look like a baby. And if not, would not the photographs reveal that the relativity-theorists in one or both trains are *mistaken* in their judgments of the date on the other train, and of the age of the people in it? [1]

E. The Relativity of Simultaneity

Men have always supposed that there is a single universal Time-order, and that every event has a single, definite position in it. Einstein denies this, in his chapter entitled *The Relativity of Simultaneity*. And it is now universally agreed by relativists that events spatially distant from one another may have different temporal relations to one another relatively to different frames of reference. Of two such events, not too far apart in time, one is the earlier with respect to some frames of reference, and the other is the earlier with respect to other possible frames. Thus "the time-order of events is in part dependent upon the observer; it is not always and altogether an intrinsic relation between the events themselves." [2]

We have already seen that, for relativity-theory, events

---

[1] The implications of the relativity of time have often been discussed by relativists, but usually in a half-hearted and evasive way. A clean-cut exposition of the implications may be found in two articles by A. O. Lovejoy in the *Philosophical Review* for January and March, 1931 (vol. XL, pp. 48, 152).

[2] Bertrand Russell, *The A.B.C. of Relativity*, p. 44.

proceed at different time-rates (relatively to one another) on bodies in relative motion. The result is that there are local times and relative times, but no common Time. But now, this relativity of Time is shown by Einstein to be not only an hypothesis invented to explain the result of certain delicate experiments, but a logical implication of what he takes to be the "natural" *definition* of Simultaneity. Two events at a distance from each other are 'simultaneous,' he says, when light-rays from each event reach an observer situated midway between the two events at the same instant. But what do we mean by 'midway'? Since there is no absolute Space, and no one privileged set of measurements, we can only mean 'midway-as-measured-on-any-reference-frame.'

Take our express-trains passing each other on parallel tracks. A light flashes from a signal-post between the tracks just where and when the engine of train *A* is passing the billionth car of train *B*. And a light flashes from another signal-post between the tracks where and when the billionth car of train *A* is passing the engine of train *B*. A signal-man at a signal-post exactly halfway between the two posts from which flashes are sent, would see the two flashes at the same instant. Supposing the two trains to have the same speed relative to the tracks, we can see that when the flashes were sent, the five hundred millionth car of each train was passing this post. But by the time the flashes *arrive* at this post, another car, say the eight hundred millionth car of each train, is passing it. Mirrors set at right-angles to each other enable the signal-man there to see the two rays simultaneously; they also enable an observer in train *A* (or *B*) to see the rays simultaneously, if he is looking out of the window at the right moment. But since he is in the eight hundred millionth car of his train, he calculates (and *rightly*, according to relativity-theory) that the two flashes were *not* simultaneous; for in *his* space-frame (that of his train) he is *not* midway between the engine and the billionth car.   He will judge that the flash (call it *x*) which his engineer saw took place *before* the flash (*y*) which the observer in the billionth car of his train saw. Conversely, an observer in the eight hundred millionth car of train *B* would judge (correctly, from his standpoint) that flash *x* took place *after* flash *y*.

If the mention of tracks, signal-posts, and observers stationary with respect to them, smacks too much of absolute Space to seem fair, the illustration can just as well be put in terms of two processions of rockets, evenly spaced, passing each other, and a helicopter keeping to a point where identically numbered rockets of each procession pass each other.   The people in the rockets and helicopter do not know whether both processions are moving, or only one, and whether the helicopter is moving or just hovering.   (On relativistic principles there is *no difference* between these alternatives.)   So each set of observers must perforce accept its own judgments of simultaneity and time-order.   In fact, *by definition*, each set of judgments *is* correct.

The believer in absolute Time may point out that a definition of 'simultaneity' might have been given in terms of sound-signals.   In that case, imagine two cannon, a few miles apart, booming out the noon hour simultaneously, as judged by carefully synchronized earth-clocks. The successive reports are a minute apart.   A listener on the earth, midway between the cannon, hears each pair of reports simultaneously.   A traveler in a fast airplane is exactly over this midway-observer at noon, precisely.

But he hears first the cannon toward which he is flying. If he is flying at the proper speed, he will hear *two* reports from that cannon before he hears the first report from the cannon behind him. The rate of firing of the cannon in front will seem faster than the rate of the cannon behind him, the time-lapse between its reports shorter, and their time-order different from that heard by earth-observers... If we may suppose the traveler flying in a fog, and not knowing his speed of flight, his situation will be similar to that of the observer of light-signals in Einstein's world. Having nothing to correct his sound-signals by, he can only say that the reports were not simultaneous with respect to *his* frame of reference. We earth-bound observers *correct* his judgments by ours. He may even correct his own, in favor of the earth-stand-point, if he knows his speed, or if he knows that the cannon were to be fired simultaneously by earth-time. But the observer who uses *light*-signals has nothing to correct them by.

If we could correct our light-ray reports by means of signals traveling *instantaneously* (as, e.g., by telepathic communication, which many people believe to be real and to be instantaneous), we should avoid *our* conflicts of judgment. And though (unless we *can* develop telepathy), we are not in a position to supersede our differing judgments as to date and duration by knowledge as to which judgments are correct, it is easy to see that One universal Time-order *would* be revealed if there were observers of all events in telepathic (or other form of instantaneous) communication with one another.

We have been discussing in this chapter Einstein's Special Theory of Relativity, which is fairly simple, though its implications are far-reaching. It has been very widely accepted by physicists and philosophers, though, one suspects, few have clearly realized its implications, and few have clearly seen what the assumptions are upon which the theory is based. Certainly most of the popular accounts, and many of the more technical presentations of the theory, are loose in statement and seriously misleading.

The assumptions upon which the theory is based are, let us repeat, that bodies have motion only with respect to other bodies (and not with respect to Space itself, or the Ether); and that the velocity of light is invariant in all directions for all observers. These assumptions are neither necessitated nor disproved by any experiments yet made. The definition of simultaneity is, of course, like all definitions, arbitrary but legitimate; it goes neatly with the rest of the theory, which is, altogether, a self-consistent *Weltanschauung*, all the more intriguing because of its paradoxes.

The General Theory is far more difficult to understand, and its point of view even more upsetting to common sense. It is the General Theory which is supposed by relativists to be verified by Einstein's calculations as to the extent to which light-rays should be bent in passing close to the sun, and the extent of the change in the perihelion of the orbit of Mercury. But as we pointed out in Chapter XI, these corrections in the calculation of accelerations due to gravitation do not hinge upon the relativistic assumptions of their author. In fact, the importance of Einstein's calculations would not be lessened if we should discard his relativistic philosophy. It is perhaps unfortunate that it is all called by the *name* Theory of Relativity. For, great as is his mathematical genius, it is quite conceivable that his mathematics is correct but his interpretation of the physical *meaning* of his equations mistaken. Pending some decisive experiment, our decision for or against Relativity will doubtless be made according to our taste in universes!

SUGGESTED READINGS

Albert Einstein, *Relativity*, Part I.
J. H. Dotterer, *Philosophy by Way of the Sciences*, pp. 135–150.
C. D. Broad, *Scientific Thought*, III, IV.
Bertrand Russell, *The A.B.C. of Relativity*.
Herbert Dingle, *Relativity for All*.
J. H. Jeans, *Relativity*, in *Encyclopedia Britannica*, 13th ed.
J. M. Bird, ed., *Einstein's Theories of Relativity and Gravitation*, esp. III, IV.
A. S. Eddington, *The Nature of the Physical World*, pp. 5–62.
James MacKaye, *The Dynamic Universe*.

CHAPTER XV

CAUSALITY AND NATURAL LAW

SEVERAL times in our argument we have had occasion to recommend belief in something essentially unobservable on the ground that the hypothesis of its existence helps to *explain* facts that *are* observable. By 'explanation' we have meant the pointing out of *causes* adequate to account for those facts. We must now ask what we mean by 'causation.'

To understand current answers to this question, we must distinguish causation from another aspect of Nature which seems also very fundamental and somehow very closely connected with it — *natural law*. For there are two sharply contrasted tendencies in modern philosophy, the one considering causality as a mere aspect of natural law, the other considering natural law as a generalization of causality.

THREE VIEWS OF CAUSALITY

1. *Causality as an Aspect of Natural Law*

By 'natural law' we mean a uniformity of sequence in events, an undeviating habit of Nature, the invariable recurrence of similar phenomena under similar conditions. Or we may mean by the term the formulas which *state* these discoverable regularities. Such formulas are very important for human life, since they enable us to predict, and in some measure to control, future events. To accomplish anything, we must discover some of these correlations between present and future events, these routes which events follow, so as to know what preliminary steps to take to secure the desired result. 'Natural law' is simply our name for these recurrent patterns in the temporal structure of the universe.

The view we are first to discuss considers causality as a mere aspect of natural law. A 'cause' is simply the antecedent in a uniform sequence; the 'effect' is the consequent. Just as geometrical laws state the spatial correlations between objects, so causal laws state the correlations between events at different times. And that is all there is to it.

> That a certain sequence has occurred and recurred in the past is a matter of experience to which we give expression in the concept 'causation.'[1]
> Events can be collected in groups by their correlations. This is all that is true in the old notion of causality.[2]
> The metaphysical conception of a cause lingers in our manner of viewing causal laws: we want to be able to *feel* a connection between cause and effect, and to be able to imagine the cause as 'operating.' This makes us unwilling to regard causal laws as *merely* observed uniformities of sequence; yet that is all that science has to offer.[3]

This view frankly discards what common sense regards as the very essence of causation, the notion that the cause somehow *brings about* the effect. That notion is considered primitive, illegitimate, unworthy of sophisticated science. All that physics offers us is such and such equations, describing *how* events occur. There is no such thing discoverable as cause and effect in the popular sense; there is only the fact that events recur in certain ways. Mr. Russell explicitly says that the concept of 'cause' is so loose and misleading that it had better be given up altogether.

[1] Karl Pearson, *Grammar of Science*, 3d ed., p. 113.
[2] Bertrand Russell, *Philosophy*, p. 115.
[3] Bertrand Russell, *The Analysis of Mind*, p. 89.

The untrained mind looks upon the relation between cause and effect as if the cause *produces* the effect.   The cause is a kind of *agent;* it does something to the effect; there is a process of *enforcement* between the cause and the effect.... [But] the conception of cause as an *agent*, which does something to the effect, no doubt is a kind of analogy carried over to nature from our own experience as agents.   When I put forth effort and use strength in overcoming obstacles, as in moving physical objects, there is a feeling of *enforcement*, a feeling of myself as agent, effecting changes.   When we do things or suffer things done to us, there is the feeling of *power* or *force;* and so, when we see things happening in nature, we carry over this inner experience of effort, or agency, which we think causes things to happen in our own lives, and assume that causation in general is just such a case of power or enforcement.   This is called an *animistic* or *anthropomorphic* explanation of causation, explaining things in nature by our own feelings and experience.   And it is wholly unnecessary for science to make assumptions of this kind, since its end may be fully served by the observation of uniformities as seen in the mere routine of experience.[1]

Certainly we must agree that we should not, without good warrant, read our *sensations* of effort, and our own *sense* of agency, into nature.   As a matter of fact, even in the case of our own agency, it is very doubtful if the sensations of effort of which we are conscious are *causes* of what we do.   They are, more likely, reverberations, by-products.   And if they are the causes, the linkage which binds them to their effects is really as mysterious, as hidden from our observation, as any causal linkage in the outer world.

In short, we must admit that we cannot *discover* anything in *any* cause that *produces* the effect.   All we can ever find is — a series of *links;* we cannot discern the *linkage.*   Certain events regularly follow other events. But *why?*   Since we cannot answer this question, should

[1] G. T. W. Patrick, *Introduction to Philosophy*, pp. 18-19.

we not, as good empiricists, content ourselves with the observable fact of recurrent sequence?

When we say 'recurrent sequence.' we do not mean that concrete events ever exactly repeat themselves. We mean that concrete events are the exact resultant of underlying causal uniformities, so that if we had a clear grasp of all the component factors, we could predict the exact nature of the resultant event, however unique and unprecedented it might be. Causal laws are, therefore, *tendencies*, directions that events will take in so far as other tendencies are not conjoined with them to produce a convergent result.

But the definition of causation as uniformity of sequence will not quite do. For we are not willing to label as cause and effect events remote from each other in Time and Space, however regularly the one may follow the other. A thousand alarm-clocks quite regularly go off at 7 A.M.; shortly thereafter a thousand workers more or less reluctantly get out of bed. However unfailing the sequence between these many alarms and this or that person's rising, only *one* of the signals is really the *cause* of his rising. Even then, there must be air-waves from the reverberating bell, and ears that function, and, in short, a whole series of intervening events, if we are to admit a causal relation. We do, indeed, speak of remote causes, but only in the sense that they produced events which, in turn, produced other events, which finally resulted in the effect in which we are interested. When speaking guardedly, we agree quite generally that a cause must be contiguous to its effect in Space and Time.

May we not agree, then, that wherever there is an undeviating route of procedure in Nature, the earlier of two consecutive links in the procedure is to be called 'cause,' and the later of the two is to be called 'effect'?

2. *Causality as an Individual Occurrence*

But, after all, why should we limit causality to *recurrent* tendencies? When I decide to do something, is not my decision a cause of my deed, even if, as many hold, my will is an independent variable, obeying no uniformities of behavior? Could conformity to law make it any more a case of causation? If God created the world, was not his fiat the cause of its coming into being, though the event was not a case of any recurrent tendency? If miracles happen, surely they are caused, though, by very definition, they are not cases of natural law. It is not necessary to discuss here whether any such cases actually occur; it is sufficient to realize that they may be conceived to occur, and that, therefore, causation *means* something other than the prior fact in a recurrent sequence. And, in fact, we very often recognize the presence of causation when we have no intimation of any natural law. This does not prove that it may not *be* a case of natural law, it simply proves that, in common usage, causation means something quite different from uniformity of sequence.

The converse of this is also true. We may admit a relation of uniform sequence where we do not admit causality. Day has always followed night, in human experience; yet we do not call night the cause of day. There is a theory (to be presently discussed) which holds that facts of conscious experience are never causes of physical events, however unvarying the correlation between them. A sensation of dazzling light is always followed by a wink of the eyelids; but the cause of the wink is a physical event, a nerve-current from brain to eye, which, in turn, was caused by an antecedent physical event, and so on back; the *sensation* is not, itself, a *cause* of anything. Now, whether or not this theory is true, it shows that we *mean* something else by 'causation' than uniform sequence.

In short, causality is one fact, invariability of recurrence is another fact — even if the two facts actually always go together. To explain a given case of cause-and-effect by saying that it is a case of a given natural law is not to *explain* it at all. Why it should happen thus over and over again is, indeed, a question; but a more ultimate question is why it happens *once*. If we could understand a single case of causation, we should doubtless see why it *always* happens that way — if it does.

Suppose, then, we define causation, with C. J. Ducasse, as "the relation between two events when the first event was the only change occurring immediately *before*, and *contiguous* to the place of, the second." Such a definition implies nothing beyond the individual event. If there is a natural law, we discover it by *generalizing* from individual cases of causation.

Most of us will feel that this is better. But have we done anything more here than to locate what we mean by a 'cause'? Have we even tried to say what the relation which we call 'causation' *is?* And may there not be cases in which this definition breaks down? Let us take a case which Ducasse himself suggests: A brick hits a window; at the same instant the air-waves from a canary's song hit the window; the window breaks. We should naturally say that the impact of the brick caused the window to break, and that the impact of the sound-waves did *not* cause it, though both events occurred

contiguously, in Space and Time, to the event which was
the breaking of the window, and therefore, by the definition, have equal right to be considered as cause of that
event.

Ducasse's answer to this (put very briefly) is, that,
considering this particular concrete case, the impact of
the air-waves *is* a part of the 'cause,' since it is a part of
what happened in the immediate environment immediately before. But when we consider what is common to
cases of this *sort*, cases of the breaking of windows, we
find that something of the general nature of an impact
by a solid substance occurs as a cause over and over
again, whereas the sound-wave-impact may just as well
not occur. So, if we say that the canary's song was not
a part-cause of the breaking of the window, we really
mean (or should mean) that the song "had nothing to
do with what occurred *in so far as what occurred is viewed
merely as a case of breakage of a window.*" [1]

This is subtle, but to many of us not convincing. We
feel that the term 'cause' implies *competence to produce
an effect;* and that the canary's song had no such competence. We feel there must be some sort of equivalence
between cause and effect, some force, some push, some
bond — and not a mere juxtaposition. There must be
some reason why a particular cause produces a particular
effect. Causation, we feel, is not just a series of links,
it is the *linkage* that joins the links. Physics, to be sure,
cannot discover this linkage; physics is, as we have already noted, very limited in what it can find. But the
fact that we have no way of discovering the nature of
causal linkage, or that we cannot even define clearly
what we mean by it, is no indication that there is not

[1] *The Journal of Philosophy*, vol. 23, p. 67.   Italics in original.

something *there*, some pushiness, something dynamic, efficacious, which *brings about* the effect. When we are told that a cause is an event immediately prior and contiguous, we feel that we are being pointed to the cause, told where to look for it, but are not being told what causation *is*.

3. *Causality as Efficacy*

The concept of 'causation' roots back into our very primitive experience of being in the presence of Powers that threaten us, that are likely to *do* something to us. And into the equally primitive experience of being able to do something, ourselves, to other people and to physical things. In short, it stems from the *active* side of our experience. It implies realism, and is one of its supports. In spite of Kant's endeavor to persuade us that causation is a merely subjective category, most of us continue to feel that it is one of the most objective of facts. We speak of causes because we feel ourselves *shoved*, this way and that, and we shove back. All this is much earlier and more fundamental than the conception of natural law, or the emasculated concept of merely contiguous events. The fact seems to be that causes are observable all about us, in the rough, although to find out *exactly* what the causes of events are, in fine detail, is a matter for patient scientific investigation. And to understand *why* certain causes produce certain events eludes us entirely. *Causes* are observable, but *causation* (the linkage between cause and effect) is not observable.

Unless, however, there *were* some linkage, some bond, some power that *makes* events follow these particular sequences, the recurrences would be, as Montague says, merely "outrageous runs of luck"; and the course of

Nature would cease to be even theoretically explicable.

> Not to assume a causative process behind the causal relation is to abandon the postulate of *explanation*, the hope nourished by most philosophers of discovering in what manner and by what means one event manages to influence another.[1]

There is a strong tendency in contemporary philosophy to believe, so far as it is feasible, only in what is observable. But most philosophers, as Mr. Loewenberg says, have sided with common sense in this matter of believing that there is more to causation than can be observed. For example:

> We have no definite idea of what we mean by cause, or of what causality consists in. But the principle expresses a demand for *some* deeper sort of inward connection between phenomena than their merely habitual time-sequence seems to be. The word 'cause' is, in short, an altar to an unknown god; an empty pedestal still marking the place of a hoped-for statue.[2]

> It seems to me very plain that, whatever the obscurities of its meaning, there is a sense attaching to the term causality in its everyday usage which cannot be satisfied to drop the reference to a connecting bond, or to effective agency.[3]

We need not be too much abashed if we cannot define what we mean by 'causation' except in synonymous phrases — e.g., that causation is the process of *bringing about* results, of *effecting* changes. The ultimate things — such as Existence, Time, Space, Sentience, Happiness — are indefinable; for there is nothing more ultimate in terms of which to define them. All we can do is to talk about them in such a way that our hearers shall guess what we are talking about; and to refuse to be satisfied

---

[1] J. Loewenberg, *University of California Publications in Philosophy*, vol. 15, p. 27.

[2] William James, *Principles of Psychology*, vol. 2, p. 671.

[3] A. K. Rogers, *What is Truth?* p. 143.

with definitions which leave out the essence of what we mean. Causation seems to be one of these ultimate things. Perhaps we shall never understand the inner *go* of it. But at least we can refuse to let philosophers palm off on us as definitions phrases which omit the very kernel of the fact to which we refer.

TWO VIEWS OF NATURE

1. *Nature as Determinate*

A 'natural law,' we have said, is a uniformity of procedure in Nature. If we believe in causation in the third sense, just discussed, we shall believe that natural laws exist because the very essence of causation is such that a certain cause must inevitably produce a certain specific effect. Whenever such and such causes exist, such and such effects will necessarily follow. It is not a *logical* necessity; we should not be guilty of self-contradiction if we asserted the existence of a certain antecedent and also the existence of a consequent different from that which experience shows to be brought into being. It is a *causal* necessity, which we can learn only from patient observation and careful experiment.... And now, our question is, Is the whole course of Nature a tissue of such causal connections? Does everything happen in accordance with natural law?

If the answer is Yes, this uniformity of Nature, this 'reign' of natural law, is one of the most fundamental and striking facts about the universe. It means that the world is through and through orderly, a cosmos, not a chaos. The apparent confusion of events is merely due to the extreme complexity of the tissue of underlying uniformities. There is no chance, no caprice, no real uncertainty, in the history of the universe, except, perhaps, in the original set-up from which everything else has rigorously followed. The strangest happenings are as orderly as the most familiar routines; they are merely the result of a less usual group of antecedents. Causes never operate alone; but effects follow, calculably, from the convergence of all the causes that operate at a given point at a given moment. So, if we had a complete knowledge of the stuff of the universe, and of its arrangement, at any one date (including, of course, a knowledge of all the changes which the innumerable units are in process of undergoing at that date), and if we had a complete knowledge of all the causal laws in accordance with which changes occur, and the brain-power necessary to make the enormously intricate calculations required, we could *deduce* the history of the universe from that moment on. The poet was right in declaring that

> the first morning of creation wrote
> What the last dawn of reckoning shall read.

What reason have we for holding such a sweeping view? Sequences there are, all about us, in Nature; primitive man must have recognized them. Summer follows spring, and autumn follows summer. Fire burns, water runs downhill, things operate according to their several, unchanging natures. Yet there seems also, to the plain man, to be a considerable measure of caprice in Nature; and he is not greatly surprised when things turn out in unexpected ways. The growing belief, in modern times, in the regularity of Nature is a result of the increasing triumphs of science in *finding* regularity underneath the surface-appearance of confusion. In addition, the simplicity, and the sublimity, of the conception appeal to many minds; it gives to many an esthetic, and even a quasi-religious thrill. We enjoy the contemplation of so marvelous a cosmos. And, of course, it is only if, and so far as, Nature *is* orderly, and her processes essentially predictable, that we can hope to master our environment and turn it to our uses. With chaos, with chance, with caprice there is nothing to be done. So idealists, if they are *practical* idealists, and not mere dreamers, usually *hope* that Nature is uniform in her processes and therefore dependable in manipulation.

The whole progress of science depends upon the discovery of uniformities; where they are undiscoverable, there can be no science. It is not uncommon, therefore, to hear the doctrine spoken of as a 'necessary postulate of science.'... But to 'postulate' something is merely to assume it, not to make it so, or to prove that it is so. In other words, scientists work with the hope, and expectation, of finding more and more uniformity in Nature. But they cannot know in advance how much there is to find. And even if there is a certain amount of free play in Nature, they have plenty to do in discovering and formulating such laws as there are. We might have a good deal of indeterminateness in Nature without driving science to bankruptcy.

There is, clearly, an enormous amount of evidence for this and that specific law. But there is also a good deal of apparent evidence for exceptions to many of these laws. And for no law is the evidence *complete*. That is to say, a single instance where the law *doesn't* hold may, for all we can say, turn up at any time. And one such clearly proved instance would be enough to upset any law. Bertrand Russell points out that a chicken who has been fed every day of his life by his owner might very well assume it to be a natural law that he should thus be fed; but one fine morning the man wrings his neck. So, for all we know, Nature may some day surprise us by acting in a way totally different from that which we have set forth as her unvarying 'law.'... And we must add, in honesty, that in some fields of inquiry very little uniformity has as yet been found. The scientist's big talk of the universal reign of natural law is a matter more of faith than of works.

Still, we may fairly claim a certain *presumption* in favor of the doctrine. It does seem to be true, in general, that the more nearly alike things are, the more nearly alike they act; whence we may properly suspect that whenever things are exactly alike (as the ultimate units of existence may perhaps be), they act in exactly the same way. We never do have two complex things, two things of observable size, exactly alike. For even the purest bit of a 'homogeneous' substance contains so many millions of millions of millions of units, moving at such enormous speeds, and weaving so intricate and rapidly changing a pattern, that its similarity to other bits of the 'same' substance is only roughly statistical. But such bits of an elementary substance come far *closer* to identical behavior in similar situations than bits of matter chosen at random. By choosing 'pure' substances we are approaching uniformity of behavior. And the farther we analyze things down to their minute components, the more uniformity we find. From all this a presumption arises that differences in *behavior* follow from differences of *structure*, and that the underlying warp and woof of Nature is utterly regular and unfailing in its pattern.

The *mechanistic* view of Nature is the simplest, though by no means the only, variety of determinism. It asserts that every event in Nature is, at bottom, a mere rearrangement of the ultimate particles, according to the laws of mechanics. Nothing ever happens but motion. No new stuff is ever created, but merely new complexes of the original units. The properties of the complexes are the strict resultant of the motions of these ultra-microscopic units. There are probably but a few simple 'laws,' but they result in innumerable different combinations under the changing conditions of their mutual interactions. We are far from understanding every physical event in such terms; probably we shall have to penetrate more deeply than we have yet done into the fine texture of matter and the ether before we can see why things happen as they do. But (except for mental events, which seem irreducible to material particles in motion) it is conceivable that everything that happens is mechanically explicable. Just as all European literature consists of nothing but twenty-six letters in innumerable combinations, so the whole complex universe may be built up out of vast numbers of simple units of only a few kinds, perpetually acting in accordance with a few simple principles.

At any rate, whether the mechanistic conception is valid or not, science is daily extending the range wherein we can see law at work, finding new laws in old fields, and finding laws in fields which remained for long hopelessly complex and perplexing. So it *may* be that the appearance of confusion and uncertainty in things is simply a result of our ignorance. Our remote descendants will perhaps unravel all these remaining secrets of Nature and convince themselves that she nowhere indulges in any willfulness or caprice.

2. *Nature as Indeterminate*

But it is hope against hope! For there are many first-rate minds to whom the thought of such a cut-and-dried 'block universe' is intolerable. William James was one of these, and, in our day, Bergson, Driesch, and plenty of other thinkers. These crave a world in which there is free play, where events may sprout out in new ways, without being hampered by their past. And they have a good deal to say, to balance against the presumption which we have just granted. Most of these arguments we must leave for discussion in some later context; so we cannot, in this chapter, reach any conclusion. But we can at least indicate the various types of evidence that are offered, and deal with several arguments to which we shall not need to recur.

In the first place, there is the evidence for *miracles*. Miracles are, by very definition, *exceptions* to whatever natural law there may be in the situation. But they are so frankly exceptional that, even if they exist now and then, they throw no light on the general question. We can admit, if we are convinced, the fact of this or that miracle, and believe very heartily in natural law, simply believing that miracles are cases of the *violation* of natural law by a supernatural Power. Indeed, if it is, otherwise, a strictly determinate universe, miracles must stand out all the more conspicuously, and be the more easily proved to be miracles. Hence the belief in natural law should be a welcome background for those who would convince us of the really miraculous nature of this or that event.... The reader who wishes, while engaged with this chapter, to consider all the relevant considerations, may turn at this point to our discussion of miracles, on p. 423.

Next we should consider the belief of the vitalists in an

'entelechy' or 'vital force,' which enables living organisms to breast the current of natural law. And the similar, but more restricted, belief of the indeterminists, those who hold that human beings, at least, have an undetermined free will, which introduces a new and incalculable factor into natural events. This matter so touches us all, and has become such an involved traditional controversy, that we shall devote to it a whole chapter (Chapter XXII). Bergson's *élan vital* is a quasibiological, essentially incalculable, force assumed to influence the whole course of Nature, as well as the life of organisms. But as it is essentially the same thing as the 'entelechy' of the vitalists, and based upon essentially the same sort of evidence, we shall include it in our discussion of vitalism, in Chapter XVII.

Many students of Nature hold that in the course of cosmic evolution new, unpredictable things come into being, not mere resultants of earlier processes and already existing laws. This view is called 'emergent' or 'creative' evolution. We shall discuss it briefly in the chapter following this.

In Chapter XXIII we shall discuss the view that Nature is 'teleological'; i.e., that she embodies, or realizes, *purpose;* the view that all things, or at least some things, work together to achieve desirable *ends.* Such a realization of purpose is often thought to be incompatible with determinism; the two views, the teleological and the deterministic, are often contrasted as antithetical. But there seems to be no good reason for erecting this antithesis. An absolutely determinate universe might be teleological, the *whole process* being headed toward some desirable consummation. And, of course, an indeterminate universe might be entirely without purpose, except for the separate purposes cherished by the living organisms which it brings forth. So we may lay aside this matter for the moment as irrelevant to our present discussion.

A totally different sort of argument against a deterministic conception of the universe is based upon the radical empiricism so much in vogue. Things must be taken to be what they are experienced as.

> The only character of the future that adequately identifies the temporal direction toward it is just its indefiniteness, its unsettled character. To object that this is merely human limitation or ignorance is to desert the empirical criterion altogether, and then all things may (verbally) be asserted without fear of confrontation with any contradictory evidence, even any evidence that the words employed are not unmeaning or self-contradictory.... An open future is the only kind of future we can experience or imagine; it cannot, therefore, be transcended without explaining away what is to be explained.[1]

The future is open, undecided yet, as a matter of actual experience!... But we have not yet experienced the future; we only imagine, and prophesy it. It seems undecided to us, because we cannot calculate the result of all the complex forces now in operation. Surely that may be just because of our ignorance. Certainly, in many cases where the future seemed, when it was still future, quite ambiguous, we have later come to see that it had to be what it was when it became the present, because causes were in existence which would, inevitably, have brought about such and such results. Perhaps with completer knowledge we should see that to be always the case.

Another empirical argument points to the fact that we all, actually, believe in chance; we talk of possibility and

[1] Charles Hartshorne, Journal of Philosophy, vol. 29, p. 429.

probability. But in a determinate universe there is no room for chance. And there is no such status as 'possibility' or 'probability'; whatever happens is inevitable, and any describable event either will or will not occur. Should we not, then, in consistency, uproot these concepts from our thought, or else give up the concept of a completely determined universe?

No. For these terms can be interpreted in full consistency with the deterministic view. The word 'chance' can be used in the following senses by a determinist:

(*a*) As referring to our ignorance. In 'games of chance' we cannot foretell which way dice will fall, or where the roulette wheel will stop, simply because we cannot compute the very delicate balance of forces involved. We do not (necessarily) believe that there are not laws which determine these events. We simply mean that *for us* — i.e., relatively to our knowledge and powers of prediction — they are chance events.

(*b*) As referring to the meeting of two causal series not hitherto related. If I walk past a building in winter, and a snow-slide just hits me on the head, I say it is a matter of chance. I do not (necessarily) doubt that there were causes that led me to that exact point at that moment, and that there were causes that loosened the snow and made it fall at that precise moment. I simply mean that the two sets of events were, up to that moment, causally unrelated to each other.

So when, in discussing evolution, we speak of 'chance variation,' we do not (necessarily) mean that there were not causes for the appearance of these variations. We simply mean that these causes were quite another set of events from those other causal processes that we summarize by the phrase 'natural selection.' Two separate lines of events, hitherto unrelated causally, conjoin to produce the fact of evolution.

(c) As referring to statistical frequency. We ask what chance there is of our throwing double sixes. The answer is the ratio of the number of times double sixes turn up to the number of times they do not turn up, out of a great many throws. Experience shows that, if the number of throws is large enough, the number of times that any one combination turns up is pretty accurately predictable, though on a single throw the result is, as we say, 'pure chance.' This statistical frequency certainly suggests that events of this sort, at least, are definitely law-abiding. For it is difficult to see how statistical laws can hold unless the individual cases, with all their diversity, are really following underlying causal laws.

Similarly, when we say that a given event is 'possible,' all we need to mean is that it may happen, *for all we know*. If we call it 'probable,' we mean that, in view of what we know, we should be better advised to bet on its happening than on its not happening. These terms, like the term 'chance,' are, usually, relative to our knowledge and ignorance.

Or, more objectively, we may say that possibility and probability are relative to a given *set of data*. Given such and such facts, a certain event is possible; i.e., it is consistent with them, it may happen so far as they are concerned. As more and more relevant facts are added to the data, the event becomes more and more probable, or improbable, until some decisive fact is added which makes the event inevitable, or impossible. This does not imply that there is any indeterminateness in the scheme of things as a whole; it simply means that an incomplete set of facts, taken alone, may not suffice to determine a given event.

The 'theory of probability' deals with the statistical frequencies of which we have spoken, and is therefore rather a support of the deterministic conception than an obstacle in the way of its acceptance.

But while these are clear and legitimate uses of these terms, consistent with a deterministic view of the universe, we must not beg the question by assuming that it is illegitimate to use them also as meaning the partial absence of law, the existence of radical variability.

Finally, we must deal with the statement not infrequent in the last few years that science itself is abandoning the deterministic view, chiefly because of the 'uncertainty principle' formulated by Heisenberg. It seems, from certain experiments which we cannot here describe, that there is a definite limit to the accuracy with which *both* the position and velocity of an electron can be determined. The more precise our location of its position, the vaguer our knowledge of its velocity must be, and *vice versa*. Therefore, it is said, the electron *has* no precise location, or velocity, and the world is not so determinate as we thought.

For that matter, we have no way, at present, of predicting when a given electron will jump from one orbit to another, or when a given radium atom will break up. These events are, for all we can yet see, quite arbitrary and willful. All we can do is to estimate the *probability* that a given electron or atom will act thus and so at a given time.

However, we do have calculable probabilities. We find, for example, that a very definitely predictable proportion of the number of atoms in a given mass of radium will break up in a certain definite time. And these statistical regularities certainly suggest an underlying set of determinate laws. In any case, the only reason for supposing that these ultra-microscopic events are indeterminate is that we have, as yet, *found* no law which expresses their individual movements, and cannot, as yet, predict them. Very likely these events are on too fine a scale, and too rapid, for us ever to reach the point of individual predictions. But it seems quite illogical to deduce from that the conclusion that the events are, themselves, indeterminate by nature.

The discussion is only begun, however; and the reader is counseled to keep an open mind on this matter, at least until the arguments we have postponed have been considered.

SUGGESTED READINGS

Bertrand Russell, *Philosophy*, XI. *The Analysis of Mind*, V.
Bertrand Russell, *Mysticism and Logic*, IX.
C. D. Broad, *Perception, Physics, and Reality*, II.
W. K. Clifford, *Lectures and Essays: Aims of Scientific Thought.*
Karl Pearson, *The Grammar of Science*, IV.
R. W. Sellars, *Essentials of Philosophy*, XXIII.
G. T. W. Patrick, *Introduction to Philosophy*, pp. 18–23.
W. F. Cooley, *Principles of Science*, VIII.
E. S. Brightman, *Introduction to Philosophy*, VIII.
G. W. Cunningham, *Problems of Philosophy*, IX.
M. R. Cohen, *Reason and Nature*, pp. 206–230.

CHAPTER XVI

EVOLUTION

WHETHER or not the fine texture of which large-scale events are composed invariably exhibits those stereotyped and theoretically predictable regularities to which we give the label of 'natural law,' and whether or not all changes of physical bodies are analyzable into changes of position of their elementary units, and so are, at bottom, merely changes in structure, at least it seems to be true that the whole known universe is in incessant change, and so has not only a spatial pattern, but a temporal pattern, a history. Our question now is, Is the history of things an evolution? or, To what extent is it an evolution?

WHAT DO WE MEAN BY 'EVOLUTION'?

The term 'evolution' is loosely used in a variety of senses. But it is generally applied only to long-scale processes. We hardly speak of the evolution of an individual, from birth to death; we speak rather of his development, his growth, his biography. We speak of the evolution of man, the evolution of democracy, the evolution of the solar system.

There are two essential marks of a process that is to be called an evolution. It must be a causally continuous process, each step growing out of the preceding. If there are breaks, discontinuities, an interpolation of new laws or substances, it is, in so far, not *evolution*. And it must be a one-way process, moving on from one state of existence to something new and different. A mere repetition of episodes, with no general trend, such as the daily movement of the tides, or the irregular fluctuations of the weather, is not a case of evolution. Nor is a cyclical process, like the recurrent rhythm of the seasons or the precession of the equinoxes. The term 'evolution' implies the appearance of some new pattern, or type, as the result of a long series of causally continuous changes.

Many writers have given the word a further connotation as implying a change from a lesser to a greater complexity. This usage is fostered by the fact that many of the most conspicuous longer trends which we observe are of this sort. But if the term is used in this more limited sense, other long-scale processes, which would otherwise be called evolutionary, have to be given another name. A trend from the more to the less complex may be called 'devolution,' or 'dissolution.' And trends which are partly of one sort and partly of the other have to be called partly evolution and partly devolution. On the whole, it is more convenient to let the word 'evolution' cover both trends. For the question concerning the relative complexity of structures is secondary to the question concerning causal continuity and one-way development.

Moreover, a definition of 'evolution' in terms of growing complexity tends to make us assume that the history of organic forms, and of the universe, is necessarily, or normally, of that sort, and thus to beg an important question. As a matter of fact, some organic types have become *less* complex, at least in certain respects, than their ancestral types. The horse, for example, has solid hoofs today, instead of the five-toed feet of his ancestors, and many prehistoric forms, of great complexity, vanished and left their place to simpler forms. In the inorganic realm, we know that radio active substances are continuously breaking up into their simpler constituents; and we suspect that in the terribly hot interiors of the stars matter itself is constantly being transmuted into the simpler form of radiant energy. Of course we can say that, in so far, the horse was not 'evolving'; and the inorganic processes we have mentioned can be thought of as a counter-current to evolution. But this is a bit dangerous. For the idea of evolution has great prestige. And whatever is rejected as not a part of the 'evolutionary' process tends to be thought of as abnormal, or exceptional, a mere eddy in the current. So it is best to let the term 'evolution' cover, without antecedent expectations, whatever gradual changes of structure we actually find.

We must be particularly on our guard, then, against supposing that 'evolution' implies 'progress,' 'improvement,' the production of continually 'higher' and 'higher' forms. We shall raise the question, in our final chapter, whether, as a matter of fact, the process of cosmic evolution, or the episode of organic evolution on earth, is a process of betterment, of progress toward some desirable goal, the production of more and more *value*. But we must certainly beware of assuming that at the outset, or implying it by our use of the term 'evolution.' The mere fact that certain types have yielded place to others does not imply that the later types are better; we must avoid what Santayana calls the "idolatry of success," and a "conscience enslaved to chronology."

ORGANIC EVOLUTION

The term 'evolution' was first used, and is oftenest used, to refer to the process which has slowly altered the

types of organisms existing upon our earth. This process
has produced organisms far more *complex* than those which
first came into existence on earth, and a very great *variety*
of co-existing types. But many simple, perhaps quite
primitive, types exist by the side of the later-developed
types; and in some cases, as we have said, more complex
types have given way to less complex. The process, as a
whole, cannot be described in any simple formula; in
fact, it has consisted in a great number of more or less
different processes going on simultaneously. The time
occupied by the process has been quite certainly in the
neighborhood of a billion years, perhaps considerably
longer. Doubtless it got under way as soon as conditions on the cooling and growing earth became favorable
for such a delicately balanced and unusual development
of events. Organic life was far advanced when the first
traces were left that we now find. Since then at least a
twenty-mile thickness of sedimentary rock has been
formed by the slow processes of erosion, carriage to the
sea by streams, and hardening there under the pressure
of superposed layers.

A large part of this long period was doubtless spent in
developing organic cells, the units of which plants and
animals consist. The cell is a highly complex mechanism
containing the most complex molecules of protein and
protoplasm very intricately arranged. Under the stress
of what forces, and by what stages, cells were formed and
elaborated we can but vaguely guess. They had no hard
skeleton and could leave no fossil remains. Doubtless
a great number of cellular and quasi-cellular forms came
into existence and perished before some lucky structure
fell into an equilibrium which could maintain itself.
Whether many, or only one, of these primitive cells de-

veloped a mechanism of division, so that its kind could multiply, and thus became the parent of all further organic forms, we cannot now say. There may be, for all we know, a number of different ancestral lines, from the very beginning, accounting for the myriad types of organism now extant. But it is certain that all the larger organisms have developed from very tiny and relatively simple ancestral forms, and that many, if not all, existing species have a common ancestry.

The fundamental achievement of organic life was the power of self-maintenance of a complicated mechanism under varying circumstances, through balanced processes of nutrition and excretion. Next came the power of division, each of two or more parts reproducing the original cell-form. Cells thus multiplying into aggregates gradually became differentiated in form and function; outer cells, being more affected by their environment, became bark, or shell; inner cells specialized in assimilation of food, and so on. From this time on there must have been innumerable lines of development, each group of cells, under the stress of inner and outer forces, growing in its own unique way. Most of them doubtless perished and left no trace. But here and there a group of cells functioning together — an 'organism' — was able to withstand dissolution long enough to reproduce itself and thus give rise to a line of descendants. An early demarcation divided the *plants*, which feed on relatively simple inorganic matter, transforming it by means of solar energy into their own complex molecules, and the *animals*, which feed on plants and other animals, breaking down their complex molecules and using the energy thus released. For this latter purpose — certainly for land-forms — mobility is important; and the animal branch

of the organic world early developed mechanisms of
locomotion, by means of which suitable food could be
sought. Plants, living on soil, water, and sunshine,
remained rooted in one spot.

The animals proved the more progressive line; among
them great further changes took place. Certain surface-
cells became increasingly sensitive to the air- and ether-
waves that beat upon them. Other cells, by lengthening
out, began to communicate the disturbances of the outer
cells to inner cells. Thus originated sense-organs and
nerves; the place where the nerves met became a brain.
This mechanism, even when rudimentary, permitted
reactions of the organism to its environment much more
elaborate and specific than had hitherto been possible.
Optical, auditory, olfactory, tactile, and pain-messages
were developed, and appropriate movements signaled
from the central nervous exchange to the motor organs.

The long series of changes that took place in the numerous lines of descent can be found described — by a
liberal use of conjecture — in the textbooks of biology.
Fossils tell us much of the story. But, of course, there
are many gaps in the record, since it is only rarely and
by accident that a skeleton or footprint is fossilized;
and the earth's rocks have been so bent and crushed and
eroded during these millions of years that far the greater
part of the fossils formed have been destroyed. Fortunately we have various other lines of evidence to help us
fill out these gaps. Embryology and comparative anat-
omy offer us clues; a study of the geographical distribution of types, and a study of vestigial organs —
remnants of organs useful to some long-vanished ancestor
— give supplementary facts. Altogether, we can trace
the line of man's descent from primitive life-forms in

surprising detail, as well as the genealogy of the other
types of organism, of which there are a million or two
now extant.

We cannot consider this evidence in detail. But since
certain religious bodies are still opposing the teaching of
evolution, even to the point of getting legislation pro-
hibiting it upon the statute-books of some of our states,
it may be worth while to note that the evidence for the
fact of organic evolution has long since been overwhelming. The National Association for the Advancement of
Science some years ago adopted a statement declaring
that "no scientific generalization is more strongly supported by thoroughly tested evidences"; the proofs for
the evolution of man "are sufficient to convince every
scientist of note in the world." The conservative *En-
cyclopædia Britannica* summed up the matter in its
Eleventh Edition:

> The discovery of a single fossil creature in a geological
> stratum of a wrong period, the detection of a single anatomical
> or physiological fact irreconcilable with origin by descent
> with modification, would have been destructive of the theory
> and would have made the reputation of the observer. But
> in the prodigious number of supporting discoveries that
> have been made no single negative factor has appeared, and
> the evolution from their predecessors of the forms of life
> existing now or at any other period must be taken as proved.

Sometimes one hears it said, in disparaging tones, that
evolution is "only a theory." The fact is, of course, that
every belief in past events is, strictly speaking, a mere
theory. It is conceivable that the earth, with all its apparent evidences of a long history, was created a few
thousand years ago — or, for that matter, yesterday.
But it is arbitrary to believe in the past history of the
earth and its inhabitants, as the evidence shows it to

have been, from a certain point on, and not all the way back. The evidence for the evolutionary process during the past hundreds of millions of years warrants belief in that process just as surely as our evidence for the facts of human history during the past few thousand years warrants belief in the reality of that history. It is not true that the 'special creation' theory offers an equally good alternative explanation. That theory, which has come down to us from a pre-scientific age, offers an explanation of the existence of various organic species, but it has no good explanation of a wide variety of specific facts, such as the relationships between the different fossils in a series, the preservation of antique types in isolated islands, the facts concerning vestigial organs, embryonic 'recapitulation' of ancestral forms, blood-relationships, inter-fertility, and so on.

What is in doubt among scientists is not the fact of evolution, or, in general, the lines of descent, but the *causes* and *method* of evolution. It was here that the genius of Darwin led the way. The process of *natural selection* is generally accepted as, if not the only method, at least the most conspicuous and telling method of evolution. This process may be summarized as follows:

An organic body is so complex and delicate a mechanism, and is subjected to so individual an environment, that the offspring of common parents are never exactly like their parents or one another. Each new individual, at birth, varies slightly, sometimes considerably, from the parent type. These variations are inherited, with further variation, by the next generation. In this way a wide range of organic forms would rapidly come into existence were it not for the stern weeding-out which is effected by the environment. Organic forms have a precarious tenure of life at best; any variation that unfits an individual for living and reproducing is quickly eliminated by the death of its possessor. And more than that, there is a fierce competition for survival among the many individuals born; in the long run, the more efficient ones outlive the others. Among many of the lower forms of life only one out of a million lives long enough to reproduce its kind; any variation in any one of the million that gives it a better chance to live than its rivals have will therefore tend to become common in a few generations. The fertility of most lower forms of life is amazing, the period between generations very short (sometimes only a few hours), and the waste of life tremendous. The result is what is called 'the survival of the fittest.'

The rigor of the physical environment gives an advantage to those types that develop hardihood, or some protective structure. The limited quantity of nutrition favors those that learn to live on a new diet or develop better facilities for finding and securing food. Parasites and disease-giving microbes destroy those that fail to develop superior resistance. Beasts of prey devour those that lag in developing speed of flight, unpalatability, protective coloring, skill in hiding, or means of self-defense. Whenever a vantage-ground of any sort is attained by any fortunate variation in some individual's genes (the minute structures which determine heredity), its descendants will start with that advantage. Some will vary in a retrograde direction and perish, a few may vary still farther to their advantage and develop the type further in that direction. Slight as the individual variations usually are, it does not take many generations of cumulative changes to produce a marked alteration of type. Some lines will survive because of superior fertility; some because of superior strength or speed; some because of keener eyesight, or sense of smell, or hearing; others for a thousand other reasons. So, in the long course of time the primitive forms of organic life have diverged into the million or two existing species. The course of evolution resembles the growth of a tree, which from one little shoot grows, without break in continuity, into hundreds of diverging branches. A look at the tree at any moment would reveal no change in form. But slowly, from day to day, the twigs grow farther and farther apart.

Various other factors have been suggested to account for the evolutionary process — not instead of, but in addition to, natural selection. Sexual selection doubtless plays a part, though not a very important one. Other alleged factors, such as 'orthogenesis,' a supposed tendency toward variation in a certain specific direction, are not well substantiated. Natural selection, working on random germ-plasm variations, is clearly the chief factor in organic evolution. There is no doubt about the reality of this process and its ability to account for a great deal. The question is whether it has been supplemented by this or that other set of causes. There is still vigorous controversy over the question whether characters acquired by an organism during its lifetime can be transmitted to its descendants. It is not easy to imagine how this can happen, since the germ-plasm, which gives rise to the next generation, has a very isolated existence. And though there is considerable evidence for the fact, it is probably not — if it exists at all — a very important factor. Evolution by natural selection is the main thing.

COSMIC EVOLUTION

Long as the story of organic evolution on earth may seem, it is but a brief episode in the cosmic life. And we come now to ask, Is this series of alterations in the types of bodies existing for a while on this insignificant planet, as it swings between a fiery star and the black abyss of Space, all there is to evolution? If there are other planets, somewhere in the wide universe, with similar stories, must we say that these sporadic and transient planetary dramas are alone deserving of this name? Or has our solar system, and our galaxy, an evolution? And, finally, is the cosmic life as a whole an evolution? That is to ask, Are the cosmic processes moving *on*, without return, so that the universe will be radically different, some billions or trillions of years in the future, from what it is today? Or is its life an endless succession of similar episodes, or a cyclical process, so that, however changed its state may become, it will eventually return to the general condition in which it now is?

The answer is pretty clear: *So far as we can see, at present*, the history of the universe is a one-way process, an evolution. The story, as deciphered by astronomers, runs as follows:

Once upon a time, say a hundred trillion years ago, an excessively thin nebula of simple gases, spread unevenly throughout a vast area of Space, was slowly drawing together, under the influence of gravitation, into separate islands, and, gaining rotary motion, becoming the spiral nebulæ. Within these huge islands of tenuous gas knots formed which became the stars; the spiral nebulæ thus became rotating galaxies of stars. It has been demonstrated by mathematical physics that a diffuse nebula would — physical laws being what we discover them to be — condense into galaxies and stars of the sizes we actually find. The process heats the stars to temperatures as high, in their interiors, as fifty million degrees. Matter at this temperature gives rise to extremely powerful radiation, which, passing through the mass of the star, gradually gets changed into the gentler radiation which we receive from them — and especially from our own star, the sun.

The stars have existed as stars, it is calculated, for from five to ten trillion years — not much more, or they would be in more advanced stages of senility. Our own sun, a smallish star, has been a recognizably separate entity, radiating light and heat, for some such period. But our sun has had an unusual history. Somewhere about four or five billion years ago — quite recently in its life — a serious accident happened to it. Another star came swinging by, quite close, and, by the tidal force of its gravitational pull, drew a considerable mass of matter out of the sun. Most of this matter, together, perhaps, with some matter from the intruder's mass, remained within the gravitational field of the sun, revolving round it in rapidly cooling irregular clouds. Since Space is very cold, these relatively small masses of matter solidified, and the larger lumps swept up the smaller pieces as their orbits intersected. Thus came into being the existing planets and their satellites. We are still sweeping up scattered bits of matter, which we see as shooting stars, and occasionally find as meteorites. But most of this matter has already joined the few planets and moons that now constitute our solar system.

The earth has been solid, and cool, on the surface, for two or three billion years. From this point on geology takes up the story. And for a third or half of this time, at least, the process of organic evolution has been taking place. In our final chapter we shall ask what the future of life on earth bids fair to be. But there are longer-range questions. The story that we have so rapidly outlined may be supposed to have taken a hundred trillion years, not much more. The stars seem to be roughly of the same age; their distributions and motions show pretty clearly that they are the result of a common cosmic evolution. What, then, happened *before* that time? Can we suppose that the cosmic life has been going on for an infinite time? Or must we conclude that it had a beginning, a hundred or a few hundred trillion years ago?

If present physical laws held in those long-past ages, and if the cosmic life is an irreversible process, it must have had a beginning. The stars cannot have been condensing and radiating away their energy for an infinite time. Were we to suppose the process extremely slow in getting under way, we might push back its beginning indefinitely, but not to an infinite time. And, in any case, the *interesting* part of the cosmic life, the period during which planets could be formed and organic life arise, can not have lasted more than, say, ten trillion years or so. Apart from the study of the rate of stellar evolution, it is evident that if radiation had been going on for an infinite time, Space would contain far more radiant energy than it actually has, and our earth would be receiving at every moment far more heat than it does. Jeans has stated that the minuteness of the radiant energy which we receive (apart from the sun's energy) proves that the stellar universe cannot have been radiating energy for more than two hundred trillion years.

Looking toward the future, we can foresee that the final state of the universe will be reached when every bit of matter that is capable of transformation into radiant energy has been so transformed, and the universe has attained thermodynamical equilibrium. It makes some difference whether Space is infinite in extent or curved and limited in area. In the former case, the radiant energy will go on and on and be lost to the universe of matter. In the latter case, it will go round and round through Space forever (unless radiation ultimately peters out), a small fraction of it striking the stars and giving them a constant slight renewal of heat. Space is so vast, however, and the stars such infinitesimal dust-specks in it, that they would not intercept enough energy — even when Space is far fuller of it than now — to lift them back into life.

The cooling-off of the stars means a slackening of the motions of their molecules. At a certain point in the cooling a star ceases to be visible to the human eye. So that, even if human beings could still survive to that far future time, there would be nothing to *see*. As the temperature of the stars approaches the absolute zero of Space, the molecular motions will slacken almost to motionlessness (the two statements are equivalent). The *life* of the universe will be over.

If Space is curved, and the galaxies evenly distributed through it, each galaxy may condense into a single frozen lump. If, on the other hand, the physical universe has a gravitational center, it seems that all the galaxies must ultimately gravitate together into one huge frozen lump. There would be many collisions, rebirths of stars, and rediffusions of matter to protract the process. But the end can apparently be nothing else than the aggregation of all matter at the center of gravity of the universe. During the process vast quantities of energy will be radiated away and lost. The cosmic life, consisting essentially of the process of contraction of matter from a primitive widely diffused tenuity to a final frozen lump, will have run its course. It had a beginning and will have an end.

This conclusion hinges, however, upon the assumption that there are no causes at work which will reverse the process. Eddington has suggested that "whoever wishes for a universe which can continue indefinitely in activity must lead a crusade against the Second Law of Thermodynamics." [1] This law is the generalization, based on wide experience, that all physical processes are forever wasting heat, most of which becomes irrecoverably lost. But there are some physicists — Millikan is the best known — who believe that atoms are constantly being formed in the interstellar spaces out of radiant energy. If this is so, it may be imagined that an equilibrium has been, or will be, reached, a re-creation of matter balancing its dissipation into radiation.

Millikan believes that the so-called "cosmic rays," which he has been foremost to investigate, bring us tidings of the birth-pangs of atoms. Most physicists, however, believe that this theory is highly improbable. It is difficult to imagine how radiant light and heat could 'condense' into electrons and protons, especially since radiation is so thinly diffused that there is apparently insufficient concentration of energy at any such minute points in Space. The amount of energy liberated from matter in radiation is enormous, and an equal amount of energy must be reconcentrated, if units of matter are to be re-formed.

However, we are as yet so ignorant of the fine scale of

[1] *The Nature of the Physical World*, p. 85.

material and ethereal events that we must consider the matter open. There may be some way, not now known, by which the energy which is lost to matter can get back again, so that the heat-death of the universe is stayed. Perhaps it is easier to assume that than to accept the alternative view that the cosmic life had a beginning and will have an end. Such evidence, however, as we positively have points to a constant and irrecoverable loss of energy from the material universe. Life is motion; and the possibility of the motion of matter seems to be slowly but inexorably ebbing.

We have had to omit many interesting features of the world-life in our highly generalized account. One point that is just now (1932) agitating the astronomical world is the shift in the spectrum of light reaching us from the distant galaxies, which *seems* to indicate that they are, almost all, receding from us at enormous speeds. We hear talk of our 'expanding universe.' The apparent velocities are, however, too great to be plausible; the universe cannot have been expanding at this rate for anything like the length of time that all our other evidence points to as lying behind us. It seems likely that some other interpretation of the spectrum shift will presently be generally accepted.

So our cosmic story begins with a diffused nebula in an early stage of contraction, and ends with the prophecy of a universe frozen, dark, and still. Why, and how, did the cosmic life begin? Has matter existed from all eternity? Or did Time itself begin? And will nothing more happen, to all eternity, after the cosmic drama is over? Will the universe vanish, and Time itself end? Or is the process, somehow, reversible, so that the whole story of cosmic evolution, as we have told it, is but an episode which has been, and is to be, endlessly repeated, world without end? And whatever the answer, Is there meaning, design, purpose in it all, or is the whole thing haphazard and blind?... To these questions we shall later return.

EMERGENT EVOLUTION

One philosophical question of importance remains: Does evolution proceed without break in continuity of law or substance, so that each stage would be, theoretically, predictable from the earlier stages, once the universal laws were known? Or are there points in the process where new substances, or laws, appear, which could not, even by omniscience, have been predicted on the basis of pre-existing laws? The latter view is currently called emergent, or creative, evolution. In so far as it is accepted, it means giving up the very concept of evolution, as we have defined it. The 'emergence' of unpredictable properties is not evolution at all; it is spontaneous generation, it is miracle — though not necessarily with the theological connotations usually attached to that latter term. But we must not beg the question by a definition. It may be that the cosmic history, and the history of organic life, are for the most part evolutionary, but that at certain critical points new laws or substances or kinds of existence just come into being. This would be inexplicable; or, if explained by the fiat of a Creator, or the urge of an *élan vital*, that fiat or urge would be, itself, inexplicable. But the very existence of the universe, with such and such laws and substances, is inexplicable. And the question merely is whether there are many inexplicabilities or only one.

The argument for the theory of emergence is empirical.

Large-scale phenomena, it is said, are not completely explicable in terms of analysis into their small-scale constituents. The later stages in evolution bring into existence complexes which exhibit, clearly, new properties and new behavior, not merely resultant from the pre-existing laws of behavior of their component parts. The term 'holism' has come into use to express this idea that *wholes* have their own laws, not deducible from anything that existed before they came into being. Two plus two does not always make four; in certain cases it makes five. There are 'levels' in evolution, each level being marked by the appearance of radically new entities or new laws. These new entities may be as determinate in their behavior as the primitive world-substance; these new laws can be counted on, perhaps, with as great a confidence. But they are something more than new exemplifications of the old substances or laws. There is no agreement among the upholders of this view as to how many levels we find, as to what specific things are radically new entities or what laws are irreducibly new laws. But they agree in regarding as hopelessly inadequate the mechanistic view which believes the whole cosmic life theoretically explicable in terms of a few simple elements and their laws of behavior.

Broad points out, for example, that the completest knowledge of the structure and properties of sodium and chlorine atoms would not enable us to predict the properties of salt, though the molecules of salt are composed merely of atoms of sodium and chlorine combined. If salt had not yet been made, no one could possibly foresee that it would be white, that it would taste salty, or that it would have such and such reactions with other substances. Once we discover these qualities and properties, we can count on the fact that salt will always be, and act, like this. But these are new, unique, ultimate facts. The formation of chemical compounds out of elementary substances constitutes a new 'level' in cosmic evolution.... Similarly, digging deeper, the formation of those complex structures which we call atoms out of their constituent electrons and protons constitutes an earlier level. And perhaps the formation of electrons and protons themselves a still earlier level. In the other direction, we shall be likely to consider the formation of crystals, and perhaps of colloids, new levels, and then the formation of organic cells, of complex organisms, and, most plausibly of all, the emergence of conscious life.

How would a mechanist answer this? He would say that the scientific facts about salt, the facts which physics and chemistry study, *could* be predicted, if we knew enough about the constituent atoms and their constituent electrons and protons. The behavior of salt-molecules is a mere resultant of the behavior of these constituent units, as they find themselves in close juxtaposition, in certain conditions of temperature, etc. In many cases the behavior of new compounds *is* now predicted, before they have been synthesized. And while there are many gaps in our knowledge, we know enough already to be able to correlate structure with behavior in considerable detail. There seems to be no positive reason for asserting that the electrons and protons have to obey any new laws when they find themselves in this new situation, or that the behavior of the salt-molecule as a whole is not the mere resultant of the behavior of each of its component electrons and protons. The *situation* is unique, and naturally leads to new *results*, according to the same old laws of motion and of attraction and repulsion which the electrons and protons have always followed.

The *qualities* of compounds — the whiteness and saltiness of salt — are a different matter altogether. Here we have to do with the *look*, the *taste*, the *feel* of things — in other words, with *effects* produced in our conscious experience when we look at, taste, and feel of things. These qualities do not belong to the salt at all, as we have been at pains to point out in our discussion of the epistemological problem. They are qualities produced in the conscious experience of perceiving organisms, by molecular and electronic motions, and the elementary attractions and repulsions of electrons and protons. These motions, attractions, and repulsions are the properties of the salt itself; they fall within the subject-matter of the preceding paragraph. But the consideration of *qualities* can lead us, at most, only to a belief in the emergence of *conscious experience*.

As a matter of fact, the argument about emergent evolution rages chiefly about the alleged emergence of organic life out of the inorganic, and the emergence of mind, or consciousness, out of the unconscious. It seems to many patently absurd to suppose that *life* could arise out of 'non-living' matter, by merely mechanical forces and a mere complexification of structure. And perhaps even more obviously absurd to suppose that *consciousness* could arise as a mere additive resultant of the simple laws of matter. Broad, for one, admits that the apparent emergence of new laws in the intra-physical realm *may* be due to our imperfect knowledge of the fine structure of things, and their simple laws; but he insists that "trans-physical laws are *necessarily* of the emergent type." [1]

[1] C. D. Broad, *The Mind and Its Place in Nature*, p. 79.

In order to judge the probabilities in these elusive matters, we shall have to know as clearly as possible what organic life is, and what consciousness is. The former question we shall proceed to discuss in the following chapter, the latter we shall consider in the chapters following that. But we may say here that it is impossible, at the present stage of human knowledge, to answer with anything approaching certainty the questions which here beset us. *Are* the novelties which appear in evolution commensurable and explicable? Or are they ultimate and unanalyzable? Is there a fundamental continuity to the cosmic life? Or are there sharp breaks, new motifs, new creation? At least, we must keep *trying* to explain the more complex and 'higher' developments in terms of the simpler and 'lower.' For explanation means not only satisfaction of our craving to understand, but power in manipulation and control. As Montague says:

> The emergence of new properties and laws constitutes a question rather than an answer; and it should act as a stimulant rather than as a sedative. The history of science is the history of replacing empirically given emergence by rational etiology.[1]

But the fact that we hope and try to explain the apparently novel in terms of the old and universal must not bias our belief in advance. If there are a series of breaks, of inexplicabilities, in evolution, we must simply make the best of it, as we must make the best of our universe as a whole, which is inexplicably what it is.

SUGGESTED READINGS

H. H. Newman, *Evolution Yesterday and Today.*
Frances Mason, ed., *Creation by Evolution.*
Geddes and Thomson, *Evolution,* I, II, VIII.

---

[1] W. P. Montague, *Essays in Honor of John Dewey,* p. 264.

W. B. Scott, *The Theory of Evolution*, I.

H. E. Crampton, *The Doctrine of Evolution*, IV.

H. H. Newman, in *The Nature of the Universe and of Man*, XIII.

J. A. Thomson, *The Outline of Science*, II, XI.

G. T. W. Patrick, *Introduction to Philosophy*, VIII.

Karl Pearson, *Grammar of Science*, X.

Columbia Associates, *Introduction to Reflective Thinking*, VII.

G. E. Hale, *The Study of Stellar Evolution*, I, XX.

P. Lowell, *The Evolution of Worlds*, I, VI, VII, VIII.

C. Snyder, *The World Machine*, XXXI–XXXIV.

J. C. Duncan, *Astronomy*, XVIII.

G. W. Cunningham, *Problems of Philosophy*, Part IV.

C. G. Abbott, *The Earth and the Stars*, XIV.

J. H. Jeans, *The Stars in Their Courses*, pp. 115–122.

C. Lloyd Morgan, *Emergent Evolution*.

PART FOUR
LIFE AND MIND

CHAPTER XVII

VITALISM

FOR a passing moment out of the ages of cosmic history an equilibrium of conditions has been maintained on this little planet favorable to the agglomeration of atoms into those extraordinarily complex structures that we call organisms. Brief, on the cosmic scale, as is the period of existence of these organic forms, and tiny as is the corner of the universe which they occupy, their life is to us the all-important fact. So we must try to understand as clearly as we may what this organic life is.

WHAT IS ORGANIC LIFE?

In the broadest sense we may say that all movement, all change, is life. But usually we mean by that term the highly complex motions of organisms; not the atomic and sub-atomic motions, which are similar to those of inorganic bodies, but those large-scale motions which are peculiarly their own, and which cease when, as we say, the organism is dead. If we could analyze these motions into their ultimate constituents, they would be seen to consist, no doubt, of such and such motions of such and such electrons and protons — or whatever the ultimate physical units may be. But if we were to consider, one by one, or even in their molecular interrelations, these motions of the elementary units, analyzing out the components of their motion due to electrical, gravitational, and chemical forces, we should miss the resultant large-scale movements which, in the case of organic bodies, are so distinctive and so important. These large-scale movements comprise the special subject-matter of physiology and behavioristic (as contrasted with introspective) psychology. They *are* 'life.' A 'living' body is a body which is capable of these distinctive types of behavior.

The mechanist believes that these movements of organic bodies, like the movements of inorganic bodies, result by simple addition from the motions of their component atoms and electrons, and that these small-scale motions are, like the motions of atoms and electrons in inorganic bodies, the inevitable result of the ordinary physical forces to which they are subjected in their particular environment, according to the same laws that hold everywhere and always. The distinctive movements of organic bodies result from their distinctive structure. We may speak of biological forces and laws, as we speak of biological structures. But the new laws and forces are merely complex resultants of the same old laws and forces functioning in new situations.

On the other hand, the vitalist believes that the behavior of organisms is, to some extent, a radically new, 'emergent' characteristic, unpredictable, not deducible from the simpler, sub-biological laws of nature. Some vitalists hold that there is a peculiar entity which enters every organic body, an 'entelechy' or 'vital principle,' which acts as a sort of steersman, giving its movements an extra guidance, freeing it, to a degree, from the control of mechanical laws. Others prefer to say, more simply, that organisms exhibit unpredictable behavior, that new laws come into being when nature attains this level, without assuming the existence in the organisms of any mysterious controlling agency.

In any case, it is clear that the behavior of organisms is, in some respects, very different from the activity of non-organic bodies. So, before raising the question whether we can consider it as a mere resultant of mechanical forces, we must consider what its peculiar characteristics are. When we have enumerated them, we shall have our definition of organic 'life.'

In the first place, the peculiar structures which we call organisms maintain their existence by a very delicate equilibrium of upbuilding and tearing-down processes. The matter of which they consist slowly changes; new matter is assimilated, old matter excreted. But the characteristic *form* of the organism is maintained — for a period of hours, weeks, or years. When this equilibrium breaks down, when the balance of intake, assimilation, and outflow is broken, the organism 'dies.' In the more complex organisms, like our own, the line between life and death is an arbitrary one; we usually choose to consider the cessation of the beating of the heart the decisive moment, although many vital activities may persist for some time afterward. For once the heart stops beating, it rarely recovers its power to beat again, and the maintenance of the complex biological processes becomes no longer possible.

But organic bodies do not merely maintain a static equilibrium, they *grow*. Each organic cell is formed by the differentiation into two of an earlier-existing cell. The two cells split apart, but remain conjoined, so that the organism grows in size. The variously located cells take up various functions, so that the complexity of the single cell gives rise to a vastly greater complexity of an organized group consisting, in the larger organisms, of many millions of millions of cells. The growth is possible by an excess of intake and assimilation of matter over outflow. The energy necessary for the upbuilding is supplied by the breakdown of complex molecules taken in as 'food'; or, in the case of plants, by a direct utilization of the energy of sunlight. The direction of growth is determined by the ultra-microscopic structures known as 'genes,' which keep each organism true (with minor variations) to the ancestral type.

In certain cases cells separate entirely and become independent entities. In the more complex organisms, complex structures of cells separate themselves from the parent organism and start to grow as new organisms of the same type. In sexual reproduction we have a complication of this original process whereby two such groups of cells, each bearing its own set of genes, unite to give rise to the new individual. The power of reproduction has enabled organisms to multiply and infest the earth.

In order to get food wherewith to maintain their activities, and grow, the simplest organisms had to have a mechanism of some rudimentary sort whereby they could react to outer stimuli. As the evolutionary process has gone on, they have become increasingly sensitive to their environment, and increasingly capable of adjusting themselves thereto. Their impression-reaction mechanisms have been developed and differentiated, serving their needs in various ways, till they have attained the complexity of the human nervous system and brain.

Thus we have (a) maintenance of structural type by balanced intake, assimilation, and outflow of matter, (b) growth, (c) reproduction, and (d) impression-reaction activities, as the essential features of what we call 'organic life.'

THE ARGUMENTS FOR VITALISM

To the vitalist it seems incredible that these very distinctive biological activities are a mere resultant of simple mechanical laws. He recognizes, of course, that new types of behavior always arise when new types of structure are found. A clock, for example, has its own very distinctive behavior, of a rather remarkable sort, although it is explicable by the laws of mechanics. A mechanical chess-player, a robot such as has been constructed now and then by some ingenious and painstaking mechanician, is capable of a wide repertoire of nicely directed activities, responding appropriately to many subtly changing stimuli. Doubtless many astonishing achievements along these lines will interest and amuse our descendants, and perhaps do a large part of their work for them. But even so, they will probably not be within hailing distance of the complexity and delicacy of response of vegetable and animal organisms. The structure of these is so minute and so complex that we cannot even investigate it, in its fine detail, much less reproduce it. The best robot we can make is likely to be a very clumsy and rude imitation of a man, or even of a mouse.

'Atoms,' we recall, are complex structures of from two to several hundred electrons and protons. The more complex 'molecules,' such as are found in organic bodies, are composed of hundreds of atoms. A single hemoglobin molecule, for instance, is a very intricate structure of 1894 atoms ($C_{600}H_{960}N_{154}FeO_{179}$). A single 'cell' may contain several quintillion (10^{18}) molecules, of many sorts; it is a whole world in itself. The adult human body contains some sixty trillion (6×10^{13}) cells. Conger tells us that if each cell were a printed letter, there would be enough, in a single human body, to fill all the pages in all the books of the vast collection in the Congressional Library. A 'gene,' one of the bearers of hereditary characters, has a diameter of the order of fifty millionths of a millimeter. It must be an extremely complex structure, composed of vast numbers of cells arranged in an unknown but doubtless very intricate and delicately balanced pattern.

There are evidently *parts* enough, and there is structure enough, in any organism, to account for any degree of complex and delicately adjusted activity, if such activity can be supposed to be simply a function of this enormously complex structure. Nature has had hundreds of millions of years to work up to existing organisms, by millions of steps, some of them doubtless taken under conditions not now reproducible, certainly under conditions of which we are hopelessly ignorant. It is not surprising that we cannot produce these organisms offhand, in our laboratories. It would require a library to *describe* the structure of a single organism, even supposing we had the means of discovering its minute structure. We cannot experiment freely with organisms without destroying their intricate balance of functions. We can only watch their large-scale activities, and guess at the underlying detail. But it is clear that the extreme complexity of structure and delicacy of balance of organic bodies *would* lead to new and delicately balanced types of behavior, in a purely mechanical way.

The argument for vitalism is, then, not the fact of the *novelty*, or the *complexity*, of organic activity, but its *uncertainty*. Many biologists, as well as ordinary observers of animal life, are impressed by the unpredictability of the behavior of organisms, especially of animals. An animal of a given species, or even the same animal on different occasions, when put into a certain definite situation may act in any one of the ways which are open to it. This seems to show that there is present some non-mechanical autonomous power of choice between alternatives; a *part* of the creature's behavior is not a mere resultant of its specific structure and the specific situation, but is due to some undetermined and variable inner factor possessed by organic bodies.

However, in order to prove this, it would be necessary to prove that the apparently similar individuals do not, after all, possess some difference in internal structure which would account for the difference in behavior. The ultra-microscopic structure of organisms, and especially of the nervous mechanism which is the guide to the behavior of all animals except the most primitive, is so intricate, and so changing from moment to moment, as new impressions are received from the sense-organs, that the necessity of an additional, non-mechanical factor cannot possibly be proved. No two organisms are ever so exactly alike as to necessitate identical behavior in all circumstances; each follows the laws of its own individual structure. And each organism changes its structure, in minute detail, with every additional moment of its life-experience. A rat put for a second time into the same position in a maze is not the same rat as he was the first time; his first experience in the maze has affected his nervous mechanism in ways which, though minute in scale, may be determinative of his behavior.

We can agree, however, upon this: organisms are, to a far greater degree than inorganic bodies, *inwardly* determined. By the decomposition of complex molecules (or, in the case of plants, by the direct use of sunlight), they generate great quantities of internal energy. This energy is controlled and liberated by their internal mechanisms (in the case of animals, the nervous system).

The result is a great deal of autonomy in their activity; it is self-generated, self-directed. This fact is peculiar to organisms only in its degree. The disintegration of radio-active matter, for example, is so completely self-determined that no change of external conditions to which we can subject it seems to influence it in the least. And in many describable respects inorganic matter of every sort carries on its own internal life in spite of great changes in its environment. But organisms display a far greater *variety* of inwardly generated activities, and so have a far greater appearance of spontaneity and independence.

They also have a far greater *individuality*, and far greater potentialities of *change* in their individuality. In particular, the brain-structure of the higher animals may be likened to a vast assemblage of guns with triggers set. A slight current from some sense-organ suffices to set off one of these triggers, and thereby to initiate a large-scale movement of the organism. On another occasion, a similar current from the same sense-organ may find a slightly changed balance of forces in this intricate network of triggers, and may set going a discharge of energy in a very different direction. This mechanism by means of which animal movements are controlled is understood to some extent; but it is hidden from us within the animal's body, and the exact nature of the small-scale processes is only partially known. It is quite possible to *conceive*, however, that this great variety of inwardly controlled reactions is strictly determined, in purely mechanical ways, by the delicate and continually changing brain-structure, together with the continual impact of influences from the animal's environment. Hence, the fact that an animal may act in any one of several ways in a given external situation is not decisive, one way or the other.

A more arresting argument of the vitalists is that organisms do special sorts of things which no mechanism, however complex, could do. For one thing, they pursue *ends*. In spite of wide variations in the environment, they act in such a way as to attain certain sought-for results. They find their food, in one way or other; they escape their enemies, by hook or crook; they find their mates and propagate their species. Of course they very often fail; an environment too unfavorable defeats them. But to a surprising extent they adapt themselves to changing circumstances and, by this route or that, reach their destination of survival and reproduction. Could mere mechanisms be so flexible, and so obstinate in working toward a definite goal?

Well, a good watch (a relatively very simple structure) manages to keep time, to a second, in spite of the continuous changes of tension in its mainspring, the continual changes of temperature to which it is subject, and its various changes of position. Keeping time is its *end*, the goal which it might be said to pursue. For that matter, a spinning top rights itself, no matter how it is pushed; *its* purpose is, to keep upright. Organisms have, it is true, vastly more difficult ends to achieve, but they have vastly more intricate structures, gradually built up during the long evolutionary process, to keep themselves righted and oriented toward achieving them. All such cases *look* like cases of conscious purpose. But in the vegetable world and in the lower animals there is, almost certainly, no conscious prevision of the ends toward which they are moving. Even such marvelously adapted creatures as bees, performing their elaborate and mutually adjusted tasks, have presumably no conscious realization of the ends for which they are working. They are simply driven from moment to moment by internal urges. The end is achieved, the colony survives, but not because it is consciously sought. It is *either* the inevitable result of the delicate structure of the bees' bodies and brains, *or* the result of that plus some new, unknown factor which pushes their reactions this way and that in equal unconsciousness of the ends it is helping to attain.

Thus the teleological way of describing animal behavior seems to be of no help in explaining how it comes about. *We* look ahead, and see that the hen sits on her eggs 'in order to' produce chickens (for us to eat). But the 'in order to' is a feature that we import into the situation; it is our gloss. The hen sits on her eggs because some inner urge, whether mechanical or non-mechanical, drives her to do it. It is often convenient for our purposes to describe animal activity in terms of the results which it achieves. But the vitalist must not suppose (as some do seem to suppose) that they have *explained* the activity by calling it teleological. It still remains to discover the causes which were at work. And our question is, Do we discover any factors determining the activity which are non-mechanical factors? Or (if that is asking too much), is it easier to *imagine* how the results are brought about by postulating some non-mechanical factor, operating in some describable way, than by confining our hypothesis to the assumption of some sort of delicately adjusted nervous (plus glandular, etc.) mechanism?

Organisms certainly do very remarkable things; there is no dispute as to that. And many 'lower' organisms do remarkable things that the more highly developed organisms cannot do. We human beings could not find

our way as carrier pigeons can. We could not track a
criminal as a bloodhound can. We could not grow a new
leg when one is cut off, we could not restore the normal
form of our bodies when it has been destroyed, as some
lower organisms can. The vitalist is convinced that
these remarkable achievements are not explicable mechanically. But how shall we know, until we have discovered,
in detail, just how they *are* caused? In some cases we
are almost wholly ignorant of the correct answer. In
such cases our question must be, Which is the more promising hypothesis, the hypothesis of mechanical causation,
or that of causation by an entelechy or vital principle?
Until we know, in great detail, what actually happens
within the organism, we can do no more than guess
whether all the steps are mechanically determined, or
whether some new 'emergent' factor or law enters upon
the scene.

It is true that animals react, in some sense, to past and
future, as well as to the present, environment. That is,
memory and anticipation are causative factors. Some
vitalists assert roundly that no mechanism could possibly
do that.... We must leave out of consideration in this
chapter the questions concerning *conscious* memory and
anticipation; but it is quite clear that 'memory' and
'anticipation' have a physiological sense; and it is possible to conceive that the distinctive physiological activities thus connoted are purely mechanical. Many
animal-reactions colored by memory and anticipation
have been studied in mechanistic terms. Pavlov's cele-
brated experiments on dogs are noteworthy. Such exact
results are obtained, and the animal's reactions can be
so definitely predicted, as changes are made in his memories and anticipations, that the general effect of these

experiments is to increase the probability that such reactions are mechanically determined.

All sorts of cases are adduced by the vitalists, in overwhelming variety.   But it is not clear that anything
definite is proved thereby.   It all amounts to saying,
How can you account for such and such facts in mechanical terms?   And the answer is, How can you account for
them in any other terms?   We must not suppose that
bringing in a new *term* — Entelechy, Vital Principle, or
just Emergent Law — solves any problems.   We must
locate the new factor or principle, discover what brings
it into being at this point, and just how it works, in detail.
In short, until someone, mechanist or vitalist, or perhaps
someone with a new label, discovers exactly what *happens*, in ultimate detail, the whole matter remains one in
which alternative hypotheses are legitimate.

THE ARGUMENTS AGAINST VITALISM

The arguments for vitalism seem to be weak; are the
arguments against it any stronger?

The mechanist points out that the vitalist's arguments
are all 'arguments from ignorance'; i.e., they consist in
reiterating that the mechanist cannot fully explain such
or such facts.   But neither can the vitalist explain them;
all he offers us is a *word*.   No positive evidence is given
us that there is something real corresponding to this
word.   As a recent writer says, vitalism "simply fills up
the gaps in mechanistic descriptions after the fashion of
Columbus' map-maker, 'Where Unknown, there place
Terrors.'" [1]

Where we are ignorant, it is a good rule of procedure
not to postulate new entities or laws unless they serve to

[1] J. Needham, in *Science, Religion, and Reality*, p. 245.

explain observed phenomena better than is otherwise possible. But the concept of an entelechy or vital force is so vague and mysterious, and its manner of working so wholly conjectural, that most students feel it to be an added burden rather than a help in solving problems. *Where* does the entelechy exist? How does it get connected with a given body? How does it move the body? Is it conscious, foreseeing the ends it wishes the body to attain? Or is it blind and merely by good fortune steering the body well? One can answer these questions as one chooses; but the fact remains that anything we may say is only a guess. On the other hand, the laws of mechanics are known to be actual fact. It is not certain that they cannot account for all the movements of bodies. Would it not be wiser, then, while keeping our minds open for any evidence that may be found, to explore freely the possibilities of mechanical explanation before concluding that other, purely conjectural factors are involved?

It is well known that organic bodies are made of the same substances as inorganic bodies. So far as our explorations have been able to go, the matter in organic bodies seems to follow the same laws as matter anywhere else in the world, including the fundamental law of the conservation of energy. As the biologist Hogben says, "There is no evidence that momentum and kinetic energy, that chemical transformations, that electrical and magnetic phenomena, occur in the living body in any manner, or to any extent, which differs from that obtaining in the more readily investigated non-living world."

Year by year organic processes are being more and more fully explained in terms of the ordinary laws of physics and chemistry. Biology, to be sure, dealing with large-scale phenomena, must have its own categories and laws, just as chemistry or any other science does. But just as chemical reactions are coming to be more and more clearly seen to be the inevitable resultant of the laws of physics, so biological reactions are coming to be more and more understood as the resultant of physical and chemical laws. All the real achievement of biology, all the actual *knowledge* that we have won, is along mechanistic lines. This surely encourages us to believe in the fundamental simplicity and continuity of Nature.

Another reason for believing in the continuity of sub-biological and biological processes lies in the impossibility of drawing any sharp line between organic and inorganic bodies. We can offer a definition of organic life, as we have done. But there are borderline cases, which show that any such definition is essentially arbitrary. Biologists are far from agreeing what the best definition of organic life is, and whether such and such microscopic bits of moving matter are properly to be called organic or not. Every characteristic small-scale activity of living matter is found in non-living matter; it seems to be only the large-scale movements of an organism which are distinctive. And even these are sometimes paralleled by inorganic bodies. Some crystals, for example, *grow*. You need a small piece to get any; but if you have a small piece, you can presently have a good deal. Some metals are subject to contagious 'diseases.' And so on.

It is manifestly impossible for us to reproduce in our laboratories the unknown and unimaginable complexities of any existing organism, or to produce any other body as intricately organized. But some biologists have created bodies which may be called quasi-organic, bodies whose movements have so closely imitated those of some tiny natural organisms that they might be said to be semi-alive. Recently, for example, Dr. Leduc made osmotic growths that resembled a great variety of living things. Algæ, mushrooms, grasses, seeds, leaves, flowers, corals, clam shells and many other types of organisms were faithfully reproduced in form, color, texture, and structure. Some of the mineral mushrooms were mistaken by experts for real fungi. Many osmotic growths swam about in the mother liquor under the stimulation of the slightest disturbance in their environment. Many underwent rhythmic movements connected with their nutrition. Some reproduced crudely by budding. Under certain circumstances the vitality of a faltering individual was rejuvenated, wounds were healed much as in live tissue. With age the membrane of an osmotic growth thickens, growth slows down and finally stops when the osmotic force in the membrane is exhausted. As in a child whose cells are young and under high osmotic pressure, the young osmotic mineral growth is plump and well formed. With increasing age flaccidity overtakes the cells of both man and mineral. Death comes ultimately to both, and with it the decay of form and structure.[1]

If the ordinary laws of physics and chemistry can account for the movements of these quasi-living things, it is natural to suppose that they can account for the similar movements of the simplest organisms, and the subtler, more complex movements of the more complex organisms. It would be easy to describe the movements of these quasi-organisms in terms of 'instinct,' 'vital force,' and so on. But this dramatic phraseology would not help us to understand the causes of their movements. Similarly, we can say that a moth has an instinct to fly toward a flame; but that does not help us to understand the causes of this behavior. It is like saying that opium puts us to sleep because it has dormative properties. The biologist must discover just what *happens*, in detail, when opium is taken into the system; then he will have at least a glimmer of *why* opium puts us to sleep. So the biologist must study

---

[1] From a report in the *New Republic*.

what happens in the moth's body when it sees a flame. Certain areas of the retinas of the moth's eyes are affected by the light, certain groups of muscles are contracted, by a nervous reflex. We now know, in some detail, what *makes* a moth fly toward a flame. To speak in terms of the moth's 'instinct,' or *élan vital*, or to say that it is a case of a new, emergent law of behavior, is simply to shirk the task of detailed explanation. Thus vitalism is not *fruitful*. Whatever theories a biologist may fancy, it is the discovery of mechanical links of cause and effect that forwards his science.

Let Santayana sum up the case as a philosopher sees it:

> Both possibilities will always remain open, because however far mechanical analysis may go, many phenomena, as human apprehension presents them, will always remain irreducible to any common denominator with the rest; and on the other hand, wherever the actual reduction of the habits of animals to those of matter may have stopped, we can never know that a further reduction is impossible.
>
> The balance of reasonable presumption, however, is not even. The most inclusive movements known to us in nature, the astronomical, are calculable, and so are the most minute and pervasive processes, the chemical. These are also, if evolution is to be accepted, the earliest processes upon which all others have supervened and out of which, as it were, they have grown. Apart from miraculous intervention, therefore, the assumption seems to be inevitable that the intermediate processes are calculable too, and compounded out of the others. The appearance to the contrary presented in animal and social life is easily explicable on psychological grounds.[1]

SUGGESTED READINGS

H. Driesch, *The History and Theory of Vitalism.*
Sir Oliver Lodge, *Life and Matter.*
C. D. Broad, *The Mind and Its Place in Nature*, pp. 56–81.
L. Hogben, *The Nature of Living Matter*, Part I, ch. III.

---

[1] George Santayana, *Winds of Doctrine*, p. 71.

Benjamin Moore, *The Origin and Nature of Life.*
R. W. Sellars, *Essentials of Philosophy*, XXIII.
G. T. W. Patrick, *Introduction to Philosophy*, VII.
J. S. Haldane, *Mechanism, Life, and Personality*, I–II.
Jacques Loeb, *The Mechanistic Conception of Life.*
H. H. Newman, *The Nature of the Universe and of Man*, VI.
J. A. Thomson, *The Outline of Science*, vol. III, ch. XIX.
J. H. Ryan, *Introduction to Philosophy*, V.
M. R. Cohen, *Reason and Nature*, pp. 240–282.

CHAPTER XVIII

BEHAVIORISM AND MENTAL STATES

LIFE consists of activities — inward activities, such as breathing and digestion, and outward activities, reactions of various sorts to the environment. These activities are simply movements of masses of matter; it is at least possible to conceive that they are the resultant of ordinary physical laws. So long as we consider an organism as merely a physical body, it is not clear that we need to postulate anything unique about it except its extraordinary complexity and delicacy of balance, and its consequent capacity for complex, varying, and distinctive movements. But organisms, at least some organisms, are *conscious;* and conscious life is something added to mere physical motion. Can we believe that consciousness, too, is an inevitable resultant of the universal laws of Nature, something that comes into being when the necessary factors combine, as naturally as flowers appear in the spring? Or do we here at last come to a clear break in the continuity of evolution? Must we regard consciousness as an unpredictable novelty, somehow 'emergent' at certain points in the process? Or does it, perhaps, belong to a totally different realm of being, which we have so far ignored, in our concentration upon the laws and substances of the physical world?

There is no more difficult problem than this. Here, if anywhere, we find ourselves at the limit of human capacity to understand. But at least we should be able to see what the problem is, and what are some of the current attempts at its solution.

BEHAVIORISM

The simplest, most radical solution — if, indeed, it can be called a solution — is that of behaviorism. The behaviorist asserts that consciousness is nothing but externally directed, adaptive behavior; psychology is simply the science of the behavior of animal organisms. The physiologist studies the fine detail of the processes, the psychologist studies them in their large-scale relations to the environment. He considers what changes in the environment produce what changes in reaction, what happens when the response is delayed, when various stimuli re-enforce or inhibit one another, and so on. He catalogues the impression- and reaction-capacities of the various types of organism, and the particular responses of individuals. When an animal acts in a certain way, he calls it a fear-reaction; another sort of reaction is play, or making love, or curiosity. But nothing is discoverable except reactions, i.e., nerve-currents, movements of muscles, activities of glands, and so on. These reactions *are* the animal's consciousness; there is nothing more to it.

The behaviorist evidently has plenty to do in studying these animal reactions; behavioristic psychology has made important contributions, it has brought into prominence the fact, not before clearly realized, that wherever there is consciousness there is behavior. Even in thinking, or in dreaming, we are reacting, though merely in slight, tentative ways, not visible to a spectator. Whatever we are conscious of (whether in perception or in conception, with our eyes open or in a brooding reverie) we are reacting *to*. The behaviorists have dragged to light these multitudinous, minute, incipient reactions, and shown us that all organisms, and especially the higher organisms, are incessantly performing these delicate reactive movements, and, in that way, keeping in touch, as it were, with their world.   Since all definition is, at bottom, arbitrary, we might be content to call this incessant play of reactions, incipient and overt, the organism's consciousness of things, *except that we need the term 'consciousness' for something else!*

When I look at a red flag, my head turns, my eyes focus themselves at the proper distance, certain tensions and inhibitions are produced which I call 'paying attention' to it, incipient reactions of various sorts are engendered, according to what the flag means to me, and what thoughts, or esthetic feelings, or purposes, or emotions it arouses. All this is grist for the behaviorist's mill.   But *in addition* to all this, I have the sensation 'red.'   The behaviorist who is studying my reactions cannot find that sensation 'red' anywhere in me.   He may have a similar sensation himself if the flag is within his field of vision; but we are talking, not about his sensation of red, but about mine. The completest possible account of my bodily reactions leaves out of account what I *see*, my sense-data; and, likewise, what I *hear*, and so on.   Nor can the behaviorist discover my feelings and emotions, my thoughts and dreams.   He can guess at them, from studying my reactions; but the quality of my feeling eludes him.   He may see me writhing, but he cannot feel my pain.   He may see my smiles, measure my muscular tensions, count my heartbeats, discover what my glands are doing, but he cannot feel my happiness.   That, and all the rest of my conscious experience, is private.

I, too, may study my own reactions, may react, that is, in certain specific ways to them.   But I may also study my *conscious experiences*, my sensations, emotions, and the rest; when I react to *them*, I am reacting differently from the ways in which I react to my bodily reactions. One sort of reaction to conscious experience we call 'introspection.' But other people know of my experiences only as I describe them. In the case of animal psychology, since our subjects cannot tell us what they see and feel, there is nothing for us to do but to study their behavior; the rest is mere guesswork. Even in studying human beings, it is so difficult for the subject to measure, to describe with any exactness his own sensations, emotions, and dreams, that the behaviorist has cast aside the data of introspection as hopelessly unscientific. It is mere 'literary' psychology. He wishes exact, measurable facts. But in discarding the story of what we see and feel and suffer and enjoy, he is missing consciousness altogether and studying only its accompanying behavior.

It is quite *conceivable* that our bodies might have carried on their outward behavior as they do their inward behavior (such as digestion) without this play of accompanying consciousness. Some years ago a discussion took place in the philosophical journals anent an 'automatic sweetheart.' Suppose a girl who *acts* in every way as your sweetheart acts — smiles, blushes, kisses, caresses, speaks in tender voice, looks at you with melting eyes — yet is absolutely unconscious, in the ordinary sense; she sees nothing, feels nothing, enjoys nothing, knows nothing; she is just cleverly made to act *as if* she felt and thought and cared; would such a sweetheart be wholly satisfactory, or not? At any rate, that is not the case. We may be merely delicately adjusted machines from the physical point of view. But what *matters* is, that we are *conscious* machines. The *only* thing that matters is precisely what the behaviorist ignores, the constant play of color and feeling, the *qualitative* life that accompanies our physical movements.

No one, of course, can deny the fact of this qualitative life that we call 'conscious experience,' or 'mental states.' The behaviorists who seem to deny it probably mean no more than the physicists mean when they deny that the *qualities* of physical things come within *their* purview. Qualities are not a proper subject-matter for science, because they are so essentially private, so incessantly varying and evanescent. Moreover, not being usually careful students of epistemology, they perhaps take it for granted that color, sound, etc., exist out there in Nature. The flag itself is red, the so-called red 'sensation' is merely the fact of the reaction of the organism to the red flag; if a place must be found for this 'red,' it is the physicist's business to find it rather than the psychologist's. *Seeing* something red is nothing but reacting in a certain way; *feeling* anger, or pain, or happiness, is merely reacting in certain other complex ways. This puzzle about qualities, how they fit into the world — why should the behaviorist concern *himself* with it, any more than anyone else?

Well, *someone* must concern himself with it. For here we have the whole pageant of sense, of imagination, of dreams. We do not *mean* motions of matter, of any sort, when we speak of these infinitely various qualities of our conscious life; we know what we mean. And we have found good reasons, in our study of epistemology, for believing that these qualities are not qualities of outer objects, but are *effects* of outer objects, produced *in us* — i.e., as we have constantly said, *in our conscious experience.* But where *is* our conscious experience? The physicist says nothing of it, and now the behavioristic psychologist ignores it too! To whom shall we turn?

Fortunately, the great majority of our psychologists are fully aware of the problem; they see their distinctive task as the study of the data of introspection. The result is, that in addition to the knowledge given us by the physical sciences (including behavioristic psychology), which is, as we have seen, at bottom a knowledge of the structure and motions of masses of electrons and protons, we have a radically different kind of knowledge, a knowledge of private 'mental states,' or 'data of consciousness.' These qualitative data cannot, for reasons which we gave in Chapter VI, be regarded as parts, or aspects, of the physical things about us; they are organism-engendered. Each of us has his own private flux of mental states, their nature clearly dependent upon the nature of his particular organism. Yet they are not discoverable by any observer *in* the organism. They do not seem to belong *anywhere* in the public spatial world. Their status seems to be unique. In short, we have upon our hands the world-old problem of the relation of mental states to physical bodies, of mind to matter.

THE DEPENDENCE OF MIND UPON BRAIN

In seeking to determine the status of 'mental states' (or 'data of experience'), we cannot fail to be impressed by the fact that they seem to be somehow connected with brain-processes. We may *believe* in disembodied spirits; but the only cases of conscious life which are so indubitable as to convince us all are cases of consciousness-in-connection-with-brains. The various theories of the nature of consciousness hinge upon the precise relation which is assumed to hold between mind and brain. So, before considering these theories, we must have as clear an idea as possible of the empirical facts.

Consider first perception. Those particular data of consciousness which we call sensations, sensa, or data of perception, are clearly dependent upon brain-stimulation, and appear only when certain specific motions occur in certain specific brain-tracts. It is true that our visual sensa (the colored shapes which appear when we open our eyes) seem to be out there in the external world; our tactile data (e.g., the smooth feel of velvet) seem to be where our hands are touching objects; auditory data (the sounds we hear) seem to be somewhere in the air about us. Yet if the nerves which run from the eye to the optical area of the brain are severed, or if the optical area of the brain is destroyed, the colored shapes vanish; they are somehow brain-engendered. Similarly, it is only as the proper nerve-currents reach the proper areas of our brain that tactile data, auditory data, pains, pleasures, etc., appear in our conscious experience. Objects will still be there about us, musicians may still be playing, our hands may rest upon objects, fire may be burning them badly; but we shall see, hear, feel nothing. For, though many steps are necessary — light-waves, or air-waves, sense-organ-events, nerve-current-events — in the end we see, feel, hear, taste, smell, enjoy, suffer by means of our *brains*.

Incidentally, we may add that if the nerve which runs from eye to brain is stimulated by electricity, so that a nerve-current flows into the brain, a sensation of light is felt, even in a pitch-dark room, or even if the eyes are blind. So, after a man has lost a limb he still sometimes seems to feel it; the nerves that used to bring messages from it are agitated, and they arouse something of the

customary activity in the brain. In cases of hallucination and mirage, and in all sorts of everyday experiences
of visual illusions, we see things that are not there; our
brains have been misled by the messages reaching them.
We see what we see; perhaps just as vividly as in veridical
perception. We hear what we hear, whether or not there
are air-waves of the appropriate sort beating upon our
ears. Whatever may or may not be going on in the world
about us, our perceptual experience is — whatever our
brain-activity causes it to be. The rest of our bodies,
and all the world beyond our bodies, affects our consciousness only as it affects our brains.

Now, what is true of our perceptual experience seems
to be equally true of the other items in our conscious life:
they all involve brain-activity and are possible only when
specific brain-processes take place. If certain definite
portions of the cortex are removed, or diseased, certain
definite sorts of conscious experience are impossible, or
possible only in a distorted way. We cannot think, or
wish, or dream, without using our brains, and without
tiring our brains.

Everyday experience shows that whatever affects the
brain affects the mind at once. Alcohol, reaching the
brain through the stomach, produces its characteristic
effects upon our mental life. Ether, reaching the brain
through the lungs, paralyzes brain-activity immediately;
our mental life abruptly ceases. Fatigue affects the
brain more slowly; but when the effects have accumulated,
the mind goes to sleep. Later on, when the brain is re-
freshed, a noise or a jar sets up renewed activity in it, and
our mental life begins again. If, during the body's rest,
the brain carries on activity not well adjusted to the
body's actual environment and needs, we dream fan-

tastic dreams. If we lack proper food or fresh air, the brain works with difficulty; we are depressed, worried, stupid. Injuries to the brain may cause profound changes in a person's character; a person formerly kind and cheery may become ugly, melancholy, morose. Organic or functional disorders of the brain produce various forms of insanity. Physical impediments to the growth of the brain cause idiocy or feeble-mindedness. The loss of memory, the petulance, the weak wit of old age are the result of the degeneration of brain-tissue, or the inability of the brain to function properly.

The study of evolution gives us good reason for believing that the development of conscious life goes hand in hand with the development of brains. The cerebrum of man is far more developed than that of any other animal. But animals with a certain sensory power or mental faculty highly developed have the corresponding tract of the brain highly organized. Dogs, for example, with a far keener sense of smell than man, have the portion of the brain reached by the nerves from the nose more highly developed. The higher types of man have better developed brains than lower types. We can confidently trace the growth of intelligence in primitive man by measurements of the skulls that are unearthed. It is possible that the lowest animal organisms, and even that all plants, are conscious in some sense or degree. But mental life in any appreciable degree like our own seems to arise only when brains, with their incoming and outgoing nerve-systems, arise. So far as ordinary, everyday evidence goes, consciousness begins in the child with the first functioning of this brain-nerve system, and ends when that system ceases to function. And throughout a man's life, the *sort* of mental life that he has seems at least very largely determined by the messages received by his brain from his body and the outside world, together with the inherited pattern of his brain-structure.

The attribution of mental life to the animals, and, indeed, to other human beings is, as we have long since noted, a mere hypothesis. Yet it is an hypothesis which we cannot help making; no one can really believe the contrary hypothesis that all animals, and all human beings save himself, are unconscious automata. But physiology and behavioristic psychology have advanced so much farther than introspective psychology that we can often understand conscious life — even our own conscious life — better in terms of the brain-life which it somehow accompanies, than in purely mental terms. Mental *habits*, for instance, are inexplicable to introspection; *why* should we tend, almost irresistibly, to think and feel and act and believe in certain peculiar, stereotyped ways? It is only when we consider the make-up of our brains and bodies that we can begin to understand. Our brains, because of their inherited pattern and the influences that have been reaching them since our birth, have a very specific, individualized character. Currents tend to pass through them along the lines of least resistance. Each time that a current passes in a certain channel, it leaves that channel a little more permeable than it was before, and strengthens the likelihood that we shall think or feel or desire, and so act, in a similar way next time. This greater permeability of certain nerve-paths through the brain is the physical side of habit.

Again, the mental fact of memory seems pure magic. *How* can we remember events that are past and gone? Consider what happens physically: a certain configuration of brain-cells is excited, by conduction from neighboring points, that was formerly excited from incoming sensory nerves. This configuration tends, by the law of habit, to arouse the same reactions that those earlier excitations aroused. We react *as to* that earlier object which impressed our senses and (through the sensory and association-nerves) excited this particular pattern of points in the brain. This is the physical side of memory. And by studying these physical processes, we can begin to see *why* we remember. As new channels are formed, the old ones tend to be disused, configurations once easily innervated are now no longer, or only very partially, re-innervated; we have 'forgotten' the particular experiences which we had when those particular groups of brain-cells gave rise to some (perhaps only momentary and slight) reaction. The faculty of memory evidently depends upon (or is constituted by) the laws of the conductivity of nerve-currents through the brain and out to the various reactive mechanisms of the body.

Perception is, from the purely mental point of view, as much of a mystery as memory. *How* can we get out of our skins, as it were, and perceive objects distant from us in Space? The answer is simple in physical terms: we receive brain-impressions from these distant objects, through our sense-organs; the particular brain-configuration excited arouses a particular set of reactions of the organism. Physically speaking, perception is simply reacting to objects which are affecting our sense-organs, just as our memory of objects is reacting to them when they are no longer affecting our sense-organs. In both cases the brain acts as a sort of central telephone-exchange, receiving and co-ordinating impressions, and initiating the multitudinous reactions of the organism thereto. But in the case of perception the sensory tracts in the brain are violently aroused, by impact from without, and the organic reactions are immediate. In the case of memory (and imagination) the brain-tracts are aroused from within, by conduction (association), in feebler degree, and give rise to slighter organic reactions. Perception is immediate reaction to stimulus, memory is revived reaction, imagination is novel reaction instigated by novel, inwardly engendered brain-configurations. Emotion is a complex bodily phenomenon, with return-wave sensations pouring into the brain from the muscles and bodily organs.

Now all this sounds very 'materialistic.' And it certainly *would* be materialism if we were to say, as the radical behaviorists say, that the organism reacting in such and such ways is *all there is to* consciousness. But we are insisting, on the contrary, that *in addition to* these organic facts there are the mental facts, our conscious experiences. In *one* sense of the terms, perception, memory, emotion, etc., are what we have just described them to be, various types of behavior of the organism. And these forms of behavior are more easily studied scientifically than the mental states which accompany them. To be sure, the exact nature of the events that take place in body and brain is none too well known. But at least we can formulate a pretty good theory of what happens, step by step, and of the causal laws involved. But when we have done all this we still have the mental states on our hands; *they* have not yet been explained. Nowhere in the complex processes of the reacting organism do we find the colors which the person is seeing, the scenes which he is remembering or imagining, the emotions which he is feeling. These conscious experiences somehow accompany the brain-processes; there is a rough parallelism between the two sets of events. What the exact nature of this correlation is, we have yet to consider.

THE UNITY AND DISUNITY OF BRAIN-LIFE

The brain, acting, as we have said, like a central telephone-exchange, gives to the reactions of an organism a considerable degree of unity. It retains traces of a long series of former excitation- and reaction-patterns, and determines current reactions on the basis, not only of the messages pouring in at the moment from the various sense-organs, but also of its complex past history. Exciting outer stimuli sometimes dominate its action, and thus the body's activity. At other times inwardly engendered brain-currents, whether in revived or novel configuration, are predominant in determining our reactions. Our conscious life, which accompanies these various types of brain-control, is in the one case a vivid consciousness of outer objects, and in the other case a stream of memories, or of thoughts and plans. But all the way along, it has a unity roughly parallel to the unity of our functioning impression-reaction mechanism. All the things which we are simultaneously receiving impressions from and reacting to, we are simultaneously perceiving consciously; to the degree that vaso-motor sensations and inwardly excited currents are *integrated* with these excitations, so that they form a common pool out of which our action flows, to that degree our consciousness of the moment includes emotional, memory-, and thought-elements.

There are, of course, simultaneously going on, a vast number of bodily processes — breathing, digestion, circulation of the blood, and so on. But these processes do not seem to affect our consciousness except as messages come from them, by the afferent nerves, to the brain. It is brain-life with which our conscious life is connected. And by 'brain-life' we mean here the conduction of nerve-currents. For even in dreamless sleep, and after death, there is a great deal of activity of a sort going on in the brain. Cells are being supplied with fresh blood, electrons are flying about their atomic centers, and so on. But only as nervous energy percolates about from this set of brain-cells to that, and percolates off down the efferent nerves, do we seem to have conscious life.

And now we must note that this nervous activity of the brain is only more or less integrated into a whole. There are striking cases where two, or even more, elaborate impression-reaction processes are carried on simultaneously in a brain without intermingling and affecting one another. In these cases the mental life of the individual is split up, and we speak of dual, or multiple, personality. Only one of the impression-reaction systems can control the same set of motor nerves at a given time; only one, for instance, can express itself through the voice. But the other system may simultaneously be writing messages with a hand. The consciousness directing the voice and the consciousness directing the hand may be entirely ignorant of each other. Or the two brain-systems may gain possession in turn of the voice and the rest of the bodily mechanism; in that case we have alternating personality, as expressed, for example, in Stevenson's story of *Dr. Jekyll and Mr. Hyde* — which is a fantastic and impossible story, but illustrative, in its main theme, of a well-known situation. In such cases, both brain-systems are really in simultaneous existence; the one which is unable to dominate the major reactions of the organism is at the same time producing minor bodily effects.

Marked cases of multiple personality are unusual.

But less striking instances of the same principle abound. Hypnotism has revealed the fact that many bodily disturbances are due to the existence of emotions and haunting ideas of which the main stream of conscious life of the patient is unaware. In many cases of anesthesia, where the proper stimuli fail to produce sensations in the patient's dominant stream of consciousness, the hypnotist discovers that the sensations have really been produced, but have been isolated, pocketed, as it were, instead of merging into the dominant conscious life and helping to determine the main bodily reactions. Many cases of ill health are due to the presence of disturbing emotions and ideas unknown to the patient; in physical terms, these are isolated brain-configurations, incessantly producing slight bodily reactions, entirely uncontrolled by, because entirely outside of, the main control-system of the brain.

We may include in the same general category the everyday cases where habitual activity is carried on 'unconsciously.' A musician may be talking earnestly and quite oblivious to his fingers — which, nevertheless, go on correctly playing a complicated piece of music. The impression-reaction system which controls his playing is, for the most part, cut off from that other system which is controlling his voice; each system is carrying on its activity independently of the other. For the time being, he is a dual personality.

It is probable that many cases where we fail to see or feel or hear something which is impressing our sense-organs are not cases where the sense-organs failed to send nerve-currents to the brain, but cases of cleavage between the brain-events produced by these currents and the main body of nervous energy which is dominating the body's reactions. In fact, cerebral activities are continually

separating and reuniting. Our brain-life — and our concomitant mental life — have a very varying degree of
unity.

Many things inexplicable in other ways become intelligible in the light of this fact. A religious conversion, for
example, or a sudden change of mood, may be due to the ir-
ruption into the main stream of consciousness of phases of
mental life previously submerged and isolated. What is
commonly called 'the subconscious' consists, doubtless, of
phases of mental life thus cut off from the main stream.
Now and then a current rushes over from such an isolated
system into the main system; ideas jump into our minds
out of the unknown. Much of the work of thinkers and
poets seems to be done in this region outside the main
field of consciousness. Ideas ripen and mature there,
and come to us in moments of relaxation; our energies
not being then needed by the main system, enough energy
is appropriated by the subconscious elements to enable
them to flow over and join the main system. All sorts of
curious facts — trance-states, hysterias, crystal-gazing,
automatic writing, etc. — are probably to be explained in
terms of the more or less complete isolation of impression-
reaction systems.

It is quite plausible to suppose that our bodies have a
certain sort of consciousness in connection with various
sub-cerebral nervous reflexes. The cerebellum, the gan-
glia along the spinal column, and the lesser nerve-plexi,
have their own activity; but it is cut off from the activity
of the cerebrum (which we have been calling 'the brain').
These little brains exhibit intelligence of a minor order,
not unlike that of some lower animals — to whose brains
they are, indeed, similar. They are little telephone-
exchanges, performing their own indispensable function

in the bodily economy.   But if there is consciousness of a sort accompanying these little impression-reaction mechanisms, it is not *our* consciousness, but so many additional threads of conscious life accompanying our bodily life.

The upshot of all this seems to be that our conscious life is *more or less* a unity; its degree of unity varies from person to person, and from moment to moment.   It seems to be as much of a unity as is possessed by our impression-reaction mechanism, which controls the main reactions of the organism to its environment.   Our conscious experience is something other than this integrated nervous process.   But it accompanies it.   And it is easier to understand the unity and disunity of conscious life in terms of this accompanying, or underlying, activity of our central nervous system.   The very word 'consciousness' means 'experiencing together.'   The togetherness, the unity-in-plurality of conscious life, has always been a mystery.   And it still is!   But at least we should recognize, before erecting our theory of mental life, that there is a corresponding unity and disunity in our brain-life. Here, as everywhere, the study of brain-processes seems to be our best clue for understanding mental life.

THE ALTERNATIVE THEORIES

The problem of mind and body presents itself to us as the problem of relating two apparently disparate kinds of knowledge.   On the one hand we have the knowledge of the physical world, which we get through perception and systematize in the physical sciences.   On the other hand we have the knowledge which we get through introspection, first-hand acquaintance with our own private mental life, with its vivid and inexpressible qualitative nature.   The two kinds of knowledge are so incongruous that it is not easy to see how they fit together; we cannot readily imagine how the intricate motions of electrons and protons, and the dance of colors, sounds, thoughts and dreams, go together to make up the life of animal organisms. Somehow consciousness is connected with brain-life. But *how?*

To sum up the empirical evidence: first, our mental states appear *at the time when* our brain-activity occurs, and only *if* it occurs. Secondly, the diverse phases of our mental life *vary concomitantly with* the variations in the impression-reaction activities of the brain. There is some sort of correspondence, as well as synchronism, between specific conscious experiences and specific brain-events. A part of our experience reflects, symbolizes, reveals, to some degree, the nature of those outer objects from which our brains are receiving impressions and to which they are initiating reactions. But they correspond indirectly to those outer events; they correspond *directly* only to the brain-activities which those outer events produce. The rest of our experience consists of memories, thoughts, and so on. We know less concerning the brain-processes which are correlated with them; but it is clear that certain specific brain-events must exist in each case. The mental states are known directly by introspection, the brain-events have to be inferred by the laborious studies of physiologists. But the *causal connections* of brain-processes are easier to reconstruct than those of mental states. Brain-processes and mental life have at least a roughly parallel degree of unity and disunity. Mental life seems largely teleological, brain-reactions seem developed largely to attain the ends which secure the welfare of the organism.... Here, then, are two kinds of reality, closely concomitant, yet apparently utterly unlike.

Many theories have been advanced to account for these facts. But some of them are crude, some of them ignore the facts which we have found in our study of epistemology. There remain three types of theory which are deserving of serious consideration. They can be graphically illustrated by the following diagrams, in which little circles symbolize mental states, little crosses symbolize physical brain-events, and arrows symbolize causal influence.

The first theory postulates the existence of a 'Self,' or 'Soul,' an invisible, intangible, non-physical entity, which *has* mental states. Each animal organism has, somehow attached to it, though not actually anywhere in Space, a Self of this sort. The Self interacts with the animal's brain-processes, receiving impressions from them and, in turn, initiating motions in them. This theory is an out-and-out dualism of substance and of causation; that is, two complex existents, belonging to utterly different orders of existence, reciprocally affect each other. The Self, dependent upon the brain for its knowledge of the world, and for its opportunity of influencing events in the world, is like a telephone-operator who listens to what the various subscribers report, through the mechanical network of wires, and utilizes another network of wires to issue orders.

The second theory holds that there are no such entities as Selves, or Souls. Mental life is a mere by-product of brain-life, an evanescent accompaniment of it, much as noise accompanies certain other physical events. The mental states are engendered by the brain-life, but are insubstantial, and have no causal efficacy. They accompany and reflect what is going on in the brain; and, because the impressions received by the brain reproduce,

A. INTERACTIONISM

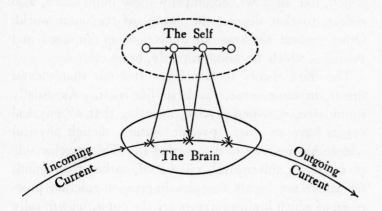

B. EPIPHENOMENALISM

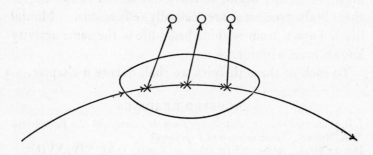

C. THE IDENTITY THEORY

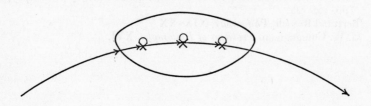

to a degree, the nature of outer events, the mental states which, like shadows, accompany these impressions, also reflect, to that degree, the nature of the outer world. Other mental shadows are reflections of impulses and volitions, which are also, primarily, brain-events.

The third theory is monistic. It holds that mental life *is*, in some sense, the brain-life itself. As usually formulated, it is pan-psychic, asserting that *all* physical events have an inner, 'psychic' nature, though physical science has no way of discovering it. This psychic side of matter is sub-mental, mind-stuff, rather than mind; for *minds* are highly complex impression-reaction processes, of which brain-processes are the outer, scientifically discoverable aspect. Minds are, therefore, not immaterial entities interacting with brains; they are the very inner life of the brain, causally efficacious to the degree that brain-processes are causally efficacious. Mental life is known from within; brain-life is the same activity known from without.

To each of these theories we shall devote a chapter.

SUGGESTED READINGS

J. B. Watson, *Behavior. Psychology from the Standpoint of a Behaviorist.*
A. A. Roback, *Behaviorism and Psychology.*
Durant Drake, *Mind and Its Place in Nature*, V–VI, XIV, XVII.
G. T. W. Patrick, *Introduction to Philosophy*, XVI.
R. W. Sellars, *Essentials of Philosophy*, XX–XXII.
DeW. H. Parker, *The Self and Nature*, I–II.
William James, *Essays in Radical Empiricism*, I.
W. S. Gamertsfelder and D. L. Evans, *Fundamentals of Philosophy*, pp. 522–544.
Bertrand Russell, *Philosophy*, XIX–XX.
G. W. Cunningham, *Problems of Philosophy*, XVI.

CHAPTER XIX

MIND AS INTERACTING

THE first of our three psycho-physical theories — the one perhaps most in accord with our naïve notions — postulates the existence of an immaterial Soul, or Self, which interacts with the brain-process in a constant causal interchange. Sensory brain-states produce in it sensations; in return, its purposes and volitions affect the brain, and through it the motor nerves and the movements of the body. We may call this theory Interactionism.

THE BELIEF IN AN IMMATERIAL SELF

We must consider carefully this concept of an immaterial Self. It is supposed to be an entity of a totally different order from the entities studied by physics. It exists in Time, but not in Space; it does not have extension, or mass, or motion; its activity lies in sensing, feeling, thinking, willing. And whereas matter consists of a vast number of extremely tiny separate units, mind consists of integrated Selves, each possessing a peculiar sort of unity, each using the brain of some animal as its instrument, but perhaps capable, since it is itself immaterial, of surviving the brain's decay.

This view is favored by the grammatical structure of our language; we say, *I* feel, *I* see, *I* will thus and so. It is favored by our religious and moral education; we are taught to think of ourselves as something other than our bodies, or than mere products of our bodies' life. We realize that we are much affected by the sort of bodies we inhabit; but, after all, is not the body a mere habitation for the Spirit?   For that matter, the greater part of my own conscious experience seems external to *me;* this colored landscape in front of me, this music that seems to float in the air, these painful and pleasant bodily sensations, inescapable as they are, are not my inner life. For, inextricably fused with our awareness of the world, and of our bodies, we have a continual, if not continuous, sense of ourselves as *having* this awareness.   Experience has a fundamental polarity: there are always the objects or feelings or impulses which the Self is conscious of, and there is always the subject, the Self, that is conscious of them and conscious of itself as being conscious of them. "All consciousness is in the form of self-experience." [1]

Now, as far as grammar goes, we must be on our guard. Language develops according to practical convenience, rather than with regard to metaphysical accuracy.   Perhaps it would be fairer to say, 'It is feeling,' as we say, 'It is raining'; i.e., feeling, or thinking, or willing is going on.   But this would be a needless purism; for there is certainly *something* to be called 'I' and 'myself,' whether it be an immaterial Soul or a sentient body.... We must be on our guard, too, against the vague dualistic assumptions which are a part of our literary and religious tradition.   The matter must be decided on the evidence. Do we actually *find* a subject-of-awareness when we examine our experience introspectively?   Or, if not, is the hypothesis that we have (or *are*) immaterial Selves, or Souls, the hypothesis which best explains the peculiarities of our experience as it comes and goes?

The interactionists have no doubt about it.

[1] E. S. Brightman, *Introduction to Philosophy*, p. 200.

The experience of the philosopher and of the 'plain man' alike testify unmistakably to the personal nature of consciousness.... The only forms of consciousness we know anything about are personal; and with every psychic state there goes a reference, explicit or implicit, to a self which somehow owns or has these states, perceives these objects, acts and feels and knows in these volitions, emotions, and judgments.... Each self is of course characterized by its present conscious state, but its present conscious state forms only a small portion of its nature.... Any given passing conscious state is merely an aspect or activity of the self. The self may be called a center of psychic powers whose characteristics necessarily transcend any given section of conscious content or phase of conscious experience, and which are essentially inexhaustible by any passing moment.[1]

Introspection is notoriously difficult, and psychologists give sharply divergent accounts of what they find. But the majority confess that they cannot find this Self. As William James said, 'experience has no inner duplicity.' We find sensa, images, ideas, purposes, all sorts of data, but we do not find a self-being-conscious-of-these-data. What at first may be taken for such a subject-of-consciousness is merely the most intimate and personal part of our stream of data. When we pause and look, as it were, for ourselves, we become conscious of the beating of our hearts, our breathing, eyeball movements, bodily tensions, emotional exhilarations or depressions, ideas and images. And in addition to these elements which we can label, there is always an elusive, unanalyzable background or margin of unnamable feelings. Taken all together, it makes up a 'stream of consciousness,' a sort of private 'movie.' There are feelings of effort, to be sure, purposes, and volitions. But these, too, are just items *of* which we are conscious. Nowhere in the flux of experience can we find a Self that is aware of it. Try it. Do

---

[1] J. B. Pratt, *Matter and Spirit*, pp. 173–179. By permission of The Macmillan Company, publishers.

you find such a Self? Do you find anything more than this or that particular item, or set of items, on a par with all the other items of which you are aware?

Some of the staunchest interactionists admit, or rather assert, that the Self cannot be found by introspection; it must be postulated. If I say that I find only *data that I am conscious of*, I imply that there is an *I* that is conscious of them. The word 'data' means 'given'; to what are the data of conscious given, to what do they appear, if not to a Self?... Well, everybody believes in a Self *in some sense*. The second and third of our three theories hold that the Self is simply the conscious organism. The question is, whether in addition to the physical organism, and its conscious life, we need to postulate an immaterial Self which has the conscious life. Is it the body, or a Soul connected with the body, that is conscious?

One of the commonest reasons for postulating the existence of an immaterial Self is to account for our persistent personal identity. Your experience is constantly changing, but you are you through it all; for it is always your Self that is 'having' the changing experiences.... But can we not explain this persistence of personal identity without postulating an immaterial Self? Your body persists. So do your abilities and capacities, your temperament, your habits, ideals and purposes — even if they are explained as the inherent characteristics of your sentient organism, or as the accompanying echo of a feeling, moving, dynamic body. Then there is the continuity of your memories and anticipations. And there is the familiarity of your physical environment and your daily routine. Is there anything more to personal identity than the persistence of these various factors, together with the abiding potentiality of recurrence of

certain memories, purposes, anticipations, hopes?...
The brain contains mechanisms for storing traces of its
activities, for keeping the body's reactions, in general, to
its own distinctive habits; it is constantly 'remembering,'
in the sense of reproducing earlier configurations of sensory and centrally excited elements, together with their
former reaction-tendencies. Here is a detailed physical
basis for continuity of personality. Of course we do not
know all we should like to know about how these mechanisms work. But we know *nothing* about how a Self
works. It is but a name.

Besides furnishing an explanation of the continuity
which our conscious life has during our lifetime, the Self
is supposed to explain the unity which our many-sided
experience has at every moment. The optical nerves
bring messages to one tract of the brain, the auditory
nerves to another, and so on. The impression-reaction
activities going on by means of incoming and outgoing
nerves are manifold. But our conscious experience,
though it too can be analyzed into many simultaneous
elements, is all felt together as *one* experience. Must
this not be because there is a unitary Self which is affected by the diverse brain-processes?

But is this anything, either, but a verbal explanation?
How does a Self unify the various elements of consciousness? The word Self (or Soul, or Subject, or Ego) is
offered us, but not the glimmer of an idea of how it produces unity out of diversity. And it seems hopelessly
incapable of explaining why the unity of consciousness is,
as we saw in the preceding chapter, so fluctuating and
partial. How about all the split-off bits of our conscious
life, the co-existent conscious activities which go on unaware of one another, the multiple personalities which,

in some degree, are very common? In cases of dual personality are there two Souls trying to inhabit one body? In the case of 'Miss Beauchamp,' who had four distinct personalities, were there four immaterial Selves, or was the one Self split into four parts?

It seems fair to say that all the actual explanation we have of the varying unity and disunity of consciousness is in terms of the more or less integrated or isolated impression-reaction activities of our nervous system. We perceive and feel as a unit what we *react* to as a unit. If we react to a single object in front of us (by 'paying attention' to it, thinking about it, talking about it, etc.), we are sharply conscious of that, and only vaguely, if at all, conscious of the other objects which are affecting our sense-organs. If we react to the scene as a whole, then we have a unitary consciousness of that landscape.... True, to point to the nature of our brain-processes is not, *ipso facto*, to explain our conscious life. But it suggests that one of the other two theories, which lean heavily on these facts, may be more intelligible than the theory which has recourse to an immaterial Self.

Finally, do we not need an immaterial Self to account for memory and perception, i.e., for the Time- and Space-transcending power of consciousness?

> If the mind be actually capable of transcending itself in such fashion as it plainly seems to do in every judgment which it makes concerning the future and the past, it is altogether a different sort of being from all material things and its ways of acting are as far removed from mechanical causation as the heavens are above the earth.[1]

In reply to this an objector may ask how the Self can accomplish this transcendence. He *can* see how the

---

[1] J. B. Pratt, *op. cit.*, p. 188. By permission of The Macmillan Company, publishers.

impression-reaction system of the brain makes the body
react to objects distant in Space, and how its storage of
traces of former activities makes the body on other occasions (or, to some degree, on the same occasion, since
perception involves memory as well as sense) react as
to formerly present stimuli.   So far as he actually under-
stands them, causally, perception and memory seem to
him to be functions of a *body* rather than functions of a
Soul.   At least, consciousness seems to reflect the specific
capacities of organic bodies more closely than the interactionist theory would have us believe.   The various
facts which the Self is invoked to explain are better explained by behavioristic psychology; in so far as they are
not yet explained, it seems to be along these lines that our
best hope lies.   All except the fact of consciousness (i.e.,
sentience) itself!

But does the Self help us to understand even the fact
that bodies are 'conscious'?   What *is* this 'Self'?   *Where*
is it?   How does it attach itself to a body, and where does
it come from?   Do all the animals have Selves?   If not,
when did they first appear in the evolutionary process?
How does a Self 'have' conscious states?   Until such
questions as these are answered, the Self remains an utterly vague and mysterious entity; to believe in it raises
many questions and answers none.   All the actual knowledge which we have of a person is knowledge of his bodily
characteristics and habits, plus what he tells us of his
mental states as they pass.   The hypothesis that he has
an immaterial Self somewhere in the background remains
a useless and unfruitful hypothesis.   Thus, except where
traditional religious ideas influence thought, the dominant tendency among philosophers and psychologists is
to discard that mysterious entity and regard mental

states simply as, in some sense, functions of a living organic body.

THE CONCEPT OF CAUSAL INTERACTION

It is possible to be an interactionist without believing in a Soul or Self. We may hold that mental states are 'emergent' at a certain point in evolution. They appear in connection with brain-processes, but they are a radically different sort of thing. Evolution here attains a new 'level.' The nature of mental states is such that the outside observer cannot discover them; they do not reflect light-rays or affect any of our instruments. But they interact with the brain-processes, and help to steer the organisms which have generated them. The real Self is the psycho-physical organism, part physical, part mental — the physical body shaping the mental life and the mental life in turn guiding the body's reactions.

This version of psycho-physical dualism does away with the necessity of believing in an unobserved and mysterious Self. But in its place we have a new perplexity. How *can* a physical organism generate something so utterly different as mental states, which are invisible, intangible, without mass, size, or shape, yet are capable of affecting causally the brain that generates them? All theories of 'emergence' leave us with a mystery unexplained, with the humble admission that our human intelligence simply cannot understand it. But of course it is conceivable that if we knew enough about the ultimate nature of matter, and about the various possible types of existence, we should see how a mental sort of existence can grow naturally out of physical existence at a certain point in its development.

Both forms of interactionism, however, have the very

grave difficulty of conceiving clearly how material processes can have causal effects upon mental existents (whether Selves or groups of mental states), and how these mental existents, having so different a *sort* of existence from that of brain-processes, can affect *them* causally. It is easy enough to speak in general terms of such reciprocal causation. But when we imagine the brain-processes in fine detail, electrons whirling around protons, nervous currents flowing this way and that, can we make any suggestion as to just where mental states get into the game, or how they succeed in altering these electronic and molecular motions?

Many thinkers have said flatly that the interactionist conception is absurd; what is not physical, and has no physical energy, cannot be conceived to affect the motions of matter. Obscure as is all causation, at bottom, we can at least trace some likeness, and some quantitative relationship, between cause and effect in the physical world. But between physical motions and mental states there is, according to the interactionist himself, nothing in common; they belong to different realms. So, to interpolate a mental link in a sequence of physical causes offends our sense of congruity. Try to think of a railway train proceeding on its way, with a mental state — the *sensation* or *idea* of a coupling — serving as the coupling between two cars! Events in our brains are on a scale so much smaller that the incongruity does not strike us so readily. But if we magnify these processes in our imagination, and try to think of a mental state as the coupling between any two of them, is it not really just as absurd?

The interactionist replies that the *fact* of the interaction of mind and body is undeniable, and we must accept it as a fact, even if we can frame no theory of how it is possible.

We are asked, *How can* two things so dissimilar affect each other at all? To which the obvious reply is the further question, Why can they not? Is it so certain that dissimilar things must fail to influence each other? Whether they can do so or not must be settled, not by an appeal to the imagination, but by an appeal to experience. Our inability to answer the question, *How can* the sun attract the earth, is not generally held to make it impossible for the sun actually to do so.[1]

We must, indeed, agree that our inability to conceive something does not disprove it. And, further, *if* the interactionist hypothesis seems, in the end, the least incredible theory, we must accept as a fact this reciprocal causation of two disparate sorts of existent, however mysterious it may be. But it must be acknowledged that a theory which involves no such supposition has in so far the advantage — though, of course, it may involve us in equally great incredibilities of some other sort.

It should be noted, too, that experience does not even *seem* to present us with the fact of a mental state affecting a brain-process. When we will to do something, or obey some mental impulse, our minds are set on the *end* we wish to achieve. We have not the least idea of how our mental state can set the right nerve-impulse going to initiate the bodily movement which we desire. We have no consciousness of affecting that nerve-process. We will, and — we know not how — our body moves. Our mental state is certainly not the *immediate* cause of what we do, though it does seem to be the remote cause of it. We can only *infer* that, without any conscious direction, our will-impulse has struck the brain-process in just the right place, and set going just the right motor currents to the proper muscles. So the case for the causal efficacy

[1] J. B. Pratt, *op. cit.*, p. 138. By permission of The Macmillan Company, publishers.

of mental states is not so direct and clear as the dualist often seems to suppose.

On the other hand, we do have continual evidence, in the large, of the dynamic efficacy of our own planning and purposing and willing. And, looking at the course of history, we have constant evidence of what is sometimes called the 'creative power of Spirit.' To preserve this gratifying and stimulating sense of the power of human purpose seems to be the chief motivation of interactionism. Any theory which hopes to supplant it must take due account of this very important mass of evidence.

Moreover, though the actual causal connections are hidden from our observation, we must note that there is an inner *relevance*, in each case, between what we plan and will to do and what we presently find ourselves doing. It was just those movements of our bodies that we foresaw and desired. So it does seem that, however unable the interactionist is to explain the detailed connection between purpose and the physical events which follow it, we are justified in assuming that there is a causal connection between them. Many would go further than this, and say that it is from just such experiences that we get our conception of causation. As we suggested in our chapter on causation, that concept roots down into the fact that we feel ourselves shoved by outside forces, and feel ourselves shoving back.... However, the other theories also have their explanations of these facts. So we must keep our minds open till we see what they have to say.

THE CONTINUITY OF PHYSICAL PROCESSES

It is from the physicist that the chief objection to causal interaction comes. He points out the great mass of evidence which has accumulated for the principle of the conservation of energy and the laws of motion. If mental states interfere with the working of the brain, pushing the molecules this way and that, they violate these physical laws. They do *work* — which, according to these laws, can only be done by energy, i.e., by actual or potential motions of material particles. Of course these laws are not proved to be universally valid; it is quite possible to believe that they hold everywhere *except* in the brain, where a mental factor interferes. But they are so beautiful and simple, and rest upon so much empirical evidence, that the physicist is apt to hope that they hold throughout Nature, and to prefer one of the theories which grant their universality.

It is possible for the interactionist to agree that the amount of energy informing bodily processes remains always an exact function of the food assimilated and the oxygen breathed, and that what the mind does is simply to determine the *direction* taken by brain-currents. But to interfere with the laws of motion is just as bad, to the lover of continuity in physical laws, as to add to the total amount of energy which the body exhibits. If the interactionist were to say that mental states are a *form* of 'energy,' he would be thereby giving up the idea that energy is simply a quantitative name for the motion of physical units. For, according to all dualistic theories, mental states (or events) are not motions of physical units. Consequently, all changes in the motion of brain-currents made by the interference of mind would still involve a break in the laws of motion. True, it is not always possible for us to *see* that these laws are followed in purely physical processes — e.g., in the jumps of electrons from one orbit to another, or in radio-activity.

But at least we can believe that they are followed in these cases which lie beyond our powers of observation. On the other hand, interactionism explicitly affirms that the physical laws of motion are *not* obeyed, whenever the body is influenced by the mind.

Let the interactionist reply:

> There is absolutely no reason of either an a priori or an empirical kind for maintaining the universal applicability of the theory of the conservation of energy. The only argument in favor of such a view is the argument from analogy that since the theory holds in the inorganic world therefore it must hold in the organic and conscious world.... So far as I am aware, there is absolutely no experimental or empirical evidence of any kind which gives any support whatever to the denial of the mind's power to modify the workings of the laws of physics and chemistry.[1]

Another argument offered by the physicist is that voluntary action arises by imperceptible stages out of reflex actions where no mental state enters in. The lowest animals may be assumed to exhibit purely physical reflexes. Or, if mental states are thought to interfere even in the most primitive animal reflexes, they may be assumed not to enter into the reflexes of the vegetable world, or into the activities of sub-organic aggregates of matter. At some point the dualist must assume that mind is generated, or enters upon the scene from without, and begins to interfere. This, again, offends the lover of continuity. If the reflexes of primitive organic or sub-organic bodies get along without interference by mind, why may not the more complex reflexes of more elaborate organisms get along without such interference?

As a matter of fact, many of our most delicate and elaborate reactions are automatic, or even quite un-

[1] J. B. Pratt, *op. cit.*, pp. 152–156. By permission of The Macmillan Company, publishers.

conscious. A series of stimuli affect our sense-organs, currents reach the brain, innervate motor nerves, and move the body, without any help of mental states. In the cases where we *are* conscious, a similar train of physiological events occurs. Why should we assume that the physiological mechanism is insufficient, in these cases too, to account for the movements of the organism? To the behavioristic psychologist the mental states seem a mere superfluity, not needed, or of any help, in his explanations.... Still, here *are* mental states. Is it not incredible, as William James put it, "that consciousness should have nothing to do with a business which it so faithfully attends?" [1]

Shall we say, in summary, that although interactionism remains a vague theory, raising many questions which it does not answer, it has a pretty good *prima facie* case? Mental states do seem to result from brain-stimulation, and do seem to affect the body's movements. The question is, whether any other theory can explain the situation more plausibly, while avoiding the physical implications of interactionism — which many of us, at least, would be glad, if possible, to avoid.

SUGGESTED READINGS

J. B. Pratt, *Matter and Spirit*, IV, V.
W. McDougall, *Body and Mind*, especially ch. XXVI.
G. T. W. Patrick, *Introduction to Philosophy*, XVIII.
William James, *Principles of Psychology*, vol. I, ch. V.
C. D. Broad, *The Mind and its Place in Nature*, pp. 95-121.
C. A. Strong, *Why the Mind Has a Body*, VI, XIII.
C. W. Cunningham, *Problems of Philosophy*, XVII.
E. S. Brightman, *Introduction to Philosophy*, VI.
J. H. Ryan, *Introduction to Philosophy*, IV.

---

[1] *Principles of Psychology*, vol. I, p. 136.

Chapter XX

MIND AS BY-PRODUCT

WHAT we are trying to explain is the synchronism and co-variance, and the apparent reciprocal influence, of brain-processes and mental states. There is a sort of rough parallelism between these two so apparently disparate sets of events. But the term 'parallelism' is metaphorical, and explains nothing. How *can* mental events and brain-events be 'parallel'? Whatever the degree and sense in which they are 'parallel,' that is the fact to be explained. Interactionism explains it by postulating an immaterial Self which 'has' mental states, or just a flux of immaterial states, existing in connection with brains, causally affected, point by point, by the brain-processes, and, in turn, affecting those processes. This detailed reciprocal causal influence explains the co-variance and 'parallelism' which we discover.... We now turn to a second theory, which goes by the formidable name of Epiphenomenalism. 'Epi-phenomenon' is Greek for 'by-product'; the theory holds that mental states are all caused by brain-processes, but exert no causal influence in return. They have no part in the dynamic life of the organism, but are a mere accompanying comment or echo.

THE CASE FOR MATERIALISM

This view is sometimes simply called 'materialism.' It does not deny the presence of mental states in connection with brain-processes, but it asserts that all that counts causally is the motions of matter. It is the impression-reaction nervous system developed by the organism that steers its movements. The belief "which attributes to thought a power, by virtue of its intent, to bring about what it calls for, as an incantation of exorcism might do," is

> a superstition clung to by the unreconciled childishness of man.... The consequences of reflection are due to its causes, to the competitive impulses in the body, not to the wistful lucubration itself; for this is mere poetry.... Consciousness is a lyric cry in the midst of business.[1]
>
> There are not two parallel streams, but one stream which, in slipping over certain rocks or dropping into certain pools, begins to babble a wanton music; not thereby losing any part of its substance or changing its course, but unawares enriching the world with a new beauty.[2]

This theory escapes most of the objections offered to interactionism. We do not have to strain our imaginations to conceive how an immaterial Soul, or immaterial mental states, can push material molecules about, and thus affect the body's action. We can retain full belief in the accepted laws of motion as universal and un-tampered with, in the brain as elsewhere. There is an enormous amount of concrete evidence of the determination of the body's behavior, and also of our conscious states, by physico-chemical conditions — our inherited bodily, and especially cerebral, capacities, the amount of oxygen and of food that we get, the functioning of our hearts, livers, stomachs, glands, and so on. There is no evidence at all, *in fine detail*, of the influencing of our behavior by our mental states; we cannot point to a single concrete brain-process, or bodily movement, and show where, and to what extent, a mental state produced or altered it. It is doubtless too much to ask for such evidence, since these processes are hidden within our bodies and cannot be observed. But it is fair to say that all the

[1] George Santayana, *The Journal of Philosophy*, vol. 3, p. 412.

[2] George Santayana, *The Realm of Essence*, p. 134.

causes we actually *find* at work, or can even clearly conceive, in detail, are physical causes.

There is considerable reason for believing that the bodily processes go on uninterrupted; a brain-process does not produce an effect upon an immaterial Self and, itself, peter out in doing so. Even when we are most vividly conscious, one set of brain-processes apparently produces another set of processes, and so on continuously. The brain-physiologist has no clear need of assuming any causative factors other than physiological factors to account for all that the body does. The more detailed our studies of organic activity, the more the body seems to be self-regulated, self-steering, in no need of the help of mind. And even when sensory stimulus is at a minimum, in pure thinking, or reverie, the brain is working hard, using up a rapid blood-supply, and getting tired.

Moreover, although planning, thinking, willing do often precede bodily movements, they by no means always precede even very complicated movements. The body is *capable*, at least, of doing a great deal, and perhaps everything that it does, without this preceding conscious life. We walk, we talk, we play the piano, we hum a tune, without taking thought, or knowing what we are doing. Indeed, the expert musician, or athlete, has to gain the habit of carrying on his complicated and delicately adjusted movements without conscious thought or direction. He has to develop a physical impression-reaction system which can do it automatically. The more urgent and rapid and accurate is the action needed, the less consciousness, in general, accompanies it.

And there are all sorts of experiences which impress upon us how helpless consciousness is, in the grip of hidden forces. We try to recall a familiar name, but we are tired, or our energies are engaged on other matters; we have to wait until uncontrollable inner mechanisms somehow, perhaps quite unexpectedly, produce the wanted word. If we find ourselves thinking of some associated memory, we know we are warm, and become hopeful; some sort of process is going on which is likely, soon, to revive the lost name.   We are not, of course, directly aware of the physiological processes which are going on; but when we do learn that such processes are going on all the time, it is easy to believe that it is those processes at whose mercy we are.   So, in literary composition, or in writing a letter to a friend, we constantly have the experience of taking up our pen and just letting the activity go ahead of its own momentum.   We are aware of a rush of thoughts, but often the pen moves before we are clearly aware of what we are going to write; there is little, if any, sense of *guidance* of its movements.   The whole thing flows out of us, like water tumbling over a waterfall.

Many other experiences could be cited which fall in naturally with the conception of mental states as a mere accompaniment of bodily life, powerless to interfere with it.   The question is, whether this conception is adequate to explain *all* the facts, and whether, even if it can be made to cover all the facts, it does not raise questions as difficult to answer as those which interactionism raises.

THE EFFICACY OF CONSCIOUSNESS

Now, although there are many cases in which consciousness seems helpless, there are also many cases in which consciousness seems to be the controlling factor. Whenever we plan, will, exert effort, our mental life feels active, efficacious, rather than a passive accompaniment of our bodily life.   Many think that this constitutes direct evidence of the untruth of the by-product theory; we have immediate experience of our minds as affecting our bodies, and that is the end on't. "The efficiency of consciousness is so obvious that it is futile to deny it." [1]

However, as we have already noted, it is *not* true that we *directly experience* the causal efficacy of our consciousness. We experience ourselves as willing, and we find our bodies moving. But the movements of our muscles are due to nerve-currents from specific motor areas of our brain. If our states of consciousness caused the movements, they caused them indirectly, by causing certain specific brain-events to take place. And we have no experience of *that*. If the motor nerves are severed or paralyzed, no amount of willing can move the muscles. And if the appropriate brain-tracts are injured or drugged, we cannot even will to move them. The belief that our conscious feelings of will and effort are causes of the motor events is an *hypothesis*, which is to be preferred to the by-product hypothesis only if it seems to explain better the observed facts.

The real argument against materialism rests upon the relevance of these mental states to the end achieved. An architect, for example, remembers houses he has seen and built, looks about him at other houses, thinks about them in detail, plans, decides, wills to take up his pencil and draw the plans which he thereupon proceeds to draw.

To tell the architect that the true reason why his process of selection and organization took the course it did is adequately stated by giving, for each of a series of moments, the distances and mechanical relations between the molecules composing his body and other co-existent masses of matter — to tell him this is to talk what to him, at least, must appear offensive nonsense. However little or however great

[1] J. B. Pratt, *Matter and Spirit*, p. 29.

the efficacy of a plan as a force in the physical world, it is the inner developing logic of his purpose, not the laws of mechanics, that inevitably seems to the planner to determine what the plan itself shall include and how its elements shall be combined with one another.... Never, surely, did a sillier or more self-stultifying idea enter the human mind than the idea that thinking as such — that is to say, remembering, planning, reasoning, forecasting — is a vast irrelevancy, having no part in the causation of man's behavior or in the shaping of his fortunes — a mysterious redundancy in a cosmos which would follow precisely the same course without it.   Nobody at a moment of reflective action, it may be suspected, ever believed this to be true.[1]

This forceful argument deserves very careful consideration.   In the first place, to present the materialistic view fairly, we must speak, not of the motions of individual molecules, but of the relatively large-scale impression-reaction activities of the organism.   The behaviorists have been showing us how the organism, by means of this extraordinarily complicated and delicately balanced set of processes, does, in a sense, take cognizance of its environment, and react appropriately to it; how it does, in a sense, remember, balance impulses, and determine its behavior, not merely in response to the impact of sense-currents, but with regard to the stored traces of its past activity.   Through an age-long process of evolutionary development, the human organism has become capable of this marvelously adjusted adaptive behavior, which is today being studied quite without any regard for the mental states which accompany this behavior.   The behaviorist is certainly wrong if he denies the existence of mental states.   But is it clear that he is wrong in saying that the behavior of organisms can be understood without any reference to them?

[1] A. O. Lovejoy, in *The Journal of Philosophy*, vol. 17, p. 630.

Most people, when they first grasp this idea that the body may be a self-steering automaton, are rather horrified, as if it meant that *they* were helpless spectators, in the grip of a sort of soulless and remorseless robot. But the theory means that *you* are, primarily, your *body*. When your brain receives impressions, balances, revives stored traces, and sends messages to your muscles, it is *you* who are perceiving and acting. If the *mental* states which you are simultaneously having reflect, and, as it were, picture these dynamic processes, that merely means that you are not only perceiving and acting, but are *conscious* of your perceiving and acting. Planning and willing are, essentially, forms of behavior; the planning and willing which your brain-processes are carrying on are *your* planning and willing. Your *consciousness* of your planning and willing is just something extra to be thankful for.

The pragmatists have advertised the phrase "creative intelligence." And we all must agree that intelligence is of extreme importance. The question is, what intelligence essentially *is*. The materialist says that it is such a happily adjusted receptivity to stimuli, past and present, as to generate happily adjusted reactions of the organism to the complex and changing situations of life. Some of our most intelligent activities are, at times, accompanied by very little, if any consciousness. And in calling conscious awareness of our own activities a mere accompaniment, the materialist does not in the least disparage intelligence in the sense of intelligent *activity*, delicately appropriate behavior. If people *act* intelligently — i.e., appropriately — why should we care what sort of mental states they are having?

Can we suppose that all cases of apparent power of

mind over body are explicable in behavioristic terms? 'Suggestion,' and 'auto-suggestion,' are undoubtedly potent in influencing the body's behavior; they may even, when intense, produce physical effects which are ordinarily beyond our control, such as the forming of blisters on the skin, and the 'stigmata' of the Cross. 'Mental healing' of every sort has marvelous cures to its credit. Hypnotists can often control their patients by a word.

Startling as are some of these cases, we must remember that in 'suggestion' there is a physical air-wave, nerve-current, and brain-excitation, which undoubtedly spreads and awakens sensitive configurations already set, like so many triggers, for explosion. In 'auto-suggestion,' which is inwardly aroused, there is undoubtedly elaborate brain-activity; and if we could trace back the history of that brain we should find earlier excitations from spoken words, or printed pages, which may account for its being so 'set' as to explode into action of a determinate sort when the inwardly engendered stimulus provides the spark.... Of course the details of these physiological processes are hidden from our view. But the behaviorist has this advantage, that he is constantly discovering more and more of the physical mechanisms involved. The interactionist can do nothing, apparently, but say, A conscious idea caused this bodily behavior. *How* it caused it remains blank mystery.

But can we seriously believe that the whole course of history would have been the same if consciousness had never developed? Would Shakespeare have written his plays, would Napoleon have fought his battles, would art and science and religion have been developed by mere *bodies*, however complex and delicately adjusted?... Well, why not? It is all very marvelous. But it is marvelous *anyway*, on any theory. Human bodies do act in these ingenious ways; and it is not clear how their mental states help them to, if they do.

Sometimes a *reductio ad absurdum* of materialism is attempted.

Take the familiar syllogism:

All men are mortal.
Socrates is a man.
Socrates is mortal.

The materialist assures us that we should be falling back into the primitive superstitions of a pre-naturalistic age should we suppose that either of the premises had anything to do with our arriving at the conclusion. We finally assert that Socrates is mortal, not because we have in mind the mortality of all men and the humanity of Socrates, nor for any other logical or psychological reason; but because certain mechanical processes in our brains force that thought into consciousness. Thus no conclusion is ever arrived at because of logical necessity. There is no logical necessity among mental processes, but only physical necessity. The truth is, according to materialism, we think the way we *have* to think, the way our mechanical brains constrain us to think. We may *happen* to think logically; but if we do, this is not because logic had anything to do with our conclusion, but because the brain molecules shake down, so to speak, in a lucky fashion. It is plain, therefore, that no conclusion that we men can reach can ever claim to be based on logic. It is forever impossible to demonstrate that any thesis is logically necessary. If we happen to entertain it we do, that is all; for demonstration is out of the question.[1]

This passage, like most controversial writing, caricatures the view it is attacking. We "arrive at our conclusion" because the molecules in our brains "shake down" in a lucky fashion! One might as well assert the ridiculousness of the idea that a watch could keep time, under changing conditions, by its molecules shaking down in a lucky fashion. The materialist believes that the

[1] J. B. Pratt, *op. cit.*, pp. 19–20. By permission of The Macmillan Company, publishers.

human brain has developed, through hundreds of millions of years of evolution, into a marvelously delicate mechanism capable of reacting to the spoken or printed words, "All men are mortal," etc., in an appropriate way. 'Drawing the correct conclusion' means, in behavioristic terms, enunciating the words "Socrates is mortal" (out loud or silently), or getting such a 'set' of the neural mechanism that one *would* say that rather than its contradictory, if occasion called for a statement.   Whether or not the brain-processes need the help of mental states to reach this new adjustment, *logic* is not the *cause* of the outcome.   Logic is not, itself, a series of causes and effects, whether physiological or psychological.   Logic is simply the fact of the consistency of one proposition with another.   It is the *knowledge* of these consistencies and inconsistencies which is (to some slight extent) the cause of our reaching an equilibrium with one reaction-tendency rather than another.   And the question merely is whether it is knowledge in the behavioristic sense which has the causal influence, or whether the *consciousness* of our body's 'knowledge' enters into the game. In any case, if the final proposition which we enunciate *is* consistent with the earlier propositions, then we have been 'logical,' whatever the processes by which we reached the goal.   Actually, we reach our goals in all sorts of different ways; sometimes we just find ourselves uttering a correct conclusion without any consciousness of what made our lips say *that* rather than something else. Logic is not the story of how the mind, or brain, works. It is just a set of checks, by contemplation of (reaction to) which we may test our conclusions and learn, gradually, to disuse habits of thinking (mental or cerebral) which have led to erroneous conclusions.

What, then, about the fact of the *relevance* of our mental states? If conscious states are a mere shadow-accompaniment of the activity of our brain-processes, why are they the *sort* of mental states that *seem* to be (at times) causes of our behavior?... Well, if they are 'shadows' of (or perhaps a better metaphor would be a 'luminescence' accompanying) our cerebral processes, they *should* seem causative. The conscious experience which we call 'willing' is the 'shadow' of the bodily process of willing; and as the latter *is* causally effective, the former naturally *seems* to be. A will-experience feels like the sort of thing that is going to produce such and such results — because it 'pictures' a process which *is* going to produce it. It feels active because it is the glow, the music, the sentience, accompanying an activity. Sensory-events are produced in the brain from without; so conscious 'sensations' have the *feel* of being produced from without. Volitions are usually the end-result of a process of inward activity, of which we have been conscious; therefore they seem to emanate, and do emanate, from *us*. In short, if materialism is true, we should naturally be supposed, if we are conscious at all, to have just the *kinds* of consciousness that we do have — a feeling of receptivity in sensation, and a feeling of activity in willing, reflecting the difference in the two sorts of cerebral events.

When we watch a 'movie' on the screen, the events *seem* to follow one another causally. The hero speaks to the heroine, she answers him. The hero smites the villain and he falls. But actually, these events are *not* causally connected with one another. Each picture, existing on the screen for a fraction of a second, is caused by light-rays coming from the projector; one picture does not causally affect the next. The figures on the screen are not dynamic, efficacious, they are merely shadows. The *apparent* causal process merely reflects a *real* causal process which went on when the picture was filmed.... Similarly, the Lady of Shalott, looking forever into her mirror, saw a continuous procession of figures, which may have come to seem very real, and very dynamic. But they were only mirror-images, not a part of the dynamic world.... So, all the pageant of our conscious life may be a sort of private 'movie,' mirroring, reflecting, expressing the dynamic life of the body. Even if telepathy be a fact, it may well have some physical basis, as wireless telegraphy and telephoning have.

If the theory is true, we are no worse off than on any other theory. We shall simply cease identifying ourselves so exclusively with our conscious life, we shall think of ourselves as psycho-physical organisms. Our activity may be just as free or bound on one theory as on another. A living organism may be conceived to be, to some degree, autonomous, self-directing, as readily as a Self or a stream of mental states. The freedom which we experience mentally may be just our *sense* of freedom, reflecting the dynamic freedom of our reactive-tendencies. On the other hand, the dualist's interaction between minds and bodies may follow perfectly regular laws and be causally determined throughout. This is a problem which we must still postpone.

If materialism is true, it is only our cerebral activities and bodily processes which are causally efficacious. But it is the accompanying music of consciousness which counts, in another, and deeper sense. For it is only the qualities of conscious life that matter at all, in the last analysis. Consciousness may be, from the physical, dynamic point of view, a by-product. But it is this by-product alone which gives *worth* to the activities of organisms and the universe that gives them birth.

HOW DO BODIES GENERATE CONSCIOUSNESS?

The materialistic theory cannot be disproved by the facts of experience; it has an answer to all the objections based upon the observed characteristics of consciousness. But it has, in common with the later form of interactionism, a very difficult problem to solve, viz., How *can* physical bodies generate consciousness? What is this process of producing a 'by-product' so strikingly disparate from the brain-events? Consciousness is said to 'accompany' brain-life; but just *where* is it? It is its 'shadow'; but that is plainly a metaphor. In short, the behavioristic side of the theory, the conception of the physical organism as a self-steering structure, needing no mental life to make it go, is a clean-cut theory, going beyond the evidence, to be sure, but perfectly conceivable. Where the theory halts is in explaining how it happens that consciousness appears at all, if it is not needed, what is the particular process that brings it into being, and what is its status when it has been produced. This whole side of the theory is usually left a blank. The body may be conceived to be self-sufficing, yes. But after all, consciousness is here. How did it get here? And *where* is *here?*

The believer in emergent evolution is content to leave the emergence of radical novelties a mystery. But it is one thing to say that matter begins at a certain point to behave in a new way, and another thing to say that it 'generates' something so utterly different as mental life.

Wherever mind is taken to begin, it bursts into being like a shot out of a pistol that is not previously in the pistol....

The supposed production of mind by matter is entirely foreign to and discrepant with the whole order of nature in the material world.... [But this is] asserting the miracle of creation out of nothing, where the creator is not an omnipotent being, but a finite and transient complex of material phenomena.... The supposed production of mental by merely material occurrences, considered in the only way in which it can be considered, as an example of causal relation, is quite unintelligible.   By this I mean not that *we* cannot understand it but that it is from the nature of the case sheer nonsense.[1]

But surely it is rash to say that the situation as the materialist conceives it is, in the nature of the case, nonsense, especially in view of the fact that the alternative theories postulate facts equally hard to understand.   Do we, for example, know anything more about where a Self comes from (or how it gets created), and how it gets attached to a given body, than about how brains generate mental states?   After all, we really know nothing about the inner nature of matter; we cannot say offhand what potentialities it may contain.   And materialism has this advantage, that it requires us to believe only in known entities — brains and mental states, whereas the believers in a unitary Self require us to believe also in that unobserved and hypothetical entity.

It may be asked, however, why, if organic bodies are self-steering automata, mental life should have appeared at all.   Interactionists can say that consciousness was produced, as eyes and ears and brains were produced, in order to help the organism to survive.   They do not usually say this, because they usually think of mind as on a par with matter — even, perhaps, more aboriginal, but, anyway, not generated by matter; they think of Selves as having independent existence, and only condescending, as it were, to have dealings with matter, to use ma-

[1] G. F. Stout, *Mind and Matter*, pp. 110–116.

terial brains as their instruments. But the interactionist who believes in emergent evolution may say that bodies gave birth to minds, and that minds survived and developed because they were of use to the organism in planning, foreseeing, guiding its movements more wisely than a mere mechanical automaton could guide itself. To the materialist, however, this answer is barred; since mental states have, on his hypothesis, no causal efficacy, they are of no *use* to the organism, and would not have been developed by natural selection.

Nevertheless, evolution *does* produce many useless things: shadows are useless, the noise made by a locomotive engine is useless, beauty is (certainly for the most part) useless. So are, so far as we can see, a good many of the features actually developed by organic bodies. The fact is, variations in type seem to be quite blindly produced, at random. Natural selection weeds out those that are positively dangerous to the organism, those that handicap it in any way. But so long as these new structures or functions are not *harmful*, they may persist indefinitely, and develop *ad lib*. Consciousness may be such a fortunate superfluity, like the beauty of a sunset, or the prismatic curve of a rainbow. Or, if the course of Nature is providential, consciousness may have been produced for its own sake, that we may *enjoy* living, although it was not needed to help us to live. As a matter of fact, materialism plays into the hands of supernaturalism rather better than interactionism does. For if the latter theory is true, it is not implausible to suppose that consciousness was developed naturally, by a blind process of natural selection, because of its usefulness; whereas, if materialism is true, though we cannot say that Nature *might* not have produced and developed it, it may seem unlikely that unconscious and purposeless energies should have given birth to something so useless, yet so elaborate and so delightful.

A decisive way to refute materialism would be to accumulate thoroughly convincing evidence of the existence of minds apart from bodies. Alleged evidence we have, in great abundance, sufficient to convince many investigators. We cannot, in this short volume, attempt to appraise this confused mass of testimony. But we must recognize that, vast as it is in bulk, it fails to convince many earnest seekers who have tried their hardest to be convinced. The matter must be considered open for the present. And in the mean time, we are all confronted with the obvious and inescapable facts, which we noted in Chapter XVIII, of the apparent dependence of mental life upon the activity of a brain. So far as we actually *know*, consciousness occurs only when brains function. The specific kinds of consciousness seem to depend upon the specific sorts of brain-processes which occur; and they, in turn, depend upon the inherited structure of the particular brain in question, together with the causal influences coming from the sense-organs, and the indirect influence of food and air and everything else that sustains life and gives it specific direction. Unless we can find definite proof that mental life can go on independently of the brain's life, we shall have to allow materialism, i.e., epiphenomenalism, as at least a tenable hypothesis.

SUGGESTED READINGS

T. H. Huxley, *Method and Results*, V.
Friedrich Paulsen, *Introduction to Philosophy*, ch. I, §§ 1–3.
C. A. Strong, *Why the Mind Has a Body*, V, XIV.
William James, *Principles of Psychology*, vol. I, pp. 128–138.
J. B. Pratt, *Matter and Spirit*, I.
C. E. M. Joad, *Mind and Matter*, I–II.
William Macdougall, *Body and Mind*, XI.

CHAPTER XXI

MIND AND BRAIN AS IDENTICAL

BOTH interactionism and materialism are, in a sense, dualistic; they take mental life to be something quite distinct from matter, having a totally different *sort* of being. They are both faced with the apparently insuperable problem of fitting these two sorts of existence together. In the one case, we have to ask in what realm immaterial Selves, or mental states, have their existence, and how they interact with matter. In the other case, we have to ask how brains can generate mental states, and where they exist when generated.

THE IDENTITY THEORY

The theory which we are now to discuss escapes these problems by asserting that mind and brain are the same thing, known in two different ways. The apparent duality of mind and matter is an epistemological, not an ontological, duality — a duality of our knowledge, not a duality of substance. The whole world of matter outside of your brain-process is known to you only at second hand, through the effects it produces upon your mental life; physical science is the analysis and organization of this second-hand knowledge. But you also know your own inner life at first hand. You are on the inside, so to speak, of your brain; that active brain-life is *you*. Your stream of mental states is the inner, throbbing reality which, known from the outside, via perception, is called your integrated, reactive brain-processes. You are, indeed, your whole organism, with its distinctive looks, capacities, habits, and mannerisms.   But your brain-life is the *conscious* part of you.   Consciousness is not something extra, interpolated into the impression-reaction mechanism of the organism, or accompanying it, it *is* that flux of impression-reaction activities, it is its inner, private nature.   This theory has had various names. We shall call it the identity theory, or psycho-physical monism.

In order to grasp the theory clearly, let us remember the outcome of our discussion of epistemology, and illustrate it by a concrete example, the sight of a star. The star itself is a vast globe of incandescent gas, many light-years distant.   Radiating from the star are trillion-mile-long light-rays.   A few of them strike my eyes and produce certain effects there.   A nerve-current flows to the optical tract in my brain.   Certain events take place there.   The activity spreads to neighboring motor tracts. A motor nerve-current flows out to my arm.   I raise an opera-glass and look up at the sky.... Concerning all these events we have whatever knowledge physics and physiology can give us.   However complete it is, or may become, it is, in the nature of the case, only structural knowledge, knowledge of the spatio-temporal pattern of these events.   It can tell us nothing of their inner nature. They are for physical science, as we have said, only x's, y's, and z's.

But now I have *another* sort of knowledge, which I call introspection.   I know that *at the time when* this particular bit of brain-activity is going on, a twinkling point of light appears in my conscious experience.   This is evidently not the same thing as the star itself.   For the star may have ceased to exist long ago; and, if not, it has probably moved, during the years since the light-rays which have just now reached my eyes started their journey, so that it is not now in the direction where I see the twinkling point of light. My twinkling-point-of-light experience is followed, at once or after deliberation, by a conscious impulse to raise the opera-glass. These conscious experiences take place while my brain-events are taking place. There seems, if I compare the two sets of events, to be at least some sort of rough parallelism, or co-variance, between them. As the sensory brain-events change, my concomitant mental events change, *pari passu*. As the motor brain-events change, my conscious impulse to action changes. Why not adopt the simplest hypothesis, and say that there is, actually, but one set of events? Seeing-the-twinkling-point-of-light, and having-a-conscious-impulse-to-raise-the-opera-glass, *are* the inner nature of the events which physiology studies from the outside and calls a certain activity of my impression-reaction mechanism.

But the question will at once be raised, How does it happen that brain-processes alone have this inner, mental nature? And the answer is, They are not alone in having an inner nature. It just happens that these particular bits of reality are the only bits of reality that we know at first hand, and whose inner nature, therefore, we can get *at*. Your brain-processes are *you*, the conscious part of you. All the rest of the restless, moving world has its own inner nature; but it has no mechanism of introspection, or of speech. It cannot tell us, it does not *know*, what its own inner nature is. Because it has no mechanism of introspection, or of perception, or memory, we cannot properly call these other bits of matter *minds*. But we can say that their inner nature is homogeneous with that of our brain-processes. Ordinary matter is the stuff out of which brains develop; its inner nature we may call 'mind-stuff.' Or we may use the term 'psychic' to connote the common inner nature of all matter. We may then call our theory 'pan-psychism.' Or we may call it 'pan-materialism,' or just 'monism.' The substance of the world is called 'matter' when we look at it from the outside. If we were on the inside of it, we should call it 'psychic stuff,' or 'sentience.'

The term 'pan-psychism' has proved misleading. It suggests a denial of the existence of matter, and its replacement by a different sort of reality, an airy, insubstantial world. But the theory does not deny any of the teachings of physics, it merely rounds it out by telling us what matter *is*. It says that the world of matter-in-motion is the real world, but that physics has no means of discovering its inner nature, and needs to be supplemented by an inference drawn from the special knowledge we have of our little corners of the world.

The term 'pan-psychism' also suggests that all the world is *conscious*. But, though, according to this theory, the whole universe is of the same *substance* as our conscious life, it lacks — except where brains have developed — the peculiar *organization* of elements which make up a *mind*. The brain is not a special sort of *stuff*, it is a very special sort of *mechanism*.[1] So the mind, which *is* the brain, considered in its inner nature, is not a different sort of stuff from the rest of nature, but is a highly complex and delicately adjusted mechanism. It is a mechanism which carries on the processes of perception, memory, imagination, thought, and emotion. These are all extremely complex processes; and where they are absent, we cannot properly speak of a 'mind.'

[1] We are not using the term 'mechanism' to imply complete determinism. We raise that point in our next chapter.

Our conception of what all the other processes of the world-life *are*, in their inner nature, must remain very vague. They cannot properly be called 'will,' as Schopenhauer thought. For willing is a very complex process, involving a revival and recombination of sensations, anticipation, a sense of balancing between alternative possibilities of action, and a sense of choosing. In behavioristic terms, this must involve a highly complex set of brain-processes of certain very definite sorts, which occur nowhere outside of brains. Willing is one of the most distinctively human of activities.... Perception and memory and emotion are also highly complex processes, for which only the higher organisms are endowed. So the life of the world outside of brains must be blind, dark, isolated, unremembered, without awareness of anything else, without desire or intent. But it is these *functions* that constitute 'consciousness'; so it would be inaccurate to call the life of nature 'conscious.'... Still, since physics can tell us nothing at all about the inner nature of what exists, we may be thankful if our awareness of our own inner life gives us some clue, however vague, to the inner nature of the world-stuff out of which we were born, and of whose very substance we are.

THE CASE FOR THE THEORY

The arguments in favor of the theory may be put in summary form, since they are clear and have already been noted explicitly or by implication:

(1) It solves very simply the tough problems which confront the other two theories, as to where mind comes from, where it exists, and how so disparate a reality can be 'generated' by, or can interact with, the brain. Minds are just complexifications of the universal world-substance.

Mental life is just a very specialized and integrated resultant of the universal activities of what we have blindly
called 'matter.'   There is no break in continuity; the
origin and development of consciousness is a natural
event in evolution.   It *is* the development of the impression-reaction nervous system centering in the brain,
considered in its inner nature.

(2) Thus it is the only theory which can explain the
whole known universe as a single, coherent spatio-temporal
order, the only theory that can fit mind and body together into one homogeneous realm of existence.   Other
theories may give us a coherent physical world, but they
leave us with mental states dangling outside of this world-
order, existing when brain-events exist, but not *in* the
brain, and not in any exactly describable relation to the
brain-events.

(3) The empirical parallelism between brain-events
and mental events suggests, though it does not prove,
their identity.   Sensory brain-events vary concomitantly
with the outer events of which they are the distant effects,
and thus are, in a sense, representative of them.   But
our conscious sensations (our sensa) are *also* representative of the outer objects, so much so that the naïve man
mistakes them for those outer things themselves.   We
thus seem to have two representations of outer reality
produced simultaneously, a set of physical events and a
set of mental events.   The behaviorist thinks that the
physical events determine the reactions of the organism;
the plain man (and the interactionist) thinks that the
mental events determine them.   Why should we have
two sets of events so mysteriously parallel?... And so
right through the gamut of brain-activity and of mental
life.   The brain remembers, recombines, purposes, in a

behavioristic sense; meantime our conscious life is be-
having in the way which those terms more familiarly
connote.   The theory which identifies the two sets of
activities is surely a great simplification.

(4) The monistic theory preserves the law of the conservation of energy and the laws of motion, as surely as
epiphenomenalism does.   There is no break in the continuity of physical processes, no interpolation of non-
physical causes.   On the other hand, it preserves our
natural belief in the efficacy of our mental life, which is
the chief motif of interactionism and the chief deterrent
to the acceptance of the by-product theory.   Our mental
life is our brain-life, in its full-blooded reality, an integral
part of the causal nexus of Nature, as dynamic as explod-
ing gunpowder.

(5) Our mental life is the nearest bit of reality to us,
the only portion of reality that we know at close range.
Is it not plausible to suppose that the rest of reality,
which we know only at arm's length, as it were, is homogeneous with this bit that we know so intimately?   If
we can believe the theory to be true, it should make us at
home in our world.   For not only are our bodies built up
of the world-substance, but our minds too are not alien
intruders, but a natural and beautiful outgrowth of the
universal world-life.

> Deftly doth the dust express
> In mind her hidden loveliness;
> And from her cool silence stream
> The cricket's cry and Dante's dream.
> For the earth that breeds the trees
> Breeds cities too, and symphonies;
> Equally her beauty flows
> Into a savior or a rose.[1]

[1] John Hall Wheelock, *Earth*.

THE CASE AGAINST THE THEORY

However, it is one thing to present the theory in general terms, another thing to analyze its meaning in detail. Some of the objections raised to it are mere misunderstandings, or are based upon an inadequate epistemology. But there are some searching questions to which the upholders of the theory are hard pressed to find plausible answers. We shall consider the former objections first, very briefly, and then weigh the really puzzling questions.

(1) The commonest objection is that brain-events and mental events are such disparate sorts of reality that they cannot possibly be the same thing. Inspect a brain, at the height of its activity: what we see is, some convolutions of gray matter occupying a few square inches of space, together with a set of incoming and outgoing nerve-fibers. We know that currents are flying through these circuits in elaborate detail, that the little mass of gray matter is full of seething activity. But even so, what an inadequate thing to *be* our mental life!

But, we may reply, the inadequacy is simply the inadequacy of our powers of *perception*. A few, relatively occasional, extremely minute events in the brain reflect light-rays, which affect the eyes and brain of the physiologist who is examining it. He therefore has the visual datum, 'a complicated mass of gray matter,' in his experience. But we must remember that it is *his experience* that we are now talking about — a meager, arm's-length *effect* of the brain. What the brain itself is like is obviously very inadequately reported by the effect which light-rays reflected by it produce in the observer's consciousness. The visual picture which the observer has is undoubtedly representative of one aspect of the reality he is trying to observe, viz., of its spatio-temporal in-

terrelations; but that is all. It is to be *expected* that the
report which perception gives us of some bit of reality
will be as different from the reality itself as a telegraphic
report is different from the events which it describes.
We must always remember that the brain-processes
themselves do not get into our experience at all; they are
separated from us by the light-rays, and other intervening
events. Thus, their nature may be anything at all, so
long as it is such as to permit this perception-report to be
evoked in us.

(2) Physics, however, by its patient indirection, tells
us quite a good deal about the real nature of the brain-
processes. Yes, but as we have long since seen, it gives
us merely the spatio-temporal *pattern* of those events.
In other words, it simply carries out into finer detail,
with the aid of instruments, the reports of perception.
And it tries to formulate the laws, the regularities of recurrence, which it may find exemplified in the processes.
At best, it furnishes us with a map of the existents it
studies, as unlike them as a geographer's map is unlike
the earth's surface which it represents. There is a concomitant variation between its descriptions and the
existents it is trying to describe, no more. We saw in an
earlier context that it is illegitimate to think of matter
as having the color, or brightness, or hardness, or any of
the qualities that we have in our experiences of it. Physicists are insistent upon this point; their formulas are
purely algebraic. Physical science gives us, as it were,
the skeleton of reality, but never its flesh and blood.

In short, the apparent disparateness of mind and body
is due simply to the fact that we have two different sorts
of *knowledge* of this one reality, the sort of knowledge that
physics gives us, and the intimate knowledge that we get
(of our *own* minds) by introspection.

Many physicists could be quoted in support of this conclusion.

> There is nothing to prevent the assemblage of atoms forming the brain from being a thinking-machine in virtue of that nature which physics leaves undetermined and undeterminable.... We create unnecessary difficulty for ourselves by postulating two inscrutabilities instead of one.[1]

So Russell speaks of

> the extremely abstract character of physical knowledge, and the fact that physics leaves open all kinds of possibilities as to the intrinsic character of the world to which its equations apply. There is nothing in physics to prove that the physical world is radically different in character from the mental world.[2]

(3) Objectors say that it strains their credulity to think of sticks and stones and dirt and the ocean as 'psychic' in nature — vague as the theory leaves that term.... But what *is* their nature? They must have *some* nature. Science cannot tell us anything except some external facts about their spatio-temporal interrelations. Is it not simplest, in the lack of positive knowledge, to believe that their inner nature is homogeneous with our own?

(4) The brain exists during dreamless sleep, and for a while after death. If the brain-processes *are* mental life, why is mental life not going on then?... Because human mental life is not the sub-biological motions of the brain-atoms, it is a set of elaborate, integrated impression-reaction nervous processes. These stop during dreamless sleep (if there is such a thing as entirely dreamless sleep), and at death.

(5) The brain acts mechanically, by pushes from be-

---

[1] A. S. Eddington, in *Science, Religion and Reality*, p. 208.
[2] Bertrand Russell, *The Analysis of Matter*, p. 270.

hind, as it were.   The mind acts teleologically, by fore-
sight of future consequences, and in order to attain desired ends.... But as we said in discussing vitalism, mechanism and teleology are not incompatible.   On the contrary, it is not at all clear how ends *can* be attained except
by some determinate causal process, in which each cause
exists prior to its effect.   It is not the *end* which brings
itself about, it is a *foreseeing* of the end — a *planning*
for it.   And according to behavioristic psychology, foreseeing and planning are bodily events, expressible in
terms of a certain 'set' of the organism, certain incipient
tendencies to action, and so on.   What the monistic
theory adds is, that this determinative activity of the
organism *is* the conscious foreseeing and planning.   We
are talking about the same set of events; in the one case,
in terms of its large-scale and dramatic achievements, in
the other case, in terms of the fine-scale processes that
brought it about.

(6) Our mental life is evidently not extended, not in
Space.   Mental states do not have size, shape, mass.
They are not composed of an enormous number of tiny
units — which physics calls electrons and protons —
whirling about at enormous speeds.

Here we reach a very serious objection.   We must admit that introspection does not reveal any such structure
underlying our mental states.   So, if we are to hold to the
theory, we must modify our statements about 'first-
hand' knowledge of our own mental life.   We must admit
that introspection, too, is a very inadequate means of
knowledge.   Introspection does not reveal that our
mental states do *not* have size, mass, etc.   But it totally
fails to reveal that they *do* have these attributes.

The monist, however, may ask, How *could* we know,

think about, report these fine details of our mental life? Introspection, after all, is, behavioristically speaking, a series of *reactions*. In introspection we are reacting to our own just past, or just passing, mental states. But our reactive-mechanism is far too gross to catch anything but mass-effects. Our mental life *has* all the fine details which physics attributes to the activities of matter. But we cannot think about them, we cannot report them, because thinking-about, and reporting in words, are large-scale activities, initiated only by other large-scale activities, and consisting in reactions to these large-scale activities as a whole, not to their innumerable, unseizable details. And this is, of course, desirable, both from a utilitarian and an esthetic point of view. It is our mental processes *as wholes* that concern us, as ways of living, not their minute sub-structure. And it is our processes as wholes that are interesting to contemplate. An emotion — love, fear, or anger — is a highly complex set of processes, based upon return-wave sensations from a great many bodily organs and muscles. But it is the particular *whole* that is important, in determining our action, and in memory. In purpose, it is the net outcome that is important, the resultant set of the organism, not the innumerable details that co-operate to that common end. And obviously in sensation, it is not the effect of each individual light-ray that is important, but the total image produced. Thus, our self-conscious, thinking, talking life concerns itself entirely with these wholes, and we have no way of reacting to our own innermost life in its fine detail.

(7) A similar answer can be given to the objection that brain-life consists of innumerable *separate* particles in motion, whereas mental life consists of relatively simple,

unitary states.   William James, who was drawn to the
theory in its then available expositions, felt this objection
to be insuperable:

> All the 'combinations' which we actually know are *effects*,
> wrought by the units said to be 'combined,' upon some en-
> tity other than themselves.... No possible number of entities
> (call them as you like, whether forces, material particles, or
> mental elements) can sum *themselves* together.   Each re-
> mains, in the sum, what it always was; and the sum itself exists
> only *for a bystander* who happens to overlook the units and
> to apprehend the sum as such; or else it exists in the shape of
> some other *effect* on an entity external to the sum itself....
> The mind-stuff theory, in short, is unintelligible.   Atoms of
> feeling can not compose higher feelings, any more than atoms
> of matter can compose physical things!   The 'things,' for a
> clear-headed atomistic evolutionist, are not.   Nothing is but
> the everlasting atoms.   When grouped in a certain way, we
> name them this 'thing' or that; but the thing we name has
> no existence out of our mind.   So of the states of mind which
> are supposed to be compound because they know many differ-
> ent things together.   Since indubitably such states do exist,
> they must exist as single new facts, effects, possibly, as the
> spiritualists say, on the Soul... but at any rate independent
> and integral, and not compounded by psychic atoms.[1]

To this the monist replies, Of course the atomic events
which make up our life cannot "sum themselves together"; the "bystander" that sums them up is the
further event, the *reaction*, which consists in attending to,
thinking about, introspecting, attributing meaning to a
mass of those atomic events.   Our mental life gets just
exactly as much unity as our reactions give it.   Whatever group of minute events we react to as a whole, that
is a unitary fact for our mental life, just as a particular
group of atoms-in-motion in front of the body is a 'thing'
for us, if, and in so far as we react to it as a single thing.
Consciousness consists, precisely, in these broad sweeps

[1] William James, *The Principles of Psychology*, vol. I, pp. 158–162.

of vision and action, which give to our mental life the units about which we think and talk. And it is, precisely, these mass-effects which are the different *qualities* which make of consciousness such a glorious pageant.... But here the theory becomes rather too technical for brief presentation.[1]

(8) Brain-life is in our heads. Mental life does not seem to be in our heads, it seems to be, as a slangy student put it, "all over the place." Our visual sensa seem to be out there in front of our bodies, the sounds we hear seem to be in the air about us. And so on.... But we have long since learned that physics cannot find these sensa of ours anywhere out there; and we have learned that they are all, in some sense, organism-engendered. They are *not* out there in the world, they only *seem* out there. In the act of reacting to outer objects, we 'project' our sensations into the things we are reacting to; i.e., we take them to be characters of these outer objects, instead of characters of our own inner life. It is a perpetual illusion. As active animals, in danger from environing things, and acting upon them, we and our ancestors for millions of years have ignored our own conscious experience as such, and have clothed the world with the colors which our own brain-life has produced, when acted upon by messages coming from that outer world.

Our familiar objects — the chairs, tables, trees, and all the rest, as we visualize and think about them — are thus hybrid objects; their spatio-temporal interrelationships are those of the groups of atoms which are really out there, about our bodies, but their dress of sense-qualities is of

---

[1] See, for an elaboration of the theory, and a discussion of the whole mind-body problem, Durant Drake, *Mind and Its Place in Nature* (The Macmillan Co., 1929).

our own make.   The physical things are really out there, and the mental life is really in our heads.   But these pic-torialized objects that swim before our vision are mere fictions, floating, as it were, between two worlds.   They *are*, in a sense, by-products; and epiphenomenalism is true of them.   So perhaps these two theories converge to the same conclusion when they are thought through to the end.   On the other hand, the mental states which, when thus 'projected,' form these sense-pictures, are really dynamic events going on in our heads.   Our mental life is causally efficacious, and interacting with the rest of the world-life, of which it is a peculiarly vigorous and individualized part.   If the interactionist would only be content with this version of interactionism, the three factions could sign a treaty of peace!

But that is, of course, utopian.   The three ways of interpreting the situation will remain, side by side, for a long time to come.   Each has its perplexities, each has its loyal advocates.   And all the while there are those who say that the problem is too deep for our solving, and man will never know the truth.

SUGGESTED READINGS

W. K. Clifford, *Lectures and Essays: Body and Mind.*
Morton Prince, *The Nature of Mind and Human Automatism.*
C. A. Strong, *Why the Mind Has a Body,* VII, XV.
Durant Drake, *Mind and Its Place in Nature,* VII–VIII, XIX.
Friedrich Paulsen, *Introduction to Philosophy,* Book I, ch. I, §§ 4–5.
C. A. Strong, *The Origin of Consciousness, Preliminary,* etc.
C. A. Strong, *Essays on the Natural Origin of the Mind,* esp. VIII.

CHAPTER XXII

FREE WILL

WHATEVER theory of the nature of mind is true, there is no doubt that we are thinking, purposing, willing creatures. And we come back now to complete our discussion of natural law and causation by asking whether our acts of purposing and willing exemplify those regularities of sequence which we formulate as 'natural law,' or whether there is reason to suppose them, to some degree, exceptions to the general causal uniformity of Nature.

DETERMINISM VS. INDETERMINISM

It is clear that organic reactions take place in general along well-worn grooves; they are, as we say, instinctive or habitual. Each type of animal has its own distinctive ways of acting. Each human cultural group has its own characteristic manners and morals. Most of our daily routine we follow, without much conscious deliberation or will, simply because our organisms are set, like alarm-clocks, to go off in such ways when the proper stimulus occurs. At meal-times we eat, at night we go to bed, at the appropriate time of life we fall in love. And so on. *Homo sapiens* has a particular sort of organism, wound up by heredity, and capable of being further wound up by education and his particular environment, to do certain definite things in certain definite ways.

But human beings exhibit far more *individuality* than the lower animals. One of the trends of organic evolution on earth has been toward more and more marked individuation. Each human being is unique in his make-up, not quite like any other human being who has ever lived.   Inevitably, then, each man's conduct is, to some extent, different from that of every other man. Even if determinism is true, we could not deduce from the general laws of human behavior the concrete acts of a given man, unless we knew in exact detail the nature of the mind and body of that particular individual.

Everything about an individual human being is more or less unique — his looks, his bodily organs, his brain, his ways of feeling, his ways of acting.   And, for all we can say, there may be a certain amount of indetermination all along the line.   But though that would be an interesting fact, it would not help us particularly.   So there is just one point at which the indeterminists usually take their stand, and that is the exercise of the *will*.   Your will, they say, is the real *you*, the very inmost core of your personality.   Though nine tenths and more of your behavior may be mere mechanical reflex, you may, by the exercise of your will, at any moment interpose a veto. However your heredity and education may have molded you, your will remains free; and because it is free, your destiny is yours to shape.   It is not true that everything is already predetermined; things can happen that are not on the bills.   Human conduct is not only *practically* unpredictable because each one of us is a unique individual whose nature, in detail, is hidden, even from himself; it is *essentially* unpredictable, because the will is not a resultant but an originating cause.

It is very necessary, then, to know, as clearly as possible, what the will *is*.   The line between willed (or 'voluntary') action and behavior that is merely instinctive, impulsive, or habitual, is evidently not a sharp line.   Thoughtless behavior shades into thoughtful behavior, and that into voluntary behavior. In so far as there is wavering, with alternative pictures of possible conduct before the mind, so that the outcome is felt as a choice, a rejection of one course and adoption of another, we speak of our action as willed. The 'will' is the name we give the impulse which emerges after reflection; it expresses not just one particular reactive tendency, but the longer-range interests of the individual. It is in reflection that we are most clearly conscious of ourselves, stirring up as we then do those aspects of our inner nature that are most personal — our hopes, plans, ideals, purposes, and accumulated wisdom; hence the tendency to action which emerges with the right of way is apt to (though it does not always) represent most adequately the net direction of our desires, and so to be most peculiarly and fully our own. It is these will-impulses that we especially care to be able to form and to carry out. It is here particularly that we want to be free.

Voluntary action is not necessarily *better* than impulsive or habitual behavior; it may very well be worse. We may voluntarily decide to do a passionate or malicious deed, when to follow the kindly or cautious impulse which we overrule would have been wiser and more moral. And our more instinctive or impulsive acts may be said to express our own natures as truly as the more deliberate acts. Nevertheless, if we are to *improve* our conduct, it must be by taking thought and exercising will. Hence the will is, in a very real sense, a sort of internal steering-apparatus, with which the moralist, the reformer, the teacher, the parent, especially concerns himself.

The distinction between determinism and indeterminism in the matter of the will is quite clear. The determinist believes that natural law holds in cases of willing, as well as in every other natural event. The indeterminist believes that the act of willing, at least, is exempt from the ordinary laws of cause and effect; 'the will' is an independent variable inserted into the causal nexus of nature. On the former view, it would be theoretically possible, from a complete knowledge of present facts, to predict *how* a given individual would will, under given circumstances. On the latter view, not even an omniscient God could do that; he might be conceived to *foresee* how that person was going to will, but he could not *deduce* his choice from the fullest knowledge of his personality and experience up to the very moment of willing.

It is important to distinguish 'fatalism' from both of these views. Fatalism is a doctrine, not of the will, but of future events; it holds that, by one route or another, a certain definite end will surely be attained. Whatever you do, whichever way you will, it cannot affect the outcome. You are caught in a net; you may struggle, but you cannot escape your destiny. You are like a poor chess-player pitted against an expert; you may move this piece or that for a while, but you are bound to be beaten. Or, looking on the optimistic side, no matter what mistakes you make you cannot hurt yourself; you will meet with no ill that you are not fated to meet anyway; you will not die, however brave you are in battle, until your hour has come.

Fatalism is a contagious doctrine, or mood; and there are striking instances that seem to justify it. But on the whole the evidence is overwhelming that human choice does matter, and that a real difference is made in our future destiny by what we do today. Moreover, to make fatalism plausible to the thoughtful mind, we should have not only to point out cases of apparent corroboration but to show, or at least to suggest, the concrete ways in which our decisions are constantly being thwarted, and our feet turned toward the fated goal. That is never done; fatalism remains hopelessly vague, a mood rather than a clear hypothesis worthy of debate.

Predestination is a theological doctrine compatible with either determinism or indeterminism. It asserts, essentially, that God has determined in advance who shall be saved and who damned. In some versions of the doctrine this happens because God predetermines our natures and our environment, so that we inevitably will to do right or wrong, as the case may be, and thus steer ourselves inexorably toward Heaven or Hell. In other versions we have the apparent liberty which fatalism grants us; we can exercise our poor little wills as a dog tied to a cart by a rope can dart this way or that. But God is driving the cart; and though we have a little free play, it makes no difference in the end, we shall arrive at our fore-ordained destination.... Obviously we cannot prove this doctrine true by any study of human life itself, nor even if we could discover that such and such people actually go to Heaven, and these others to Hell. The only way to prove whether their reaching these destinations was *pre-destined* would be to read the mind of God.

Leaving aside, then, these picturesque doctrines, we shall try to weigh fairly the arguments for determinism and for indeterminism in the matter of the human will.

THE EMPIRICAL ARGUMENTS

(1) The indeterminist declares that we *feel* ourselves to be freely choosing, exercising free will; we have the *consciousness* of freedom. Determinism must assert that this is mere illusion. And unless it can be definitely

shown to be illusion, the experience should be taken at its face value.

The determinist replies that there is no illusion about it, except as the indeterminist cherishes his particular *interpretation* of the experience. We do choose, we do will, of course; that is one definable form of behavior. We are 'free' to choose, and to will — well, just as far as we *are* free; that depends upon the various other forces in the field. The particular impulse which emerges after reflection, and which we label our 'will,' is free to express itself in action just in so far as there are not obstacles sufficient to hinder it from carrying itself out into action. Other impulses, passions, habits, or mere inertia, may block this will-impulse and reduce it to impotence. That is, of course, a very common experience. In these cases, it turned out that the will was *not* free to express itself; some *other* tendency got the right of way.

Everyone admits that our behavior, including our re-flective processes and our acts of willing, is to a very con-siderable degree determined by our heredity, education, and environment. The question at issue concerns the possible existence of some free play. When the will-impulse is finally formed, is it an exact resultant of earlier perceptual and thought-processes, or is it merely in-fluenced, not actually determined, by all that has gone before? Does the experience of willing throw any light on that question? Does it reveal the fact that the process of willing is exempt from ordinary causal law? A little introspection certainly reveals causal processes at work shaping our decisions; does it show us that they were not adequate to determine them completely? In the moment of willing, we feel *ourselves* acting, we feel that our will is expressing our own nature and desire at the moment.

And so it is. But that is not the whole story. At that moment we are only conscious of desiring and willing; we are no longer conscious, at least clearly and in detail, of the processes of thought and sensation that led up to this particular desire and will. That does not prove that there were *not* such processes leading up to this outcome and making it what it is.

(2) But, says the indeterminist, no matter how well we know a person, we can never safely predict his behavior. People continually do the most unexpected things. In spite of apparently excellent heredity and education, this one drifts into vice or crime; another, reared under adverse circumstances, becomes a hero or a saint. Twins who look so much alike that few can tell them apart sometimes turn out very differently. Do not such facts suggest strongly that there is an upsetting factor which forever makes calculation of human conduct impossible? If determinism is true, men are just very complicated machines. But can we conceive any machine, however complicated, having as much independence and as much variability as men apparently have?

But in the non-human world, too, processes are often so intricate and delicately balanced that we cannot predict their outcome. Here is an aged oak; will it withstand the forces of decay within and the force of storms from without and continue to carry on its life-processes? Here is a man struggling with temptation; will he be able to withstand the forces of impulse and passion within and the incitements that reach him from without, and keep his life from shipwreck? In both cases the forces at work are too intricate, too evenly balanced, and too hidden from our observation for us to know what the result will be. But that does not prove that, if we *could* follow all the processes, in fine detail, from moment to moment, we should not see the outcome, whatever it is, to be the resultant of the forces at work.

Any judgment that a given person's heredity, education, and environmental influences have been 'excellent,' or 'adverse,' is far too sweeping and too precarious, except as we can actually see the results they have produced. Sometimes what we call an adverse environment may be better for a person's development than what we stupidly consider favorable. Our education, elaborate and costly as is our equipment, is still so rudimentary and blind, and so little adapted to the infinitely varying needs of individuals, that we need be surprised at no result — or absence of result — from years of exposure to it. As to heredity, we know very little of value for prediction, since traits long recessive may suddenly appear, and since in studying a person's ancestors it is impossible to know how far their character and conduct were due to inherited nature and how far to environment. We *do* have clear evidence that identical twins are, in general, far more nearly alike in their behavior than other brothers and sisters. But however evenly they start their lives, all sorts of incidents happen to one that do not happen to the other; and it is impossible to know in advance what apparently trifling happening — some book read, some conversation, some physical accident — may give a decided bent to this life that was not given to that. No one knows enough of any human being, not even of himself, to predict his behavior with complete assurance. But what does that prove but the intricacy and unique individuality of each human being's life?

When it is asserted that men are 'not mere machines,' just what do people mean? Man-made machines have no consciousness, no purpose, no will; even the most complicated of them have a very narrow range of performance, and do the same thing over and over again. Naturally we resent being called machines. But the determinist no more believes that man is a machine in *that* sense than the indeterminist does. If he ever does liken man to a machine, he has in mind just the one point, that he believes man's complex life to be as definitely determined by the structure of his organism and his varying environment as is the simple behavior of a machine. If men are machines in *this* sense, they are machines which can do all that the heroes and saints have done, machines that feel and think and love and will.

(3) Still, says the indeterminist, we know that we *can* do *either* this thing *or* that. Afterward, in looking back, we know that we *might* have done differently. We know that we are not compelled to choose, to will, as we do.

But what does it *mean* to say that I *can* do this or that? Does it not mean simply that my *will* to do it is just the one additional thing necessary to make me do it? I am capable of doing either thing, the decisive factor is to be my decision as to what I want to do. There is nothing in that even suggestive of any indetermination. To say that I *might* have done differently means that I *should* have done differently *if* I had wanted to badly enough, *if* I had willed to do it. It was only I myself that stood in the way. Man is freer than any other animal, because he has more alternatives open to him, he is capable of greater variety of response. But whether he will choose this response or that is not a matter of mere chance; it obviously depends upon the comparative strength of his various impulses and desires — including his long-run purposes and ideals as well as his momentary mood.

We must beware, then, of supposing determinism to mean that we are compelled, by forces outside of us, to act as we do. There is compulsion upon us only when we desire to do something and are prevented from doing it by some outer force. In free activity our compulsion comes from *ourselves*. For we are a bundle of conflicting desires; and whichever desire wins the day, there is something in us that must be constrained. It is true that all causes are, themselves, effects of earlier causes; if you choose as you do it is because you have become the sort of person you are. But now that you are that sort of person, it is *you* who are choosing. The links of causation go *through* your life; the 'you' of today is a dynamic part of nature, free — to a degree — to express itself. The greater part of our behavior is *externally* indeterminate; i.e., so far as external causes go, it may be either this or that. It is the complexities of the inner life of the individual that determine the reaction which is chosen. Any being whose activity is thus self-determined may properly be called free. But that is not to say that this autonomous life of the individual does not proceed according to regular laws of cause and effect.

(4) We have already mentioned, in discussing natural law, the Heisenberg principle of indeterminacy, and pointed out that there is no positive reason to suppose that it implies anything more than an indeterminateness in our *knowledge*. We cannot *discover* accurately both the position and the velocity of an electron; but that does not mean that it *has* no definite position or no definite velocity. There are many minute events in Nature whose causes we have not found; e.g., the jump of this particular electron from one orbit to another, the break-up of this particular radium atom. But that is not to say

that they do not *have* causes, which may, perhaps, some day be discovered.

Nevertheless, some indeterminists have seized upon this physical principle of indeterminacy as empirical evidence of their doctrine. Nature is at bottom capricious, each tiny electron does as it pleases; the appearance of regularity on a large scale is merely the result of the statistical fact that out of the vast numbers of electrons and atoms an approximately equal number do the expected thing from moment to moment. But if even electrons are 'free,' how much more surely are men free! We have been frightened by a bogey of our own invention; natural law is merely statistics.

It seems worth considering, however, whether we should get statistical regularity if the individual occurrences which we are collating were not the effects of causes acting in regular ways. If the break-up of a radium atom is really a random event, a mere uncaused caprice on its part, how does it happen that a predictable proportion (exact to the limits of our powers of measurement) break up in a given length of time, so that we can confidently predict, through years and centuries, how large a proportion of a bit of radium or uranium will have disintegrated? *Whatever* be true of the minute constituent events, the large-scale events are (at least approximately, and perhaps exactly) uniform. Would this be true if the constituent events were not, themselves, law-abiding, rather than lawless, in their acts?

And in any case, human behavior is a large-scale phenomenon. Whether the causal laws exemplified in our mental and physical processes are the resultant of underlying exact laws, or whether they are 'statistical' laws, seems quite irrelevant to the problem of free will.

What good can it do us if electrons jump in capricious ways? If any indeterminateness should result in our behavior, it would be a mere random, crazy indeterminateness, without any value for our moral life. Who wants the vagaries of electrons to influence his conduct? The only sort of freedom that is of any value to us is freedom to determine our behavior by our intelligence and our wills. We can safely leave the physicist to grapple with the behavior of electrons and tend to our own business.

The position of the determinist has been perhaps sufficiently elucidated in these replies to the indeterminist. We shall merely add three points that determinists may properly make:

(1) So much natural law has been discovered that a presumption has been created that all events (or at least all large-scale events) are law-abiding. Moreover, there is a vast amount of evidence for the exemplification of law in human behavior. The more closely we study people's lives, the more clearly we can see the causes of their conduct. Sociology, studying the behavior of groups, is constantly speaking in terms of cause and effect. Literary and artistic criticism consists, in part, of pointing out the causes which produced this particular sort of writing or art at this particular time. Psychology unearths causal relations that are not suspected by the individual whose behavior and conscious experience has exemplified them. On the other hand, the fact that we are *not* aware, for the most part, of the causes that have led us to do what we do, proves nothing. We cannot be forever introspecting and making note of our motives, desires, and inhibitions; and on the physiological side the whole thing is hidden from us and can only be laboriously

inferred.   There is no way in which we *could* discover all
the causes of our own conduct, let alone the conduct of
others.   It is noteworthy that in cases of post-hypnotic
suggestion the patient does exactly what the hypnotist
told him to do; we as onlookers see that this conduct
of his had a definite cause.   But the patient is quite unaware of this fact, and thinks that he is doing it 'of his
own sweet will.'

The indeterminist replies that we can discover law in
human behavior to only a very small extent; as to the
rest, the burden of proof rests upon the determinist to
show that behavior so unpredictable as human conduct
is really the result of regular laws.

(2) Reflex action merges insensibly into voluntary
action.   There is no sharp line.   The 'will' is not a separate 'faculty,' like a steersman at a wheel.   Will-impulses
are just impulses that emerge after reflection, or are accompanied by more *self*-consciousness than other impulses.
As a refinement upon mere impulsive action, voluntary
action is intelligible; it has been gradually developed by
the human race out of the simpler types of conscious
reaction. Determinism has no need to postulate any new
and mysterious factor.   Will-impulses are free (so far
as they are free) in exactly the sense in which any other
impulse is free.   They are free if they are not inhibited
by some more powerful passion or desire.   Indeterminism remains, by contrast, vague and mysterious.
Why should a will-impulse be 'freer' than any other impulse?   Why should it be exempt from causal law? Does
the will-impulse, or whatever it is in the will-impulse
that is uncaused, just well up out of nothing?

The indeterminist's best recourse is the Soul, or Self.
Your Soul is to be regarded as the real *you*.   It is from

it, from *you*, that the will-impulse emerges. It is, indeed, caused by *you*, but your *causing* it is not caused. There is something in you which is independent of the whole causal nexus.... There may, of course, be indetermination in human behavior without any Soul to set it going. But the source of the novel push to our behavior lacks then even a name, to give it a respectable status. It certainly cannot be definitely proved that there is not some sort of internal originating apparatus in us; but the indeterminist has heavy going to explain exactly what it is, where it is, where it came from, and how it works.

(3) Perhaps the best thing the determinist can do is to demand a careful definition of 'freedom,' and to insist that all the empirical evidence points to freedom *in one sense*, whereas the indeterminist means by 'freedom' something quite different. Here is a good statement of this position:

> What is it to be free? You cannot be free unless you are free *from* something; what is it from which the will is free? It is free, first, from the necessity of deciding upon any one course of action, rather than its opposite, or than no action at all. It is free, antecedently, from the necessity of deciding at once, in advance of the most mature deliberation. In a word, we can choose, and take our time about it. We can weigh what it is we contemplate doing, and realize how our feelings and inclinations and previsions and deepest instincts bear upon it. We can make quite sure what we want before we speak the final word. So that, when the decision finally comes, it will be the expression of our innermost, our entire nature. Now this is what we originally and properly mean by our wills being free. And this is the only kind of freedom essential to morality. Moreover, it is an obvious and undeniable fact, a fact of experience; nobody can question that we are free in this sense. I propose to call this our *empirical* freedom.
>
> You cannot then say, in this sense, that we feel as if we were free, and therefore we probably are so. This is to in-

troduce the other kind of freedom, the uncausedness of our decisions — *speculative* freedom, as I shall call it, because it could only be established by speculation — and make the feeling of freedom an argument for it.   But the feeling of freedom is the feeling of our empirical freedom — it is the feeling of freedom in the sense in which freedom can not be denied without absurdity.   Speculative freedom, on the other hand, is one theory of choice, the theory that it is uncaused, with another theory, the theory that it is caused, opposed to it.   To argue from empirical to speculative freedom is thus to offer the *fact* of choice as a proof that one *theory* of choice rather than another is true.[1]

THE MORAL ARGUMENTS

The indeterminist is apt to put the weight of his argument not so much upon any positive evidence that his theory is true as upon the supposed bad consequences of believing determinism to be true.   This is a typical 'pragmatic' attitude, subject to the criticism which we gave that point of view in Chapter V.   We shall not repeat that general criticism here, but the reader may well have it in mind as we distinguish the various aspects of the indeterminist's argument.

(1) Belief in determinism tends, and quite logically, to paralyze our moral efforts.   By teaching us that our acts are the inevitable products of heredity and circumstances, that whatever will be, will be, it gives us a feeling of helplessness.   We are but puppets, of little importance in the universe.   On the other hand, indeterminism gives us individual importance and dignity.   As William James put it, in one of his Lowell lectures:

Most persons [feel that] what is called their free-will... is a principle, a positive faculty or virtue added to man, by which his dignity is enigmatically augmented.   He ought to believe in it for this reason.   Determinists, who deny it, who

[1] C. A. Strong, *The Origin of Consciousness*, pp. 325-326.   By permission of The Macmillan Company, publishers.

say that individual men originate nothing, but merely trans-
mit to the future the whole push of the past cosmos of which
they are so small an expression, diminish man.   He is less
admirable, stripped of his creative principle.[1]

The determinist replies that the only sort of freedom
which we need, or should desire, is the freedom which we
demonstrably *have*, the freedom to express our own nature, to do what we want to do.   The 'speculative freedom' of the indeterminist, an exemption from the laws of
cause and effect, would not add to our power or dignity.
The value of freedom is that we do not have to do as
other people say, or as our own lower impulses push us.
We can determine our conduct by our ideals and long-
range purposes — *if* we have the 'will-power' to do it.
If we haven't, it is no use to mock ourselves with the
comforting talk of our 'free will.'   Freedom from enslave-
ment to our passions has to be *won*.   And determinism
alone can point the way; it teaches us that every effort
counts, that there is a mechanism of self-control.   We
can cure our weaknesses, we can make ourselves what we
want to be.   It is just a question of finding the right
method of self-education and applying it.   On the other
hand, the indeterminist leaves us helpless; he gives us no
clue as to how to make ourselves do right.   If our will-
impulses are as lawless, as capricious, as he says, we may
train ourselves never so patiently, and that little imp of a
'free will' may just as well jump the other way.   The
indeterminist can scold, the determinist diagnoses and
seeks the appropriate cure.   Belief in indeterminism may
be vaguely inspiriting, but it is not concretely *applicable*.
If our wills are 'bad,' what is there to do about it?   Experience shows that it is dangerous to rely upon mere

[1] *Pragmatism*, pp. 115–116.

'free will' to do the right thing when a crisis comes; we need a *trained* will. If we have failed to do right, it is because there is something definite the matter with our system of inner controls; a way can be found to correct the situation. Morality is a great art, and an art that has to be *learned*, just as playing the piano well has to be learned. We must study and apply the right technique.

(2) But, says the indeterminist, this means that you can do right *if* you want to badly enough to train yourself to do it. If you do not care enough, you cannot do it. And whether you do or do not care enough depends upon your heredity and environment. But this is not fair. And, as a matter of fact, the worst sinner knows that he has certain duties, certain obligations. But to say that you have a *duty* implies that you *can do* your duty, heredity and environment to the contrary notwithstanding. You can assert your will against overwhelming forces. Though you have contracted vicious habits, **you** *can* shake yourself loose from them by the sheer exercise of your free will.

This is certainly good preaching. Speaking to a man in this vein may create just the necessary additional inner force to make him overcome his fault. A dead heave of effort can do wonders. But the ability to *make* a steady heave of effort is the result either of a strong hereditary obstinacy, or combativeness, or else a skillful training. The Puritans could master their impulses because they practiced resisting temptations from childhood on. They kept themselves in training by hours of prayer, meditation, Bible-reading, and church-attendance. They often exercised their wills in disastrous ways, but they did exercise them. It would be very foolish of an indeterminist to think that he could skip the necessary training, and yet depend upon his will to do what he believes is right in the face of fierce temptation. He *can* do it, no doubt — if he wills hard enough. But will he *will* hard enough? Probably not, if he has never developed the habit of making his will the master of opposing passions and desires.

Experience shows that freedom is a matter of *degree*. We are freer to be *ourselves* — i.e., to behave in accordance with our deepest purposes and ideals — as our wills grow stronger, and as our habit of reflection preceding willing becomes stronger. As a matter of fact, we are still *ourselves* when we act according to a gust of passion or an unreflective desire. *Those* aspects of our nature are freer when our reflective habits and our wills are *not* strong. But in reflection we usually identify ourselves rather with our wills than with our impulses and passions, and we feel ourselves free when **our** *wills* dominate the situation. Weak-willed people waver between this impulse and that; strong-willed people determine their conduct more by a steady inner group of ideals and purposes. Reflective choice more and more replaces mere reflex or impulsive action. Most of us, however, are still the battleground of opposing desires; we are not free to become saints, because our contrary desires and interests are too strong. We *could* become saints, if we wanted to persistently and ardently enough. But we do not want to persistently enough; or we are not wise enough to adopt the right technique to make ourselves over. For we have ourselves to deal with. And what we actually are, is a mass of conflicting tendencies. In order to make our better selves dominant, we must not only have the will, we must find a *way*.

(3) But if our freedom to do our duty is only partial,

depending upon a fortunate heredity or skillful training, how can we hold a man *responsible* for his sins or, in fairness, blame him? It is really God, or Nature, that is responsible, for having made him what he is. And if a man realizes that he is not really responsible, what is to prevent him from feeling that he might as well 'eat, drink, and be merry'? After all, he is 'made that way'; the blame rests upon God rather than upon him. If men get to realizing this, what will become of their morality?

Well, no doubt God, or Nature, has produced him, the creature that he is. But it would do us no good to hold God or Nature 'responsible.' 'Responsibility' is a very practical concept. To hold a man 'responsible' is to hold him accountable to the community for his acts; it is a useful and necessary thing to do. By cultivating a sense of responsibility in men, we help to keep them to their duties, i.e., to what is due the other members of the community. We do not hold babies or insane people responsible, because that would do no *good*. If determinism is true, this attitude of the community, reflected in the individual's sense of responsibility, has its definite part in helping to determine people's conduct. Praise, blame, punishment, are necessary precisely because determinism is true; they are important new causes brought into a situation to help determine the outcome.

Nor is there any illusion about this sense of responsibility. Our acts *are* the result of our character; *we* are the causes of what we do. The fact that a cause is itself the effect of earlier causes does not make it any the less a cause. We praise good deeds because they are good, we blame sins because they are bad — whatever their causes. Praise and blame are, primarily, expressions of our emotional reactions toward good and bad conduct and character. They are justified because of their value in spurring men to the good and deterring them from the bad. They are safety-measures, like fire-engines and the police. We are sorry to have to blame people, and sorrier to have to punish them. We have (or should have) no desire for *vengeance*, we merely wish to protect ourselves from harm, to deter the wrongdoer, and, if possible, to reform him. The excuse of blame and punishment is their *efficiency;* they are like surgical operations, a mere addition to the evil in the world unless they *cure*.

Even remorse is justifiable — just in so far as it is *efficacious*. The sort of remorse that is a mere wallowing in distress, without help in reforming our conduct, is sheer evil. Remorse of this wasteful sort should be turned into concrete planning how to prevent a repetition of the sin. Determinism does tend to make us less unhappy in our remorse, but it tends to substitute for mere self-flagellation a clear-eyed program for self-reform. And so with the punishment of criminals. Determinism helps us to realize the wickedness of cruel punishments, and spurs us to find the sort of punishment that really reforms. And it shows us that what we really need is not so much blame, remorse, punishment, as proper education to start with, which shall prevent folly and sin. If a young person, under the influence of determinism, decides to 'eat, drink, and be merry,' instead of living a decent and useful life, it shows that he is unintelligent, in that he prefers the lesser to the greater good. The thing to do is to show him wherein his true good lies.

Bertrand Russell declares that "the conception of 'moral responsibility' is 'responsible' for much evil." It has made us angry and hard, or fruitlessly remorseful,

when we should have been discerning and eager to understand.   We must be tender and charitable toward those
who have had unfortunate bringing-up, or have inherited
unhappy dispositions.   We must be careful of our influence over others.   We must study our own failures,
and find out how to circumvent our weaknesses.   We
must never let ourselves think that 'this time don't count.'
We must keep away from bad influences; they will not
prevent us from expressing our own free will, but they
will help decide what that free will is to *be*.   Education
and criminology, so far as they have developed really
good techniques, are deterministic in their outlook; they
study the causes of crime, and of socially and personally
advantageous behavior.   We have scolded children and
punished criminals for centuries.   Now at last we are
beginning to see that our job is to avoid breeding bad
habits and passions in them; we have learned that by
getting hold of them early enough we can, if we are intelligent and patient, bring them up to be useful and
reasonably happy men and women.

May we suggest, in conclusion, that the concept of
'free will' is essentially a *practical* concept; it expresses
our sense that our conduct is *as yet* undecided.   The
decision hangs in the balance, and we can still *do* something about it.   According as we put our wills into the
scales will the matter be determined.   'Free will' expresses the situation *before the fact*.   *After* the fact we can
see, perhaps, the causes which led us to decide thus and
so.   Preaching and pleading and education, and all the
arts, are prospective.   Science is retrospective.   The
moralist and educator need the term 'free will'; the psychologist and physiologist have no need of it.   But there

is no contradiction between their points of view. For every art, including the great art of successful living, must be based, even though unconsciously, upon the laws which hold in its field. Indeterminism *may* be true; it certainly cannot be disproved. Belief in it is evidently a comfort to some types of mind. But it seems safe to say that all advance in the arts of life comes through better and better understanding of the laws of human nature and of the materials with which human nature has to work.

SUGGESTED READINGS

F. Paulsen, *A System of Ethics*, Book II, ch. IX.
G. T. W. Patrick, *Introduction to Philosophy*, XIX.
W. G. Everett, *Moral Values*, XII.
William James, *The Will to Believe: The Dilemma of Determinism.*
T. de Laguna, *Introduction to the Science of Ethics*, IV.
J. M. E. McTaggart, *Some Dogmas of Religion*, V.
F. C. Sharp, *Ethics*, XIII.
C. A. Strong, *The Origin of Consciousness*, Epilogue.
Durant Drake, *Mind and Its Place in Nature*, XVIII.
H. H. Horne, *Free Will and Human Responsibility.*
Bertrand Russell, *Scientific Method*, VIII.
G. H. Palmer, *The Problem of Freedom.*
J. H. Ryan, *Introduction to Philosophy*, VIII.
C. E. M. Joad, *Mind and Matter*, IV–V.

PART FIVE
VALUES

Chapter XXIII

NATURALISM VS. SUPERNATURALISM

So FAR we have been discussing the facts of Nature, and of our conscious experience, without making any evaluations. We turn now, in conclusion, to the intensely practical questions concerning the *meanings* and *values* to be found in our own lives — and perhaps throughout the cosmos.

Our first question is to be, precisely, Are our human values *merely* human, or are they, in some way and in some sense, superhuman, dear to Nature herself, or to a cosmic God?

We may use the term 'supernaturalism' to mean any belief or doctrine which holds that behind, or at the heart of Nature, there is design, purpose, interest in *the good*. According to this view, the universe is essentially a stage set for the production of values; the whole cosmic life has *meaning*, is making for a *goal*. There is, therefore, a *why* for everything, a *raison d'être*. And it is usually supposed that *we* are the leading actors, that the universe is friendly to *our* interests, the stage was set for *us*. The form of supernaturalism most familiar to us is, of course, the Christian teaching that the world was created by a benevolent and omnipotent God, whose chief interest is in man and his salvation. But there are many forms of the doctrine. In one shape or other most men have had some sort of supernaturalistic belief, though often vague and inarticulate. And very many people feel that life would not be worth living at all if they could not believe that, somehow, their welfare has cosmic support, that their interests are cherished by the Power that is in, or back of, Nature.

We call this view 'supernaturalism' because it carries us beyond what is directly observable in Nature. 'Naturalism' is, by contrast, a sophisticated view growing partly out of the bitter disappointments and disillusionments of human life, partly out of the austerely empirical attitude of science. Naturalism holds that science (including history, psychology, and philosophy carried on in a scientific spirit) comprises the sum total of organized, reliable human knowledge. We know of nothing beyond, or behind, Nature. We can see values arising, as an aspect of life on our little planet; but though they mean everything to *us*, they are apparently episodic in the universe. As to the vast reaches of cosmic life before and beyond our little terrestrial episode, there is no clear indication that they have any meaning or purpose. At any rate, it is quite useless for us to ask *why* things happen as they do; all we can profitably study is *what* happens, and its bearing upon our human purposes and goods.

Undoubtedly the supernaturalistic outlook is warmer, more congenial to the human spirit, helping us, as it does, to feel at home in the universe. Unfortunately, concrete supernaturalisms, entrenched with ecclesiastical authority, have done much to cloud the clarity of human thought and to retard progress. Hence a violent reaction against all forms of supernaturalism is often to be found among reformers, as among the Russian Communists of today. But the normal human being, when unprovoked by the abuses which have become associated with supernatural dogmas, is eager to find signs of friendliness to his needs in the enveloping cosmos, and dearly hopes that some such belief is true.... Yet we must not be biased by our hopes. We must ask dispassionately, Have we serious reason to believe in any doctrine of the sort? When we study the cosmic life in detail and in the large, when we study life on earth, from its earliest tentative beginnings until now, does it look to us, honestly, as the work of purpose, and perhaps, also, of good-will and love?

It is sometimes said that until we have answered the question as to the 'why' of things we have not really understood our world; a complete philosophy must have a solution for this most insistent of all problems. And only the discernment, or conjecture, of a spiritual purpose can give us the solution we seek. But this begs the question. We cannot know in advance that there is any such solution; perhaps the problem is an illusory one, and there *is* no 'why' to things. Certainly the craving to answer such questions is no excuse for accepting any answer we find lying about, or for accepting arguments which would not convince us in our everyday affairs. Unless we have good reasons for believing a supernaturalistic theory to be true, we are deluding ourselves by accepting it, and laying up trouble for our sons if not for ourselves. We must be ready to admit the possibility that there is no answer to our wistful questioning, or that, if there is an answer, we are not in a position to know what answer is true.

In any case man has *his* purposes, and finds the meaning of his life in driving toward goals which he himself has set. Religion and morals need not cease to flourish if the supernaturalistic grounds upon which they have usually been based come to seem mere poetry or illusion. Duty has a natural claim upon our allegiance, morals and religion have to do with the right living of life here upon earth, quite apart from any cosmic sanction which they may have. Some of the most devoted people have been purely naturalistic in their outlook; and, as we shall see in a later chapter, much that is best in current religion is pure humanism, without any reliance upon cosmic support. If, to the candid inquirer, the universe about us gives no clear sign of purpose, at least *we* can formulate *our* purposes and find the worth of life in working for their attainment.

There are three main lines of approach to supernatural-istic belief. The first, and most obvious, is the apparent evidence for concrete interposition in the course of natural events by some supernatural agency. There is an enormous amount of testimony to the existence of events which, it is thought, would not have come about through merely natural causes. The general term for these alleged interpositions is 'miracles'; that term may be understood to include answers to prayer (which would not have been brought about by natural causes), special providences, miraculous healings and conversions. These occurrences are held to prove the existence, not only of purpose in general in the cosmos, but of a very personal purposer, interested in the fortunes of individual men and women.

Then there is the more philosophical Argument from Origins, of which the best-known form is the First Cause Argument. How could the universe have come into existence, it is asked, unless it was created by a God? How could life have originated, and mind, and the human soul? The argument, if sound, would prove only a Creator at the beginning of things; but it would create a presumption in favor of the belief in a continuing Providence, or a plan, at least, for the future of what was created.

In the third place, there is the Argument from Design, which asserts that the *look* of things points to purpose. The cosmos seems, as we study it, to be moving toward some great end; there are signs everywhere of the working-out of intent. Or at least, the universe seems, in the manner of its shaping, to be a stage set for the creation and triumph of values.

If any one of these three types of argument seems convincing, we shall agree that our purposes — or, at least, our best purposes — are not merely ours, but are fragments of a universal or underlying purpose. Our human drama is one act in a cosmic drama.... We shall now take up each of these three types of argument in turn.

MIRACLES

Obviously we cannot weigh here the enormous amount of testimony for this miracle or that. All we can do is to suggest some general considerations in the light of which the study of the evidence may be made.

(1) At the outset we must remember that human testimony, however honest, is notoriously fallible. If anyone doubts this sweeping statement, let him read Professor Münsterberg's delightful little book, *On the Witness Stand*, which shows the astounding errors constantly being made in the statement of fact by sworn witnesses, supposedly competent observers, in court. There is a large subjective element entering into almost every observation; and memory is a very tricky thing. So we must ask searchingly, when we are confronted with any sort of testimony, How soon after the alleged event was the statement made? Is the witness one who was antecedently inclined to believe in the miraculous? Had he been trained in accuracy of observation and state-

ment? Have we an ungarbled form of his original statement? Have we corroborating independent testimony
from others, or is the testimony of others influenced by,
or perhaps a mere echo of, the statement of one original
witness?

(2) We properly require much *stronger* testimony for
the occurrence of a miracle than for the occurrence of any
everyday event. For in the latter case we know that
sort of thing does happen, whereas in the former case we
are asked to believe in something that makes quite against
our ordinary experience. If a neighbor tells me that he
saw a bay horse trotting past my house, I have no hesita-
tion in believing him. If he tells me that he saw a zebra,
I shall be rather skeptical, thinking it more likely that he
mistook an unusually marked horse for a zebra, or that
he is trying to fool me. If he tells me that he saw a centaur trotting past my house, I shall be entirely skeptical.
He is the same witness in each case, and his statement
may be as solemnly made. But I properly require more
than the testimony of any one man for the occurrence of
an event which, from all my study of biology and history,
seems to me so antecedently improbable.

(3) We must also recognize the plain fact that testimony to miraculous occurrences abounds in uncritical
periods and among unsophisticated peoples, whereas in
scientific circles miracles are rarely if ever reported. In
Bible times, for example, even educated people were very
credulous; the early Christian writers believed the most
preposterous tales. Tertullian tells us, amid many such
marvels, that the hyena changes its sex each year, Saint
Augustine that peacocks' flesh never decays. In such
an atmosphere the Christian tradition grew. Today
stories of miraculous events are constantly coming from

naïve and ignorant folk, and from those who are so steeped in the Christian teaching that miracles seem as natural as ordinary events. By contrast, miracles do not seem to happen among people trained to investigate and analyze. This is not conclusive; perhaps God prefers to work through the simple-minded and those of ready faith. But if so, it is unfortunate. For men are gradually becoming trained to scrutinize the credentials of proffered beliefs; and unless evidence can be furnished which will satisfy the scrupulous, belief in miracles is bound to wane.

(4) In any case, there is an enormous number of pseudo-miracles. It is possible in many cases to trace the growth of a miracle-story and see how a natural event came to acquire a miraculous coloring, or how an innocent statement became twisted into something much more marvelous and exciting. In other cases, while we cannot prove that the story has grown up in such a way, it is difficult to resist the suggestion. For example, a Jewish chronicler quoted from a book of poetry, then extant but now lost, a verse to the effect that the sun stood still in the heavens to see the hosts of Israel conquer. Anyone familiar with poetry would take this to be a pleasant bit of poetic license. But generations of devout Christians have believed that the sun really did stand still (which would have to mean that the earth stopped rotating) — because the Bible says so! Again, one of the Gospel writers reports a parable from Jesus' life in which he likens the Jewish people to an unfruitful fig tree which the owner will cut down soon if it does not bear fruit. Another Evangelist tells us that one day Jesus went up to a fig tree, hoping to find figs to allay his hunger, and, when he found none, cursed it (though it was not yet the season for figs) for its unfruitfulness, whereupon the tree withered. It is

easy to surmise that the parable was mistaken, by somebody who heard it at second hand, for the story of an
actual occurrence, and thus found its way into the tradition in two forms.   Once more, when we read in one
Gospel that Jesus at his baptism "saw the spirit of God
descending like a dove," we may suppose that Jesus told
his disciples of a vision that came to him at that hour.
But another Gospel tells us flatly that "the Holy Ghost
descended in a bodily shape like a dove upon him, and a
voice came from heaven..." And a still later Gospel tells
us that John, who baptized him, "saw the spirit descending from heaven like a dove," and heard God saying to
him that this man was the Messiah.   It is evident that
the story, passing from mouth to mouth, has suffered some
change; what was in the earlier version not necessarily a
miracle at all has become a miracle of the most startling
sort.

(5) In many cases we can see that antecedent expectation preceded, and therefore very likely colored, the report of an occurrence.   For example, the pious Jews at
the time of Jesus were fervently expecting a Messiah.
They combed their Scriptures (our Old Testament) for
statements which, according to their current methods of
exegesis, could be taken to be prophecies concerning this
coming national savior.   They found reason to suppose
that he would be born in Bethlehem, and be a descendant
of their greatest hero, David.   Some Greek-speaking
Jews, reading a certain statement of one of their prophets
as rendered, rather misleadingly, into Greek, thought he
would be born of a virgin.   The first Christians, full of
these ideas, accepted Jesus as the Messiah, and naturally
supposed that their antecedent expectations held of him.
The events, of course, must have happened "according

to the Scriptures," and "in order that the Scriptures might be fulfilled." As the Gospel spread far from Galilee, where Jesus and his actual biography were known to a small circle, it is inevitable that widespread anticipation should supplant fact. For this reason, although the existence of the anticipations does not prove that the events did not happen so, it should put us on our guard and make us scrutinize with especial care the strength of the actual testimony.

(6) But whatever our attitude toward miracles, we should, in fairness, adopt the *same* attitude toward the miracles of all the faiths. Christianity has no exclusive lien on miracles. On the contrary, there is equally abundant evidence for Moslem, Hindu, and Buddhist miracles. In fact, human story *abounds* in miracles. Many good Christians, who would find little mental difficulty in accepting the miracles of their own tradition if they stood alone, are appalled at the discovery of more or less similar miracle-stories in other lands. It would necessitate very careful detailed study, with scrupulous impartiality, to justify any conclusion as to which miracles were the more strongly authenticated. The superficial appearance, at least, is that there are about equally supported miracles in connection with very different faiths, and quite apart from any religion. There is unimpeachable testimony to the performance of the most incredible acts by fakirs and miracle-men of today, merely for money. Herodotus was certainly far more of a trained and critical historian than any of the Gospel writers. He tells us of miracles happening in his own day, without a doubt of their authenticity. Objectively considered, this should weigh with us more than the stories set down, a generation or more after the event, by the unknown compilers of the Christian Gospels.

(7) In certain cases it may be suspected that the events regarded as miracles actually happened, but were not really miracles. Some of the healing-miracles, so-called, attributed to Jesus, are similar to cures wrought today by Christian Scientists, mental healers of various sorts, and the practicers of psychotherapy. Many 'answers to prayer' can be accounted for in purely natural terms. The startling conversions once attributed to supernatural agency are now explained as an inrush into consciousness of ideas and emotions which had been latent in the 'subconscious' life of the individual.... But this does not apply to the major miracles. If Jesus turned water into wine, if he walked on the waves, if he emerged bodily from the tomb after death and ascended into heaven, these are certainly miracles in the full sense of the term. Even supposing that there *are* ways to do these things by purely natural means, it would be utterly miraculous that Jesus should know how to do them. So, if these events actually happened, they are convincing evidence of superhuman power, and of the setting-aside of natural law.

(8) But, after all, what is to be gained by the acceptance of miracles? Nothing, except the realization that wonders do happen, and the presumption that there are Powers behind the scenes. The ability to work miracles does not in the least prove that the person who works them has also a supernatural knowledge of *truth*. His life might be a series of marvels, and his teaching a mass of error. As a matter of fact, we read in the Bible that "false prophets" were working miracles too. And if one teaching is authenticated by miracles, so are any number of others. True, if the miracles are *helpful* to men, they may tend to show that the supernatural Power is bene-

ficent. But actually, in many of the recorded cases, they do not seem to express love or justice. Peter was rescued from prison by a miracle — but the innocent guards met their death as a consequence. The miraculous falling of the walls of Jericho gave the children of Israel a fine chance to massacre and loot; but it was certainly hard on the inhabitants of that ill-fated little town. And the question has never been satisfactorily answered why, if there is a beneficent Power behind Nature, willing upon occasion to break the usual rules of the game, that Power does not intervene upon so many other occasions when agony and catastrophe might be averted.

THE ARGUMENT FROM ORIGINS

Belief in miracles is waning in the modern world. Perhaps for that reason there has been an increased attention to the old arguments based upon the alleged necessity of assuming a supernatural cause to account either for the universe as a whole or for some special feature of existence.

(1) The First Cause Argument asserts that nothing happens without a cause. The universe has come into being, and its coming into being must have had a cause. What can that cause be but God?

The argument assumes that the universe is not eternal; it came into being at a certain time. Of course we are very far from knowing that this is the case. But it is true that the cosmic life *seems*, from the very fragmentary data which we possess, to be a one-way process of which only the earlier part has yet elapsed. Unless there is some compensating tendency not yet known, some return of the energy which is now being radiated and apparently lost, the cosmic process seems to be running down. And if so, it cannot have been going on for an infinite time, or it would long ago have run down completely.   There is no escape from the alternative: either there is some return-swing of the pendulum of fate, of which we have as yet no clue, or else there was a beginning to the process of cosmic evolution, and will be an end.   If it *did* have a beginning, what started it, what set it going, if not God?

In reply, we may say that if everything must have a cause to account for it, the existence of God must have a cause as surely as the existence of the universe.   We have invented the hypothesis of God to account for the universe; how shall we account for God?   From the strictly logical point of view, we seem to have gained nothing.

And we have created for ourselves new difficulties. *How* could God create a universe?   We have not the faintest idea.   Why did he create it when he did, rather than long before?   And why did he create this kind of universe rather than a different (and as it would seem to us, better) kind of universe?   The fact is that the word 'God' has a narcotic effect, paralyzing the inquirer.   It seems blasphemous, or at least presuming, to raise any further questions.   But are we really any better off, in understanding the ultimate nature of things, with a universe and God to explain, than just with a universe?

There are, of course, all sorts of other guesses.   But, *unless we have independent reason, on other grounds, to believe in the existence of a Creator-God*, this too is a mere guess.   The honest thing to say is — we don't know! The origin of the universe — if it had an origin — is an over-the-horizon problem.   Everyone has a right to guess. No one knows whose guess is right.

(2) Some theologians are more impressed with the puzzle offered us by the existence of *life, mind,* the human

soul, or the human *conscience*, than by the existence of the universe itself.   How, in a world of whirling atoms, could life arise?   How could mind arise, out of a world of matter?   And how could this divine spark, our moral sense, find lodgment in us?   All these new and wonderful things demand belief in a creative force that could interpolate something new into Nature.

In reply, we may say that all of these wonderful things *may* have had a purely natural origin.   Many, perhaps most, biologists believe that organic life is a complexification of physico-chemical processes, arising inevitably, as a resultant of the universal laws of Nature, under the special conditions of terrestrial existence.   In the case of mind, we may recall that the third group of theories, the monistic theories, offer us a prospect of solving the problem, since they regard minds as merely complex integrated structures arising as naturally in evolution as the brain-structures whose inner nature they are.   As for the soul, the dominant tendency among philosophers and psychologists is to say, "there ain't no such animal" — in any sense requiring special creation to account for it. And conscience, which used to be regarded as a sort of supernatural faculty implanted in us, is now quite generally considered a natural development of the human mind under the conditions of group life.   In short, we cannot safely rule out the possibility that *all* of these developments in the evolutionary process are *resultants*, under the peculiar terrestrial conditions, of the universal laws of Nature.

On the other hand, the emergent evolutionists think not.   They hold that there are a number of new 'levels,' occurrences unpredictable before the event.   But they do not usually think it necessary to postulate a supernatural intervention to produce the new occurrence. They talk of an 'inherent impulse,' an '*élan vital*,' something in Nature herself which struggles, buds forth in new ways, and feels its way upward.

So we have three possible views: These new things are natural resultants of universal laws; they are emergents, produced by Nature herself, out of her vast potentialities; they are interpolations, directly caused by God.... In the present state of human knowledge, it would surely be presumptuous to assert very confidently that one rather than another of these views is true.

(3) Still other thinkers put their emphasis upon the origin of *values*, and especially of spiritual values. For example, Brightman tells us that any view which dispenses with creation by intelligence "makes human values and ideals a far more miraculous and meaningless thing than a view that sees in values some clue to what really is." [1] And Fosdick declares, "The human mind will never permanently consent to think that spiritual values are a fortuitous accident born of atoms going it blind in a godless universe." [2] Those who hold this view usually believe, explicitly or implicitly, that *parts* of the universe cannot have higher qualities, or values, than the universe as a whole, or the Power back of the universe. The very existence of values implies a source at least *as* valuable from which they have come.

The naturalist, on the other hand, sees no logic in this argument. Why may not valuable things rise out of less valuable or valueless things, as water-lilies grow out of the mire? And why do valuable things require any more explanation than ugly or uninteresting things? Is there

[1] Edgar Brightman, *A Philosophy of Ideals*.
[2] Harry Emerson Fosdick, in *Recent Gains in American Civilization*, p. 244.

any more reason for saying that effects cannot be *better* than their causes than there is for saying that they cannot be *worse* than their causes? Everyday experience makes against both of those propositions.

THE ARGUMENT FROM DESIGN

The most persuasive arguments in favor of a supernaturalistic interpretation of the universe are those which point to the *look* of things. They say, Look at the world; it is the kind of world that would be designed by a benevolent God. There are *signs* of purpose, and of friendliness to our interests, on every hand — not in those exceptional events called miracles, but in the everyday processes of Nature.

(1) Paley, in his famous *Natural Theology*, put the argument in the form of an analogy. A savage finding a watch dropped by an explorer, but with no knowledge of its source, would know that it was made by an intelligent being. For it is a complex mechanism which serves a rational purpose. But the universe is far more complex than a watch, and serves a far more glorious end. May we not infer, then, that it, like the watch, was created by intelligence?

Unfortunately, arguments based upon analogies are always weak. The fact that two things are alike in one respect does not prove that they are alike in some other respect. So far as this argument can tell us, the universe may be analogous to a watch in being a mechanism that attains useful ends (at least at certain times, in certain places), but unlike a watch in its manner of coming into being. It is such a far cry from a watch (or any other man-made machine) to the universe, that whatever analogy exists between them must not be pressed.   Very likely *some* mechanisms are made by intelligent purpose, viz., those made by man, while other mechanisms, such as organic bodies and stellar systems, come into being without pre-existing purpose.

(2) Far more arresting is the Argument from Adaptations.   Here are millions of organic bodies delicately adapted to their environment: the hawk has sharp eyesight, the dog a keen sense of smell, the giraffe a long neck to reach the leaves of trees, the duck web-feet to swim with, and so on in infinite detail, each creature being adapted to the environment in which it lives, in the most complicated and admirable way.   Surely mere chance cannot have brought all this about.   How many times would you have to throw out bags of types before they fell, by lucky chance, into the text of one of Shakespeare's plays?   But the structure of even the simpler organisms is far more complex than the structure of letters that forms a play.   Is it not to the highest degree improbable that a blindly working Nature should have produced such marvelously fortunate combinations of atoms? The atoms themselves cannot be supposed to be intelligent, or to have co-operated consciously to bring about such a result.   What cause, then, can we suggest, to account for these intricate and delicate adjustments, but a supernatural design to produce them?

Before the facts of natural selection were discovered, this argument was very strong.   But now that a set of causes has been found at work producing constant variations in type, and weeding out those which are less well adapted to their environment, it is not clear that we need to assume any other cause for the evolution of the most delicate adjustments.   We can see how these remarkable results accrue through a long series of steps, each explicable (it may be believed) in purely natural terms. Useful variations tend, in a purely mechanical way, to ensure their own survival. And an accumulation of variations, handed on by heredity, may lead to any degree of adaptation.... If it seems difficult to account for some features of organisms by natural selection, we may look for other causes and processes. There may be a number of factors at work. But the point is, that in so far as we find natural causes adequate to account for the results, there is no reason for assuming any supernatural cause. And natural causes we are finding in ever-increasing degree.

Incidentally, there are grave difficulties in the theological view. For the process of evolution of properly adapted organs has been terribly long and wasteful. Uncounted billions of billions of organisms have perished because they were *not* well enough adapted to survive. It looks like a process of blind trial-and-error on a gigantic scale rather than like the outcome of intelligent purpose. And so with the embryonic development which each of us has gone through.

> Instead of proceeding steadily forward as a planned project should, the whole process is one of building up, tearing down, discarding, and remodeling.[1]

As it is, most or all organisms are burdened with useless or ill-developed organs, and with more or less harmful instincts, such as that which drives the moth into the flame.

> Each part of the human body is only just good enough to get by.... If evolution happens to be furnished with fine materials it has no objection to using them, but it is equally ready to use shoddy if it will hold together long enough to get the machine by the reproductive period.[2]

[1] H. H. Newman, in *The Nature of Man and the Universe*, p. 407.
[2] Raymond Pearl, *Studies in Human Biology*.

In short, the whole business of adaptation looks pretty hit-or-miss.

Further, the tiger's claws, the rattlesnake's fangs, the mosquito's proboscis, the ingenious adaptations of bed-bugs, body lice, and a thousand other disgusting parasites, the delicate adjustments of hundreds of kinds of disease-producing microbes, offer as good evidence of design as our own organs. But who wants to believe in a designer who planned all of these horrible and cruel devices? A wide survey of organic adaptations hardly suggests that they were designed to produce a general *welfare* or *happiness*. They are survival-devices, sometimes fairly efficient, but usually not efficient enough, even to ensure a 'normal' span of life. Most animals get eaten by other animals; if they do not, they soon wear out and die in pain.

Let it be clearly understood, *belief* in design is compatible with the facts of evolution. But the *argument* (that you must believe in design in order to have a cause for the existence of adaptations) is gone. The whole process *may*, of course, be designed. But the supposed *evidence* for that belief, in so far as it consisted of the adjustments of organisms to their environment, seems to be no evidence at all. And the belief itself has to face the facts of the clumsiness and cruelty of the process by which adaptations have been produced, and their only very partial efficiency.

(3) A third form of the argument points out the antecedent improbability of so favorable an environment. It has taken a very extraordinary combination of circumstances to make organic life possible. If our atmosphere did not have just the right proportions of oxygen and carbon dioxide, if the temperature on earth were a little colder or a little hotter, if there were not an abundance

of water, or if the atoms of which organic bodies are built did not have just the properties that they do have, these organic bodies could not have appeared.   Their existence is possible only because of

a certain unique arrangement of unique properties of matter. The chance that this unique ensemble of properties should occur by 'accident' is almost infinitely small.... Hence we are obliged to regard this collocation of properties as in some intelligible sense a preparation for the processes of planetary evolution.[1]

The stage has clearly been set for organic life.   Only an intelligent Designer can have done that.

We cannot, however, fairly use the theory of probability to prove that the particular sort of universe which we find existing could not have developed without design. For *any* sort of universe, when contrasted in imagination with the countless other conceivable universes, would seem, antecedently to the fact, equally improbable. Yet if a universe is to exist at all, it must have *some* nature; and why not this?   The theory of probability is merely a statistical theory, applying to a great number of instances of some phenomenon; it has no application to a single instance.... And if we consider our earth-environment as one instance of a vast number of local environments in the universe, we realize that out of the billions of billions of heavenly bodies, we know of only this one where organic life exists.   Perhaps the biological drama is happening just once, in this tiny corner of the universe, for a few passing moments of cosmic time. Does this suggest that the universe is 'bio-centric,' that all the vast reaches of cosmic life are just a stage-setting for this local episode?

[1] L. J. Henderson, *The Order of Nature*, pp. 191–192.

Moreover, organic forms have gradually arisen here, during hundreds of millions of years of struggle and adaptation, adjusting themselves to the conditions they found. If conditions had been somewhat different, who knows but what different structures would have been developed, adapted to *those* conditions. If so, they might have said, "Lo! how beautifully the stage has been set for *our* existence!" Who knows what glorious forms of existence might have arisen under other circumstances?... Think, too, of all the experiments which evolution on our earth has made, types of life intrinsically interesting and full of promise, which have died off because the environment was not favorable for them! It is always easy for the survivors in a struggle to believe that everything was preordained for their success. But how about the billions of organic creatures that have *not* been able to succeed? The environment was *not* favorable for *them*.

(4) Finally, it is often argued that the 'rational order' of the universe implies intelligence back of it. This phrase has several possible meanings, not usually clearly distinguished. Sometimes what is meant is that the *orderliness*, the regularity, of events point to 'a consistent will.'

As we increase in knowledge, and the amazing order is revealed by which the laws of Nature interlock, we cannot fail to gain conviction of a plan, continuous and purposeful, which we, at present, cannot comprehend. But less and less we question its existence.... Slowly, thread by thread, [science] lifts the veil from marvelous co-ordinations, reveals adjustments joining substances and forces, an order and a plan which we cannot, as comprehension grows, accept as chance.[1]

[1] Hans Zinsser, in the *Atlantic Monthly*, vol. 155, p. 90.

It is interesting that *irregularities* ('miracles') are offered by some as evidence of a supernatural Intelligence, while the *regularity* of Nature (unbroken 'natural law') is considered by others to point to the same conclusion! The former argument is the stronger. For irregularities, if they are striking and beneficent in their effect, irresistibly suggest interposition by intelligence. But it is not clear why regularity is supposed to be evidential of intelligence. If the units of matter are alike, why should they not act alike? Perhaps it is just their nature to. In the mere fact of uniformity of structure and behavior there is no logical implication of *purpose* or *plan*.

Again, the world is called 'rational' because we find it (in some degree) intelligible. It "embodies laws and meanings which mind can discover." [1]

It would seem that the striking thing is not that the world is intelligible, but that we have minds that can, in some measure, understand it. Intelligence is perhaps the most interesting product of evolution. We cannot say with assurance that it has been produced by a mere blind process of natural selection. But neither can we say with assurance that it has not been thus produced. In any case, since we *have* intelligence, we cannot help using it. *Whatever* the sort of universe we found ourselves existing in, we should observe, generalize, and organize our knowledge. *Any* sort of universe would thus be, in some degree, known to us if we lived in it. True, the universe we do live in has a great deal more *regularity* than a universe might be conceived to have, and is thus more readily catalogued and understood than a more chaotic universe. But, if that is the point of the argument, it takes us back to the point we have just considered. And the further

[1] Edgar Brightman, *The Problem of God*, p. 148.

fact that *we* find the universe (in some degree) intelligible is merely a backhand way of saying that we have (a considerable amount of) intelligence.

Or, 'rational' may mean 'valuable.' And this is perhaps the strongest argument of all. The cosmic life has attained, on this little planet, such great *values* that we must believe it to have been directed, in part at least, to this end. It is incredible that blind Nature should have given birth to such marvelous and beautiful things. Whenever we love, whenever we thrill to beauty of any sort, whenever we are profoundly happy, whenever we contemplate noble and heroic acts, we find it impossible to believe that these events and experiences should be a mere random product of unintelligent natural forces.

But the conclusion is reached by our emotional nature rather than by logic. We have no knowledge that blind natural forces could *not* produce these valuable things. If it lay within the potentialities of the cosmic stuff to flower out, under favorable (but evidently very exceptional) circumstances, into these beautiful forms, then doubtless they would appear in their due season.... And if we suppose the beautiful things to be the product of design, it would seem that, in fairness, we should consider the ugly things as also designed. We must look fairly on both sides of the picture. There is an enormous amount of misery, ugliness, frustration, and pain in human life. If much of life seems 'rational,' much seems 'irrational.' Anyone with imagination can conceive how human life on earth might have been almost infinitely happier, and more beautiful, these past million years. It is not clear why the happiness and beauty and love in life should be considered a clue to the ultimate nature of things, while the ugliness and frustration and pain are passed over as not equally significant clues. It rather looks like a case of the 'will to believe.'

It seems plain that man will have to know far more than he now knows about the causal processes which produced organic life, and then human beings, with their intelligence and their capacity for joy and pain, before he can have a basis for judgment as to whether these outcomes imply a conscious purpose behind Nature, or whether they are the result of an immanent *élan vital* in Nature herself, or whether they are a natural resultant of the cosmic laws, unplanned, unforeseen, unwilled. In the mean time, we shall believe as our emotions and our hopes impel us. And no one can rightly condemn us for that, so long as we refrain from becoming dogmatic and trying to impose our beliefs upon others, and so long as we are honest enough to recognize that the question remains open, and that no man really knows.

SUGGESTED READINGS

Matthew Arnold, *Literature and Dogma*, V.
R. W. Sellars, *The Next Step in Religion*, IX–X.
J. O. F. Murray, in *Cambridge Theological Essays*, VIII.
George Hodges, *Everyman's Religion*, IV.
W. H. Mallock, *Religion as a Credible Doctrine*, XI–XIII.
Durant Drake, *Problems of Religion*, XVIII–XIX.
J. R. Cohu, *Vital Problems of Religion*, II.
G. T. W. Patrick, *Introduction to Philosophy*, IX.
A. K. Rogers, *The Religious Conception of the World*, pp. 93–120.
F. Paulsen, *Introduction to Philosophy*, pp. 150–180.
J. M. E. McTaggart, *Some Dogmas of Religion*, §§ 156–165, 196–207.
E. S. Brightman, *Introduction to Philosophy*, VIII, IX.
L. J. Henderson, *The Fitness of the Environment*.
W. K. Wright, *A Student's Philosophy of Religion*, XVIII.
W. E. Hocking, *Types of Philosophy*, III–VII.

NATURALISM VS. SUPERNATURALISM   451

CHAPTER XXIV
BEAUTY

THERE are those who say, Unless we can believe that the
Power back of Nature is interested in our human values,
they are of little importance. If naturalism (or determinism, or atheism, or natural selection) is true, life is
not worth while, morality has scant claim upon us, nothing really matters. Conservative Christians say, If the
doctrine of the Resurrection is not true, if Christ was not
a supernatural Being, then Christianity is a great impos-
ture and should be repudiated.... In short, the worth of
human goods is held to depend upon the truth or untruth
of certain beliefs concerning cosmic or historic facts.

But surely, the answers to these cosmic and historical
questions, however interesting in themselves, have no
logical bearing upon the answers to the questions concerning the values found in human life. The *origin* of a
teaching is quite another matter from its *worth*. Whether
Jesus got his ideas by supernatural inspiration or from
his human predecessors and his own genius, if his Way of
life approves itself in human experience as a *good* Way, it
is good, whatever its source. Whether our sense of
beauty, and our sense of duty, have arisen as blind resultants of cosmic tendencies, or because of a divine purpose,
they have exactly the same value — whatever value
experience shows that they *have*. The people who really
care for beauty care for it in itself, and for what it con-
tributes to human happiness, not because they think it
part of a cosmic plan. Those who really love moral values

— kindness, courage, sympathy, love, and the rest — love
them for their inherent worth, irrespective of who has
taught them or how men have come to cherish them.
Esthetics and ethics should be autonomous disciplines,
basing their conclusions upon empirical data, rather than
formulating them as corollaries of men's varying theological creeds.

WHAT IS BEAUTY?

So we take a fresh start, and turn to an empirical study
of human values.   Our first classification may distinguish
direct, *immediate* values from the values which things, or
experience, may have as *means* to a valuable end.   Bread
is valuable as food, i.e., as a means to satisfying our
hunger.   Cognitive experiences are valuable as giving
us clues to action — which, in turn, is valuable in so far
as it secures for us direct, immediate values.   Morality
is valuable (as we shall see in the succeeding chapter)
as a means.   Esthetic experience (and mystical experience, the experience of being in love, etc.) is valuable *in
itself*.   Beauty, as Emerson said, is its own excuse for
being.

Esthetic experience is, then, a species of the genus
'experiences-good-or-bad-in-themselves.'   What, now, is
its special differentia?   How can we demarcate it from
other intrinsically good and bad experiences?   The answer seems to be, The esthetic experience is *a contemplative experience in which we project our emotion into the
object contemplated*.   This concept of 'projection' we have
already met with, in connection with the last of the
epistemological theories discussed in Chapter X.   But
whatever be the truth concerning colors and other sense-
qualities, there can be no doubt that projection occurs

in the case of what are sometimes called 'tertiary' qualities — the beauty and ugliness of things. The situation is this: A certain complex outer existent affects our sense-organs, produces in us a complex of sensations, which, in turn, evoke an emotional complex; we thereupon project into the object which appears in our conscious experience the peculiar emotional quality which has been evoked in us. We call the object beautiful or ugly, according as our emotion is pleasurable or unpleasant.[1] Thus beauty may be defined as the pleasurable emotion got in contemplation, projected into the object of contemplation. Or, more simply, as the objectification of our emotional satisfaction in contemplation.

We objectify our emotions in very varying degree. The mystic usually attributes to God, or Nature, or the All, the radiant glory of his ecstatic experience. The lover attributes to his beloved a loveliness which is but the outward embodiment of the rapture which resides in his own breast. When we speak of 'somber' or 'gay' colors we are, perhaps, aware that the depression or gaiety is our own; when we talk of a 'serene' sky, or of 'angry' clouds, we recognize the 'pathetic fallacy.' When objects awake emotion in us because of their relation to our practical needs, we are less apt to project our emotion into them; we do not call the letter 'beautiful' that brings us good news, or clothing beautiful just because it keeps us warm. But when we listen with delight to music, we objectify our delight: the music, we say, is beautiful. When we look at a Gothic cathedral, a great painting, or a glowing sunset, we project our emotion, and think of the building, the canvas, the mass of clouds

---

[1] There is, of course, no actual spatial transfer; 'projection' is simply imaginative, the *attribution* of a quality to an object.

and sky, as, in itself, possessing the attribute of 'beauty.'

This definition of 'beauty' may seem to some to over-emphasize the emotional aspect of esthetic experience. Surely, it will be said, there is an intellectual element in the appreciation of beauty. Yes, thinking and judging take place when we *analyze* the beauty of an object, when we estimate how beautiful it is, and in what respects. The critic may have little emotional response, may not actually *feel* the beauty very vividly. The performer of a work of art, even its creator, may be so immersed in the details of technique, the means, that their minds for the time being are little concerned with the end, the creation of beauty. Such attention to technique on the part of the artist, and to the artist's technique on the part of the critic, is necessary if beautiful works of art are to be created and enjoyed. By detailed attention, discrimination, labeling, classifying, we can vastly develop and enhance our esthetic reactions. But the esthetic experience itself, the actual enjoying of beauty, is an emotional experience. And it is only as beauty is *enjoyed* that there *is* beauty. For beauty is, precisely, the projection of our enjoyment.

Beauty is just the most striking aspect of the perpetual illusion which pervades perception. We suppose it to be out there, in the building, the painting, the sunset sky. But out there there are but electrons and protons carrying on their endless dance, there are light-rays and air-waves speeding across Space. A very slight change occurs in the vibration of a string and the length of the air-waves it produces. In Nature the change is negligible; but in us, who listen to the violin-note 'off the pitch,' there is all the difference between ecstatic enjoyment and acute discomfort. It is *we* who are responding to the sense-stimulation by faster breathing, by delicious tensions and relaxations, by activity of glands, and a host of obscure physiological events. Only when there is a sentient being thus reacting to the world about him is beauty born. The architect, the engineer, the physicist may know far more about a *building*, as it objectively is; but unless they are affected emotionally by it, they do not feel its beauty.

Why do we react with pleasurable emotion to some objects of our contemplation and with uncomfortable emotion to others? Well, that is a long story, which it is the psychologist's task to ascertain. There is a great variety of reasons why this and that aspect of objects (and of such *events* as sounds, fireworks, dances, which are not commonly called 'objects') arouse in our breasts these emotional reverberations. They seem to be of little direct practical use to us, and are doubtless to be reckoned as incidental by-products of evolution. The primary, biologically useful emotions are anger, fear, and love. Esthetic emotions are derivative, not directly involved in the struggle for existence, although in the long run they may be of considerable indirect value.... We may frame hypotheses as to the cause of some particular emotional reaction, as when we suggest that the color 'red' is the color of blood, and derive from that fact its special emotional flavor for us. Or we may generalize, and say, for example, that what stimulates bodily activities and gives them free, unimpeded play evokes pleasant emotions, while a lack of stimulus is boring, and blocked bodily functioning is distressing. Thus a melody is interesting, not boring like a monotonous repetition of one sound; and it can be grasped as a whole, it gives rise to a single integrated reaction, instead of being confusing, and therefore more or less distressing, as is an unmelodious series of sounds.

We cannot, in this brief chapter, consider these questions. Nor can we consider *what* aspects of objects are beautiful to us. That is the subject-matter of books of art-criticism, books on the appreciation of music, or of Nature, and so on. We must, however, deal with the abstract question, Is beauty, then, purely 'subjective'? And if so, how can we say that certain objects are 'really' more beautiful than others? What right have we to speak of 'standards' of taste? It is quite clear that the beauty which any one of us feels depends upon his capacities for emotional reaction, upon his state of health and his mood at the moment, upon his past history and particular personal associations. At different times in our lives we discover, as we say, new beauties in things; i.e., we develop new susceptibilities, new emotional reactions. We are so accustomed to thinking of certain well-known objects as, of course, beautiful — the Parthenon, the Venus de Milo, the Mona Lisa — that we fail to realize how different our actual individual reactions are. We are ashamed if we do not feel their beauty, we distrust our own reactions, we try to educate ourselves to feel as others tell us they feel. We hesitate to say how thrilled we have been, say, by a simple song heard floating across a Venetian lagoon at dusk, and how bored we have been at a Symphony concert. We are willing to admit, with Mark Twain, that classical music is really better than it sounds.

A little analysis, however, will make clear in what sense beauty is subjective and in what sense it is objective. It is subjective in the sense that it is not a quality or aspect of the physical things which we call beautiful, or a truth about *them*. It is an *effect* produced when observers contemplate them. The effect is produced, moreover, only under certain conditions. A building, for example, does not produce the beauty-effect when seen from an airplane, or when seen too close-to. It is only from certain points of view that it seems beautiful. Even the loveliest human body is not beautiful in all positions; some poses give awkward lines, as photographers well know. And the observer must be capable of appreciating the particular sort of beauty which can be felt in the object, and must be in the mood to appreciate it. Only under favorable conditions does the beauty-experience arise. And unless it arises, there *is* no beauty. Beauty does not exist out there, waiting to be appreciated; it is *created* by a favorable conjunction of object and beholder.

On the other hand, beauty is objective in the sense that it is only objects with certain characteristics which produce in observers the beauty-experience. It is possible to describe, at great length, just what combinations of line, form, color, etc., will seem beautiful to the normal human observer. Thus we may speak of an object as being, in itself, beautiful, in the sense that it has a permanent potentiality of arousing a pleasant esthetic experience in beings like us. Human beings are sufficiently alike to respond somewhat similarly to similar stimuli, and, therefore, to attribute beauty to the same objects and events.

But people differ a good deal in their esthetic reactions. And when they differ, has anyone a right to claim superior validity for his taste? Some people like hurdy-gurdies, chromos, and jazz; others like Bach and Italian Primitives. Must we say, simply, *De gustibus non disputandum?*...

True, 'cultivated' people — i.e., people with wide experience in a certain field, people who have observed certain types of art-objects long and understandingly — are deferred to as 'connoisseurs.' We seek to 'improve' our taste, to imitate the reactions of these experts. But why? If beauty is but the objectification of our pleasure in contemplation, why should we not be simply happy in whatever chances to give us pleasure? We are not ashamed of liking crackers and milk, or boiled onions, because some epicures prefer caviar and artichokes. Why should we be ashamed of preferring a popular song to a fugue of Bach's? Why should we call the standards of the art- and music-critics higher, or better, than those of any humble person who really enjoys what he enjoys?

The only answer is that the connoisseur has a richer, profounder enjoyment than the uncultivated man. We, too, are capable of that richer joy; and so we want to learn to see, to hear, to feel as he does.... But the connoisseur must guard against the distorting effect of his moods and his merely personal associations — if he is to give utterance to judgments which can be widely accepted. He must beware of first impressions, which are apt to be thus distorted, and study the object on various occasions. He must seek to understand as widely as possible the many aspects of objects which may provoke the beauty-experience. And even then, he must never be dogmatic. For no one man can feel all the possible esthetic experiences that may be evoked in different observers by a simple object. And we who are seeking to broaden our basis of enjoyment must compare the verdicts of many critics and learn something from them all. In all the arts there is a great variety of aims and effects. Different observers are sensitive to different effects, and the most gifted critic may quite miss an aspect of beauty that another feels. The differences of critics are mostly differences of emphasis and of interest, and need not blind us to the universality of esthetic verdicts in their main outlines.

WHAT IS ART?

In the broadest sense of the term, 'art' is *activity requiring skill, leading to a goal.* In this sense we speak of the art of navigation, the art of cookery, the art of strawberry-growing.... But by 'art' we often mean 'fine art,' the subject-matter of esthetics. In this narrower sense, 'art' is *the creation, by skill, of objects capable of evoking esthetic experience.* Or more briefly (in the words of Ducasse), art is "skilled objectification of feeling." Or, "art is the language of emotion."

To bring out clearly the meaning of this conception of art, several points should be noted:

(1) It is rather better, when generalizing, to say that art is the objectification or expression of *'feeling'* than of 'emotion.' For 'emotion' is too strong a word to apply to many forms of art. Making lace, or a beautiful rug, hardly involves emotion, but does express the feeling of pleasure which the craftsman has in contemplating the pattern he is creating, and which the purchaser will presumably feel when he contemplates it.

(2) There must be *skill* involved, if we are to call the product art. One may blow soap-bubbles which give a genuine esthetic pleasure; one may, by breathing on a cold window-pane, produce beautiful frost-crystals. But such simple, casual activity is hardly to be called art.[1]

---

[1] I owe a clear recognition of this point, as well as of various other points in the analysis of esthetic experience, to Professor C. J. Ducasse, whose *Philosophy of Art* seems to me the clearest and most accurate work in this field yet written.

(3) The feeling must be embodied, *objectified*, in some medium, to be art. We may express and communicate our feelings in all sorts of other ways. We express anger by throwing things around and speaking vehemently. We express apprehension by twiddling our fingers or pacing the room. We express love by caresses and smiles. But these forms of emotional release are not art. On the other hand, we have art if we express our love in a love-poem, or if we express our anger in a skillfully composed denunciatory speech.... Obviously there is no sharp line in practice. The love-poem and the denunciatory speech may be impromptu and not committed to paper. But the line is clear in theory. The mere transmission of the emotion from one person to another does not in itself constitute art. There must be an object-of-contemplation, an object which evokes *esthetic* experience. If the beloved merely feels her lover's emotion, and responds to it, there is as yet no art. But if she loves the love-*poem*, thinks of *it* as beautiful (or tender, or stirring, or thrilling), a work of art has been produced.

(4) It is better to speak of art as the 'expression' of feeling than as the 'communication' of feeling. For no communication to others may be intended or take place. A pianist may create lovely music alone at his piano; an artist may paint a lovely picture and destroy it before anyone else sees it. 'Expression' implies potential communication, but the communication may not be actual. Artists frequently do not think of a public at all, but enjoy expressing their feelings and love the beautiful things they create for their own sake. The social value of art, however, consists, of course, in the actual transmission of feeling from artist to the public, by means of the art-object.

(5) Moreover, the artist need not actually feel the emotion himself, if he is skilled in the technique of creating objects which will convey the emotion to others. Actors vary very much in the degree with which they feel the emotions they are expressing; some of the greatest actors are said to be quite emotionless. A religious painter may not himself feel the religious emotion which his Madonnas awaken in the pious who see them. Indeed, the more expert an artist becomes, the more his mind is concerned with accuracy of technique, and the less likely he is to be feeling the beauty of what he is creating. The essence of art is not the expression of feelings which the artist is actually having, but the creation of objects which will evoke esthetic feelings in the beholder. Often, too, the artist has but the vaguest idea of the feelings which he wishes to convey. His esthetic experience grows with the work of creation; when it is finished, he may well be surprised at the feeling he gets in contemplating it. He may seem to have been a mere passive instrument of a divine inspiration. Or, when his creative ecstasy has passed, the work may fail to produce even in him the feeling which he was trying to express; yet it may have its own beauty, and be a real work of art.

In the light of the foregoing explanations, we will briefly discuss two rival definitions of art.

IS ART THE EXPRESSION OF TRUTH?

Barrett Wendell defined literature as "the lasting expression in words of the meaning of life." Reginald Wright Kauffman, with the drama particularly in mind, declared that "Art is to make the truth of here-and-now dramatically and movingly clear to you.... If it inter-

prets life truthfully and dramatically, it is art."...
Among the well-known exponents of this view are Ruskin,
Balzac, and Bernard Shaw. Is this conception of art,
as a moving expression of truth, adequate?

Certainly it is one function, and an important one,
performed by the arts that employ the medium of words.
But as certainly, it is not the only, or the fundamental,
function of art. It does not apply at all to such arts as
the making of beautiful fabrics, furniture, and buildings,
or to music and purely decorative painting. Nor does it
apply without a straining of meanings to romantic and
imaginative poetry or fiction. Such forms of literature
are not so much reports of how things *are* as visions of
what they might be. If we may speak of their truth, we
can only mean fidelity to fundamental human needs and
cravings, not fidelity to actual fact. Even landscape
painting and sculpture are seldom accurate transcriptions
of existing reality, they are expressions of the artist's
dream. They give us reality glorified, made over into
the image of the heart's desire. If the artist's primary
motive is to communicate truth, his work is mere reporting, and not art at all, unless it also embodies feeling and
evokes an esthetic response. Art is never a mere set of
signs for the conveyance of information, it is something
to be enjoyed and loved for its own sake. If, in addition,
it produces in the reader or beholder a profounder understanding of life, that is a moral value superposed upon
its primary esthetic value.

We may note, however, that every work of representative art, if it is to evoke a satisfying esthetic experience,
must have truth enough not to offend. The degree of
truthfulness necessary depends upon the specific type of
art. A drama dealing with the life of today must be

reasonably realistic, if it is not to seem silly to the audience. But a play may deal entirely with a realm of fantasy. A piece of fiction may be a pure fairy-tale. A painting of a familiar scene must render it with fair truthfulness. But painting may well show us what never was on land or sea. A statue of a man must be anatomically correct. But the sculptor may prefer to give us a purely imaginary creature, a centaur or a faun.

Probably most people will agree that a work of art which has profound truth to life is, other things equal, a greater work than those which have little relation to our urgent human concerns. Realistic art touches us more deeply than fantasy-art. Shakespeare and Homer are great poets, not merely because of the magic of their verse, but because of their profound fidelity to human nature and their insight into its perennial needs. This means that moral worth has been added to and enhances the esthetic worth of the work of art.... But there are many kinds of lovely art. And it is quite clear that whereas the communication of truth is the main function of science, history, and philosophy, it is not the main function of art.

IS ART THE EXPRESSION OF BEAUTY?

To say that art is the creation or expression of beauty is to give a *normative* definition. This is what art aims to do, this is the *good* of art. It records and reminds us of the beauty of Nature, it opens our eyes to aspects of beauty we have not noticed before, it creates new forms of beauty not found in natural objects. It evokes in us happy emotions to gild the drabness of our days, it gives us objects that we can love and enjoy.... To be sure, esthetic experiences include the experience of ugliness as well as the experience of beauty. And the various fine arts actually create a good deal of ugliness as well as a good deal of beauty. A discordant or banal piece of music is bad art, but it is still art. The ugly buildings that line our streets are products of the art of architecture. Occasionally, even, an artist may consciously desire to create something ugly. But in general, neither artists nor public want ugliness; and ugly art is simply abortive art, art that has failed in attaining its goal.

By 'ugly' art we have meant art which evokes in the beholder an unpleasant esthetic experience. But, as we have noted, a work of art may be ugly to some observers and beautiful to others. Many a work of art which has seemed beautiful to its creator has seemed ugly to everyone else. In fact, there is no sharp line; beauty shades by insensible degrees into ugliness. And some esthetic experiences are so mixed that it is difficult to say whether the objects which evoke them are predominantly beautiful or predominantly ugly. Few works of art are *wholly* beautiful, for a sufficiently discriminating analysis. Thus, if we should define art as "the creation, by human skill, of beauty," we should have to say that concrete buildings, paintings, etc., are works of art only if, and in so far as, they are beautiful. So subjective and complex a criterion would be very difficult to apply. It is better, therefore, to define art in such a way as to include the ugly with the beautiful, and to say that the possession of beauty is a criterion not of art, but of *good* art.

The matter is complicated by the fact that objects are often called 'ugly' which actually evoke a pleasant esthetic experience, and may therefore also be properly called 'beautiful.' A grinning gargoyle, a portrait of an old wrinkled woman, an etching of some shocking slum, are not repellent; we enjoy contemplating them, though our enjoyment is somewhat mixed.   It would be better in such cases to speak of the gargoyle as 'grotesque,' rather than 'ugly,' and to say that we have a beautiful picture of an ugly scene.   One of the functions of such forms of art is to invest the ugly and the commonplace with an aura of beauty, and so to reconcile us to their existence.

And so with tragedy.   Life is full of tragic events.   Art invests them with its color and music, transmutes them into strange forms of beauty, and so makes them bearable — if the tragedy is not too realistic, and does not touch us too close.   Such forms of art give us a profounder thrill than idyllic art, because reality is, in the long run, more poignantly interesting to us than dreams.   The vicarious sadness which they gently evoke is a release to our pent-up pain and sorrow; by the genius of the artist our bitterness is turned into courage, resignation, or laughter.   Such works of art may be very beautiful to us, as well as morally inspiring.   On the other hand, a story, a play, or a 'movie' may be so gruesome that whatever beauty of form and expression it may have is forgotten in the impression of horror it produces, and we feel the work to be repellent.

Moral and esthetic ratings are thus inextricably intertwined.   Works of art may legitimately be used for stimulating moral attitudes, and may properly be condemned if their effects are immoral.   Tolstoy, and other earnest moralists whose zeal for right conduct has smothered their interest in beauty, would have us rate art solely with respect to its moral value.   On the other hand, artists generally assert that "Art is for Art's sake," and that moralists should keep their hands off.... This, however, is a moral problem, and has nothing to do with the comprehension of what art essentially is. Art *is* the skilled evocation of esthetic experiences. And, whatever emotional release the artist may get in creating it, and whatever ulterior uses the moralist may find for it, its main function is the evocation of *happy* esthetic experiences, the addition of beauty to life.

SUGGESTED READINGS

C. J. Ducasse, *The Philosophy of Art*, especially chs. VIII, IX, XI, XII.
George Santayana, *The Sense of Beauty*.
H. S. Langfeld, *The Æsthetic Attitude*, I–IV, XI.
H. R. Marshall, *The Beautiful*, Part I.
E. D. Puffer, *Psychology of Beauty*, II; IV–VI.
DeW. H. Parker, *Principles of Æsthetics*, II–III.
DeW. H. Parker, *The Analysis of Art*, I.
L. W. Flaccus, *The Spirit and Substance of Art*.
E. Rowland, *The Significance of Art*.
Helen Parkhurst, *Beauty*.
Vernon Lee, *The Beautiful*.
E. F. Carritt, ed., *Philosophies of Beauty*.
E. F. Carritt, *What is Beauty?*

CHAPTER XXV

MORALITY

IT IS well to begin the study of values with a consideration of beauty. For in esthetic experience we have the good in an intrinsic, indisputable form. The only things we know or can imagine that are *intrinsically* good or bad are — certain qualities of conscious experience. There are many names for these intrinsically desirable and undesirable qualities of consciousness; perhaps the least misleading are 'happiness' and 'unhappiness.' Beauty-experiences are happy experiences; their goodness is directly *felt*. Suffering of any sort is a bad sort of feeling. We may forget these primary values in our absorption in some further end. But however willingly we may renounce a happy experience, or endure pain, it remains true that the former has intrinsic worth and the latter intrinsic badness. However ashamed of our naïve esthetic preferences we may become, the pleasure that we had in them was a genuine good, while it lasted. All our esthetic education, all our preaching and propaganda, all our moral effort and sacrifice, is fruitless and of no account if it does not result eventually in the increase of happiness, or at least the lessening of unhappiness. For everything else is but means; happy experience, in its infinite variety, is alone of inherent worth.

The morally good is harder to recognize and agree upon than the esthetically good, because it is an extrinsic character. Moral conduct is conduct which is desirable as a means to an end. The end is recognizably good, but it may be so remote as to be difficult of appraisal. Thus, there is room for endless dispute as to the relative value

of ends, and as to the best means of attaining them....
Men actually have approved, at some time or other, almost every sort of conduct, without in the least realizing
why they approved of this and disapproved of that.
Morality has grown up out of animal instinct, and been
superposed upon it by tribal tradition, through a haphazard process of natural selection, and often misguided
leadership. The result is that men have sometimes approved cruel and disastrous codes, and have seldom realized with any clear understanding what morality is *for*.
They have formulated various principles to justify the
precepts which they found themselves approving. We
must examine these principles if we are to understand
the chaos to which morals have come, and if we are to
have a hand in shaping the more enlightened morality of
the future.

WHAT MAKES CONDUCT RIGHT OR WRONG?

1. *Acts are right because God commands them*

Primitive communities have usually attributed their
moral codes — one-sided and often barbarous as they
have been — to their particular god. Christendom,
inheriting the Hebraic tradition, still acquiesces, more or
less vaguely, in the idea that morality consists, essentially,
in obedience to God. There is a simplicity about this
conception — if we assume that the God of the Christian
tradition exists, and that the precepts of the Bible writers
correctly represent his will. To accept these time-
honored commandments saves men from the arduous
labor of criticizing and judging and deciding the moral
issues involved, and offers them the easier attitude of
unquestioning loyalty to a Higher Will.

But suppose God *has* given us these commandments.

Why should we obey them? Because he will damn us if we don't, and save us if we do? But in that case the brave man would scorn to obey. Or, if he did obey, it would be because he recognized it to be expedient, not because he felt it to be right. He would feel it to be *right* only if he felt sure that God, being good, commands what is really best. The mere fact that God commanded it would not *make* it best; God would be commanding it because it *is* best. So we should still have to find the answer to the question, What *makes* one act good and another act bad?... As a matter of fact, it is quite clear that kindness and courage and mercy are good anyway, God or no God, and that cruelty and meanness and hatred are bad. If God commands these virtues and forbids these sins, that may be for many an additional motive; but it cannot make them any more truly virtues and sins than they were before he spoke.

The unhappy fact is that commandments promulgated in the name of God have done a great deal to distort and confuse morality. So credulous have men been of what their priests and parents have taught them that they have allowed their bodies to be enslaved and their spirits stifled in obedience to this alleged Divine Authority. Noble heroisms and lovely deeds of charity have also been inspired by supernaturalistic ethics. Flowers and weeds have grown side by side in the gardens of the various authoritative religions. But theological morality, by its very nature, is not open to correction by experience. Even if it is not exploited by ecclesiastics and rulers, as it was in pre-revolutionary Russia, it resists change and even free discussion. So it seems necessary to insist that the accredited prophets of God are as fallible as anyone else; if there is a loving God who wishes for us what is really best, the surest way of getting into harmony with his will is not to accept blindly some tradition, but to study patiently the needs of human nature and find, by careful empirical research, what kinds of conduct observably have the best results. This is what we should have the best reason to call God's will.

2. *Acts are right because Conscience commands them*

Many who feel uncertain of the authoritativeness of any written tradition of God's will, feel that conscience (or the moral sense) is an authoritative guide. Conscience does speak, to those in whom it is strongly developed, with a voice of authority; and in many cases it is clearly on the side of right, and ought to be obeyed. But *why* should we obey it? Why not defy it, and be free of its tyranny? Obviously, we should obey it only if, and in so far as, it bids us do what is really best. It has no authority *in itself*; it deserves our allegiance only when it serves to call us to what are actually our duties. Conscience is a general name for certain inner urges and inhibitions, which have an important part to play in checking and redirecting our primary impulses. They have been developed, like our other tendencies, by a long process of natural selection, because of their usefulness. But, like our other tendencies, they are to be followed only in so far as experience shows that they really are of use.

Observation quickly shows that the dictates of different people's consciences differ very widely. Even in a single community, yes, even in a single family, conflicts of conscience are common. And if we consider the history of man, we find extraordinary divergences in conduct that is sincerely conscientious. What one people, or one religious sect, holds to be an important duty, other peoples look upon as sin. The anthropologists have shown us in convincing detail that these inner urges and checks which we call conscience, or a 'sense of duty,' are, like all our other ideas and ideals, a product of our particular environment and education, as superposed upon our own particular blend of hereditary tendencies. In the Middle Ages, when the Christian code had become crystallized and reigned undisputed in Europe, it was easy to think of Conscience as a Mystic Voice telling every child of God what was right and wrong. But as soon as men became aware of the utterly different moral judgments of other days and other races of men, this simple notion had to be relinquished. It is quite evident that in this confusion of consciences many, if not most, consciences have been *wrong*. And if some deliverances of conscience are wrong, it is clear that conscience is a very dubious guide.

Further, a little analysis shows that it is only in stereotyped cases that our consciences give us a clear command. We have been told from infancy that it is wrong to lie; it is no wonder that that teaching is reflected in an inner inhibition which sets up a protest when we find ourselves tempted to tell a fib. But when we confront a new situation, conscience cannot help us, except as we are able, by hook or crook, to classify the alternative possibilities under some familiar headings. Since conscience is a crystallization of our moral education, it embodies the prejudices of the group to which we belong, and has little to say concerning problems lying outside the range of its code.

Even, however, if conscience were far more standardized than it is, acts would not be right *because* our conscience urged them. Conscience is, at best, simply a psychological mechanism for pushing us toward the better kinds of conduct. If we were all (as some people are) devoid of this particular sort of inner prompting and admonition, it would still be just as true that some acts are better than others. For the value of conduct lies not in the motives and forces that lead to it, but in the results which it achieves.

3. *Acts are right because approved by a Community*

The foregoing analysis brings out the fact that we usually approve such conduct as is approved by the community to which we belong, and condemn whatever our group condemns. May we not simply say, then, that morals are *mores*, the customs of a given people? Obviously these moral customs vary indefinitely.

> The wildest dreams of Kew are the facts of Khatmandu,
> And the crimes of Clapham chaste in Martaban.

According to this conception, there is no one universal right and wrong; there are merely local and temporary standards, like the local spaces and times of relativity-theory. Indeed, this view of morality is frankly relativistic. What is right for us, as a member of our community, may be quite wrong for a member of an alien group. It is a mortal sin for a Catholic to commit suicide, but it is a glorious deed (under certain circumstances) for a patriotic Japanese. Praying for rain was a sacred duty, in time of drought, for the Orthodox Russian; to the young Communist, it is stupid and misleading superstition. Thus, even in the same land, and within the same home, widely divergent codes clash. To be moral is simply to be true to the code of the group to which you belong.

This view of morality, which is becoming very widespread in our day, agrees with the preceding conceptions in making morality consist in *conformity* — in this case to our group, instead of to God or to the voice of our conscience. It gives us no reason to think that the particular code of our group is a *better* code than that of some other group. It gives us no leverage by which to *criticize* and *improve* the morals of our group. It allows no meaning at all to the concept of moral *progress*. However superstitious and stupid, or even cruel, the customs of our community are, they are, by definition, what is right — for us. The unthinking conformist is the moral man, the moral reformer is the immoral man — unless he converts his fellows to his view.

But we do not really believe this. We are all constantly criticizing the morals of our own group — not to say the morals of other peoples. And while a prophet is apt to be without honor in his own country during his lifetime, he is often rated by a later generation as the most moral man of his day, precisely because he rejected the inadequate moral code of his people. We all feel that moral judgments are more important than this definition of morality makes them out to be. There are really better and worse ways to live, whether or not they are approved by a group. It may be expedient to follow the crowd; but it is braver to lead the way to something better. And it is only as people have a conception of morality totally different from this that they will move on toward the millennium.

4. *Acts are right because they conduce to Self-Realization*

A more progressive doctrine, and one very widespread among the youth of today, is that which makes self-realization the highest good. Each of us has his own life to mould, his own happiness to secure; his business is to develop his latent potentialities, to make the most of himself. Not conformity, but *growth*, is the ideal; whatever acts expand our horizons, enrich our experience, bring out what is in us, are *ipso facto* good. We must, of course, respect the right of others to realize themselves; and that involves a certain amount of personal sacrifice as well as the widest tolerance. Moreover, it is only in group-life and in co-operative activity that we can realize our highest potentialities. But the end is essentially atomistic, the development of each of our specific personalities, the production of a great many fine types of men and women.

There is a great deal that is admirable in this ideal — especially in view of the almost universal human tendencies to sloth and to stupid conformity. But it does not dig deep enough to satisfy the inquiring mind. After all, *why* should we develop our latent potentialities? If a man prefers to dream away his days, to go fishing, to bask in the sun, or to carry on a simple and familiar routine, why should we urge him to get up and 'realize' himself? It is not clear that there is anything intrinsically desirable about the realization of potentialities. The process of developing them may be irksome; are we sure that the end is worth achieving? Many people, especially young people, feel the urge to try their powers, to taste life to the full, to become something different from what they are. Well and good, let them have their fling, give them rope. But can they prove to us that they have chosen a better way than that of quiet satisfaction in what we have and are?

Moreover, the moment we set out to develop our potentialities, we are confronted by the question, Which potentialities? For at every moment — and especially in youth — all sorts of divergent paths lie before us. If we choose to become scientists, we cannot become as cultured as we should like in poetry and art. Life is too short to develop a tithe of our potential powers. To be a first-rate musician or lawyer or research-worker means giving up being almost everything else. Some of our capacities are obviously not much worth developing, some are even dangerous to develop. And among those which we should like to develop it is very hard to choose. The criterion of 'self-realization' gives us no clue as to *which* potentialities, among so many, are most worth developing. A clever man may develop himself into a successful criminal, racketeer, floater of specious investments. Why not? Nero, Ghenghis Khan, Attila, Tamerlane realized themselves — at uncounted cost in human pain and tears.

True, if we keep in mind that *everyone* has a right to self-realization, we shall condemn those who carve their own way at the expense of others. But if a man's heart is in realizing himself, he is sadly likely to overlook the harm he is doing others, and unlikely to spend his strength in helping them to realize themselves. And if the gospel of self-realization *for a group* is preached, the danger is still greater. Self-realization for Germany, for Japan — there is no greater menace to humanity. The doctrine must be expanded to mean self-realization for all mankind, with only as much self-expression for individuals and groups as is consistent with that.

Many of the world's greatest moralists have felt that what the individual needs is not a call to self-realization, but a call to self-denial. We have *too much* concern for our own needs, too little willingness to sacrifice what we, individually, might do and be, for the general good.

Particularly in America, we are 'out for ourselves.' The gospel of individualism has been preached so long, and brought to our attention by such brilliant examples of personal success, that the slogan 'self-realization' falls on willing ears. But it is only a half-truth. There are cases where the realization of some potentiality is highly desirable, and cases where it is not. To decide what the particular situation demands, we need a more ultimate criterion than this.

5. *Acts are right because they conduce to the maximum satisfaction of desire*

Human society is the scene of conflicting interests, needs, desires. But so is the individual human heart. One desire is as intrinsically deserving of satisfaction as another; satisfaction is always, in itself, a good. But they cannot all be satisfied, for many of them are mutually incompatible. If we try to satisfy each desire as it comes along, we shall find ourselves acting at cross-purposes, and losing out in the end. Experience shows, moreover, that some desires are more persistent and ineradicable, while others fade out if denied. By carefully picking our way amid the solicitations which beset us, we can satisfy those desires which will fit together, and can achieve a harmonious, integrated life. Every bit of satisfied desire is an intrinsic good; the maximum of co-attainable satisfaction is, therefore, the highest attainable good. So, in a society, each person's needs and desires should be considered as equally deserving, and the social ideal should be the maximum of co-attainable satisfaction for everyone.

This is a useful picture of the moral problem. But we must make certain qualifications. There are desires which are so inimical to any synthesis of goods that they must just be killed off, or kept enchained. And we must include in our synthesis not merely *felt* desires, but potential desires, unrealized needs. Otherwise we might achieve harmony at too low a level. We must *awaken* desire, as well as trying to integrate existing desires; the reformer, the moral leader, is usually a disturber of equilibrium rather than a mere arbiter of conflicts in the interests of harmony.

And, after all, it is not the existence of desire for something that makes that thing a good. There are desires — call them 'pathological,' if you like — whose fulfillment would bring good to no one. In a rage a man wishes to murder his wife; in depression he longs to commit suicide; on the edge of a cliff he has the urge to jump off. The carrying-out of these impulses would be of no value to anyone. The fact is, our desires and purposes do not always point to actual goods, just as perceptual experiences do not always point to actually existing things. Either may be hallucinatory.... On the other hand, many of our best experiences are not *desired*, or anticipated at all, they just come to us — as, the sudden glory of a sunset sky, music stealing to us from some unexpected source, ecstatic dreams, mystical experiences that descend unsought upon the soul.... The *anticipation* of the fulfillment of desire may be, itself, a very considerable good. And the *recollection* of past joys is another, added joy.... In short, the worth of an experience is intrinsic, it lies in its conscious quality; it does not depend upon the extrinsic fact of its having been desired.

We must, then, include in our total life-plan such ways of living as will tend to give us as many as possible of these overtones of joy which we cannot specifically seek.

And we should not be too insistent upon making out of our lives one single integrated pattern. We may properly be, to some extent, pluralistic in our interests, picking up all sorts of pleasant experiences which are irrelevant to our main purposes. Organization, synthesis, is necessary, if our lives are not to be helter-skelter and full of conflict. But organization is only a means, and may be overdone. The only thing that is *intrinsically* good is the happy experiences themselves. Everything else, including all morality, and all religion, is only a means.

6. *Acts are right because they conduce to the greatest attainable happiness for all concerned.*

All of the standards which we have discussed lead us, when thoughtfully considered, to the realization that happiness is the only ultimate good. There *is* no other kind of good, except in the derived sense of being a *means* to happiness.... If we clearly realized this, we should see that no act is wrong unless it tends to bring unhappiness to someone. And we should thereupon become more sympathetic and tolerant of the manifold forms of happiness which we ourselves cannot feel. We should also realize that the attainment of the greatest possible human happiness is a very great art, which we have only begun to learn. It is that art which is morality — or rather, what morality ought to be. It is impossible to be *lastingly* happy, or to attain to anything like the richest life, without taking a great deal of pains and making many sacrifices. In other words, if we are to be happy, and make those around us happy, in the long run, we must be moral. For that is what morality is, the technique of securing the greatest attainable happiness for everyone.

For us who are reared in the Christian tradition, which

emphasizes self-denial, the thought of happiness as the ultimate end sounds pagan and vaguely sinful. We feel that we should follow virtue for virtue's sake, without any regard to results. But the question is, What *is* the 'virtuous' thing to do? The *really* virtuous act is the act that will tend to bring about the greatest happiness. Any other sort of conduct, however hallowed by tradition, is simply cruel, since it gives people less happiness than they might have had. As yet, it is true, the greater part of morality is concerned with getting rid of *un*happiness, avoiding the manifold dangers and pitfalls of life. It is remedial, like medicine, and therefore rather unpalatable. But we ought to learn the A B C's of life quickly, and go on beyond that to the vast reaches of positive effort for happiness. If people who are now bored with morality, or restive under it, could be made to see that it is not mere convention, or tyranny, but is just the art of life, they might adopt it with zest, and show some moral creativeness, instead of a grudging conformity.

It is very difficult, of course, to see in detail what sort of conduct will be best in the long run. And so we accumulate traditions, and put the gathering wisdom of the race into precepts, commandments, and codes. But the wide divergences between these codes show how complex and difficult the problems are. Happiness is not measurable; and no one can know what joy or pain others are feeling, except very inadequately, as they tell him. So there will remain a wide margin of uncertainty in ethics. Life is experimental; we cannot know in advance what ways will prove best. We need warm sympathies, wide experience, and cool, unbiased thinking. The moralists of the past have seldom seen clearly what morality is *for*. And so, although their sympathies were often sensitive

and their judgments sound, we cannot accept their conclusions blindly. Our current codes will probably have
to have a good deal of correction and expansion before
they are really fit to pattern our lives by. This is what
makes ethics so interesting today. We are just beginning
to realize that morality is made for man, not man for
morality. We are beginning to study morals empirically,
and to base our conclusions upon the observable *results* of
conduct.[1]

Some readers will still feel that many ways of getting
happiness are immoral, and that moral living by no means
always secures happiness.... But *why* are some ways of
getting happiness wrong? Simply because they make
against our own ultimate happiness, or, more likely, diminish the possible happiness of others. In the first case
the act is imprudent, in the second case it is selfish. Im-
prudence and selfishness are the two great sins, of which
all other sins are cases. Often it is not easy to see why
we must do this, or renounce that. And, in fact, there is
much that is simply stupid in accepted moral codes. But
we must not too lightly assume the irrelevance of a duty
whose concrete value we cannot at the moment see.
Human nature is very complex, and the results of acts
are often quite different from what we foresee. We may
chafe under moral restrictions, and fancy that we should
all be happier to ignore them. But we are very apt to
learn, too late, that our judgment was immature, and that
it would have been wiser to curb our immediate desires.
We shall not be sure of happiness for ourselves or for
those about us, even if we follow the moral way. For
many things which affect human happiness are beyond our
control. But morality is simply doing our part toward it.

[1] Cf. Durant Drake, *The New Morality* (The Macmillan Co., 1929).

And even if ill fortune intervenes to spoil our efforts, there is a satisfaction in having done our part.

There is no field in which we need creative thinking more urgently. Our problems are growing in number and complexity as civilization advances. We have in many ways outgrown the codes of simpler societies, and are floundering amid the many conflicting standards which call for our allegiance. We must utilize the findings of the anthropologists, sociologists, economists, psychologists, and all other serious students of the various phases of human life; we must watch the experiments being tried in various lands, with a dispassionate desire to see, in each case, to what degree they are forwarding or retarding human welfare. It will undoubtedly be possible to avoid a large part of the misery which now attends human life, and to secure for the community of mankind a far richer and securer happiness than is attained as yet by more than a fortunate few. We need for this many things besides morality; but there is nothing that we need more.

SUGGESTED READINGS

Durant Drake, *Problems of Conduct*, VI–VIII, XII–XIV.
H. W. Wright, *Self-Realization*, Part I, ch. IV.
F. Thilly, *Introduction to Ethics*, III, IV, V.
W. Fite, *Introductory Study of Ethics*, IV, V, IX, XI.
R. B. Perry, *The Moral Economy*, I.
W. James, *The Will to Believe: The Moral Philosopher*, etc.
W. K. Clifford, *Lectures and Essays: On the Scientific Basis of Morals*.
F. Paulsen, *System of Ethics*, Book II, ch. I, V.
F. Harrison, *The Philosophy of Common Sense*, IX.
T. deLaguna, *Introduction to the Science of Ethics*, II.
Bertrand Russell, *What I Believe*, III.   *Philosophy*, XXII.
W. G. Everett, *Moral Values*, IX.
S. E. Mezes, *Ethics*, III, V, VIII, IX.
L. Stephen, *Science of Ethics*, II, VII, IX, X.
Durant Drake, *The New Morality*, I–III.

CHAPTER XXVI

RELIGION

PRIMITIVE man was beset by moral injunctions, taboos, duties forced upon him by his tribe and reflected in his own conscience. He was also beset by vaguely understood Powers that peopled his world — ghosts, spirits, djinns, fauns, demons, gods. In such an animistic and oppressive world religion was born. It is impossible, of course, to draw a line and say, At such and such a moment religion appeared. It was, like every other phase of human life, a very slowly developed set of attitudes and acts. But we may perhaps venture to say that religion appeared with man's dawning sense of wonder, of dependence upon the mysterious Powers about him, of thankfulness and praise for their beneficence, of fear and awe, of loyalty and devotion, as he came to attribute to them the moral law which was really the product of his tribal life and his own developing conscience.

These confused emotions gave rise to three sorts of reaction, which have been blended in varying proportions in historic religion. In the first place, they found expression in *rites* of various sorts — sacrifices, petitions for help, ceremonies such as ablutions, bodily mutilations, dances and chanting — caused by the overflow of excitement and the more and more explicit intent to placate the Powers and win their favor. They also began very early to crystallize into *beliefs* as to the nature of these vaguely felt Powers; and these surmises gradually became standardized, petrified, into dogmas, creeds, theologies. At the same time these emotions acted as a powerful re-enforcement to the tribal morals, turning conformity into loyalty, injunctions into ideals, willfulness into sin. This *devotion to ideals*, this taking sides for good against evil, is the slowest fruit of religion to ripen, but it tends to outlive the earlier expressions of religious emotion, and fills the foreground in the teaching of the great religious prophets and saints.

There are types of religion in which emotional experience itself remains the central and important thing, as with the mystics (who form a sort of esoteric fellowship drawn from all the folds), or with certain forms of modern 'revivalism.' There are religions in which the rites are focal and of fundamental importance, as with the older Judaism, some forms of Hinduism, and perhaps Roman Catholicism, which puts forward its sacraments as necessary to salvation. There are religions in which the creed is central, and orthodox belief the chief concern, as with the Christianity of the Athanasian period and with some forms of modern Protestantism. There are religions in which devotion to moral ideals is the one thing needful, with the other aspects of religion absent or peripheral, as in the teachings of Buddha, Amos and Isaiah, Jesus, Saint Francis, and modern 'liberal' Christianity.... Our problem, then, is to decide which of these developments of historic religion are important, are consonant with our modern world-view, are deserving of our adoption or retention, and destined to play a part in the religion of the future — if the future is to have a religion. It is our varying answers to these questions which lead to our divergent conceptions of what constitutes the 'essence' of religion.

RELIGION AS AN EMOTIONAL EXPERIENCE

Religion, we have said, was in its inception, or grew out of, certain emotional experiences. It is not easy to formulate a definition that will cover the rather wide range of religious emotions without including the kindred emotions, such as love and patriotism. In fact, it is only gradually that religious emotion differentiated itself from these other great emotional patterns. We can mark out love, by saying that it is a certain type of emotion felt toward a fellow human being; while patriotism is a somewhat similar emotion felt toward one's home land. But when love widens its horizon, becomes a love of one's fellowmen in general, or of God, it becomes religious; when patriotism passes from being a mere animal attachment to a familiar portion of the earth into a loyalty to the ideals for which one's country stands, it too merges into religion. Perhaps we cannot be more exact than to say that religious emotion has for its object a Reality felt to be greater than an individual human being, a political or economic group, or a natural object. It is emotion felt in the presence of something deemed *supremely* worthy of our attention and devotion.

There is no doubt that the religious emotions are among the most precious of human experiences, and that some of them have very desirable effects. Perhaps, in their finest forms, they are the most precious and most valuable of human experiences. So it is natural to conceive them as the core of religion. The following quotations reveal differing conceptions of the essential nature of the religious emotions, but agree in making the emotional experiences central.

Unfailing testimony repeats that the religious experience is in itself the most delightful, and as a dynamic of conduct the most energizing, of our experiences. Once it comes to you, it possesses you; willy-nilly it has established itself as the goal of your heart's desire and the ineffable measure of value for all other experiences that make up your subsequent history.[1]

Religion is a feeling-adjustment to the deeper things of life, and to the larger reality that encompasses the individual life.[2]

Religion appears to me an unrational emotion, more akin to the esthetic sense than to any other. It is a going out of the emotional nature similar to that which is produced by the appreciation of a beautiful vase. Some men can appreciate beauty and some cannot. It is largely a matter of temperament. And it is as irrational, or rather as unrational, as falling in love.[3]

What, then, is religion? Is it a theory of the universe? Is it creeds, dogmas, speculations of any kind? It is none of these things. Religion is the recognition and cultivation of our highest emotions, of our more beautiful instincts, of all that we know is best in us. What these emotions may be varies in each people according to their natures, their circumstances, their stage of civilization.... The creeds are but the theories of the keener intellects of the race to explain, and codify, and organize the cultivation of these feelings.[4]

What shall we say to this conception of religion as consisting essentially of emotional experiences?

Well, in the first place, we cannot be content with the subtle selfishness of those who think of religion chiefly in terms of private exhilaration, personal consolation, inner peace or rapture. We *need* religion to affect *character* and *conduct*. The hermits and mystics and common folk for whom religion is a *refuge* from life, a dream-world, are not helping to solve our common human problems, they are shirking them. They are suffering from 'ingrowing religion.' The more admirable forms of religion

[1] H. M. Kallen, *Why Religion?* p. 79.
[2] E. S. Ames, *The Psychology of Religious Experience*, p. 321.
[3] H. B. Mitchell, *Talks on Religion*, p. 10.
[4] H. Fielding-Hall, *The Hearts of Men*, pp. 298–299.

are those which tap moral energies and widen social vision. "Men need emotional experiences; that spring of conduct and will must be stimulated. But if emotional experiences are to have value, the stimulus must stimulate *to* something; it must be a beginning and not a terminus." Religion is, indeed, largely an emotional experience; but these emotions should not be allowed to run to waste, their potentialities for *moralizing* human life are too precious. The searching test for appraising the value of religions was stated by Jesus: "By their *fruits* ye shall know them."

The second point to note is that some religious emotions are morally superior to others. It is not merely pleasant religious emotions that are to be cultivated, but *morally desirable* religious emotions. The delight in mystery, for example, is a sort of satisfaction with ignorance; it is, for many minds, a congenial emotion, but surely not so useful an attitude as that of curiosity, searching inquiry, the attempt to understand. So the feelings of dependence, of resignation, and humility, tend to slacken effort; we need rather to realize our power to remake our environment and ourselves. Pious acquiescence in things as they are, as "the will of God," has been a tremendous obstacle to human progress. The raptures of the mystics have seldom borne much moral fruit; the ecstatic visionary has not often been a socially minded person, he is too happy in his own dream-world. The smug thankfulness and praise that well up from the hearts of the well-dressed rich in their comfortable pews is offensive to any sensitive spirit. On the other hand, the emotions of love and sympathy, of charity and pity, of reverence and loyalty toward the highest a man knows — whether he calls that Highest "God," or not — are usually salutary emotions, productive of far-reaching good. The dedication of a man's heart and will to the noblest ideals he can formulate, the surrender of all willfulness, worry, and grieving that stand in their way, and the joy that springs from devotion to a Great Cause, in the midst of so wonderful a world as this, are not only an enrichment of his emotional experience, but at the same time a stimulus and guide to his moral life.

Surely, too, it is not necessary to be in a state of emotional excitement to live a noble and fruitful religious life. Relatively unemotional people can be religious in that practical and important sense. But it is doubtful if these ideals of religion-in-practice would ever have spread and attracted great numbers of men if it had not been for the deep emotional experiences of the saints and seers. The *fountain-head* of religion lies in man's emotional life.

RELIGION AS RITE AND CEREMONY

Religion often seems to the historian to be mostly a matter of varying rites or ceremonies, designed to placate or please the gods and ensure the salvation of the believer. Even today the orthodox Jew regards circumcision as essential, the orthodox Christian thinks that unless he is baptized he cannot be saved. The Buddhist turns his prayer-wheel, the Moslem prostrates himself toward Mecca, the poor Catholic peasant buys a candle to burn at the shrine of the Virgin, the Protestant listens with bowed head while his minister invokes the blessing of God upon all and sundry from the President to those present. Family prayers and grace-before-meals are vanishing survivals of an older day, but elaborate liturgy and ritual maintain their hold in church services. The

Jew continues to avoid pork, the Catholic to deny himself meat on Friday, and multitudes of believers refrain from innocent amusements and recreation on their Sabbath — Friday, Saturday, or Sunday, as the case may be. The sacrament of the Communion remains important to most Christians, as does confession and absolution to the Catholic.... What shall we say to all this ceremonial side of religion?

Certainly, if any of these believers are justified in assuming that their rites have direct, magical efficacy in securing for them the desired blessings, they are right in deeming them of central importance. If non-baptized infants must suffer eternal torment, if the uncircumcized cannot participate in the Kingdom of God, if absolution really saves us from the punishment which our sins deserve, if attendance at Mass really disposes God in our favor, if petitions for the blessings we crave are really answered, then we should be fools not to utilize these short-cuts to our heart's desire. But the modern mind (if, for convenience, we may use such a vague expression) finds itself unable to retain these consoling beliefs. And our problem today is not so much whether rites of some sort are to be considered of prime importance as whether they are of any importance at all.

Sociologists tell us that religious rites have played a considerable part, historically, in binding communities together and increasing their morale. Perhaps today, with our individualistic tendencies and our great need of a communal spirit, the adoption of some sort of common cult would help cement our fellowship and give nations, and the world-community, a greater sense of oneness. But since we cannot possibly agree, for the indefinite future, upon a common cult, the influence of our separate forms of worship seems to be divisive rather than unifying. Separate groups are indeed bound together, but they are arbitrary groups, having no relation to the realities of our political and economic life; their effect is to create needless divisions in our society rather than to integrate it.

At their best these religious practices have a psychological effect upon the individual of considerable value, keeping his mind focused upon his religious ideals, counteracting the turmoil and fret, the self-centered ambitions and rivalries which his daily life engenders, giving him a measure of balance and inner peace. People vary greatly in their responsiveness to the 'suggestion' given by religious ceremonies; but there are not a few, of a very 'modern mind,' who hold them to be indispensable.

Where there is no ceremonial there is no religion.... It is certainly possible that in a community where various religious rites are regularly practiced by groups of worshipers, many individual persons who never participate in these rites may be most devoutly religious. In such a case, however, it may be questioned whether such persons do not constantly have the fundamental problems and sentiments of religion thrust upon their attention by the very ceremonials which they themselves abstain from witnessing and perhaps regard with loathing.... Ninety-nine persons out of a hundred who hold my fundamental views in regard to the principles of ethics, religion, and politics incline to disbelieve in ritual altogether.... But in assuming such an attitude they are doing nothing less than refusing to naturalism, democracy, and national idealism a system of signs by which the deepest personal responsibilities of social life might be announced and established among the many. They are unwittingly robbing humanism of indispensable organs, and reducing it to the most beggarly and inarticulate means of actualizing its ideal throughout the community.... In the past, religious ceremonies, being anti-democratic, unscientific, and occult, have strangled liberty and intellectual honesty. They have overpowered the imagination of the people, and allured them into willing subjection to human and superhuman monsters.

But the worst of all their effects has been this unthinking
and bitter hatred and distrust aroused in naturalists and
democrats for any and every form of religious ritual.... Until
a ritualistic religion be constructed on the basis of science
and democracy, science and democracy will be almost exclusively confined to the domain of material wealth and politics.
They will be occupied with the machinery instead of the
dynamics of social justice. They will fail in the supreme
art of generating the enthusiasm and guiding the loyalty of
the masses of the people.[1]

Powerful as is this plea for ceremony in religion, there
are grave dangers to be faced. Ritual tends easily to
usurp attention for itself, deflecting it from what is of
ultimate importance, the daily *life* of the worshiper.
'Attending service' takes the place of the actual render-
ing of service. Many believers have a comfortable sense
of having done their duty for the week when they have
gone to church; as the saying is, they "pray on their
knees on Sunday and on their neighbors the rest of the
week." Where religious rites become elaborate and
require considerable thought and sacrifice, they become
a needless burden upon conduct and a poor substitute
for the devotion to concretely useful ideals, such as justice,
charity, and brotherliness. It is noteworthy that most of
the great religious founders and saints have disapproved
of religious ceremonial; such leaders as Buddha, Amos,
Isaiah, and Jesus warned their followers in no uncertain
tones that it was in danger of choking their spiritual life,
which alone was of ultimate importance.

Can we not say, then, that religious ceremonial, like
religious emotion, must be judged by its *fruits*? If
prayers, liturgies, rites actually produce in those who use
them a nobler type of life, they are justifiable; if their

[1] Stanton Coit, *The Soul of America*, pp. 344–365.

net effect seems rather to be that of an opiate, a subjective substitute for an objectively religious *life*, they
must be reckoned as morally harmful, however soothing
or exhilarating to their upholders.   Probably in many
cases there is no great effect one way or the other; the
ritual is esthetic in its effects rather than religious, a
pleasant variation in the week's activities, an intermittent
contact with impressive architecture, music, and group-
expression, but irrelevant to any important human
decisions.... At most, these religious practices are to be
appraised as means to an end, the living of a truly spiritual
life; they cannot be considered as constituting in themselves the essence of religion.   "Why call ye me Lord!
Lord! and *do* not the things which I say?"

RELIGION AS COSMIC BELIEFS

Perhaps the commonest view of religion in our contemporary world is that it consists of *beliefs* — in the
existence of a God, the supernatural status of some
Saviour, some supernatural plan of salvation, some transcendent destiny for the human soul.   If a man in our
circles doubts that Jesus was superhuman, that there is a
Supreme Being who created and runs the universe, that
he has a soul, or that it is immortal, he is generally held to
be irreligious.   In liberal circles the vaguest faith that
"the universe is friendly to us," or that "all important
values are somehow conserved," is thought to suffice.
But there must be some theological, or at least cosmic,
creed to set apart the religious from the 'merely moral'
man.   A recent and widely used *Introduction to Philosophy*
asserts that without a "belief in superhuman forces and
powers" religion "loses its very heart."   And, to quote
another contemporary philosopher:

Religion is man's sense of the disposition of the universe to himself.... Religion is belief on the part of individuals or communities concerning the final or overruling control of their interests.... It involves... an interpretation of the environment at large, in other words, a cosmological judgment.... It is characteristic of religion to insist, so far as possible, upon the favorableness of the environment.... Religion is man's belief in his salvation, his confident appeal to the overruling control of his ultimate fortunes.[1]

Gilbert Chesterton is even more emphatic in his assertion that religion implies some cosmic belief:

Don't say, "I look forward to that larger religion that shall have no special dogmas." It is like saying, "I look forward to that larger quadruped who shall have no feet." A quadruped means something with four feet; and a religion means something that commits a man to some doctrine about the universe.[1]

By contrast with these views, we may quote writers of a diametrically opposite persuasion:

'Religion' is a word of many meanings; and perhaps its least worthy, certainly its least living, and practical, meaning is that of a belief in supernatural powers, and a hope of a super-terrestrial existence.... Speculation as to supernatural intelligences, future existences, and so forth...must strike many thinking people as, at the least, waste of time. I say 'at the least'; for it may be even worse than waste of time. The withdrawal of our minds from the tangible, the visible, the intelligible, to the consideration of the vague, the unseen, the incomprehensible, the possibly non-existent, may well result in a warping of our mental vision in its outlook upon things which undoubtedly are.[3]

Civilization cannot be saved by people not only crude enough to believe these things, but irreligious enough to believe that such belief constitutes a religion.[4]

[1] Ralph Barton Perry, *The Approach to Philosophy*, p. 66; *The Moral Economy*, pp. 218–231.

[2] Gilbert Chesterton, *A Miscellany of Men*, p. 308.

[3] Kingsley Tarpey, *Hibbert Journal* (1919).

[4] Bernard Shaw, *Preface* to *Back to Methuselah*.

Right here is perhaps the sharpest clash in contemporary thought about religion: Is some sort of cosmic belief necessary, or may a purely humanistic religion be worthy of the name?   Our answer will be apt to depend upon our belief as to whether or not man has actual knowledge of these cosmic matters, and knowledge of importance to his religious life.   In other words, if we are convinced that the theological (or cosmic) doctrines of some religion are *true*, we shall probably hold that a knowledge of these great and inspiring truths is so important that it deserves a central place in our religion.   If, on the other hand, confronted by the vast number of conflicting religious dogmas, and unable, with the best of good-will, to find solid empirical justification for any of them, we conclude that man has no actual knowledge of these matters, but only conjectures, hypotheses, and hopes, we shall probably wish to disentangle the religious life from these conjectural and probably obsolescent doctrines; at least we shall cease to hold them as essential and central.   Or we may say, as many are now saying, These pre-scientific speculations, these unhistorical assertions, this supernaturalistic outlook, are of the essence of religion — therefore religion is something to be discarded by intelligent and intellectually scrupulous men.

We can hardly overestimate the consolation and the inspiration which the sense of a cosmic setting, and of a cosmic backing, for their moral effort has given to men. And the briefest survey shows that such beliefs have played a major part in most religions, from earliest times to the present.   Nevertheless, there are strong reasons for calling these cosmic beliefs the 'setting' within which religion has grown up, rather than religion itself.

The very fact that humanity has been, historically,

chock full of such beliefs (most of them, of course, very naïve and grotesque) makes us pause. Surely not all these myriads of people are to be called 'religious,' just because they accepted current cosmological and theological beliefs. Satan himself may be supposed to be correctly informed as to these matters, without thereby becoming religious. It will perhaps be less readily accepted by some that one who accepts none of these beliefs may be truly religious; but certainly there are atheists who, except for their rejection of the supernaturalistic outlook of their church-going friends, have all the earmarks of a genuine spiritual life. There is quite obviously no *logical* connection between devotion to high ideals, between the religious *spirit* and *life*, and any cosmic or historical beliefs whatsoever. Practical idealism is justified empirically, by its fruits in human happiness on earth, quite irrespective of our ideas concerning the ultimate nature of the universe or the ultimate destiny of the soul. And the *psychological* connection is much weaker than we are apt to suppose. In the Middle Ages, when practically everyone believed the theological doctrines of the Church, human morality was at rather a low ebb; in our twentieth century, in spite of a very widespread loss of belief in these doctrines (and no widespread acceptance of substitute doctrines), the general level of idealism is certainly higher. There is no reason to suppose that if everyone became agnostic in theology, the religious spirit would be less widespread or less vital than in past generations. And does it really *matter* greatly whether or not a man believes in God, or the Devil, in Heaven or Hell or Nirvana, or whether he is agnostic on all these matters, if he lives an unselfish, devoted life, loyal to the best he knows?

However this may be, if we were right in our earlier discussions, religion has no special way of finding out whether these cosmic and historic beliefs are true or not; that is the task of science and a scientific philosophy. If we are honest and dispassionate, we must agree that empirical study does not — as yet — yield convincing evidence that any of these traditional creeds are true. To hold them up as true is, then, to answer momentous questions glibly, to prejudge the issue, that is, to be prejudiced. The whole body of what, for convenience, we may call 'theology' has not the status of actual knowledge; it is hypothesis, assumption, or hope. We men do not really *know* even that "the universe is friendly to us," or that "all values are conserved." Those are but happy hopes.... But is not vital, living religion too important a thing to be made in any way dependent upon what is merely conjectural? Suppose it should increasingly appear that these optimistic cosmic beliefs are *not* true; any religion closely entangled with them will go by the board. In fact, religion *has* gone by the board for millions of people precisely because the beliefs which have been preached as its base and support have come to seem to them untrue. The only hope that religion will continue to appeal to people who are trained in the rules of evidence lies in the possibility of its divorce from doctrines which at their best are unverifiable and at their worst are absurd.

At least, there is no likelihood that men are going to agree in theology. If theological beliefs continue to be held essential to religion, sectarianism will continue, and perhaps grow worse.... But nothing is more obvious than that people of the most diverse beliefs may be profoundly religious. A Roman Catholic may be a saint, so may a

Methodist or a Unitarian, or a Buddhist who believes in no God. Since, then, no one really knows which belief is correct, and since the variation in belief need make little practical difference in the essential quality of a life, and since it is the life that is of fundamental importance, not the theological belief, it seems strange that religious people should lay so much emphasis upon profession of belief. The explanation is, of course, that the believers feel their beliefs to be more or less precarious, and cannot bear to think of losing them; they therefore set them up as creeds, insist upon them, keep hammering in the 'suggestion' that they are true, resent bitterly the 'skepticism' of those who cannot agree with them. All of which, unhappily, diverts their attention from what is really important.

A study of history shows that to center religion about theological doctrines is more dangerous even than to center it about emotional experience or about ceremonial. Think of the innumerable holy wars; think of the Crusades, with their tragic waste of human life and happiness; think of the persecutions, the Inquisition, the unimaginable sufferings inflicted in the name of the various world-views which have usurped the place and name of religion. Even in our humaner day, it is the writer's opinion that the habit of thinking of religion as a set of theological beliefs does more than anything else to obscure its vital essence. A man is thought to be anti-Christian if his beliefs about God and Christ are not respectable. Relatively few see that he is really anti-Christian when he is selfish, greedy, a grafter in politics, a profiteer in business, an inciter to war. This shift of conception goes back to the theologians of the early Christian centuries, whose spirit was far from that of the Founder. To Jesus, religion was the way of love and forgiveness, the doing unto others as we would that they should do unto us. How could we possibly forget this if the churches had not clouded the issue with their insistence upon theological and historical beliefs? A changeling has been substituted for the Christ-Child, a pseudo-Christianity for the real thing.... And much the same thing has happened with other faiths. The great Teachers offer men a vision and an example of how life might be lived. The followers are more interested in persuading themselves that they *are* to be saved than in practicing that arduous way of life which alone can actually save them.

RELIGION AS A WAY OF LIFE

The conception of religion held by the great Jewish prophets is condensed in Micah's question, "What doth the Lord require of thee but to do justly, to love mercy, and to walk humbly with thy God?" The New Testament conception is summarized in the Book of James, "Pure religion and undefiled is this: to visit the fatherless and widows in their affliction and to keep oneself unspotted from the world." By general consent, Jesus' teaching finds its climax in the "Sermon on the Mount," where he declares that what is important is not obedience to specific injunctions, but the spirit of love, forgiveness, and personal purity which permeates a life. He certainly conceived his function to be not that of inculcating correct beliefs, or appropriate rites, but that of creating in men a clean heart and renewing a right spirit within them.

When we turn to the non-Christian religions, we find Buddha declaring that the gods, if they exist, are of no religious importance, and that religion is just a Way of Life, which anyone may adopt. If we turn to Taoism,

we find that the word Tao means, precisely, the Way.
Confucianism is another Way. Zoroastrianism was essentially a dramatization of the war against Evil, in
which we are all called upon to take sides. The sense
of inner harmony and peace, which all religions seek, is
found by the best religions through the forgetfulness of
self in sacrificial service. To get consolation and peace
by holding certain optimistic beliefs, or by performing
certain rites, is a cheap substitute for the real thing, and
usually betokens the decay of a really vitalizing religion.

One who has been brought up on what Santayana has
called the Christian Epic — the gorgeous dream of orthodox Christianity — is apt to look upon Jesus' own gospel
as too simple, too uninteresting, too obvious. That is
"mere morality." It is what anyone might believe, it
is a teaching adopted by most of the higher religions,
and not distinctively Christian.... Well, whatever we are
to call it, it is not *mere* anything; it is the most important
lesson we can learn. And we should be profoundly thankful that a recognition of it has not been limited to Christendom. It is simple, yes, to understand; but it is desperately
hard to put in practice. It is much easier for most people
to believe an elaborate theological creed than to live a
simple Christian life.

Religion, in this sense, begs no questions, rests upon
no dubious postulates; it has verifiable values. It does
not antagonize science or corrupt education. It may
unite men of every fold, instead of dividing them into a
hundred sects. It is the view of religion held by an increasing number of thinking people.

A conscience and a code of honor is the essence of religion.[1]
Religion comprises... first, the intuition of a personal

[1] Bernard Shaw, *Preface* to *Misalliance*.

and social ideal above the present reality; secondly, a movement of our whole being towards that ideal, as well as the
whole of our efforts to realize it; finally, the act of faith by
which, when we have affirmed the ideal, when we feel we are
made for it, we also feel, despite all obstacles, that we are
capable of attaining it.[1]

[Religion is] the selfless, untrammeled life in the whole,
which frees man from the prison-house of eager wishes and
little thoughts.... The soul of man is a strange mixture of
God and brute, a battleground of two natures, the one particular, finite, self-centered, the other universal, infinite, and
impartial.... The infinite nature is the principle of union in
the world, as the finite nature is the principle of division....
The transition from the life of the finite self to the infinite
life in the whole requires a moment of absolute self-surrender.
The self-surrender in which the infinite life is born may be
made easier to some men by belief in an all-wise God to whom
submission is a duty. But it is not in its essence dependent
upon this belief or upon any other.... It has become a matter
of the first importance to preserve religion without any dependence upon dogmas to which an intellectually honest assent grows daily more difficult.[2]

Religion is the will in action — the free and determinative
choice between the better and the dearer, between what is
felt to be right and what is felt to be pleasant.[3]

I conceive the essential task of religion to be to develop
the consciences, the ideals, and the aspirations of mankind.[4]

What counts is not creed, but conduct. By their fruits
ye shall know them and not by their beliefs. Religion is not
correct belief, but righteous living.... Every great religion
has cured its followers of the swell of passion, the thrust of
desire, and the blindness of temper.[5]

From the cold necessity of obedience to moral laws and of
self-repression religion leads men to a love of righteousness
and purity; from an enforced tribal loyalty and a legally pre-
scribed justice religion lifts them to a love of their fellows, to

[1] Paul Sabatier, *A Frenchman's Thoughts on the War*, p. 96.
[2] H. A. Overstreet, in *The Hibbert Journal*, vol. 11, p. 46 ff.
[3] "The Author," in H. B. Mitchell's *Talks on Religion*, p. 19.
[4] R. A. Millikan, in *The Forum*, vol. 82, p. 194.
[5] S. Radhakrishnan, *The Hindu View of Life*, pp. 51–60.

a genuine unselfishness and charity; from a mere stunned submission to fortune or defiance of its injuries, religion lifts them to a peace that comes from complete self-surrender in the service of the Ideal. This disposition of the heart and will, through which a man comes to care for the highest things and to live in gentleness and inward calm above the surface aspects and accidents of life, we call, in its inner nature, Spirituality; when it is embodied in outward forms and institutions, and spreads among whole communities, we call it a religion.[1]

The great, the momentous fact is that there *is* a Way of Life so much better than ordinary living as to seem different in *kind*. This is the good news, the gospel, preached by all the prophets. The masses of mankind have always failed to catch the vision; they have supposed it to be their duty to be religious, they have not realized it to be their greatest privilege. Many have conformed to religious practices, have accepted religious beliefs, have had moments of religious emotion; few have learned to live the religious life. But those few have been like pillars of flame leading the way out of the confusion and pettiness of ordinary human existence. They are the ones who no longer feel the constraint of the moral law, because their *delight* is the Law of the Lord, and on that law do they meditate day and night. To serve it is their passionate desire and their steadfast intent. Thereby they integrate their random impulses, give their lives depth and meaning, find for themselves an abiding underglow of joy and radiate blessing to their fellowmen.

Definition — let us say again — is arbitrary. One may pick what one likes out of the confused and multifarious phenomena of the historic religions, and say, This is the essence of the thing, this is what I mean, essentially, by

---

[1] Durant Drake, *Problems of Religion*, p. 244.

the term 'religion.' But in this case it is more than a matter of definition. Upon our conception of religion hinges, in no small degree, the future of human happiness. If we define religion as rites, or as theological beliefs, we shall continue to witness its slow disintegration — or its rapid dissolution, as in the Russia of today. Or, if sacramental and creedal religion continue to live on, fostered by Catholics and Fundamentalists, they will continue to obstruct intelligence and the development of a rational morality. If, on the other hand, we define religion as the self-transcending Way of Life, the devotion of heart and will to the Highest Good — that is, to God; if we conceive prayer as consecration to this Highest Good, and communion with it, as a "fight for the power to see and the courage to do" the right; if we see that worship is the outpouring of our love and veneration, our loyalty and devotion, to this Highest Good; then we shall in that very definition be setting up before men something which has transformed the lives of men and women here and there through the ages, and may yet transform this human scene, with its unhappy conflicts of purpose and its needless, self-imposed disasters, into that ideal human brotherhood which all lovers of mankind have looked forward to, and which we of the Christian inheritance call the Kingdom of God on earth.

SUGGESTED READINGS

Durant Drake, *Problems of Religion*, XIV.
J. B. Pratt, *The Religious Consciousness*, I.
W. K. Wright, *A Student's Philosophy of Religion*, V.
R. B. Perry, *The Approach to Philosophy*, III, IV.
R. W. Sellars, *The Next Step in Religion*, I, XVI.
G. A. Coe, *The Psychology of Religion*, IV, VIII, IX.
J. M. E. McTaggart, *Some Dogmas of Religion*, I.
G. Galloway, *Philosophy of Religion*, IV.

George Hodges, *Everyman's Religion*, I, II, VI.

H. S. Coffin, *What is There in Religion?*

B. H. Streeter, *Restatement and Reunion*, I.

E. S. Ames, *Psychology of Religious Experience*, Part IV.

J. H. Haydon, *The Quest of the Ages*, I, IX.

Reinhold Niebuhr, *Does Civilization Need Religion?* especially ch. IV.

R. W. Sellars, *Religion Comes of Age*, especially chs. I, XVI.

Kirsopp Lake, *The Religion of Yesterday and Tomorrow*.

Chapter XXVII

GOD

RELIGION has usually, though not always, been centered about gods, or God. There were pre-theistic religions, which had not yet definitely personified the Powers that threatened and blessed their lives, and there have been post-theistic religions which, like primitive Buddhism, ignored the gods as of no religious importance, or, like some forms of modern humanism, reject belief in God as a mere relic of superstition. But these exceptions, by their rarity, emphasize the fact that thus far, historically speaking, the central concept of religion has been that of gods, or a single God.

THE SOURCES OF OUR CONCEPT OF GOD

Our modern conceptions of God are, of course, the product of a long process of evolution. But it is not difficult to go back in imagination and trace the sources of this belief. One of its roots is the personification of the powers of Nature.

> We must remember that all those physical events, the intricate causes of which our modern science explores, are to the savage pure mystery, inexplicable and arbitrary. Having no idea of natural causation, as we now understand it, he instinctively regards all the moving objects about him after the nearest analogy he has, his own life. When they harm him, he ascribes to them the feelings he has when he injures another; when they favor him, he imagines them kindly disposed; by a naïve and natural fallacy he reads into them his own emotions and thinks of their activity, now beneficent, now baneful, as caused by intermittently friendly and malicious impulses such as he finds in his own heart.[1]

[1] Durant Drake, *Problems of Religion*, p. 12.

The process of making winds and rivers into anthropomorphic gods is, for the most part, not the result of using the imagination with special vigor. It is the result of not doing so. The wind is obviously alive; any fool can see that. Being alive, it blows; how? Why, naturally, just as you and I blow. It knocks things down, it shouts and dances. It whispers and talks. And, unless we are going to make a great effort of the imagination and try to realize, like a scientific man, just what really happens, we naturally assume that it does these thinks in the normal way, in the only way we know.[1]

Another root of theism lay in the inability of primitive man to realize the fact of death — especially to realize that the Great Chief, so powerful, so fearful, is really gone for good. Many see him in dreams, and wake with a strong impression that he is still about, though invisible. In this way tribal chiefs often became tribal gods, prayed to, placated, invoked for the protection of their people. Or the god may have been a great spiritual teacher; the deification of founders of religions has taken place within historic times, notably in the case of Gautama and of Jesus.

In such ways, and in other ways which space does not permit us to describe, the world became peopled, in prehistoric times, with all sorts of spirits and supernatural beings. They are properly to be called 'gods' only in so far as they were *worshiped* — i.e., in so far as it was thought that great blessings might be secured by devotion to them and they became the focal points of a religion.

As a result of various causes, and in ways which are traceable in some detail, the polytheism of primitive peoples gradually developed into, or was superseded by, a quasi-monotheism. Among the Greek philosophers, who were too sophisticated to take the popular pantheon

[1] Gilbert Murray, *Four Stages of Greek Religion*, p. 25.

very seriously, a feeling that mind, reason, a principle of good and of order, must lie behind and explain the world of appearances led to a world-view not perhaps quite monotheistic, but easily blending with monotheism. A very different train of events led, somewhat later, to the development by the prophets of Israel of an explicit monotheism, not philosophic, but intensely religious and practical. When Christianity swept over the Western World, it assimilated the current Greek thought, to a degree, with the result that orthodox Christian doctrine is a blend of Greek philosophy and Jewish feeling.

As a matter of fact, monotheism has seldom been clear-cut or complete — except for the Mohammedan world. The Jews took over the conception of Satan from the Persian religion, and a dualistic strain has persisted in Judaism and Christianity to this day. In addition, from another series of causes, early Christianity evolved a Trinitarian doctrine, which was primarily an attempt to reconcile its emphatic monotheism, taken over from Judaism, with the empirical fact that Jesus was being worshiped as a God. And then the deep-rooted pagan tendencies of the peoples among whom the new religion spread manifested themselves in the semi-deification of the Madonna and the saints — who to all intents and purposes took the place of the former local and subsidiary gods.

Philosophers and theologians, church-fathers and the popular mind have been at work down the centuries deepening, and in various ways modifying, this monotheistic belief. The Greek Orthodox and Roman Catholic churches succeeded in defining their standard doctrines of God in lengthy and subtle exposition. Protestant thought has, naturally, taken many variant forms. But the Protestant theologian, while arguing many moot points, thought that he knew a great deal about God. Even a generation ago, such a book as Clarke's *The Christian Conception of God*, with its complacent elaboration of God's attributes, could regard as obvious heresies the conceptions now most astir in the world, and devote the bulk of its five hundred pages to the various lines of supposed proof that the God of orthodox dogma, with his omnipotence, omniscience, aseity, and what not, exists.

The striking fact about contemporary conceptions of God is, by contrast with this cut-and-dried orthodoxy, their plasticity and variety. A co-operative volume, published in 1927, under the title *My Idea of God*, presents conceptions of God formulated by nineteen leaders of American theological thought; there are there nineteen distinct and different concepts. The question for the world of today is not, Can we believe in the fixed theistic doctrine of traditional theology? But rather, Is there *any* conception of God that we can accept? The God-idea has become fluid again, and we are once more in the midst of a creative period in religious thought. A priori and authoritarian arguments are being rejected, and conceptions of God are being formulated as firmly empirical as anything else in which we are asked to believe. This emancipation from the fixity of the conception that had become traditional in the churches has led many thinkers who would never have concerned themselves seriously with the God of popular belief to look afresh at this concept, and to seek to mold it into a form more consonant with man's maturer experience and more serviceable for his spiritual life.

THE PERSONAL GOD

The gods were originally *persons*, of course, conceived as more or less like ourselves. Intelligent, sophisticated Greeks and Romans (and doubtless men of earlier civilizations) came to see clearly that they were really personifications of natural forces, or of abstract powers and virtues — or else mere ghosts of departed heroes. And throughout the history of Christianity there has been an esoteric circle who have taken the Christian God as a popular and poetic symbol for a natural force or a moral ideal. But the great mass of Christians have believed, and believe today, that their God (but not, of course, the gods of other religions) is an actually existent Person, a loving Father, Creator of the world and Arbiter of its destinies. We must consider, then, what reasons we have, as disinterested reflective thinkers, for believing or disbelieving in the existence of such a Being.

Our Christian belief in God derives principally from the belief of a nomadic Semitic tribe in their tribal god Jahveh (miscalled Jehovah). Jahveh was perhaps a fire-god of Mount Sinai; at any rate, he was, in those early days, hardly different from the other patron-gods of the various tribes. He was a god of battles, jealous, vengeful, favoring his particular people to the extent of helping them in their massacres, their looting and rapine. Under the influence of the great Jewish prophets he came to be thought of as a very different sort of being, an august, just, but merciful Father of mankind. But, although the conception of the nature of their god changed gradually, each generation believed in him primarily because their fathers had done so before them. Our current theism is, essentially, the result of the belief of that primitive Jewish tribe in their Jahveh. The apologetic of the philosophers and theologians is clearly secondary, the momentum of a continuous tradition is the underlying cause of belief.

But no sophisticated and impartial person believes today that Jahveh really walked with Adam in the Garden of Eden "in the cool of the evening," or handed the tables of the Ten Commandments to Moses on Mount Sinai. We do not actually believe the tradition, though we cling to the belief which the tradition has produced. Indeed, if we assent to the argument of the First Part of this volume, we discard the authority of the tradition, anyway, and of the Bible, which preserves it, and of the Church which teaches it. We must find new grounds for this old faith.

And of course the arguments which are offered are endless. It is impossible to discuss them all, even very briefly, in a chapter or two. Therefore, it is impossible for us, properly, to reach any conclusion here on this important matter. The two leading arguments are the First Cause Argument and the Argument from Design, which, in varying forms, continually reappear. To many minds one or the other or both of them seem fairly conclusive, while to others they remain inconclusive and seem rather 'rationalizations' of a pre-existent belief than an expression of disinterested thought. There is nothing approaching consensus of opinion as to the evidential value of any of these arguments. So we cannot honestly say that man *knows* of the existence of a personal God; it remains a matter of individual opinion or faith, or the partisan dogma of a Church.

The belief in a personal God has waned pretty rapidly in recent years among the intelligentsia all over the world. The reasons are manifold. Among them we may mention the historical study of the Biblical documents, which has revealed their naïveté and thus cast doubt upon the beliefs of their authors.   The change from a geocentric conception of the universe to the conception of modern astronomers has led naturally to asking *where* Heaven is (so close by on the old scheme), and where God exists. The change from an animistic view of Nature, with miracles the natural thing, to a conception of the universe as a cosmos, following those regular habits which we call natural laws, has made increasingly insistent the question, *How* does God control events?   Our increasing sensitiveness to pain has made more acute the question, which Job could not answer, how there can be so much agony and frustration in a world created and ruled by a loving God.   And finally, the loss of belief in the old folk-tales has led men to ask why, if there is a loving God, he does not speak out, explain these riddles, manifest himself to us unambiguously.   The *silence* of God is perhaps the greatest obstacle to the traditional belief.

Many signs are, of course, offered as evidence — answered prayers, special providences, miraculous cures, dramatic conversions, which seem to imply a supernatural power.   Quantitatively this testimony is enormous; but it is all sharply questioned by those who are trained in estimating evidence.   We must not rule it out cavalierly because of any a priori belief in natural law.   But we should need to have a far more thoroughgoing scientific study of these phenomena than has yet been made before we should be warranted in saying that the hypothesis· of supernatural causation is more plausible than the naturalistic explanations.

The upshot of this seems to be that, in the conflict of counsel, each of us must consider for himself whether any of these arguments is convincing, in spite of the objections which have been raised. If one or several of them do seem to him convincing, he will be fortunate in being able to hold this most inspiring and comforting of human beliefs. If not, he will either "will to believe" in it, anyway, if that course seems to him honest, or he will discard it in favor of some conception of God that seems to him more tenable — or he will give up the belief in God altogether.

THE GOD OF PANTHEISM

The advantage of pantheism is that it is, at least in some of its forms, purely empirical. It can *point* to its God. For its God is only another name for Nature, or for the Power, whatever it may be, that is manifested in Nature.

We must get rid of the great moral governor or head-director. He is a fiction of our own brains. We must recognize only Nature, the All; call it God if we will, but divest it of all anthropological conceptions.... Here is this vast congeries of vital forces which we call Nature... the sum and synthesis of all powers and qualities, infinite and incomprehensible. This is all the God we can know, and this we cannot help but know.[1]

The Infinite Spirit pervades the universe, just as the spirit of a man pervades his body, and acts, consciously or unconsciously, in every atom of it. [It is] one omnipresent, eternal Energy, informing and inspiring the whole creation at every instant of time and throughout the infinite spaces.[2]

When I say God, I mean the mysterious Power which is finding expression in the universe and is present in every tiniest atom of the wondrous whole.[3]

[1] John Burroughs, *The Light of Day.*

[2] C. W. Eliot, *The Religion of the Future*, an address delivered at the Harvard Summer School of Theology, July 22, 1909, and subsequently printed in the *Atlantic Monthly* and in pamphlet form.

[3] Rev. R. J. Campbell, *The New Theology.*

God is the all-pervading principle in each growing plant, in each human soul. I see him in each individual blade of grass, in each sparkling bit of water. When I see the sun shine, I see God's smile. When I see trees shiver in the wind, when leaves turn into startlingly gorgeous colors in the fall, when I see a sunset on a dark mountain lake, I see God.[1]

Pantheism has often appealed to poets, because of the added glamour with which it invests Nature. It has sometimes appealed to scientists, because it emphasizes the unity of Nature. The objection to it comes, in part, from matter-of-fact people, who see no adequate evidence that Nature is conscious, or has a purpose or intended goal, or is in any way worthy of being deified. There are really two distinct questions here. First, Is there convincing or even highly suggestive evidence that there is in Nature (outside of the animal kingdom) anything resembling consciousness? Or is there, if not a cosmic consciousness, at least an *élan vital*, a life-force, striving unconsciously toward some goal? These questions, touched upon in earlier chapters, we cannot here take up. In any case the second question remains, Is Nature, as we may legitimately conceive it, deserving of the attitudes of worship, reverence, love, obedience which have usually been implied by belief in God? And, if not, is it desirable to apply this sacred word to the existing world, or to the manifold of forces that manifest themselves in its life?

The chief objection to pantheism comes, not from prosaic people who see no point in deifying Nature, but from morally minded people who see great harm in it, because Nature is so cruel in fact and so apparently indifferent in intent, so completely callous to suffering. The pantheistic God, being omnipresent, being all the power there is, has to answer for the evil as well as for the

[1] Flora McClellan, in a paper written at Vassar College.

good in the world. How can we tolerate a God who includes evil in his being or as the expression of his nature? In John Stuart Mill's famous essay on *Nature*, the ruthlessness of Nature is convincingly portrayed, with the conclusion that "the scheme of Nature, regarded in its whole extent, cannot have had, for its sole or even principal object, the good of human or other sentient beings." In such a book as Richard Jefferies' *Story of My Heart* — surely one of the most beautiful books in our language — this empirical conclusion is expressed with passionate conviction. A more moderate statement can be found in — for example — Mr. Hobhouse's words:

> The moral indifference of Nature forces itself upon us; and it becomes evident that the real as such is not spiritual nor the creation of anything that is purely spiritual, just, or good, in the human sense. The spiritual is an *element* in reality.[1]

Mr. H. G. Wells, feeling this very keenly, has contrasted sharply the two "antagonistic" conceptions of God, God-as-Nature (or as Creator of Nature) and God as the Holy Spirit in our hearts — the God of humanism. He says that he, the author,

> cannot bring the two ideas under the same term God. He uses the word God, therefore, for the God in our hearts only, and he uses the term 'The Veiled Being' for the ultimate mysteries of the universe; and he declares that we do not know and perhaps cannot know in any comprehensible terms the relation of the Veiled Being to that living reality in our lives who is, in his terminology, the true God.[2]

On the other hand, Mr. William Archer has made himself the spokesman of those who prefer to worship Power rather than Goodness.

I beg leave strongly to urge the claims of the Veiled Being

[1] L. T. Hobhouse, *Development and Purpose*, p. 202.
[2] H. G. Wells, *God the Invisible King*, Preface.

as against the Invisible King.... It is the moral pretensions tagged on by the theologians to metaphysical Godhead that revolt and estrange reasonable men — Mr. Wells among the rest.... But if you divest the Veiled Being of all ethical — or, in other words, of all human — attributes, then there is no difficulty whatever in admiring, and even adoring, the marvels he has wrought.... We cannot but own that the Power which set all this whirl of atoms agoing is worthy of all admiration. And approbation? Ah, that is another matter; for there the moral element comes in.[1]

A recent writer has said that the trouble with pantheism is that "if everything is divine, then nothing is peculiarly divine, and all the distinctions of good and evil are meaningless." It would be more accurate, perhaps, to say that pantheism, by calling everything "divine," removes from the words 'divine' and 'God' the connotation of goodness. For nothing is clearer than that not everything that is is good. Many people, acknowledging this, admitting that "His ways are not our ways," will nevertheless prefer to bow down before Nature — or the Force, or Spirit working in Nature — in awe and reverence and exultation. Here there is power, beauty, sublimity, mystery, and *allness*.

On the other hand, the more sensitive spirits will refuse to worship such a God and will turn elsewhere for the focus of their religious life.

THE GOD OF PLATONISM

We may, for convenience, use the name 'Platonic' for a conception of God found in Plato and Aristotle, and in somewhat esoteric circles to our day. According to this conception God is not an existent Being, but an essence, the Supreme Good, that perfection which eludes us in

---

[1] William Archer, *God and Mr. Wells*, pp. 131–133.

earthly things, but which we must ever love and follow. This is too abstract, too elusive a conception for the popular mind, but is one that has appealed to thoughtful people and to mystics through the ages. It makes literal truth of the sayings "God is a spirit"; "God is love"; God is not just a single loving Person, God is Love itself, the spirit of love, wherever found, or imagined; nay, a spirit that transcends all actual embodiments of love and is to be found in its fullness only in the realm of the Ideal. There is a strong Platonic strain in Emerson, as when he says, "I, the imperfect, adore my own perfect."

> By conversation with that which is in itself excellent, magnanimous, lowly, and just, the lover comes to a warmer love of these nobilities, and a quicker apprehension of them. Then he passes from loving them in one to loving them in all; and so is the one beautiful soul only the door through which he enters to the society of all true and pure souls.... And, beholding in many souls the traits of the divine beauty, and separating in each soul that which is divine from the taint which it has contracted in the world, the lover ascends to the highest beauty, to the love and knowledge of the Divinity, by steps on this ladder of created souls.[1]

So T. H. Green spoke of God as "our unrealized ideal of a Best."[2] George Gordon declared God to be "the meaning, beauty, spirit, and power of our whole experience.... God as the perfect good or satisfaction moves the universe.... He moves the rational spirit of man through love of the highest, and thus draws the soul to himself." And again, he spoke of "the good, that is only another name for God."[3] And Bousset asserts that "the Christian belief regards God and moral good as one."

---

[1] Ralph Waldo Emerson, Essay on *Love*, in *Essays, First Series*.
[2] T. H. Green, *The Witness of God*.
[3] G. A. Gordon, *Aspects of the Infinite Mystery*.

When the soul seeks God she seeks her final escape from this incessant gathering and heaping and never coming to an end. It is not an additional object that she seeks, but it is the permanent in all that is impermanent, the highest abiding joy unifying all enjoyments.[1]

The following excerpts are from the spontaneous writing of contemporary college students:

God is the ideal which contains within itself all ideals, bearing much the same relation to them that philosophy does to the sciences. God is the goal of perfection toward which we are striving, the star toward which we are rushing.

God is the archetype of those qualities toward which evolution is leading us. As man makes progress in mental, moral, and spiritual evolution, he can increasingly be said to be "made in the image of God." For God is the perfection of wisdom, the perfection of justice, the perfection of love, the perfection of whatever is embodied in our highest aspirations — and the perfection of other qualities to which we have not even aspired.

Walter Lippmann suggests, in his eloquent *Preface to Morals*, that the run of people have always craved a more or less anthropomorphic God, a definite Person, to whom they could pray and from whom they might expect favors; while the relatively few *disinterested* people, the really surrendered souls, the true saints, have more or less clearly seen through that symbolism to the truth symbolized, that it is love itself, and mercy, courage and honor and purity of purpose, which are worthy of our love and loyalty. It is the ideal itself which we follow, not just some specific embodiment of the ideal; it is love itself that we love, *wherever* we may find it, not merely this or that loveworthy person, or even a supremely powerful and loving Person, supposing that He exists. The personification of an ideal is merely a step toward realizing its intrinsic claim upon our hearts.

[1] Rabindranath Tagore, *Sadhana*.

Samuel Butler tells us that the Erewhonians were horrified when their English visitor denied personal existence to Justice, Hope, and the other virtues; for no one surely would be interested enough in abstract virtues to love and follow them.

"Can you not see," I had exclaimed, "that the fact of Justice being admirable will not be affected by the absence of a belief in her being also a living agent? Can you really think that men will be one whit less hopeful because they no longer believe that Hope is an actual person?" She shook her head, and said that with men's belief in the personality, all incentive to reverence of the thing itself, as justice or hope, would cease; men from that hour would never be either just or hopeful again.[1]

Will men live and die for an abstraction? Yes, yes. Patrick Henry, when he said, "Give me liberty or give me death," did not regard Liberty as a Person. Nor do we, in spite of her statue in New York Harbor. The loyal Englishman will die for Britannia, yet he knows that her figure is but a symbol. Just so, it is not true that men who frankly regard the term God as a symbol, as a name for a spirit, an ideal, will therefore cease to love and pursue that ideal. In fact, to many a reflective person who has been confused and discouraged by the difficulties of believing in a Person God, this conception of God as a Spirit, as an Ideal, comes with a sense of relief, as to one who has found at last his spiritual home.

THE GOD OF HUMANISM

Humanism is not inconsistent with the Platonic vision; it may well worship the transcendent God, the supreme Essence or Ideal. But it is more concerned with the immanent God, the spirit of love and good-will actually

[1] Samuel Butler, *Erewhon*, ch. XVI.

living and working in human hearts.   Matthew Arnold
did much to popularize this conception, with his definition
of God as the Power in the world, greater than our individual selves, making for righteousness and all good.
In our own day many writers have championed this
conception:

> The reality of religion deals wholly and exclusively with
> the God of the Heart.... God... works in men and through
> men.... Modern religion bases its knowledge of God and its
> account of God entirely upon experience.   It has encountered
> God.   It does not argue about God; it relates.... He is the
> undying human memory, the increasing human will....[1]
>
> The God-life is our own deeper and more permanent life...
> that larger life in us of law and ideality which is at once the
> condition and the stimulus of our growing existence.... In
> the light of spiritual maturity, the god of magic, the god of
> miraculous power, the god of loving protection, the god of
> all-seeing care — the Parent God — must give way to the
> God that is the very ideal life of ourselves, our own deep and
> abiding possibilities of being, the God in us that stimulates
> us to what is highest in value and power.[2]
>
> We are realizing nowadays that the old guardian God of
> our childhood never existed.... What then is to take his
> place?... We are abandoning the idea of God the Father, and
> we are realizing the idea of God the Holy Spirit.   We are
> giving up the idea that the Kingdom of God is in Heaven,
> and we are finding that the Kingdom of God is *within* us.
> We are relinquishing the old idea of an external God, above,
> apart, and separate from ourselves; and we are taking on the
> new idea of an internal spirit working within us — a con-
> straining, immanent influence, a vital, propelling impulse
> vibrating through us all, expressing itself and fulfilling its
> purpose through us, and uniting us together in one vast
> spiritual unity.[3]

This is William James's conception of a "striving God";
not omnipotent or omnipresent, but growing in power as

[1] H. G. Wells, *God the Invisible King*, pp. 5 ff.
[2] H. A. Overstreet, *Hibbert Journal*, vol. 13, p. 155.   *Forum*, vol. 52, p. 499.
[3] Sir Francis Younghusband, *Within*, p. 52.

we grow toward our ideal, a God that is *potentially* al-
mighty, but dependent upon our effort and our loyalty,
in need of our help, as we are individually in need of God.

> A battle is constantly going on, in which the humblest
> human creature is not incapable of taking some part, between
> the powers of good and those of evil, and in which every
> even the smallest help to the right side has its value in pro-
> moting the very slow and often almost insensible progress
> by which good is gradually gaining ground from evil, yet
> gaining it so visibly at considerable intervals as to promise
> the very distant but not uncertain final victory of Good.   To
> do something during life, on even the humblest scale if noth-
> ing more is within reach, towards bringing this consumma-
> tion ever so little nearer, is the most animating and invigorat-
> ing thought which can inspire a human creature; and that it
> is destined, with or without supernatural sanctions, to be
> the religion of the Future I cannot entertain a doubt.[1]

This God striving in us is "not ourselves," individually,
as Arnold was wont to say, but is above and beyond our
individual selves and our particular groups.   Thus God
is super-personal; or, if you prefer, inter-personal.   We
are caught up, swept on, at our best we are 'inspired' by
something higher than our ordinary selves.   This something, that we call God, is the indwelling idealism of
humanity, coming to us in part from without, in part
welling up in us out of our own natures, pushing us up
and on toward our proper goal, toward the Kingdom of
God, the ideal community for which we work and sacrifice
and yearn.

GOD OR NO-GOD

Noting these striking variations in the conception of
God, we may ask whether it is possible to formulate a
definition broad enough to cover such diverse usages....

[1] John Stuart Mill, *Three Essays on Religion*, last page.

The common fact seems to be that the God of any group of people is the object of their highest loyalty, adoration, allegiance, awe, reverence, devotion. These emotional and moral reactions vary: for instance, the pantheistic God excites chiefly awe and admiration, a sense of wonder and mystery and resignation, while the humanistic God evokes rather loyalty, allegiance, devotion. Worship is perhaps the most general term; understanding it so, we may say that the catholic, inclusive meaning of the term 'God' is, *the object, or being, deemed supremely worthy of worship*.... We may then proceed to state what we consider to *be* supremely worthy of our worship. The Platonist says, Goodness itself, in all its forms (including Beauty), is alone worthy of that attitude of happy praise, reverence, and loyal devotion which we call worship. The humanist says, it is not so much Goodness itself, in the abstract, as the concrete good-will, love, idealism in our fellowmen, in our own hearts, in the human race as a whole and especially in its spiritual heroes, that evokes our admiration, our praise, our love, and our loyalty. The pantheist is intoxicated by the wonder and mystery and power of the universal Life, and bows down before that. The personalist believes in the existence of a Person, somewhere, who embodies power, wisdom, love, whatever he admires, in supreme degree, and thereby becomes the object of his worship.

What shall we say, then, if we are asked whether we believe in God? We may well say that we believe in God, in some sense, if we believe there is, in fact, any Object or Being supremely worthy of our worship, or devotion. The 'atheist,' then, would be the cynic, the moral and esthetic skeptic, the amused spectator of life, or the despairing pessimist, who thinks that nothing

matters, and nothing is worth while. "The conception of
a godless world is the conception of a world with the
bottom dropped out, a world from which all the high
values have disappeared." If we believe in something,
in anything, which gives great worth to human life, something bigger than our personal ambitions and passions,
something that can lift us out of ourselves and give our
little lives a deeper meaning and value, then, in the widest
sense, we may be said to have a God.

> The word 'God' is used in most cases as by no means a
> term of science or exact knowledge, but a term of poetry and
> eloquence, a term *thrown out*, so to speak, at a not fully
> grasped object of the speaker's consciousness, a *literary*
> term, in short.... What is the common substratum of idea
> on which, in using it, they all rest?... In the sense *the best*
> *that man knows or can know*, as a matter of fact and history,
> mankind constantly use the word. This is the common sub-
> stratum of idea on which men in general, when they use the
> word 'God,' rest; and we can take this as the word's real sense
> fairly enough.[1]

There is evidently a great deal of vagueness about most
people's conception of God — probably more nowadays
than ever before, because there are so many conceptions
current. In general, and for practical purposes, this
matters little; it is more important to *use* God than to
understand clearly what God is. But it is very confusing
to find that many who call themselves atheists have essentially the same beliefs as many who call themselves
believers. For many people, disbelief in a *personal* God
is atheism, and the pantheist or Platonist or humanist
merely an atheist in disguise. But that is on a par with
the feeling that only Christianity is really religion, Buddhism, Mohammedanism, and the rest being mere dam-

[1] Matthew Arnold, *Literature and Dogma*, pp. 11 ff.

nable error; or, for that matter, with the feeling of the Fundamentalist that only his brand of belief is really Christianity. Whatever our own conception of God, we must realize that there are other, very different conceptions, equally vital to their believers. And many a man (like Richard Jefferies, for example) who calls himself an atheist has actually a more vital, saving sense of God than the multitude who suppose themselves to believe in God, but in whose lives the belief makes no practical *difference*.

It would seem to matter little whether we use the *word* 'God,' so long as we retain the values which that hallowed word has enshrined. Indeed, there would be a gain in clarity in discarding a term which has such mythological connotations for the great mass of people, and has given prestige to so many tyrannies and inhumanities. In Russia the Communists have been so disgusted and embittered by the use of religious sanctions to perpetuate ignorance, superstition, and entrenched privilege, that they have discarded the whole ideology of religion, including the term 'God.' And even in countries where the churches have been far less obscurantist, there are many who look upon the traditional terminology of religion as more potent for harm than for good. Mr. Wells felt at one time that the word 'God' is hopelessly bound up with

the self-contradictory absurdities of an obstinately anthropomorphic theology... that barbaric theology which regarded God as a vigorous but uncertain old gentleman with a beard and an inordinate lust for praise and propitiation.[1]

There has grown up a practice of assuming that, when God is spoken of, the Hebrew-Christian God of Nicæa is meant. But that God trails with him a thousand misconceptions and bad associations; his alleged infinite nature, his

[1] H. G. Wells, *Anticipations*, p. 306.

jealousy, his strange preferences, his vindictive Old Testament past.[1]

Is it possible to deodorize a word which comes to us redolent of "good, thick stupefying incense-smoke," mingled with the reek of the auto-da-fé?... 'God' has been by far the most tragic word in the whole vocabulary of the race — a spell to conjure up all the worst fiends in human nature: arrogance and abjectness, fanaticism, hatred and atrocity.... If the word is at best a confusion and at worst a war-whoop, should we not try to dispense with it, to avoid it, to find a substitute which should more accurately, if less truculently, express our idea? Is it wise or kind to seek to impose upon the future an endless struggle with its sinister ambiguities?[2]

But the majority of students of our Western society are more impressed by the moral and emotional values carried and perpetuated by the idea of God than by its dangers.

The word 'God' being respected by humanity, having for it a long-acquired right, and having been employed in all beautiful poetry, to abandon it would be to overthrow all habits of language. Tell the simple to pass their lives in aspiration after truth, and beauty, and moral goodness, and your words will be meaningless to them. Tell them to love God, and not to offend God, and they will understand you perfectly.... Even supposing that for us philosophers another word were preferable, and without taking into account the fact that abstract words do not express real existence with sufficient clarity, there would be an immense inconvenience in thus cutting ourselves away from all the poetic sources of the past, and in separating ourselves by our language from the simple folk who worship so well in their own way.[3]

To the present writer it seems that in twentieth-century America the man of ideals, the man who merges his own individual life in something greater than self, and finds

[1] H. G. Wells, *God the Invisible King*, p. 8.

[2] William Archer, *God and Mr. Wells*, p. 78.

[3] Ernest Renan, *Intolerance in Skepticism*, in *The Poetry of the Celtic Races and Other Studies*.

life thereby infused with profound meaning and worth, runs less risk of being misunderstood by using than by rejecting the term 'God.' Whether it is a benevolent Creator and Ruler of the universe in which he believes, or the idealized figure of Christ, or a Life-Force making for good throughout Nature, or the Spirit of Good in human hearts, or just Goodness itself, there is no other name for the object of his devotion that has the associations, the emotional overtones, and the continuity of meaning that binds him to the devoted souls of every race who have found the deeper values of life.

But however this may be, the important thing is, not to assent to the truth of God's existence, but to *feel* his reality and be dominated by it; to recognize a law above our private wills, to cast aside all willfulness and cynicism and little-mindedness, to acknowledge the infinite worth of life and the infinite importance of duty.... There is no merit or value in a belief in God that makes no practical difference: the only important thing is to get into our lives the great experiences and the vital faith which that word connotes. For though our definitions of God be different, and our opinions vary from age to age, if we have the fear and love of God in our hearts, our theological opinions are of little moment.[1]

SUGGESTED READINGS

Durant Drake, *Problems of Religion*, IX.
J. B. Pratt, *The Religious Consciousness*, X; *Psychology of Religious Belief*, III, IX, X.
W. K. Wright, *A Student's Philosophy of Religion*, XIX, XX.
E. H. Rowland, *The Right to Believe*, II–III.
J. R. Seeley, *Natural Religion*, Part I.
Samuel Butler, *God the Known and God the Unknown*.
J. M. E. McTaggart, *Some Dogmas of Religion*, VI–VII.
H. N. Wieman, *Religious Experience and Scientific Method*.
H. N. Wieman and others, *Is There a God?*
J. E. Haydon, *The Quest of the Ages*, IV–V.
J. F. Newton, ed., *My Idea of God*.
H. G. Wells, *God the Invisible King*.
J. Middleton Murry, *God*, pp. 225–250.

---

[1] Durant Drake, *Problems of Religion*, p. 149.

CHAPTER XXVIII

HUMAN DESTINY

WE HAVE now taken a rapid glance at human values, esthetic, moral, and religious. We realize that the *rating* of the values which appear in human life is a totally different problem from the problem of their cosmic setting, their origins and their future. But although it is true that their origin and the foothold which they have in existence does not affect their value while they are here, it is also plain that they are entirely dependent for their appearance and continuance upon the causal processes of Nature. And the most searching question which man can formulate is the question, How assured, or how precarious, is the status of human values? Can we be legitimately optimistic about the success of this strange and exciting human adventure, can we believe that what we prize is destined to prosper? Or, as we look forward, can we read an inevitable doom awaiting all that is precious in our experience and our hopes?

THE COSMIC SETTING

Belief in evolution has been taken by many to mean belief in progress. We hear not only of the 'ascent of man,' but of the *élan vital* animating all Nature, generating ever higher and higher forms of life, from matter to mind, from mind to spirit, and, in some accounts, from spirit to God. The primitive nebula was pregnant with the promise of life; and the stage of life which we have reached forecasts dimly an unimaginable but ever more marvelous future.

Undoubtedly there is much truth in this picture. Man

is, quite objectively speaking, the highest product of the cosmic life of which we know. As compared with the other animals on earth, he is far more independent of his environment, and has far more control over it. His sense-organs tell him more of what is going on around him, his reaction-potentialities are more numerous and more delicate, his brain is a better instrument, his experience is wider and more varied, his happiness is richer and more lasting. In him alone, as far as we *know*, Nature has become self-conscious and intelligent enough to continue by collective planning the progress which has hitherto been haphazard and fumbling. Not only is human life the best thing of which we know, it seems to be the beginning of something that may be almost infinitely better. We hardly dare set a limit to the future achievements of man.

When we read the story of evolution as the story of *our* evolution, it is easy to think of Nature as, by some irresistible inner impulse, or some guidance from without, surging onward and upward from dull beginnings toward some glorious goal. But we must not forget that man is but one of a million species which evolution has produced on earth. Improvement, progress, is by no means a universal fact, even among organic forms on earth. Beside the story of *our* evolution is the story of the evolution of sponges, of jelly-fishes, of poisonous snakes and disgusting parasites, of swarming hordes of insects and unimaginable millions of microbes. Many instances of organic evolution are not instances of progress, in any intelligible sense; the later phases are no *better* than the earlier. There is no one story of evolution, there are a million stories, *one* of which has become a really significant drama.

Moreover, we remember that our earth is an extremely tiny speck in an inconceivably vast universe. It is a terrific leap to infer from this instance of progress-to-something-better, on this little planet, that Nature as a whole has any bent toward progress. It is, indeed, conceivable that more or less similar dramas have been enacted, on other planets swinging about other stars. If the formation of our solar system was due, as is generally believed today, to a chance encounter of two stars, we may ask the astronomers how often such an incident may be thought to have occurred. The consensus of present opinion — if there is anything approaching consensus — seems to be that possibly one star in a hundred thousand may have had some sort of eruption, with consequent formation of planetary bodies. Even then a planet must be at just the right distance from its sun to have the proper temperature for life as we know it. And so many other conditions must be fulfilled — as, the right amount and composition of atmosphere, a sufficient amount of water, and of various other substances — that anything even remotely resembling organic life on earth must be very rare indeed. Still, so vast are the cosmic reaches in Time and Space that it seems unlikely that there should not have been, somewhen and somewhere, other life-dramas comparable to our own.

It is altogether likely. But there seems to be no way in which man could ever hope to know. Each such story would be an isolated, self-contained story, with no influence upon the other life-stories and no common goal. Only if there is intelligent life upon one of the other planets of our own group would there be any hope of intercommunication. It is fascinating to speculate whether intelligent life is possible upon Venus or upon

Mars.   We all know of the markings which some observers have thought they discovered on Mars, and have
called 'canals.'   But as yet we can only say that there
may be a possibility of some sort of organic life on Mars,
and a bare possibility for Venus.   Conditions are so different from conditions on earth that any life-forms that
may exist there must be very different from those on
earth.   The chance of there being any development of
life that we could call intelligence, or, if so, intelligence at
all comparable with our own, and therefore capable of
establishing communication with us by light-rays or
radio-signals, seems to be extremely slim.   So, to all intents and purposes, at least, man is alone in the universe,
building his civilization as a tiny oasis in the vast im-
mensities of Space.

Moreover, the process of evolution does not end with
the development of man and his civilization, as if that
were its preordained goal.   Our sun is wasting its mass at
a rate estimated to be in the neighborhood of four million
tons a second.   At this rate it will lose something like a
tenth of its mass in a trillion years.   Astronomers tell us
that it may shine, with increasing feebleness, for possibly
ten trillion years to come.   What interests us more, however, is to know how long a time man has ahead of him
on earth before he is frozen out.   The answer seems to be
that in a trillion years the mean temperature on earth
will have fallen about thirty degrees centigrade; all water,
including the oceans, will be frozen solid.   If man survives so long, it will be in an increasingly uncomfortable
and monotonous environment.   And eventually the sun
will grow too cool to sustain life at all on our earth.

There are many other ways in which life on earth *may*
come to an earlier end.   It is conceivable that another

star should come near enough to ours to produce a second cataclysm, similar to that which gave the start to our earth-story. It is possible that the moon will break up, as Saturn's moons have done, and that some of the pieces will fall into the earth. It is possible that a huge meteorite may strike the earth and produce widespread destruction. It is possible that the earth will lose so much of its atmosphere that man will die off for lack of oxygen. It is possible that tidal friction will so slow up the earth's rotation that there will be a gradual approach to an end of the alternation of day and night, with the result that one side of the earth will be too hot and the other side too cold for habitation. But whether or not these catastrophes befall, it seems clear that the earth is only a temporarily habitable abode for man.

Though the future of our own planet is our chief concern, we also want to know about the future of the cosmos. Here the answer is less certain. But if our conclusion was correct, that evolution is a one-way process, the cosmic life is slowly approaching an end. Like our sun, all the stars are wasting away their mass in radiant energy. Minute bits of this energy are intercepted by the other stars, and their planets. What happens to the rest? If Space is infinite, it must, apparently, fly out and out forever; at least, it is hopelessly lost. If Space is curved and finite, it would apparently go round and round, but with little more advantage to the specks of matter that float in Space. When the stars have lost all the energy which they can radiate, there will not be enough radiant energy in Space to light them again. So, unless there is some compensating tendency not now known, the stars are dying embers, and will presently be burned out. And this will happen, we are told, within a few trillions, or tens of trillions, of years.   This is what is called the 'heat-death' of the universe.   What may happen thereafter to these dark, frozen specks of matter is of little moment to us.   Life of any sort will long since have become impossible.

We must be humble about this forecast.   New discoveries may conceivably open up new vistas.   We have as yet only begun to glimpse the mysteries of the universe. Our little gleams of knowledge are

Like scattered lamps in unfrequented streets.

So if the picture we have drawn seems oppressive, it is legitimate to hope that it will presently turn out to be untrue.   All sorts of strange facts of observation seem, at present, to be incommensurable with the world-picture which the main currents of contemporary physics, as-tronomy, and psychology portray.   Possibly the world is quite different from what it seems to be.   Possibly the sun's energy will in some way be renewed.   Possibly 'psychic research' will presently prove to us that the human mind survives the body's death, and continues its adventures of conscious experience in some other di-mension of existence.   We cannot at present say that man *knows* any of these pleasing possibilities to be true. But there is vast room for speculation and for hope.

HUMAN PROGRESS

But suppose that man has only a trillion years, or even somewhat less, to survive.   That is a million times the period that man has yet had on earth, and a hundred million times the length of what we can, by any stretch, call civilization.   We are evidently dawn-men.   When we see what man has done during the past few thousand years, there seems hardly a limit to what he may ac-complish during the next few million years.   Surely the time ahead of man is long enough to enlist all our energy and our idealism to create new types of civilization, new potentialities of happiness. For whatever man's cosmic setting may be, what is worth while is the happiness of men while they live. And to further that, for our own generation, and for the uncounted generations that lie ahead, should be our passion and our determined will.

What is the outlook for the future? Is the human race making satisfactory progress? Is it probable that progress will continue?... If we go back far enough, there has obviously been a great deal of progress. But there have also been many backwaters, many periods of decadence. Progress is not steady, continuous, certain, nor is it usually progress all along the line. It is irregular, spasmodic, uncertain. Many civilizations have arisen, flourished for a while, and decayed. Many observers are telling us today that our civilization has passed its prime and is going downhill. And thus, they say, it will be through the centuries to come; there is no assurance that man's future will be, on the whole, better than his past.

To reach a well-based decision on this point, we should have to study the tendencies now at work in careful detail, balancing the forces making for progress against those making for stagnation or decline, and forecasting which will carry the day. Space does not permit this undertaking here. We can merely make a few discriminations which would be of use to one who should undertake this task. We can analyze progress into its various strands, and call attention to some of the classes of facts which would have to be studied in detail.

In the first place, we can safely say that *material progress* has proceeded during this past century at a more rapid pace than ever before.   So far, it seems that the farther it goes the faster it goes.   We have considerable reason to expect that the men of the future will have far more of the comforts and conveniences of civilization than even the more fortunate have today — better homes, better transportation, higher living standards, greater security from disease, famine, wild beasts, shipwreck, and the other dangers that have always beset human life. Their health will reach a higher average level, their longevity will be greater.   Many more goods of all sorts will be produced, so that men will have a greater abundance of things; at the same time they will have a greater amount of leisure.   They will get rid of the smoke and dust, and to some extent of the noise, of our civilization, eradicate slums, end poverty and want.

That is to say, they *can* easily do all these things. Whether they will or not depends upon their moral progress.   The destructiveness of war has increased so tremendously during the past few years that it is quite possible that a really desperate war on a large scale might wipe out human civilization.   Russia in 1920 was on the verge of relapsing into barbaric chaos.   In the future the danger will be much greater.   For the more advanced a civilization, the easier it is to put it out of gear.   A few skillfully placed bombs could destroy the bridges and highways that give access to a city, put its water-supply, its sewage-system, its electric lights, its central heating systems out of commission, and make the city quickly uninhabitable.   In situations like this, with whole populations starving and in danger of bombs and poison gases, or whatever other diabolical devices our war-offices now have or will presently have in readiness, all the processes of law and order, all economic and political life, would quickly disappear, and men would be savages again.... It is true that every intelligent person knows of these terrific dangers. But intelligence has as yet proved a feeble force when pitted against passion. Our nationalistic patriotisms and tensions continue unabated, while such hopeful developments as the League of Nations and the World Court are still, by comparison, pathetically weak.

It also depends upon moral progress whether men will distribute the benefits of material progress to everyone or keep many of them for a relatively small possessing class. The latter has been the almost invariable practice hitherto. This radical injustice always tends, sooner or later, to provoke rebellion, revolution, civil war. And such internecine conflicts may be as destructive as wars between nations.... It is true that much progress has been made in diffusing the benefits of civilization. And one great community of peoples, the Soviet Union, has not only set as its explicit goal the approximately equal distribution of the good things of life to every man, woman, and child, but has already taken gigantic strides toward that achievement. But the forces of selfishness are still very strong. The possessing classes in the more advanced nations, such as our own, will probably bitterly resist the curtailment of their privileged status. No one can predict what depressions, what crises, what revolutions may try our bodies and our souls before we shall solve this pressing moral problem.

If we can avoid war, the *intellectual progress* of man seems assured. Day by day there is extension of what is known by mankind; and year by year there is extension of what the average man knows. Our educational systems are, on the whole, becoming more and more efficient in method, reaching more people, and doing more for them.   Illiteracy is being gradually wiped out, super-stition is slowly decreasing, the general level of intelligence is rising.   The number of books and magazines and news-papers read will undoubtedly continue to increase.   The post-office, the telegraph, the telephone, the radio are all recent inventions, and are profoundly shaping the minds of men.   Science is as yet in its infancy, but it has already transformed human life, and will doubtless transform it still more, in ways which we cannot predict.... But a few days' war on a great scale could destroy our libraries and laboratories and schools, and kill off a large proportion of our educated people.   The permanence of what we have already achieved, as well as the further development of human intelligence, depends upon the determination of those who guide our destinies to keep out of war.   And until moral progress has gone to heights hardly hoped for now, the danger of war will hang like a sword of Damocles over the world.

Esthetic progress has not always gone hand in hand with material progress; and many phases of human civili-zation, including a large part of our own, are very depress-ingly ugly.   Yet the urge toward beauty is insistent and widespread, and is chiefly blocked by a lack of sufficient material prosperity to allow a surplus of money and energy to satisfy this secondary need of the human spirit. If material and intellectual progress continue, and war's black hand is stayed, man will doubtless repair much of the damage he has done to Nature, and make the earth-scene in many ways more beautiful than ever.   Art and music and literature and drama will flourish; and, if the stronger and cleverer folk, the people entrenched in strategic positions, will allow, they will become the herit-age of all.

As to *eugenic progress*, we are probably not making headway at all. It is doubtful if we are a better stock than the ancient Greeks or Romans, or even than the stone-age men. We are keeping alive our degenerates, our morons, our pathological types, and letting most of them breed. We are allowing the 'lower classes' to out-breed, by a big margin, the 'upper classes.' Hitherto we have killed off many of the strongest and best in war, leaving the race to be propagated by the weaker ones who stayed at home.... But *if* man continues to progress intellectually, there is ground for hope that he will presently realize the importance of eugenics, and will turn some of his ingenuity now spent in breeding better varieties of trees, flowers, and domestic animals, into producing a human stock of higher quality than our present human race.

Everything rests, clearly, upon our ability to make *moral progress*. But precisely here is our greatest weakness. *Are* we going ahead morally? If so, can we rely upon the continuance of this progress? The matter is far too complex to discuss in a few paragraphs. But it is perfectly plain that sufficient moral progress to ensure a happy future for man on earth is by no means assured. Very difficult problems lie ahead. Some of our important natural resources are being shamelessly wasted, and will presently give out. Food-resources may be strained eventually, if the population keeps on increasing. This means increasing tension and danger of moral dissolution. The supernaturalistic religions are losing their hold on men's minds and hearts. The money-making motive stands grimly athwart all programs of social betterment.

On the other hand, morality is largely a matter of intelligence, and intelligence is increasing. More different kinds of experiments in living are being tried than ever before; and there is, on the whole, more tolerance and mutual understanding than in earlier days. Human life is becoming liberated from many of the taboos that have hitherto stifled it. Women are rapidly becoming the equal partners of men, instead of their property, and are doubling the brains and purposiveness available to plan and realize progress. International-mindedness and a determination not to spoil everything by getting into war are slowly spreading. There are many useful movements afoot, many currents making in the direction of moral and social progress. It will be a long struggle; but there is much ground for the faith that intelligence and good-will are going to win.

IS OPTIMISM RATIONAL?

The term 'optimism' is highly ambiguous. In the first place, it may be taken to mean the belief that everything that happens is really good and that, therefore, evil is merely illusion, unreal, 'mortal error.'... However, suffering is still suffering under the new label 'illusion,' 'error,' or 'unreality.' No new name, and no belief, however obstinate, can alter the fact that human beings (and our dumb cousins, the animals) do suffer, that their suffering is often agonizing, and that its sum-total is appalling. If we reject the statement that suffering is *bad*, an *evil*, we have no reason to trust any statement whatever about 'good' and 'bad'; the words have lost all their significance. If we call everything 'good,' we blur one of the most important distinctions of human speech, that between good and bad. If we say that only what is good is 'real,' we use the term 'reality' in a way which may have some significance for our metaphysical system, but which must not make us forget that suffering is *here*, and that it is as bad as it is. Suffering has, *empirically*, the same sort of status that happiness has; it is an indubitable feature of human experience. An 'optimism' that consists in denying, or blurring over, the fact of suffering, is irrational, callous, brutal, blind.

Another brand of optimism consists in believing that 'all is for the best.' The existence of evil is not denied, but is held to have a necessary place in a Divine Plan; it serves some glorious end, which could not have been attained without it. Or it is an inevitable consequence of the nature of the material which the Creator of the universe had to deal with, and is bound to be overcome and left behind as the Divine Plan is achieved.... Such beliefs as these — which, of course, have many variants — are inspiriting in times of effort and comforting in times of sorrow. And if there is any case where the 'will to believe' is justifiable, this would seem to be such a case. But in whatever form this optimistic belief is held, it must be recognized as an 'overbelief'; it must not lead to a slackening of our energies because of our reliance upon the assumed inevitability of the triumph of good; it must not become dogmatic, and so a barrier to candid discussion, or a badge of respectability. Intellectual honesty requires that we admit freely that such beliefs as these are a matter of faith or hope, or plausible hypothesis, but have not yet, at least, attained the status of scientific probability.

There is a pseudo-optimism which consists in ignoring evil, or at least minimizing it. The cheerful Rotarians who are complacent in face of the crudities of our business world, the Babbitts who perpetuate the ugliness and hypocrisy of our Main Streets, the smug pew-holders who thank God for his mercies to them with never a thought for the unemployed around the corner, the hundred per cent Americans whose patriotism is offended if you 'knock' America — such people justify the definition of a pessimist as one who has to live with an optimist. Better to look squarely at the facts than to live perpetually in a fool's paradise. Indeed, it is necessary, and our evident duty, to look unflinchingly at the facts, if we are ever to build a better world.

But there is at least one kind of optimism which we can all share, and which is all to the good. It is the optimism which is born of courage and determination that man *shall* continue his march toward the millennium. From this point of view cynicism is simply slackness. And optimism, in this sense, is not so much a belief as an attitude. Such an optimist, whatever his cosmic creed, has a truly religious spirit. For him Christianity is not so much a doctrine as an invitation. Whether or no there are unseen forces battling for us, at least *we* can battle for the right and the good, and spend ourselves gladly in their service. Long before the days of aviation, Leonardo da Vinci wrote in his notes, "There shall be wings." So the optimist says, There shall be beauty and joy, security and peace, beyond anything the world has yet known, for the generations of men that are to live during the coming thousands of millions of years. To work consciously and unremittingly for that end is the most inspiring and the worthiest aim that we can set before ourselves. With sufficient faith, with sufficient determination, there is hardly a limit to what the human race may some day achieve.

A hundred million ages it may be until he comes; what does it matter?...
A hundred million ages; and yet, sometimes,

Here and now, in these small primeval days — in this dull gloaming
    of creation's dawn —
Here and now, sometimes, there crackle out a tiny shimmering spark,
Some hint in our blind, protoplasmic lives,
Of that far, infinite torch
Whose ray shall one day touch the utmost reaches of space....
One that has made brotherhood with the eagle and the hawk;
One that has made voices speak across the emptiness;
One that has laid cheer and comfort to the tired heart —
These and a thousand others are the prophecy:...
He that will come will know not space nor time, nor any limitation,
But will step across the sky, infinite, supreme — one with God.[1]

SUGGESTED READINGS

Durant Drake, *Problems of Religion*, XXIII.
R. W. Sellars, *The Next Step in Religion*, XII.
J. H. Snowden, *Is the World Growing Better?*
H. S. Jennings, *Prometheus.*
Ralph Sockman, *Morals of Tomorrow*, I, XIV.
Durant Drake, *The New Morality*, XXII.
Glenn Frank, *Thunder and Dawn*, IX.
Stanton Coit, *The Soul of America*, XIV.
H. W. Wright, *Faith Justified by Progress*, especially ch. VIII.
Bertrand Russell, *Skeptical Essays*, XVII.
Percival Lowell, *The Evolution of Worlds*, VII–VIII.
Irwin Edman, *The Contemporary and His Soul*, especially pp. 51–76,
    163–191.
Albert Schweitzer, *Civilization and Ethics*, XVII–XXII.
Norman Thomas, *America's Way Out*, XVII.

[1] Albert Bigelow Paine, *The Superman.* By permission of the authors.

INDEX